CIMA
STUDY TEXT

Intermediate level Paper 5

Business Taxation

BPP's NEW STUDY TEXTS FOR CIMA's NEW SYLLABUS

- Targeted to the **syllabus** and **learning outcomes**

- **Quizzes** and **questions** to check your understanding

- Incorporates CIMA's new Official Terminology

- Clear layout and style designed to save you time

- Plenty of **exam-style questions**

- **Chapter Roundups** and summaries to help revision

- **Mind Maps** to integrate the key points

New in this September 2001 edition

- A bank of **objective test questions** at the back

BPP's **MCQ cards** also support this paper.

BPP Publishing
September 2001

First edition September 2000
Second edition September 2001

ISBN 0 7517 3161 7 (Previous edition 0 7517 3143 9)

British Library Cataloguing-in-Publication Data
A catalogue record for this book
is available from the British Library

Published by

BPP Publishing Ltd
Aldine House, Aldine Place
London W12 8AW

www.bpp.com

Printed in Great Britain by W M Print
45-47 Frederick Street
Walsall, West Midlands
WS2 9NE

We are grateful to the Chartered Institute of Management Accountants for permission to reproduce past examination questions and questions from the pilot paper. The suggested solutions to the illustrative questions have been prepared by BPP Publishing Limited.

Contents

	Page

(iii)

Contents

REVIEW FORM & FREE PRIZE DRAW

ORDER FORM

MULTIPLE CHOICE QUESTION CARDS

Multiple choice questions appear in Section A of the exam. To give you further practice in this style of question, we have produced a bank of 150 **multiple choice question cards**, covering the syllabus. This bank contains exam style questions in a format to help you revise on the move.

COMPUTER-BASED LEARNING PRODUCTS FROM BPP

If you want to reinforce your studies by interactive learning, try BPP's **i-Learn** products, covering major syllabus areas in an interactive format. For self-testing, try **i-Pass** which offers a large number of objective test questions, particularly useful as multiple choice questions form part of the exam.

See the order form at the back of this text for details of these innovative learning tools.

BPP PUBLISHING

THE BPP STUDY TEXT

Aims of this Study Text

To provide you with the knowledge and understanding, skills and application techniques that you need if you are to be successful in your exams

This Study Text has been written around the **Business Taxation** syllabus.

- It is **comprehensive**. It covers the syllabus content. No more, no less.

- It is written at the **right level**. Each chapter is written with CIMA's precise learning outcomes in mind.

- It is targeted to the **exam**. We have taken account of the pilot paper, questions put to the examiners at the recent CIMA conference, the latest syllabus guidance notes and the assessment methodology.

- It is fully up to date for the provisions of the **Finance Act 2001**. This Act will be examined in the May and November 2002 exams.

To allow you to study in the way that best suits your learning style and the time you have available, by following your personal Study Plan (see page (x))

The BPP Study Text has a variety of features, highlighted by icons. You can use these features in different ways to suit your learning style.

You may be studying at home on your own until the date of the exam, or you may be attending a full-time course. You may like to (and have time to) read every word, or you may prefer to (or only have time to) skim-read and devote the remainder of your time to question practice. Wherever you fall in the spectrum, you will find the BPP Study Text meets your needs in designing and following your personal Study Plan.

To tie in with the other components of the BPP Effective Study Package to ensure you have the best possible chance of passing the exam (see page (vi))

BPP
PUBLISHING

Recommended period of use	Elements of the BPP Effective Study Package
Three to twelve months before the exam	**Study Text** Use the Study Text to acquire knowledge, understanding, skills and the ability to use application techniques. You might also use BPP's **i-Learn** product to reinforce your learning.
Throughout	**MCQ cards and i-Pass** Revise your knowledge and ability to use application techniques, as well as practising this exam question format, with 150 multiple choice questions. **i-Pass**, our computer-based testing package, provides objective test questions in a variety of formats and is ideal for self-assessment.
One to six months before the exam	**Practice & Revision Kit** Try the numerous examination questions, for which there are realistic suggested solutions prepared by BPP's own authors. Then attempt the two mock exams.
From three months before the exam until the last minute	**Passcards** Work through these short, memorable notes which are focused on what is most likely to come up in the exam you will be sitting.
One to six months before the exam	**Success Tapes** These audio tapes cover the vital elements of your syllabus in less than 90 minutes per subject. Each tape also contains exam hints to help you fine tune your strategy.
Three to twelve months before the exam	**Breakthrough Videos** Use a Breakthrough Video to supplement your Study Text. They give you clear tuition on key exam subjects and allow you the luxury of being able to pause or repeat sections until you have fully grasped the topic.

HELP YOURSELF STUDY FOR YOUR CIMA EXAMS

Exams for professional bodies such as CIMA are very different from those you have taken at college or university. You will be under **greater time pressure before** the exam - as you may be combining your study with work. There are many different ways of learning and so the BPP Study Text offers you a number of different tools to help you through. Here are some hints and tips: they are not plucked out of the air, but **based on research and experience.** (You don't need to know that long-term memory is in the same part of the brain as emotions and feelings - but it's a fact anyway.)

The right approach

1   The right attitude

Believe in yourself	Yes, there is a lot to learn. Yes, it is a challenge. But thousands have succeeded before and you can too.
Remember why you're doing it	Studying might seem a grind at times, but you are doing it for a reason: to advance your career.

2   The right focus

Read through the Syllabus and learning outcomes	These tell you what you are expected to know and are supplemented by Exam Focus Points in the text.
Study the Exam Paper section	The pilot paper is likely to be a reasonable guide of what you should expect in the exam.

3   The right method

The big picture	You need to grasp the detail - but keeping in mind how everything fits into the big picture will help you understand better. • The **Introduction** of each chapter puts the material in context. • The **Syllabus content, learning outcomes** and **Exam focus points** show you what you need to **grasp.** • **Mind Maps** show the links and key issues in key topics.
In your own words	To absorb the information (and to practise your written communication skills), it helps **put it into your own words.** • **Take notes.** • Answer the **questions** in each chapter. As well as helping you absorb the information you will practise your written communication skills, which become increasingly important as you progress through your CIMA exams. • Draw **mind maps.** We have some examples. • Try 'teaching' to a colleague or friend.

BPP PUBLISHING

Give yourself cues to jog your memory	The BPP Study Text uses **bold** to **highlight key points** and **icons** to identify key features, such as **Exam focus points** and **Key terms**. • Try **colour coding** with a highlighter pen. • Write **key points** on cards.

4   **The right review**

Review, review, review	It is a **fact** that regularly reviewing a topic in summary form can **fix it in your memory**. Because **review** is so important, the BPP Study Text helps you to do so in many ways. • **Chapter roundups** summarise the key points in each chapter. Use them to recap each study session. • The **Quick quiz** is another review technique to ensure that you have grasped the essentials. • Use the **Key terms** highlighted in the index as a quiz. • Go through the **Examples** in each chapter a second or third time.

Suggested study sequence

Tackle the chapters in the order you find them in the Study Text. Taking into account your individual learning style, you could follow this sequence.

Key study steps	Activity
Step 1 **Topic list**	Each numbered topic is a numbered section in the chapter.
Step 2 **Introduction**	This gives you the **big picture** in terms of the **context** of the chapter, the **content** you will cover, and the **learning outcomes** the chapter assesses - in other words, it sets your **objectives for study.**
Step 3 **Knowledge brought forward boxes**	Not applicable for this subject.
Step 4 **Explanations**	Proceed methodically through the chapter, reading each section thoroughly and making sure you understand.
Step 5 **Key terms and Exam focus points**	• **Key terms** can often earn you *easy marks* if you state them clearly and correctly in an appropriate exam answer (and they are highlighted at the back of the text). • **Exam focus points** give you a good idea of how we think the examiner intends to examine certain topics.
Step 6 **Note taking**	Take brief notes if you wish, avoiding the temptation to copy out too much.
Step 7 **Examples**	Follow each through to its solution very carefully.
Step 8 **Case examples**	Not applicable for this subject.
Step 9 **Questions**	Make a very good attempt at each one.
Step 10 **Answers**	Check yours against ours, and make sure you understand any discrepancies.
Step 11 **Chapter roundup**	Work through it very carefully, to make sure you have grasped the major points it is highlighting.
Step 12 **Quick quiz**	When you are happy that you have covered the chapter, use the **Quick quiz** to check how much you have remembered of the topics covered.

BPP
PUBLISHING

Key study steps	Activity
Step 13 **Question(s) in the Question bank**	Either at this point, or later when you are thinking about revising, make a full attempt at the **Question(s)** suggested at the very end of the chapter. You can find these at the end of the Study Text, along with the **Answers** so you can see how you did. We highlight those that are introductory, and those which are of the standard you would expect to find in an exam. Whether you are sitting the exam in May or November 2002, attempt **all the question formats provided**. (If you have purchased the MCQ cards use these too.)
Step 14 **Multiple choice questions**	Use the bank of MCQs at the back of this Study Text to practise this important assessment format and to determine how much of the Study Text you have absorbed. If you have bought the MCQ cards, use these too.

Developing your personal Study Plan

Preparing a Study Plan (and sticking closely to it) is one of the key elements in learning success.

Step 1. How do you learn?

First you need to be aware of your style of learning. There are four typical learning styles. Consider yourself in the light of the following descriptions and work out which you fit most closely. You can then plan to follow the key study steps in the sequence suggested.

Learning styles	Characteristics	Sequence of key study steps in the BPP Study Text
Theorist	Seeks to understand principles before applying them in practice	1, 2, 3, 4, 7, 8, 5, 9/10, 11, 12, 13 (6 continuous)
Reflector	Seeks to observe phenomena, thinks about them and then chooses to act	
Activist	Prefers to deal with practical, active problems; does not have much patience with theory	1, 2, 9/10 (read through), 7, 8, 5, 11, 3, 4, 9/10 (full attempt), 12, 13 (6 continuous)
Pragmatist	Prefers to study only if a direct link to practical problems can be seen; not interested in theory for its own sake	9/10 (read through), 2, 5, 7, 8, 11, 1, 3, 4, 9/10 (full attempt), 12, 13 (6 continuous)

Step 2. How much time do you have?

Work out the time you have available per week, given the following.

- The standard you have set yourself
- The time you need to set aside later for work on the Practice & Revision Kit and Passcards
- The other exam(s) you are sitting

(x)

- Very importantly, practical matters such as work, travel, exercise, sleep and social life

Note your time available in box A.

A | Hours |

Step 3. Allocate your time

- Take the time you have available per week for this Study Text shown in box A, multiply it by the number of weeks available and insert the result in box B.

B

- Divide the figure in Box B by the number of chapters in this text and insert the result in box C.

C

Step 4. Implement

Set about studying each chapter in the time shown in box C, following the key study steps in the order suggested by your particular learning style.

This is your personal **Study Plan**.

Short of time: *Skim study technique?*

You may find you simply do not have the time available to follow all the key study steps for each chapter, however you adapt them for your particular learning style. If this is the case, follow the **skim study** technique below (the icons in the Study Text will help you to do this).

- Study the chapters in the order you find them in the Study Text.

- For each chapter, follow the key study steps 1-3, and then skim-read through step 4. Jump to step 11, and then go back to step 5. Follow through steps 7 and 8, and prepare outline answers to questions (steps 9/10). Try the Quick quiz (step 12), following up any items you can't answer, then do a plan for the Question (step 13), comparing it against our answers. You should probably still follow step 6 (note-taking), although you may decide simply to rely on the BPP Passcards for this.

Moving on...

However you study, when you are ready to embark on the practice and revision phase of the BPP Effective Study Package, you should still refer back to this Study Text, both as a source of **reference** (you should find the list of key terms and the index particularly helpful for this) and as a **refresher** (the Chapter roundups and Quick quizzes help you here).

And remember to keep careful hold of this Study Text - you will find it invaluable in your work.

SYLLABUS AND LEARNING OUTCOMES

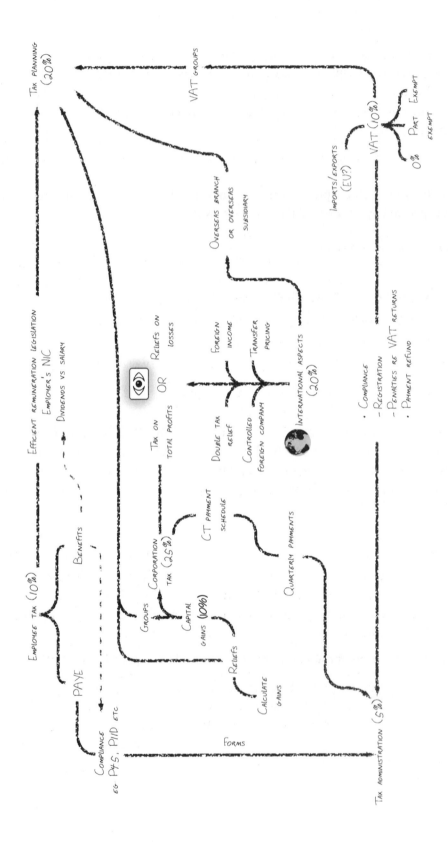

Syllabus overview

This syllabus introduces CIMA students to a wide range of taxation concepts and legislation. It recognises that Management Accountants will not be expected to become experts in taxation, but rather that they will recognise the important role that taxation can have to play in the decision making process in the business.

At the very least the Management Accountant should be able to raise relevant issues with their tax advisors from an informed point of view. While they will not be expected to produce say, a detailed tax planning report, they should be able to prepare notes or a memorandum on taxation issues to be discussed at a forthcoming meeting.

It is felt that there continues to be a need to cover a number of basic computational aspects of taxation as well as requiring students to deal with the planning issues within the subject.

Aims

This syllabus aims to test the student's ability to:

- Identify the rules imposed upon employers in relation to employee taxation
- Explain and apply the system of corporation tax self assessment, capital gains and VAT
- Identify and evaluate the impact of international aspects on a company's taxation
- Identify and evaluate the impact of different tax planning scenarios

Assessment

There will be a written paper of 3 hours. The paper will be in three sections as follows:

Section A will consist of objective testing of up to 25 marks on knowledge based areas in syllabus sections (i), (ii), (v) and (vi).

Section B will compromise a compulsory scenario which could include aspects of any section of the syllabus. It will include planning and compliance elements. The format of any report etc. will be specified.

Section C will require two technical questions worth 20 marks each (out of a choice of four) taken from sections (ii), (iii), (iv) and (v) of the syllabus. The questions could contain a minor panning element.

Note: While it is unlikely that a full question would be set on Tax Administration any of the elements could be examined within the context of another area of the syllabus.

Learning outcomes and syllabus content

BPP note: The learning outcomes below are as published in CIMA's official syllabus. The syllabus content has been taken from the syllabus guidance notes written by the examiner in November 2000 and from additional comments made to BPP Publishing Ltd by the examiner in the light of Finance Act 2001. At the time of printing this text the examiner had not issued guidance notes specifically updated for Finance Act 2001.

5(i) Tax administration - 5%

Learning outcomes

On completion of their studies students should be able to:

- Describe the system of Corporation Tax Self Assessment (CTSA)
- Identify the key dates for submission of returns
- Describe the Inland Revenues' powers of enquiry
- Identify the various penalties and interest charges in CTSA
- Identify the minimum record-keeping requirements
- Identify the compliance requirements imposed on employers in relation to employee taxation
- Identify the VAT registration/de-registration requirements and the rules and penalties in relation to VAT returns

Syllabus content

- Corporation tax self assessment - all compliance aspects including: returns; deadlines; interest and penalties; Revenue enquiries; appeals, time limits
- Returns required from employers in connection with all aspects of employee tax
- VAT administration: registration and returns

5(ii) Employees' taxation - 10%

Learning outcomes

On completion of their studies students should be able to:

- Apply knowledge of the Benefits in Kind (BIK) system for employees
- Identify the rules for different types of employees
- Calculate the total assessable benefits of an employee and explain the effect on code numbers
- Evaluate the relative tax efficiency of different methods of rewarding employees

Syllabus content

- Schedule E emoluments, pay-as-you-earn (PAYE) expenses and benefits in kind, share options, employer's and employee's National Insurance contributions (for the 2002 exams Enterprise Management Incentives and the All Employee Share Ownership Plan have been specifically added to the syllabus)
- Status issues - IR 35
- Personal pension plans (PPP) and approved occupational pension schemes
- Contrasting salary with dividends
- Tax efficient methods of rewarding employees

5(iii) Corporation tax - 25%

Learning outcomes

On completion of their studies students should be able to:

- Calculate the schedule D I profit for taxation purposes, showing knowledge of case law and statute

- Calculate the total profits of a company for CT purposes

- Calculate the capital allowances entitlement of a company

- Calculate the CT liability of a company (including that of small and intermediate companies)

- Prepare a schedule of CT payments of a large company covering a two year period under the quarterly payment system

- Identify the effect of all forms of loss relief on a company's, group's or a consortium's CT liability

- Explain the effect of the loan relationships rules on a company's CT liability

- Explain the operation of Shadow ACT

Syllabus content

- Scope of CT - what profits are chargeable?

- Adjustment of trading profits: statute and case law

- Calculation of total profits and CT liability; relevance of associated companies; application of rates and taper relief including the new small company rate from 1 April 2000

- Payment of CT liability; quarterly payment arrangements for large companies; group payment arrangements

- All forms of relief for trading losses and charges in a single company for CAPs starting after 2 July 1997

- ACT and Shadow ACT: all aspects including the calculation of shadow ACT and the use of surplus ACT existing at 6.4.1999. Surplus shadow ACT will not be examined nor will any group aspects of shadow ACT

- Loan relationship rules: all aspects including the reliefs for non-trading deficits

- Group structures: group relief; group capital gains, including rules for pre-entry losses and gains. No questions will be set on the surrender of ACT.

- Accounting periods

- Close companies and close investment holding companies; identification and consequences

- Capital allowances; plant, industrial buildings, short life assets; qualifying expenditure - statute and case law (long life assets are not examinable nor are such things as agricultural buildings or patents)

- Research and Development Expenditure

5(iv) International aspects - 20%

Learning outcomes

On completion of their studies students should be able to:

- Evaluate the taxation implications of alternative methods of running an overseas operation

- Identify the significance of company residences for tax purposes

- Calculate the CT liability of a UK company which has overseas income, using the rules of double tax relief (but excluding knowledge of Treaties)

- Identify transfer pricing problems, calculating any adjustment required and state how this will be reported in its CTSA return

- Identify a controlled foreign company (CFC)

- Calculate the CT liability arising as a result of the presence of a CFC

Syllabus content

- Company residence
- Double taxation relief (DTR)
- Controlled foreign companies (CFC)
- Transfer pricing
- UK companies trading abroad - subsidiary v branch

5(v) Capital gains (for companies only) - 10%

Learning outcomes

On completion of their studies students should be able to:

- Identify chargeable assets for taxation as capital gains

- Apply rollover and holdover reliefs for business assets

- Identify the CGT reliefs available in a group situation and the anti-avoidance rules relating to pre-entry assets

- Calculate the gain arising on the disposal of quoted securities using the pooling system

Syllabus content

- Scope, exemptions, chattels
- Reliefs for losses; rollover relief; holdover relief
- Groups of companies: inter company transactions
- Shares and securities including pooling bonus issues and rights issues
- EIS and VCTs

5(vi) Valued Added Tax - 10%

Learning outcomes

On completion of their studies students should be able to:

- Identify the significance of standard rate, zero rate and exempt supplies and those supplies outside the scope of VAT
- Identify the correct tax point of a supply and understand its significance
- Identify the significance of EU and non-EU countries when dealing with VAT
- Discuss the problems and opportunities inherent in a VAT group registration

Syllabus content

- Scope, including basic property transactions - 'opting to tax'
- Registration and deregistration: penalties, exemptions, zero rating and partial exemption
- Tax point; taxable value; payment and refunds
- Transactions with foreign companies including those in EU member states
- Applications in groups of companies. Group registrations

5(vii) Tax planning - 20%

Learning outcomes

Students are reminded that 'Tax Planning' is not a discrete area of taxation. It is the application of the knowledge you gain while studying each section of the syllabus. Try to grasp the planning opportunities when studying each section.

On completion of their studies students should be able to:

- Calculate the form of loss relief which will minimise the CT liability in either a single company or in a group or consortium
- Evaluate the tax efficiency of alternative methods of acquiring other businesses
- Identify methods of minimising employer's National Insurance Contributions (NIC)
- Contrast the tax implications of financing a company by debt or equity
- Demonstrate the planning aspects of maximising the use of surplus ACT existing at 6 April 1999 for a company
- Demonstrate the most efficient method of disposing of assets to third parties by a group of companies
- Discuss the most efficient method of arranging VAT registrations for groups of companies

Syllabus content

- Loss strategy: maximisation of group and consortia relief; intra group transfers of assets
- Utilisation of surplus ACT existing at 6.4.99; capital allowances
- Company takeovers; changes in ownership; methods of acquisition - assets or shares?
- Integration of tax planning into the budgeting process
- National Insurance Contributions planning
- Taxation implications of alternative financial structures. Balance between debt and equity. The impact of EIS and VCT
- Current issues and proposals

The planning aspects could be within a scenario or in the technical questions.

THE EXAM PAPER

Format of the paper

		Number of marks
Section A:	Multiple choice questions worth 2 marks each	25 max
Section B:	Compulsory scenario question	Balance
Section C:	Choose two out of four 20 mark questions	40
		100

Time allowed : 3 hours

Section A will be worth a maximum of 25 marks. It is unlikely that there will be more than 14 marks for Section A.

Section B could include any elements of the syllabus, including planning and compliance aspects. The format of the required answer will be specified - report, memo, letter, etc and it will be important to produce your answer in the format specified.

Analysis of past papers

May 2001

Section A

1   7 objective test questions worth 2 marks each

Section B

2   Corporation tax. Acquisition of two subsidiaries. Sale of assets. VAT groups.

Section C (2 out of 4 questions)

3   Benefits in kind. PAYE codes.
4   Capital allowances on plant and machinery. Industrial buildings allowance
5   Corporation tax. Groups and consortia
6   Chargeable gains. Rollover relief

Pilot paper

Section A

1   7 objective test questions worth 2 marks each

Section B

2   Computation of CT liability. Due payment dates. Obligations under CTSA

Section C (2 out of 4 questions)

3   Calculation of benefits in kind. PAYE code numbers
4   Capital allowances on plant and machinery. Industrial buildings allowance
5   Chargeable gains including holdover relief
6   Double tax relief. Controlled foreign companies

WHAT THE EXAMINER MEANS

The table below has been prepared by CIMA to help you interpret exam questions.

Learning objective	Verbs used	Definition
1 Knowledge What you are expected to know	• List • State • Define	• Make a list of • Express, fully or clearly, the details of/facts of • Give the exact meaning of
2 Comprehension What you are expected to understand	• Describe • Distinguish • Explain • Identify • Illustrate	• Communicate the key features of • Highlight the differences between • Make clear or intelligible/state the meaning of • Recognise, establish or select after consideration • Use an example to describe or explain something
3 Application Can you apply your knowledge?	• Apply • Calculate/compute • Demonstrate • Prepare • Reconcile • Solve • Tabulate	• To put to practical use • To ascertain or reckon mathematically • To prove with certainty or to exhibit by practical means • To make or get ready for use • To make or prove consistent/compatible • Find an answer to • Arrange in a table
4 Analysis Can you analyse the detail of what you have learned?	• Analyse • Categorise • Compare and contrast • Construct • Discuss • Interpret • Produce	• Examine in detail the structure of • Place into a defined class or division • Show the similarities and/or differences between • To build up or compile • To examine in detail by argument • To translate into intelligible or familiar terms • To create or bring into existence
5 Evaluation Can you use your learning to evaluate, make decisions or recommendations?	• Advise • Evaluate • Recommend	• To counsel, inform or notify • To appraise or assess the value of • To advise on a course of action

TACKLING OBJECTIVE TEST QUESTIONS

What are objective test (OTs) questions?

Objective test questions (OTs) are designed to ensure that there is **no need for the marker to interpret or grade** the answer as they measure distinct results. Because they **avoid subjectivity,** they can be **marked by a computer.** OTs come in **many formats,** one of which is the multiple choice question (MCQ).

So what are multiple choice questions?

MCQs are a type of objective test question to which you have to **identify the single correct answer from a number of options.**

The Paper 5 exam and objective test questions

OTs in the May and November Paper 5 exam

Of the total marks available for the paper, multiple choice questions will comprise a maximum of:

A   10%
B   20%
C   25%
D   40%

The correct answer is C. However, the examiner has said that it is unlikely that he will allocate anymore than 14% of the marks to multiple choice questions in 2002.

To help you practice MCQs, we have included them in the **Question bank** at the end of the text. And don't forget that we publish a **bank of 150 multiple choice question cards** which you can order using the form at the end of the text.

The MCQs in your exam contain four possible answers. You have to **choose the option that best answers the question.** The four incorrect options are called distracters. There is a skill in answering MCQs quickly and correctly. By practising MCQs you can develop this skill, giving you a better chance of passing the exam.

You may wish to follow the approach outlined below, or you may prefer to adapt it.

Step 1.   **Skim read** all the MCQs and **identify** what appear to be the **easier** questions.

Step 2.   Attempt each question - **starting with the easier questions** identified in Step 1. Read the question thoroughly. You may prefer to work out the answer before looking at the options, or you may prefer to look at the options at the beginning. Adopt the method that works best for you.

Step 3.   Read the four options and see if one matches your own answer. **Be careful with numerical questions,** as the distracters are designed to match answers that incorporate common errors. Check that your calculation is correct. Have you followed the requirement exactly? Have you included every stage of the calculation?

Step 4.   You may **find that none of the options matches your answer**.

- Re-read the question to ensure that you understand it and are answering the requirement

- Eliminate any obviously wrong answers

- Consider which of the remaining answers is the most likely to be correct and select the option

Step 5.   If you are still **unsure** make a note **and continue to the next question.**

Step 6.   **Revisit unanswered** questions. When you come back to a question after a break you often find you are able to answer it correctly straight away. If you are still unsure have a guess. You are not penalised for incorrect answers, so **never leave a question unanswered!**

Exam focus. After extensive practice and revision of MCQs, you may find that you recognise a question when you sit the exam. Be aware that the detail and/or requirement may be different. If the question seems familiar read the requirement and options carefully - do not assume that it is identical.

The **Practice and Revision Kit** for this paper to be published in **January 2002** will be **full of OTs,** providing you with vital revision opportunities at the fundamental techniques and skills you will require in the exam.

TAX RATES AND ALLOWANCES

A   INCOME TAX

1   *Allowances*

	2000/01 £	2001/02 £
Personal allowance	4,385	4,535

2   *Car fuel scale charges*

	2001/02	
	Petrol £	Diesel £
Cars having a cylinder capacity		
1,400 cc or less	1,930	2,460
1,401 cc to 2,000 cc	2,460	2,460
More than 2,000 cc	3,620	3,620
Cars not having a cylinder capacity	3,620	3,620

3   *Authorised mileage rates (AMR)- 2001/02 rates*

Car mileage rates

	On first 4,000 miles	On each mile over 4,000
Size of car engine		
Up to 1,500 cc	40p	25p
1,501 cc - 2,000 cc	45p	25p
Over 2,000 cc	63p	36p

Bicycle mileage rate

12p per mile

Motor cycle mileage rate

24p per mile

4   *Personal pension contribution limits*

Age	Maximum percentage %
Up to 35	17.5
36 – 45	20.0
46 – 50	25.0
51 – 55	30.0
56 – 60	35.0
61 or more	40.0

Subject to earnings cap of £91,800 for 2000/01 and £95,400 for 2001/02.

Contributions limit £3,600 (2001/02)

B   CORPORATION TAX

1   *Rates*

Financial year	Full rate %	Small companies rate %	Starting rate	Marginal relief Fraction	Lower limit for starting rate £	Upper limit for starting rate £	Upper limit for SCR £	Lower Limit for SCR £
1996	33	24	-	9/400	-	-	1,500,000	300,000
1997	31	21	-	1/40	-	-	1,500,000	300,000
1998	31	21	-	1/40	-	-	1,500,000	300,000
1999	30	20	-	1/40	-	-	1,500,000	300,000
2000	30	20	10	1/40	10,000	50,000	1,500,000	300,000
2001	30	20	10	1/40	10,000	50,000	1,500,000	300,000

2   *Marginal relief*

$$(M - P) \times I/P \times \text{Marginal relief fraction}$$

3   *Capital allowances*

	%
Plant and machinery	
Writing down allowance	25
First year allowance (acquisitions 2.7.97 - 1.7.98)	50
First year allowance (acquisitions after 2.7.98)	40
First year allowance (information and communication technology equipment - period 1.4.00 - 31.3.03, energy saving equipment, flats above shops)	100
Industrial buildings allowance	
Writing down allowance: post 5.11.62	4
pre 6.11.62	2

C   VALUE ADDED TAX

1   *Registration and deregistration limits*

	To 31.3.01	*From 1.4.01*
Registration limit	£52,000	£54,000
Deregistration limit	£50,000	£52,000

2   *Scale charges for private motoring*

For the first accounting period beginning after 5 April 2001 (VAT inclusive)

	Quarterly Petrol	Diesel
Up to 1400 cc	242	225
1401 to 2000 cc	307	225
Over 2000cc	453	286

BPP PUBLISHING

D CAPITAL GAINS TAX

1 Lease percentage table

Years	Percentage	Years	Percentage	Years	Percentage
50 or more	100.000	33	90.280	16	64.116
49	99.657	32	89.354	15	61.617
48	99.289	31	88.371	14	58.971
47	98.902	30	87.330	13	56.167
46	98.490	29	86.226	12	53.191
45	98.059	28	85.053	11	50.038
44	97.595	27	83.816	10	46.695
43	97.107	26	82.496	9	43.154
42	96.593	25	81.100	8	39.399
41	96.041	24	79.622	7	35.414
40	95.457	23	78.055	6	31.195
39	94.842	22	76.399	5	26.722
38	94.189	21	74.635	4	21.983
37	93.497	20	72.770	3	16.959
36	92.761	19	70.791	2	11.629
35	91.981	18	68.697	1	5.983
34	91.156	17	66.470	0	0.000

2 Retail prices index (January 1987 = 100.0)

	1982	1983	1984	1985	1986	1987	1988	1989	1990
Jan		82.6	86.8	91.2	96.2	100.0	103.3	111.0	119.5
Feb		83.0	87.2	91.9	96.6	100.4	103.7	111.8	120.2
Mar	79.4	83.1	87.5	92.8	96.7	100.6	104.1	112.3	121.4
Apr	81.0	84.3	88.6	94.8	97.7	101.8	105.8	114.3	125.1
May	81.6	84.6	89.0	95.2	97.8	101.9	106.2	115.0	126.2
Jun	81.9	84.8	89.2	95.4	97.8	101.9	106.6	115.4	126.7
Jul	81.9	85.3	89.1	95.2	97.5	101.8	106.7	115.5	126.8
Aug	81.9	85.7	89.9	95.5	97.8	102.1	107.9	115.8	128.1
Sept	81.9	86.1	90.1	95.4	98.3	102.4	108.4	116.6	129.3
Oct	82.3	86.4	90.7	95.6	98.5	102.9	109.5	117.5	130.3
Nov	82.7	86.7	91.0	95.9	99.3	103.4	110.0	118.5	130.0
Dec	82.5	86.9	90.9	96.0	99.6	103.3	110.3	118.8	129.9

	1991	1992	1993	1994	1995	1996	1997	1998	1999	2000	2001★	2002★
Jan	130.2	135.6	137.9	141.3	146.0	150.2	154.4	159.5	163.4	166.6	172.5	178.5
Feb	130.9	136.3	138.8	142.1	146.9	150.9	155.0	160.3	163.7	167.5	173.0	179.0
Mar	131.4	136.7	139.3	142.5	147.5	151.5	154.4	160.8	164.1	168.4	173.5	179.5
Apr	133.1	138.8	140.6	144.2	149.0	152.6	156.3	162.6	165.2	170.1	174.0	180.0
May	133.5	139.3	141.1	144.7	149.6	152.9	156.9	163.5	165.6	170.7	174.5	180.5
Jun	134.1	139.3	141.0	144.7	149.8	153.0	157.5	163.4	165.6	171.1	175.0	181.0
Jul	133.8	138.8	140.7	144.0	149.1	152.4	157.5	163.0	165.1	170.5	175.5	181.5
Aug	134.1	138.9	141.3	144.7	149.9	153.1	158.5	163.7	165.5	170.5	176.0	182.0
Sept	134.6	139.4	141.9	145.0	150.6	153.8	159.3	164.4	166.2	171.7	176.5	182.5
Oct	135.1	139.9	141.8	145.2	149.8	153.8	159.6	164.5	166.5	171.6	177.0	183.0
Nov	135.6	139.7	141.6	145.3	149.8	153.9	159.6	164.4	166.7	172.1	177.5	183.5
Dec	135.7	139.2	141.9	146.0	150.7	154.4	160.0	164.4	167.3	172.2	178.0	185.0

★ Estimated figures.

E   NATIONAL INSURANCE (NOT CONTRACTED OUT RATES) 2001/02

Class 1 contributions

£

Employee

Lower earnings limit (LEL)	3,744 (£72 pw)
Primary threshold	4,535 (£87 pw)
Upper earnings limit (UEL)	29,900 (£575 pw)

Employer

Secondary threshold   4,535 (£87 pw)

Employee contributions   10% on earnings between the primary
threshold and the UEL
(8.4% if contracted out)

Employer contributions   11.9% on earnings above secondary threshold
(Reduced rates on earnings between secondary
threshold and UEL if contracted out)

Class 1A and Class 1B contributions

Rate 11.9%

BPP
PUBLISHING

Part A
Corporate tax

Chapter 1

AN OUTLINE OF CORPORATION TAX

Topic list	Syllabus reference	Ability required
1 Introduction to the UK tax system	(i), (ii), (iii), (iv) (v), (vi), (vii)	Knowledge
2 The scope of corporation tax	(iii)	Application
3 Profits chargeable to corporation tax	(iii)	Application
4 Accounting periods	(iii)	Application
5 The charge to corporation tax	(iii)	Application

Introduction

We start our study of tax with an introduction to the UK tax system.

As the taxation of companies is a vitally important part of the business taxation syllabus we then look at corporation tax (CT). This is the tax that a company must pay on its profits.

In this chapter you will learn both how to compute the profits on which a company must pay tax and how to compute the corporation tax liability on those profits.

Learning outcomes covered in this chapter

- **Calculate** the total profits of a company for CT purposes
- **Calculate** the CT liability of a company (including that of small and intermediate companies)

Syllabus content covered in this chapter

- Scope of CT – what profits are chargeable?

- Accounting periods

- Calculation of total profits and CT liability; relevance of associated companies; application of rates and taper relief including the new small company rates from 1 April 2000

1 INTRODUCTION TO THE UK TAX SYSTEM

1.1 Central government raises revenue through a wide range of taxes. Tax law is made by **statute** and as this can be notoriously ambiguous and difficult to understand, the Revenue are currently involved in a project to rewrite it in simpler more user-friendly language. The first Act to result from the tax law rewrite project was the Capital Allowances Act 2001.

Statute is interpreted and amplified by **case law**. The Inland Revenue also issue:

(a) **statements of practice,** setting out how they intend to apply the law;

(b) **extra-statutory concessions,** setting out circumstances in which they will not apply the strict letter of the law;

(c) a wide range of **explanatory leaflets**;

(d) **business economic notes**. These are notes on particular types of business, which are used as background information by the Inland Revenue and are also published;

(e) the **Tax Bulletin**. This is a newsletter giving the Inland Revenue's view on specific points. It is published every two months;

(f) the **Internal Guidance**, a series of manuals used by Inland Revenue staff.

However, none of these Inland Revenue publications has the force of law.

A great deal of information and the Inland Revenue publications can now be found on the Revenue's internet site.

1.2 The main taxes, their incidence and their sources, are set out in the table below.

Tax	Suffered/paid by	Source
Income tax	**Individuals**	Income and Corporation Taxes Act 1988 (ICTA 1988) and subsequent Finance Acts; Capital Allowances Act 2001 (CAA 2001)
Corporation tax	**Companies**	As above
Capital gains tax	**Individuals** **Companies** (which pay tax on capital gains in the form of corporation tax)	Taxation of Chargeable Gains Act 1992 (TCGA 1992) and subsequent Finance Acts
Value added tax	**Businesses**, both incorporated and unincorporated	Value Added Tax Act 1994 (VATA 1994) and subsequent Finance Acts

1.3 **Finance Acts** are passed each year, incorporating proposals set out in the **Budget**. They make changes which apply mainly to the year ahead. This Study Text includes the provisions of the Finance Act 2001. This will be examined in May and November 2002.

1.4 **Income tax, capital gains tax and corporation tax are direct taxes. Value added tax is an indirect tax** because it is imposed on taxpayers through the chain of supply (see later in this text).

1.5 Note that you will not be expected to compute income tax or capital gains tax in your exam. The only aspects of the taxation of individuals that are in the syllabus are the computation of an individual's employment income, and advice on whether it is better to reward an employee with salary or dividends. We will look at this later in this text.

1.6 The **Treasury** formally imposes and collects taxation. The management of the Treasury is the responsibility of the Chancellor of the Exchequer. The Treasury appoint the **Board of Inland Revenue** (sometimes referred to, particularly in names of court cases, as the **Commissioners of Inland Revenue (CIR)**), a body of civil servants. The Board administers income tax, corporation tax, capital gains tax and national insurance contributions. Rules on the administration of these taxes are contained in the **Taxes Management Act 1970 (TMA 1970)**.

1.7 The UK is divided into a number of **regions** (each under a regional controller). Each region is subdivided into **districts.** There are also a number of business streams such as the IR's

Savings, Pensions and Share Schemes 'business stream'. Each district has a **district inspector** in charge and he is assisted by other inspectors and clerical staff. The official title for an inspector is **HM Inspector of Taxes** (HMIT). The main work of the districts consists of examining the returns and accounts of individuals, businesses and companies.

1.8   The collection of tax is not the responsibility of inspectors but of **collectors** of taxes. The collector will pursue unpaid tax through the courts. In extreme circumstances, the collector may seize the assets of the taxpayer.

1.9   Although the functions of 'Collectors' and 'Inspectors' are currently kept separate the Treasury is considering combining them and has enacted legislation which enables 'Collectors' and 'Inspectors' to be interchangeable terms in the legislation. The term '**Officer of the Board**' is now generally used in legislation.

1.10   The structure of offices set out above is also being changed. **Taxpayer service offices** are being set up to do routine checking, computation *and* collection work, while **Taxpayer district offices** investigate selected accounts, deal with corporation tax and enforce the payment of tax when it is not paid willingly. **Taxpayer assistance offices** handle enquiries and arrange specialist help for taxpayers.

1.11   The **General Commissioners** (not to be confused with the CIR) are appointed by the Lord Chancellor to hear **appeals** against Revenue decisions. They are part-time and unpaid. They are appointed for a local area (a **division**). They appoint a clerk who is often a lawyer or accountant and who is paid for his services by the Board of Inland Revenue.

1.12   The **Special Commissioners** are also appointed by the Lord Chancellor. They are full-time paid professionals. They generally hear the more complex appeals.

1.13   **Many taxpayers arrange for their accountants to prepare and submit their tax returns. The taxpayer is still the person responsible for submitting the return and for paying whatever tax becomes due: the accountant is only acting as the taxpayer's agent.**

2   THE SCOPE OF CORPORATION TAX

2.1   Companies must pay corporation tax on their **profits chargeable to corporation tax** for each **accounting period**. We look at the meaning of these terms below.

> **KEY TERM**
>
> A '**company**' is any corporate body (limited or unlimited) or unincorporated association.

2.2   The term 'company' includes sports clubs or political associations which are not run as partnerships. Charities and local authorities are not liable to corporation tax.

BPP PUBLISHING

3 PROFITS CHARGEABLE TO CORPORATION TAX

3.1   A company may have both income and gains. As a general rule income arises from receipts which are expected to recur regularly (such as the profits from a trade) whereas chargeable gains arise on the sale of capital assets which have been owned for several years (such as the sale of a factory used in the trade).

3.2   A company may receive income from various sources. **Most income is taxed under a set of rules known as a schedule.** Schedule D is divided into cases:

Schedule A	Income from land and buildings (rents and so on) in the UK
Schedules B and C	Abolished
Schedule D	
Case I	Profits of trades
Case III	Interest from non trading loan relationships (see later)
Case V	Income from foreign possessions (for example foreign dividends, rents, business profits and pensions)
Case VI	Any annual profits not falling under any other schedule or case (such as casual commissions)

3.3   **The schedules and cases are important because each has its own set of rules.** Once we have decided that income is taxed under, say, Schedule A, the rules of Schedule A determine the amount of income taxed in any period. Each of the types of income that a company might receive is considered in detail later in this text.

3.4   A company receives some income, known as **taxed income**, net of income tax:

(a)   Patent royalties, annuities and other annual payments are received net of tax at 22% where the payer is not a UK company

(b)   Interest on most gilt edged securities is received gross but in certain limited circumstances it is received net of tax at 20%

(c)   Prior to 1 April 2001; interest received from another UK company (such as debenture or loan stock interest) was received net of tax at 20%

(d)   Prior to 1 April 2001 patent royalties annuities and other annual payments received from another UK company were received net of tax at 22%.

3.5   **The gross amount of taxed income, ie the amount received plus the income tax withheld at source is included in the computation of a company's profits chargeable to corporation tax** (see below). For example, a patent royalty received from an individual of £7,800 is grossed up by multiplying it by 100/100-22. This gives £10,000 gross (£7,800 received plus £2,200 income tax withheld at source by the payer) to include in the computation of profits. We will see how the income tax withheld at source must be dealt with later in this text.

3.6   All taxed income other than interest income is included as a separate item in the corporation tax computation (see the proforma below). Interest income is included either within Schedule D Case I or within Schedule D Case III income. We look at interest income later in this text.

3.7   **A company's profits chargeable to corporation tax are arrived at by aggregating its various sources of income and chargeable gains and then deducting charges on income.** Here is a pro forma computation. All items are explained later in this text.

	£
Schedule D Case I	X
Schedule D Case III	X
Schedule D Case V	X
Schedule D Case VI	X
Schedule A	X
Taxed income (gross)	X
Chargeable gains	X
Total profits	X
Less charges on income (gross)	(X)
Profits chargeable to corporation tax (PCTCT) for an accounting period	X

Exam focus point

It would be of great help in the exam if you could learn the above proforma. Then when answering a corporation tax question you could immediately reproduce the proforma and insert the appropriate numbers as you are given the information in the question.

3.8 **Dividends received from UK resident companies are not included in the profits chargeable to corporation tax.** The one exception to this rule is where shares are held as trading assets, and not as investments, any dividends on those shares will be treated for tax purposes as trading profits.

Charges on income

3.9 Having arrived at a company's total profits, charges on income are deducted to arrive at the profits chargeable to corporation tax (PCTCT).

KEY TERM

A **charge on income** is a payment which tax law allows as a deduction.

3.10 Examples of charges on income include

    (a) patent royalties

    (b) copyright royalties

    (c) charitable donations paid under the gift aid scheme (see below)

3.11 **A company must withhold basic rate (see below) income tax from any patent royalties paid to a non corporate recipient.** The income tax withheld must be accounted for to the Inland Revenue. The method used to account for the income tax withheld is covered later in this text. Essentially, any tax withheld must be paid to the Inland Revenue if it cannot be matched with tax suffered on income received net.

3.12 The basic rate of income tax has been 22% since 6.4.00. This means that if a patent royalty of £10,000 gross is to be paid to an individual, the company must withhold income tax of £2,200 and make a net payment of £7,800. Prior to 6.4.00 the basic rate of income tax was 23%. Prior to 6 April 2001 basic rate income tax was also withheld when patent royalties were paid to a corporate recipient.

3.13 **The gross amount of the charges paid in an accounting period is deducted in the computation of profits chargeable to corporation tax.**

3.14 **Copyright royalties and payments to charity under the gift aid scheme (see below) are paid gross.** Patent royalties paid to corporate recipients are now paid gross. Prior to 6.4.01 patent royalties were always paid by companies net of basic rate income tax.

Donations to charities

3.15 Almost all donations of money to charity can be made under the **gift aid scheme** whether they are one off donations or are regular donations made, for example, under a deed of covenant. **Gift aid donations are paid gross.**

3.16 A donation by a close company (a company under the control of five or fewer people or of their shareholder-directors (see later in the text), will not be a qualifying donation under the gift aid scheme if:

(a) the company, persons connected with it, or persons connected with those connected persons, between them receive benefits from the charity, as a result of the donation worth more than:

Donation	Maximum benefit
< £100	25% of the total donations made in that accounting period
> £100 < £1,000	£25
> £1,000 < £10,000	2.5% of the total donations made in that accounting period
> £10,000	£250

(b) the gift is subject to any condition of repayment.

3.17 Companies are connected with anyone controlling them, with other companies under common control and with partnerships under common control.

3.18 Donations to charities which are incurred wholly and exclusively for the purposes of a trade are deducted in the calculation of Schedule D Case I profits instead of as charges on income. We will look at the calculation of Schedule D Case I profits later in this text.

4 ACCOUNTING PERIODS

4.1 **Corporation tax is chargeable in respect of accounting periods.** It is important to understand the difference between an accounting period and a period of account. A period of account is any period for which a company prepares accounts; usually this will be 12 months in length but it may be longer or shorter than this. An accounting period starts when a company starts to trade, or otherwise becomes liable to corporation tax, or immediately after the previous accounting period finishes. An accounting period finishes on the earliest of:

(a) 12 months after its start;
(b) the end of the company's period of account;
(c) the commencement of the company's winding up;
(d) the company's ceasing to be resident in the UK;
(e) the company's ceasing to be liable to corporation tax.

4.2 **If a company has a period of account, exceeding 12 months (a long period), it is split into two accounting periods: the first 12 months and the remainder.** For example, if a company prepares accounts for the sixteen months to 30 April 2001, the two accounting periods for which the company will pay corporation tax will be the twelve months to 31 December 2000 and the four months to 30 April 2001.

4.3 Where a company has a long period of account (as in the above example), profits are **allocated to the relevant periods** as follows:

- **Trading income** before capital allowances is apportioned on a **time basis**. Capital allowances are a form of tax depreciation that will be covered later in this text.

- **Capital allowances are calculated for each accounting period.**

- **Schedule A and Schedule D Case III** income is allocated to the period in which it accrues.

- **Taxed income** is allocated to the period in which it is received.

- **Schedule D Case VI** income is apportioned on a time basis.

- **Schedule D Case V income is allocated to the period to which it relates.**

- **Chargeable gains** are allocated to the **period in which they are realised.**

- **Charges on income** are deducted in the accounting **period in which they are paid.**

Question: Long period of account

M Ltd had the following results for its fifteen month accounting period ended 30 September 2001.

	£
Trading profits	150,000
Chargeable gains	
- realised 4.5.01	5,000
- realised 1.9.01	4,000
Charges paid (gross)	
- 4.10.00	1,000
- 5.8.01	2,000

The company was not entitled to any capital allowances

Compute the profits chargeable to corporation tax for the two accounting periods falling into this period of account.

Answer

	Y/e 30.6.01	3 m/e 30.9.01
	£	£
Trading profits	120,000	30,000
Chargeable gains	5,000	4,000
Less charges paid	(1,000)	(2,000)
Profits chargeable to corporation tax	124,000	32,000

---

5 THE CHARGE TO CORPORATION TAX

5.1 **The rates of corporation tax are fixed for financial years. A financial year runs from 1 April to the following 31 March and is identified by the calendar year in which it begins.** For example, the year ended 31 March 2002 is the financial year 2001 (FY 2001).

5.2 The full rate of corporation tax is 30% for FY 1999 to FY 2001.

The small companies rate (SCR)

5.3 **The SCR of corporation tax (20% for FY 1999, FY 2000 and FY 2001) applies to the profits chargeable to corporation tax of UK resident companies whose 'profits' are not more than £300,000.**

5.4 **'Profits' means profits chargeable to corporation tax plus the grossed-up amount of dividends received from other UK companies** (excluding dividends received from companies **in the same group**). Since 6.4.99 UK company dividends have been received net of a 10% tax credit. We, therefore, gross up dividends received by multiplying them by 100/90. Prior to 6.4.1999 dividends were grossed up by multiplying them by 100/80.

5.5 You may see the grossed up amount of dividend received referred to as **franked investment income (FII).**

Question: The small companies rate

B Ltd had the following results for the year ended 31 March 2002.

	£
Schedule D Case I	42,000
Dividend received 1 May 2001	9,000

Compute the corporation tax payable.

Answer

	£
Schedule D Case I	42,000
Dividend plus tax credit £9,000 × 100/90	10,000
'Profits' (below £300,000 limit)	52,000
Corporation tax payable	
£42,000 × 20%	£8,400

The starting rate

5.6 **A new 10% starting rate of corporation tax was introduced with effect from 1 April 2000. It applies to companies with 'profits' of up to £10,000 for FY 2000 and FY 2001.**

Question: The starting rate of corporation tax

Dexter Limited has the following income for the year ended 31 March 2002.

(a) Schedule D, Case I income of £9,500, and
(b) Franked investment income of £300.

Calculate the corporation tax liability for the year.

Answer

	£
Schedule D, Case I	9,500
Franked investment income	300
'Profits'	9,800
Corporation tax on PCTCT £9,500 × 10%	£950

Marginal relief

5.7 **Small companies marginal relief (sometimes called taper relief) applies where the 'profits' of an accounting period of a UK resident company are over £300,000 but under £1,500,000. We first calculate the corporation tax at the full rate and then deduct:**

$(M - P) \times I/P \times$ **marginal relief fraction**

where   **M = upper limit (currently £1,500,000)**
             P = 'profits' (see above Paragraph)
             I = PCTCT

The marginal relief fraction is 1/40 for FY 1997 to FY 2001 inclusive.

Question: Small companies marginal relief

Lenox Ltd has the following results for the year ended 31 March 2002.

	£
PCTCT	296,000
Dividend received 1 December 2001	12,600

Calculate the corporation tax liability.

Answer

	£
PCTCT	296,000
Dividend plus tax credit £12,600 × 100/90	14,000
'Profits'	310,000

'Profits' are above £300,000 but below £1,500,000, so marginal relief applies.

	£
Corporation tax on PCTCT £296,000 × 30%	88,800
Less small companies' marginal relief	
£(1,500,000 – 310,000) × 296,000/310,000 × 1/40	(28,406)
	60,394

5.8 **For companies with 'profits' between £10,001 and £50,000, the small companies rate less a starting rate marginal relief applies from 1 April 2000.** The formula for calculating this marginal relief is the same as that given above except that 'M' is the upper limit for starting rate purposes. (£50,000 – FY 2000 and FY 2001). The small companies rate only applies in full when 'profits' exceed £50,000.

Question: Starting rate marginal relief

Armstrong Ltd has the following income for its year ended 31 March 2002:

		£
(a)	Schedule D, Case I	29,500
(b)	Franked investment income	3,000

Calculate the corporation tax liability.

Answer

	£
Schedule D Case I	29,500
Franked investment income	3,000
Profits	32,500

	£
Corporation tax at small companies rate:	
£29,500 × 20%	5,900
Less: starting rate marginal relief -	
1/40 × ((£50,000 − £32,500) × £29,500/£32,500)	(397)
Corporation tax payable	5,503

Changes in the rate - Accounting periods straddling 31 March

5.9 **If there is a change in the corporation tax rate, and a company's accounting period does not fall entirely within one financial year, the profits of the accounting period are apportioned to the two financial years on a time basis.** Note that the profits as a whole are apportioned. We do not look at components of the profit individually, unlike apportionment of profits of a long period of account to two accounting periods.

Question: A change in the rate

Frances Ltd makes up accounts to 31 December each year. For the year ended 31 December 1999 its profit and loss account was as follows.

	£
PCTCT	644,000
Dividends plus tax credits	10,000
'Profits'	654,000

Calculate the corporation tax liability for the year. (Note that the full rate of corporation tax was 31% for FY 1998).

Answer

	FY 1998 3 months to 31 March 1999 £	FY 1999 9 months to 31 December 1999 £
PCTCT (divided 3:9)	161,000	483,000
'Profits' (divided 3:9)	163,500	490,500
Lower limit for SCR		
FY 1998 £300,000 × 3/12	75,000	
FY 1999 £300,000 × 9/12		225,000
Upper limit for SCR		
FY 1998 £1,500,000 × 3/12	375,000	
FY 1999 £1,500,000 × 9/12		1,125,000
Tax on PCTCT		
FY 1998: £161,000 × 31%		49,910
Less small companies' marginal relief		
£(375,000 − 163,500) × 161,000/163,500 × 1/40		(5,207)
		44,703
FY 1999: £483,000 × 30%	144,900	
Less small companies' marginal relief		
£(1,125,000 − 490,500) × 483,000/490,500 × 1/40	(15,620)	
		129,280
Corporation tax payable		173,983

5.10 The 'profits' falling into each financial year determines the rate of corporation tax that applies to the PCTCT of that year. This could be the full rate, the small companies' rate or, for periods falling into either FY 2000 or FY 2001, the starting rate.

Question: Period straddling 1 April 2000

Hewson Ltd had the following results for its year ended 30 September 2000.

Schedule D Case I	£9,500
Franked investment income	£300

Calculate the corporation tax liability for the year.

Answer

	FY 1999 6 months to 31.3.00 £	FY 2000 6 months to 30.9.00 £
'Profits' (£9,800)	4,900	4,900
Profit chargeable to corporation tax	4,750	4,750
Lower limit for starting rate (– : 6m)	-	5,000
Lower limit for SCR (6m : 6m)	150,000	150,000
Corporation tax payable		
£4,750 × 20%		950
£4,750 × 10%		475
Total corporation tax payable for 12 months APE 30.9.00		1,425

Associated companies and short accounting periods

> ### KEY TERM
>
> The expression **'associated companies'** in tax has no connection with financial accounting. For tax purposes a company is associated with another company if either controls the other or if both are under the control of the same person or persons (individuals, partnerships or companies). Whether such a company is UK resident or not is irrelevant (even though non-UK resident companies cannot benefit from the starting rate, small companies rate or from marginal relief). Control is given by holding over 50% of the share capital or the voting power or being entitled to over 50% of the distributable income or of the net assets in a winding up.

5.11 **If a company has one or more 'associated companies', then the profit limits for starting rate and small companies rate purposes are divided by the number of associated companies + 1 (for the company itself).**

5.12 Companies which have only been associated for part of an accounting period are deemed to have been associated for the whole period for the purpose of determining the profit limits.

5.13 An associated company is ignored for these purposes if it has not carried on any trade or business at any time in the accounting period (or the part of the period during which it was associated). **This means that you must ignore dormant companies.** A holding company counts as not carrying on any trade or business so long as:

- Its only assets are shares in subsidiaries

- It is not entitled to deduct any outgoings as charges or management expenses, and

- Its only profits are dividends from subsidiaries, which are distributed in full to its shareholders.

Question: Associated companies

J Ltd has two associated companies. In the year ended 31 December 2001, it had profits chargeable to corporation tax of £400,000. Dividends of £45,000 were received on 30 September 2001. What is the corporation tax payable for the year?

Answer

Year ended 31.12.2001 falls 3 months into FY 2000 and 9 months into FY 2001

	FY 2000 £	FY 2001 £
Profits chargeable to corporation tax	100,000	300,000
'Profits' for small companies rate purposes (400,000 + 45,000 × 100/90)	112,500	337,500
Lower limit for small companies rate	25,000	75,000
Upper limit for small companies rate	125,000	375,000

As there are two associated companies (plus J Ltd), the upper and lower limits are divided by 3.

Small companies marginal relief applies in both years.

	£
FY 2000	
£100,000 × 30%	30,000
Less	
$£(125,000 - 112,500) \times \dfrac{100,000}{112,500} \times \dfrac{1}{40}$	(278)
FY 2001	
£300,000 × 30%	90,000
Less	
$£(375,000 - 337,500) \times \dfrac{300,000}{337,500} \times \dfrac{1}{40}$	(833)
	118,889

5.14 **The profit limits are reduced proportionately if an accounting period lasts for less than 12 months.**

Question: Short accounting periods

For the nine months to 31 January 2002 a company with no other associated companies had PCTCT of £278,000 and no dividends received. Compute the corporation tax payable.

Answer

(a) Reduction in the lower limit for small companies' rate purposes as the accounting period is only nine months long

£300,000 × 9/12 = £225,000

(b) Reduction in the upper limit

£1,500,000 × 9/12 = £1,125,000

(c) 'Profits' = £278,000

(d) Corporation tax

	£
£278,000 × 30%	83,400
Less small companies' marginal relief £(1,125,000 – 278,000) × 1/40	(21,175)
Corporation tax	62,225

Marginal rate of tax

5.15 Note that when a company is given small companies marginal relief, a marginal rate of tax of 32.5% is being charged on the profits chargeable to corporation tax which fall into the small companies' marginal relief band. Similarly, the marginal rate of tax is 22.5% for profits which fall into the starting rate marginal relief band. You may need to be aware of these tax rates in tax planning questions.

Chapter roundup

- Profits chargeable to corporation tax are income plus gains minus charges.

- Companies pay corporation tax on their profits chargeable to corporation tax profits of each accounting period. The rate of tax depends on the level of 'profits'.

- Tax rates are set for financial years.

- Companies may be entitled to the starting rate, the small companies rate or to marginal relief, depending on their 'profits' (profits chargeable to corporation tax plus grossed up dividends received).

Quick quiz

1   When does an accounting period end?

2   How are trading profits (before capital allowances) of a long period of account divided between accounting periods?

3   How is taxed income dealt with in a corporation tax computation?

4   From which date will a company pay gross debenture interest to another UK company?

5   Which companies are entitled to the starting rate of corporation tax?

6   What is an associated company?

Answers to quick quiz

1   An accounting period ends on the earliest of:

   (a)   12 months after its start
   (b)   the end of the company's period of account
   (c)   the commencement of the company's winding up
   (d)   the company ceasing to be resident in the UK
   (e)   the company ceasing to be liable to corporation tax

2   Trading profits (before capital allowances) are apportioned on a time basis.

3   Taxed income is included in the calculation of PCTCT at its gross equivalent

4   1 April 2001

5   Companies with 'profits' of up to £10,000

6   A company is associated with another company if either controls the other or if both are under the control of the same person or persons (Individual, partnership or companies).

Now try the question below from the Exam Question Bank

Number	Level	Marks	Time
1	Exam	20	36 mins

Chapter 2

PAYMENT OF TAX BY COMPANIES

Topic list		Syllabus reference	Ability required
1	Returns, records, enquiries, assessments and claims	(i)	Comprehension
2	Payment of tax and interest	(iii)	Application
3	Advance corporation tax (ACT)	(iii), (vii)	Application
4	Income tax suffered or withheld from charges and interest	(iii)	Application

Introduction

We have previously looked at the computation of a company's CT liability. In this chapter we look at the self assessment system for CT.

Advance corporation tax (ACT) had to be paid in respect of certain payments made before 6.4.99. We will look at ACT and the system for relieving any unused ACT brought forward on 6.4.99. We shall also see how income tax is accounted for. Companies are not supposed to pay income tax so the effects of deducting income tax at source need to be neutralised.

Learning outcomes covered in this chapter

- **Describe** the system of corporation tax self assessment (CTSA)
- **Identify** the key dates for submission of returns
- **Describe** the Inland Revenue's powers of enquiry
- **Identify** the various penalties and interest charges in CTSA
- **Identify** the minimum record keeping requirements
- **Prepare** a schedule of CT payments of a large company covering a two year period under the quarterly payment system
- **Explain** the operation of shadow ACT
- **Demonstrate** the planning aspects of maximising the use of surplus ACT existing at 6 April 1999 for a company

Syllabus content covered in this chapter

- Corporation tax self assessment- all compliance aspects including: returns; deadlines; interest and penalties; Revenue enquiries; appeals; time limits
- Payment of CT liability; quarterly payment arrangements for large companies; group payment arrangements
- ACT and Shadow ACT: all aspects including the calculation of shadow ACT and the use of surplus ACT existing at 6.4.99
- Integration of tax planning into the budgeting process

1 RETURNS, RECORDS, ENQUIRIES, ASSESSMENTS AND CLAIMS

1.1 **A company's tax return (CT 600) must include a self assessment of any tax payable.**

Returns

1.2 **An obligation to file a return arises only when the company receives a notice requiring a return.** A return is required for each accounting period ending during or at the end of the period specified in the notice requiring a return. A company also has to file a return for certain other periods which are not accounting periods (eg for a period when the company is dormant).

1.3 A company that does not receive a notice requiring a return must, if it is chargeable to tax, **notify the Revenue within twelve months of the end of the accounting period.** Failure to do so results in a maximum penalty equal to the tax unpaid twelve months after the end of the accounting period. Tax for this purpose includes corporation tax, notional tax on loans to participators of close companies (see later in this text) and any tax on the apportioned profits of controlled foreign companies (see later in this text).

1.4 A notice to file a return may also require other information, accounts and reports. For a UK resident company the requirement to deliver accounts normally extends only to the accounts required under the Companies Act.

1.5 A return is due on or before the filing date. This is the later of:

(a) **12 months after the end of the period to which the return relates;**

(b) **if the relevant period of account is not more than 18 months long, 12 months from the end of the period of account;**

(c) **if relevant the period of account is more than 18 months long, 30 months from the start of the period of account;** and

(d) **three months from the date on which the notice requiring the return was made.**

The relevant period of account is that in which the accounting period to which the return relates ends.

Question: Filing date

A Ltd prepares accounts for the eighteen months to 30 June 2001. A notice requiring a return for the year ended 30 June 2001 was issued to A Ltd on 1 September 2001. State the periods for which A Ltd must file a tax return and the filing dates.

Answer

The company must file a return for the two accounting periods ending in the period specified in the notice requiring a return. The first accounting period is the twelve months to 31 December 2000 and the second is the six months to 30 June 2001. The filing date is twelve months after the end of the relevant period of account, 30 June 2002.

1.6 **There is a £100 penalty for a failure to submit a return on time, rising to £200 if the delay exceeds three months. These penalties become £500 and £1,000 respectively when a return was late (or never submitted) for each of the preceding two accounting periods.**

1.7 **An additional tax geared penalty is applied if a return is more than six months late. The penalty is 10% of the tax unpaid six months after the return was due if the total delay is up to 12 months, and 20% of that tax if the return is over 12 months late.**

1.8 There is a tax geared penalty for a fraudulent or negligent return and for failing to correct an innocent error without unreasonable delay. The maximum penalty is equal to the tax that would have been lost had the return been accepted as correct. The Revenue can mitigate this penalty. If a company is liable to more than one tax geared penalty, the total penalty is limited to the maximum single penalty that could be charged.

1.9 A company may amend a return within twelve months of the filing date. The Revenue may amend a return to correct obvious errors within nine months of the day the return was filed, or if the correction is to an amended return, within nine months of the filing of an amendment. The company may amend its return so as to reject the correction. If the time limit for amendments has expired, the company may reject the correction by giving notice within three months.

Records

1.10 Companies must keep records until the latest of:

(a) six years from the end of the accounting period;

(b) the date any enquiries are completed;

(c) the date after which enquiries may not be commenced.

All business records and accounts, including contracts and receipts, must be kept.

1.11 If a return is demanded more than six years after the end of the accounting period, any records which the company still has must be kept until the later of the end of any enquiry and the expiry of the right to start an enquiry.

1.12 Failure to keep records can lead to a penalty of up to £3,000 for each accounting period affected. However, this penalty does not apply when the only records which have not been kept are ones which could only have been needed for the purposes of claims, elections or notices not included in the return.

1.13 The Revenue do not generally insist on original records being kept but original records of the following must be preserved:

(a) Qualifying distributions and tax credits

(b) Gross and net payments and tax deducted for payments made net of tax

(c) Certificates of payments made to sub-contractors net of tax

(d) Details of foreign tax paid, although the Revenue will accept photocopies or foreign tax assessments when calculating underlying tax (see later in this text) on dividends from abroad

Enquiries

1.14 **A return or an amendment need not be accepted at face value by the Revenue. They may enquire into it, provided that they first give written notice that they are going to enquire.** The notice must be given by a year after the later of:

(a) The filing date;

(b) The 31 January, 30 April, 31 July or 31 October next following the actual date of delivery of the return or amendment.

Only one enquiry may be made in respect of any one return or amendment.

1.15 If a notice of an enquiry has been given, the Revenue may demand that the company produce documents for inspection and copying. However, documents relating to an appeal need not be produced and the company may appeal against a notice requiring documents to be produced.

1.16 If the Revenue demand documents, but the company does not produce them, there is a penalty of £50. There is also a daily penalty, which applies for each day from the day after the imposition of the £50 penalty until the documents are produced. The daily penalty may be imposed by the Revenue, in which case it is £30. If, however, the Revenue ask the Commissioners to impose the penalty, it is £150.

1.17 The Revenue may amend a self assessment at any time during an enquiry if they believe there might otherwise be a loss of tax. The company may appeal against such an amendment within 30 days. The company may itself make amendments during an enquiry under the normal rules for amendments. No effect will be given to such amendments during the enquiry but they may be taken into account in the enquiry.

1.18 An enquiry ends when the Revenue give notice that it has been completed and notify what they believe to be the correct amount of tax payable. Before that time, the company may ask the Commissioners to order the Revenue to notify the completion of its enquiry by a specified date. Such a direction will be given unless the Revenue can demonstrate that they have reasonable grounds for continuing the enquiry.

1.19 The company has 30 days from the end of an enquiry to amend its self assessment in accordance with the Revenue's conclusions. If the Revenue are not satisfied with the company's amendments, they have a further 30 days to amend the self assessment. The company then has another 30 days in which it may appeal against the Revenue's amendments.

Determinations and discovery assessments

1.20 If a return is not delivered by the filing date, the Revenue may issue a determination of the tax payable within the five years from the filing date. This is treated as a self assessment and there is no appeal against it. However, it is automatically replaced by any self assessment made by the company by the later of five years from the filing date and 12 months from the determination.

1.21 If the Revenue believe that not enough tax has been assessed for an accounting period they can make a discovery assessment to collect the extra tax. However, when a tax return has been delivered this power is limited as outlined in 1.22 and 1.23 below.

1.22 No discovery assessment can be made on account of an error or mistake as to the basis on which the tax liability ought to be computed, if the basis generally prevailing at the time when the return was made was applied.

1.23 A discovery assessment can only be made if either:

(a) the loss of tax is due to fraudulent or negligent conduct by the company or by someone acting on its behalf; or

(b) the Revenue could not reasonably be expected to have been aware of the loss of tax, given the information so far supplied to them, when their right to start an enquiry expired or when they notified the company that an enquiry had finished.

1.24 The time limit for raising a discovery assessment is six years from the end of the accounting period but this is extended to 21 years if there has been fraudulent or negligent conduct. The company may appeal against a discovery assessment within 30 days of issue.

Claims

1.25 Wherever possible claims must be made on a tax return or on an amendment to it and must be quantified at the time the return is made.

1.26 If a company believes that it has paid excessive tax because of an error in a return, an error or mistake claim may be made within six years from the end of the accounting period. An appeal against a decision on such a claim must be made within 30 days. An error or mistake claim may not be made if the return was made in accordance with a generally accepted practice which prevailed at the time.

1.27 Other claims must be made by six years after the end of the accounting period, unless a different time limit is specified. If an error or mistake is made in a claim, a supplementary claim may be made within the time limit for the original claim.

1.28 If the Revenue amend a self assessment or issue a discovery assessment then the company has a further period to make, vary or withdraw a claim (unless the claim is irrevocable) even if this is outside the normal time limit. The period is one year from the end of the accounting period in which the amendment or assessment was made, or one year from the end of the accounting period in which the enquiry was closed if the amendment is the result of an enquiry. The relief is limited where there has been fraudulent or negligent conduct by the company or its agent.

2 PAYMENT OF TAX AND INTEREST

2.1 Corporation tax is due for payment by small and medium sized companies **nine months after the end of the accounting period**.

2.2 **Interest is charged on corporation tax paid late and interest is paid to companies on corporation tax overpaid or paid early. This interest paid/received is dealt with under Schedule D Case III as interest paid /received on a non trading loan relationship** (See later in this text).

2.3 Other points to note in respect of interest on overpaid corporation tax or corporation tax paid early are:

- the earliest date from which interest can be calculated is the date for the first instalment payment of corporation tax by large companies (see below);

- interest is paid from the day after the end of the accounting period if the refund is in respect of income tax suffered on payments received (see below);

- there will be a recovery, without assessment, of interest paid to companies where subsequent events show it ought not to have been paid; and

- there are restrictions on the amount of interest paid to companies (or the amount by which interest due from companies is reduced) where reliefs are carried back.

Quarterly payments of corporation tax liabilities

2.4 A system of quarterly payments on account for corporation tax liabilities is being phased in over a four year period. **For accounting periods ending between 1.7.99 and 30.6.00 a 'large' company paid 60% of its corporation tax by four equal instalments each of 15% with the remaining 40% as a balancing payment nine months after the accounting end. Then:**

- **72% in instalments (4 × 18%), 28% as a balance for APs ending between 1.7.00 and 30.6.01;**
- **88% in instalments (4 × 22%), 12% as a balance for APs ending between 1.7.01 and 30.6.02;**
- **100% in instalments (4 × 25%) thereafter.**

2.5 **Instalments are due on the 14th day of the month, starting in the seventh month. Provided that the accounting period is twelve months long subsequent instalments are due in the tenth month during the accounting period and in the first and fourth months after the end of the accounting period. If an accounting period is less than twelve months long subsequent instalments are due at three monthly intervals but with the final payment being due in the fourth month of the next accounting period.**

2.6 EXAMPLE

X Ltd is a large company with a 31 December accounting year end. Instalments of corporation tax will be due to be paid by X Ltd on:

- 14 July and 14 October in the accounting period;
- 14 January and 14 April after the accounting period ends

Thus for the year ended 31 December 2001 instalment payments are due on 14 July 2001, 14 October 2001, 14 January 2002 and 14 April 2002.

2.7 Instalments are based on the estimated corporation tax liability for the current period (not the previous period). This means that it will be extremely important for companies to forecast their tax liabilities accurately. Large companies whose directors are poor at estimating may find their company's incurring significant interest charges. The amount of each instalment is computed by:

(a) working out $3 \times CT/n$ where CT is the amount of the estimated corporation tax liability payable in instalments for the period and n is the number of months in the period;

(b) allocating the smaller of that amount and the total estimated corporation tax liability to the first instalment;

(c) repeating the process for later instalments until the amount allocated is equal to the corporation tax liability. This gives four equal instalments for 12 month accounting periods and also caters for periods which end earlier than expected.

The company is therefore required to estimate its corporation tax liability before the end of the accounting period, and must revise its estimate each quarter.

Question: Short accounting period

A company has a CT liability of £1,000,000 for the eight month period to 30 November 2001. Accounts had previously always been prepared to 31 March. Show when the CT liability is due for payment.

21 **BPP**
PUBLISHING

Answer

88% of £1,000,000 = £880,000 must be paid in instalments.

The amount of each instalment is $3 \times \dfrac{£880,000}{8} = £330,000$

The due dates are:

	£
14 October 2001	330,000
14 January 2002	330,000
14 March 2002	220,000 (balance)

The final payment of £120,000 is due for payment on 1 September 2002.

2.8 **Broadly, a 'large company' is a company that pays corporation tax at the full rate** (profits exceed £1.5 million where there are no associated companies).

2.9 A company is not required to pay instalments in the first year that it is 'large', unless its profits exceed £10 million. The £10 million limit is reduced proportionately if there are associated companies. For this purpose only, a company will be regarded as an associated company where it was an associated company at the START of an accounting period. (This differs from the normal approach in CT where being an associated company for any part of the AP affects the thresholds of both companies for the whole of the AP).

2.10 There is a de minimis limit in that any company whose liability for its accounting period ending on or after 1 July 2000 does not exceed £10,000 need not pay by instalments.

2.11 Interest runs from the due date on over/underpaid instalments. The position is looked at cumulatively after the due date for each instalment. The Revenue calculate the interest position after the company submits its corporation tax return.

2.12 EXAMPLE

X plc prepared accounts to 31.12.01. The company has always prepared accounts to 31 December each year. It paid CT instalments of:

Date	Amount
	£
14.7.01	3.5m
14.10.01	8.5m
14.01.02	4.5m
14.4.02	4.5m
	21.0m

X plc's CT return showed a CT liability of £25m. The £4m balance was paid on 1.10.02. £22m (88% × £25m) should have been paid in instalments. The under(over) payments were:

Date	Paid	Correct	Under(over) paid
	£	£	£
14.7.01	3.5m	5.5m	2m
14.10.01	8.5m	5.5m	
	12.0m	11.0m	(1m)
14.1.02	4.5m	5.5m	
	16.5m	16.5m	-
14.4.02	4.5m	5.5m	
	21.0m	22.0m	1m

Interest would be charged (received) as follows.

14.7.01 - 13.10.01	Interest charged on £2m
14.10.01 - 13.1.02	Interest received on £1m
14.1.02 - 13.4.02	No interest
14.4.02 - 30.9.02	Interest charged on £1m

2.13 The rate of interest charged on underpayments of corporation tax under the quarterly instalment arrangements is one percentage point above base rate. For overpayments the interest rate is one quarter of a percentage point below base rate. The interest rates applying after the normal due date (ie nine months and one day after the end of the accounting period) are two and half percentage points above base rate for underpayments and one percentage point below base rate for overpayments.

2.14 There are penalties if a company deliberately and flagrantly fails to pay instalments of sufficient size. After a company has filed its return or the Revenue has determined its liability, the Revenue may wish to establish the reason for inadequate instalment payments. It can do this by asking the company to produce relevant information or records (presumably to decide if a penalty applies). The failure to supply these will lead to an initial fixed penalty which may also be followed by a daily penalty which may continue until the information/records are produced.

2.15 Companies can have instalments repaid if they later conclude they ought not to have been paid.

Group payment arrangements

2.16 Where more than one company in a group is liable to pay their tax by instalments, arrangements may be made for the instalments to be paid by one company (the nominated company), and allocated amongst the group. These provisions were introduced because groups often have uncertainties over the tax liabilities of individual group members until all relevant group reliefs and claims are decided upon following the end of the accounting period.

The arrangements are as follows:

(a) Eligible companies are parent companies and their 51% subsidiaries, and the 51% subsidiaries of those subsidiaries and so on. It is not necessary to include all group members, and it is possible to have several group payment arrangements for subgroups.

(b) Only companies which have filed their tax returns and settled their tax liabilities for the last but one accounting period (or new companies) are eligible to join.

(c) The arrangements apply to the period of account of the nominated companies, and this will normally be an accounting period for each participating companies. New companies, and companies which join the group may be included if they align their accounting date with that of the nominated company, but they cannot be included for accounting periods beginning before the start of the nominated company's period of account.

(d) A company may remain a participating company even if it has an accounting period which ends during the nominated company's period of account (for example if it ceased trading part of the way through the period), provided that it draws up accounts for the same period as the nominated company.

(e) Once the arrangements are in force, they will automatically apply to future periods. The nominated company must, before the due date for the first instalment for each future period, advise the Revenue of any companies joining and leaving the arrangement.

(f) Any participating company may be removed from the arrangement before the due date for the first instalment. Companies which leave the group or which do not have an accounting period ending at the end of the nominated company's period of account must be removed.

(g) The arrangement can be terminated by the nominated company for any period, providing notification is given before the first instalment date. The Revenue may terminate the arrangement if any of the terms are breached.

(h) The nominated company must sign an agreement to the arrangement, and must submit the signed agreement to the Revenue at least two months before the first payment is due.

(i) The nominated company agrees to pay all the instalments due by all of the companies covered by the arrangement. This includes the requirement to adjust the payments on the basis of amended profits forecasts, and the right to reclaim any amount it considers to be overpaid. The Revenue will not seek payment of tax from any other participating company before the closing date.

(j) After the closing date the nominated company must allocate the payments between the participating companies as it thinks fit. The Revenue may then seek payment of any shortfall from companies whose liabilities exceed allocated payments. The closing date is the date by which all of the participating companies have filed their tax returns (or determinations have been made if any returns have not been filed), but it cannot be earlier than the filing date.

(k) If any of the participating companies are liable to a tax geared penalty for the late filing of their returns (see above), any shortfall at the relevant date will be reallocated by the Revenue for the purpose of calculating the tax geared penalty. The shortfall will be allocated first to companies liable to a 20% penalty, and then to companies liable to a 10% penalty, and finally to companies not liable to a tax geared penalty. This maximises the tax geared penalty that can be charged.

3   ADVANCE CORPORATION TAX (ACT)

3.1   **Prior to 6 April 1999 advance corporation tax (ACT), at the rate of 20/80 = 1/4 of net dividends, was paid by a company to the Revenue when dividend payments were made to shareholders. ACT acted as an advance payment of corporation tax.**

3.2   The payment of ACT was abolished on 6 April 1999. From this date dividends carry a notional tax credit of 10% but the company does not actually make any payment of tax in respect of the dividend payment. A company does not get any relief for the notional tax credit.

3.3   ACT accounting was abolished because large companies now pay their corporation tax by quarterly instalments. Small and medium sized companies are also exempted from paying ACT even though they continue to pay their corporation tax nine months after the end of the accounting period. The Treasury are content to abolish ACT generally as their cashflow is maintained even by only applying quarterly tax payments to large companies.

3.4 The abolition of ACT is a significant cash flow advantage to those companies which regularly pay dividends and are not required to pay their corporation tax by instalments. It is also an advantage to large companies which normally pay substantial dividends early in their accounting period. Quarterly instalments of CT will be paid later and may be less than their ACT payments would have been.

3.5 Large companies which either do not normally pay dividends or pay them late in the year will not benefit from the abolition of ACT. Instead, their cash flow is adversely affected by the introduction of the quarterly instalments system.

Question: ACT

D Ltd has an issued share capital of 1,000,000 £1 ordinary shares. During the accounting period ending 31 March 1999 it declared a 10% dividend on 30 September 1998. The company received no dividend income itself. How much ACT was payable in respect of the dividend?

Answer

The net dividend was £100,000. This dividend gave rise to an ACT liability of £100,000 × 20/80 = £25,000.

The company made a total payment equal to the dividend plus the ACT. This is called a **franked payment** (FP), and in this example the franked payment is £125,000.

£100,000 went to shareholders and £25,000 to the Revenue.

3.6 ACT could be calculated as 20% of a franked payment or as 20/80 of the net dividend.

3.7 In many cases companies not only pay dividends, they also receive dividends from other UK resident companies. Such income will have been paid from profits which have already been subject to UK corporation tax in the hands of the paying company. This dividend income is therefore *not* taxable again in the hands of the recipient company. **Prior to 6 April 1999 the dividend received, plus the ACT on the dividend** (so a total of dividend × 100/80 at the ACT rate) **was set against any franked payments by the recipient company, before working out the ACT due.** The grossed up amount of a dividend received was known as Franked Investment Income (FII).

Dividends from unit trusts investing in shares are also FII.

Question: ACT when dividends have been received

In the example above, suppose D Ltd received a dividend of £75,000 from another UK company on 1 September 1998. What ACT would have been payable?

Answer

This cash receipt represents franked investment income of £75,000 × 100/80 = £93,750.

When D Ltd paid its own dividend on 30 September 1998 it had to account for ACT of (FP – FII) × 20%.

Thus it paid ACT of £(125,000 – 93,750) × 20% = £6,250.

3.8 **Dividends from foreign companies are not FII. They are chargeable to corporation tax under Schedule D Case V**. The gross income receivable is taxable in the corporation tax computation, after adding back any foreign taxes deducted at source. Credit is given for the foreign tax suffered against the company's corporation tax liability. We will look at this later in this text.

3.9   A surplus of FII over FP for an accounting period taken as a whole was carried forward and treated as though it were FII received on the first day of the next accounting period. This still applies after 6.4.99 (see below).

The set-off of ACT

3.10   If during an accounting period, ACT was paid to the Revenue and was not all repaid, the net amount paid could be set against the company's corporation tax liability. However, in any one accounting period, the maximum ACT set off was 20% × PCTCT.

Surplus ACT

3.11   Any ACT paid in an accounting period over and above the maximum available for set-off was known as surplus ACT. This could be:

- carried back and set against the corporation tax liability of accounting periods beginning in the preceding six years. This was subject to the maximum set-off available in each of these periods. ACT carried back had to be used in more recent accounting periods before earlier ones.

- carried forward and set against corporation tax liabilities of future accounting periods, again subject to the maximum set-off in each period. For a carry forward into periods after 5 April 1999 see below.

Dividends paid after 5 April 1999

3.12   Dividends paid after 5 April 1999 carry a tax credit equal to 10/90 of the net distribution. The franked payment is the net amount paid multiplied by 100/90.

3.13   Similarly franked investment income is defined as the net amount multiplied by 100/90.

Treatment of ACT surplus at 5 April 1999

3.14   Although ACT accounting ended on 5 April 1999, there were many companies carrying forward surplus ACT at that date. Thus there is a **'shadow ACT'** system which allows the set-off of real brought forward ACT in line with the old (ie, pre-6 April 1999) rules.

3.15   For accounting periods ending after 5 April 1999 companies can offset ACT brought forward subject to a maximum of 20% of the chargeable profits.

3.16   The maximum set-off is reduced by the ACT that would have been payable (at 20/80) on distributions made after 5 April 1999 had the old rules continued. **This 'shadow ACT' is only a notional amount and cannot itself reduce the corporation tax for the period.**

3.17   If the shadow ACT exceeds the maximum set-off for the period the excess is carried forward and used to restrict the set-off maximum for the following period.

3.18   EXAMPLE

Icon Ltd prepares accounts to 5 April each year and had a surplus of ACT of £200,000 to carry forward at 6 April 1999. In the year to 5 April 2000 it paid dividends of £80,000 and had chargeable profits of £240,000.

How much of its surplus ACT remained to be carried forward at 6 April 2000?

3.19 SOLUTION

	£
Maximum ACT set-off : £240,000 × 20%	48,000
Less: Shadow ACT £80,000 × 20/80	20,000
Capacity for ACT brought forward	28,000
Surplus ACT brought forward at 6 April 1999	200,000
Less: Used in the year to 5 April 2000	28,000
Surplus ACT carried forward at 6 April 2000	172,000

3.20 If a company has surplus franked investment income at 6 April 1999 this is carried forward and used to frank dividends paid thereby reducing any shadow ACT as if the system of quarterly accounting abolished from 6 April 1999 still applied.

3.21 If a company receives FII after 5 April 1999 it can also be used to reduce the shadow ACT as if the previous system still applied. However, FII is calculated as 100/90 of the net dividend received after 5 April 1999 so that figure has to be multiplied by 90/80 for set off against franked payments under the shadow ACT rules.

3.22 Certain distributions received by companies will not be treated as FII for the purpose of computing shadow ACT. The legislation in this area aims to prevent schemes where distributions are paid specifically to reduce the amount of shadow ACT. However, also included in the legislation here are intra-group distributions.

3.23 Surplus FII arising in future periods is merely carried forward and treated as received at the start of the following period.

3.24 EXAMPLE

Merlin Ltd prepares accounts to 31 March and pays a dividend of £24,000 on 10 September 2001. It receives a dividend of £16,000 on 2 February 2002 and had surplus ACT brought forward at 1 April 2001 of £50,000. Its PCTCT for the year to 31 March 2002 was £100,000. How much ACT remains unused at 1 April 2002?

3.25 SOLUTION

	£
Notional FP £24,000 × 100/80	30,000
FII for Shadow purposes £16,000 × 100/90 × 90/80	20,000
FP for Shadow purposes	10,000
Shadow ACT @ 20%	2,000
Maximum set-off – (£100,000 × 20%)	20,000
Reduction for shadow ACT	(2,000)
Set-off limit	18,000
Surplus ACT to carry forward at 1 April 2002	
£50,000 – £18,000	32,000

3.26 From a planning point of view companies with surplus ACT at 6 April 1999 should consider restricting dividends paid in subsequent periods. This restriction will reduce the shadow ACT arising and will therefore help with the set off of surplus b/f ACT. Alternatively, companies could consider maximising their PCTCT by not claiming all available reliefs. If PCTCT is maximised so is the maximum set off of surplus ACT b/f (ie 20% × PCTCT). Companies will need to integrate this type of tax planning into the budgeting process.

3.27 Companies which decide that the shadow ACT rules effectively preclude them from recovering actual surplus ACT brought forward are not obliged to involve themselves in the shadow ACT system.

Anti-avoidance rules

3.28 **Where there was a change in ownership of a company, ACT due in respect of distributions made on one side of the change (before or after it) could be prevented from being carried forward or back for set-off against corporation tax of a period on the other side of (after or before) the change.** A change in ownership for these purposes meant the acquisition of more than one half of the ordinary share capital of a company by a person, or by a group of persons each of whom holds more than 5%. **A company was prevented from carrying ACT forward or back through the change if within three years before or three years after the change there was a major change in the nature or conduct of its business. A company was also be prevented from carrying ACT forward or back through the change if there was *at any time* after the change a revival of the company's business which had become small or negligible by the time of the change.** With the abolition of ACT accounting this anti-avoidance rule has been abolished but an identical rule involving unrelieved surplus ACT has been inserted into the legislation to effectively replace it.

3.29 A change in ownership is disregarded if both before and after the change the company is a 75% subsidiary of the same company. This provision prevents the loss of ACT where there is a group reorganisation under which the ultimate ownership of the company does not change. A company is treated as a 75% subsidiary of another company for this purpose only if that company is entitled to at least 75% of its profits and to 75% of its assets if it is wound up.

3.30 A further anti-avoidance provision was designed to counter arrangements under which a group purchased a company with unrelieved ACT and transferred assets to the company shortly before their sale in order that the unrelieved ACT could be offset against tax on any gain arising. Where the acquired company brought forward pre-acquisition surplus ACT, and also had chargeable gains on assets which were:

- acquired in a no gain/no loss transfer (see later) from another group member after the acquisition of the company; and

- disposed of within three years of the acquisition of the company,

a special restriction applied. The limit on ACT set-off for the period of the chargeable gain was reduced by the lower of:

- the pre-acquisition ACT; and
- the ACT in a franked payment equal to the gain and made at the end of that period.

This provision applied whether or not there was a major change in the business of the company which has been acquired. Again, with the abolition of ACT accounting this anti-avoidance rule will not apply to disposals made on or after 6 April 1999 but a parallel rule in the shadow ACT regulations has been introduced to ensure similar anti-avoidance law remains in place for the purposes of unrelieved surplus ACT.

Interest treated as a distribution

3.31 **Companies might try to pay interest as an alternative to dividends, because interest is a deductible expense** (See later in this text). **This form of tax avoidance is not acceptable to the Inland Revenue and legislation exists to prevent equity investment being artificially characterised as a loan in order to obtain interest relief.**

3.32   Interest which exceeds a reasonable commercial return on the loan capital is treated as a distribution where the creditor is not a UK company.

3.33   Interest on **certain loans where there is a right to share in any increase in profits is also treated as a distribution.** However, this does not apply to interest on certain commercial loans with interest rates linked to profits ('ratchet loans'). These are loans where the rate of interest reduces as business results improve (or conversely the interest rate increases as business rates deteriorate).

4   INCOME TAX SUFFERED OR WITHHELD FROM CHARGES AND INTEREST

4.1   From 1 April 2001 **a paying company is not required to withhold income tax on payments** of:

(a)   annual interest
(b)   royalties
(c)   annuities
(d)   annual payments

if it reasonably believes that the **recipient is chargeable to corporation tax on the payment.**

4.2   Thus such payments made by one UK company to another UK company will be made gross from 1 April 2001 onwards.

4.3   However such payments made to individuals, partnerships etc (ie non companies) will still be made under deduction of income tax at 20% (eg debenture interest) or 22% (eg patent royalties).

4.4   **When the company pays interest or a charge on income it deducts the gross amount in its corporation tax computation. For items paid net** (such as debenture interest and patent royalties paid to non corporate recipients), **it acts as an agent for the Revenue and retains income tax at 20% (interest) or 22% (charges) on the gross amount for payment to the Revenue.** The *net* amount is then payable to the payees (for example the individual debenture holders).

4.5   **Companies may receive some income which has suffered 20% or basic rate, (currently 22%) income tax at source. For example, patent royalties received from an individual are received net of 22% tax.** This is known as taxed income, or unfranked investment income (UFII). The cash income plus the income tax suffered, that is the gross figure, forms part of a company's profits chargeable to corporation tax. The income tax suffered is deductible from the corporation tax liability.

4.6   **Income tax actually paid over to the Revenue (and therefore dealt with on Form CT61 – see below) is based on amounts paid and received. However, income tax on interest is dealt with on an accruals basis in working out a company's corporation tax liability.**

Quarterly accounting for income tax

4.7   **Income tax is accounted for by companies on a quarterly basis on a return form CT61. Returns are made for each of the quarters to 31 March, 30 June, 30 September and 31 December.** If the end of a company's accounting period does not coincide with one of these

BPP
PUBLISHING

dates, a fifth return must be made to the end of the accounting period (and a new return period started at the beginning of the company's next accounting period).

Question: Quarterly returns

S Ltd makes up accounts to 31 May each year. Show the income tax quarterly return periods for this company for the year to 31 May 2002.

Answer

(a)   1 June 2001 to 30 June 2001
(b)   1 July 2001 to 30 September 2001
(c)   1 October 2001 to 31 December 2001
(d)   1 January 2002 to 31 March 2002
(e)   1 April 2002 to 31 May 2002

4.8 **Each quarterly return has details of income tax suffered and income tax withheld from interest and charges.** (*Note: not the gross income and payment figures.*)

4.9 **The company must account to the Revenue for any income tax payable 14 days after the end of the return period. Interest runs from this date.**

4.10 The overall amount of income tax due is reduced by that suffered on income received.

4.11 **If a company has tax suffered on income exceeding its tax deducted from payments, it can reclaim the income tax suffered by recovering income tax payments already made through the quarterly accounting system or by reducing its corporation tax liability. If** appropriate a repayment of income tax will be made after the corporation tax computation has been submitted. There is no limit on the amount which can be set off.

Question: Quarterly accounting for income tax

Income plc has the following income and payments for the year to 31 March 2002.

		£
10.4.01	Patent royalty paid to ABC Ltd	20,000
30.4.01	Patent royalty paid to Mr Jones	10,000
30.9.01	Debenture interest received from X Ltd	14,000
30.11.01	Debenture interest paid to individuals	10,000
5.3.02	Patent royalty received from Smith Partnership	28,000

All of the above figures are gross. Debenture interest accruing in the year was the same as the amounts paid/received.

Set out the relevant CT 61 income tax returns.

Answer

Return period	Tax on payments £	Tax on income £	Income tax Due £	Income tax Repayable £	Due date
1.4.01 - 30.6.01	2,200	0	2,200	0	14.7.01
1.7.01 - 30.9.01	0	0	0	0	-
1.10.01 - 31.12.01	2,000	0	2,000	0	14.1.02
1.1.02 - 31.3.02	0	6,160	0	(4,200) (a)	14.4.02
	4,200	6,160			
		4,200			
		1,960 (b)			

Notes

(a) The repayment is restricted to income tax already paid in the same accounting period. The return is due by the date shown, but there is no set date by which the Revenue must make the repayment.

(b) £1,960, the net income tax suffered over the year, will be set against the company's corporation tax liability. If that liability is less than £1,960, the company will receive a repayment of income tax suffered.

(c) Amounts paid to and received from companies will be paid and received **gross** by Income plc after 1 April 2001.

Chapter roundup

- CT 600 returns must, in general, be filed within twelve months of the end of an accounting period.

- The Revenue can enquire into returns.

- In general, corporation tax is due nine months after the end of an accounting period but large companies must pay some corporation tax in four quarterly instalments.

- Shadow ACT reduces the capacity of a company to set off real ACT brought forward at 6.4.99.

- From 1 April 2001 a paying company is not required to withhold income tax from annual interest, royalties or annuities if the recipient is also a company.

- Income tax is accounted for quarterly, on form CT61.

Quick quiz

1 What are the fixed penalties for failure to deliver a corporation tax return on time?

2 What is the penalty if a company fails to keep records?

3 When must the Revenue give notice that it is going to start an enquiry if a return was filed by the filing date?

4 State the due dates for the payment of quarterly instalments of corporation tax for a 12 month accounting period.

5 Which companies must pay quarterly instalments of their corporation tax liability?

6 What is shadow ACT?

7 How can the set off of surplus ACT brought forward on 6.4.99 be maximised?

8 For which periods are CT61s due?

9 From which payments must a company withhold income tax?

Answers to quick quiz

1   There is a £100 penalty for failure to submit a return on time rising to £200 if the delay exceeds three months. These penalties increased to £500 and £1,000 respectively when a return was late for each of the preceding two accounting periods.

2   £3,000 for each accounting period affected.

3   Notice must be given by one year after the filing date.

4   14th day of:

   (a)   7th month in AP
   (b)   10th month in AP
   (c)   1st month after AP ends
   (d)   4th month after AP ends

5   'Large' companies ie: companies that pay corporation tax at the full rate.

6   'Shadow ACT' is the ACT that would have been payable (at 20/80) on distributions made after 5 April 1999 had the old ACT rules continued.

7   The offset of surplus ACT brought forward - can be maximised by:

   (a)   restricting dividends paid post 5.4.99 to reduce 'shadow ACT'

   (b)   maximising PCTCT and hence CT to allow surplus ACT to be offset

8   Returns are due for quarters to

   (a)   31 March
   (b)   30 June
   (c)   30 September
   (d)   31 December

   plus company AP end if it does not coincide with any of the above dates.

9   Payments of

   (a)   annual interest
   (b)   patent royalties
   (c)   annuities
   (d)   annual payments

   to a non-corporate body (ie an individual or partnership etc). Prior to 6.4.01 income tax also had to be accounted for when a company made these payments to a corporate recipient.

Now try the question below from the Exam Question Bank

Number	Level	Marks	Time
2	Exam	13	23 mins

Chapter 3

SCHEDULE D CASE I

Topic list	Syllabus reference	Ability required
1 The Badges of trade	(iii)	Application
2 The adjustment of profits	(iii)	Application
3 Deductible and non-deductible expenditure	(iii)	Application
4 Income not taxable under schedule D Case I	(iii)	Application
5 Deductible expenditure not charged in the accounts	(iii)	Application
6 The cessation of trades	(iii)	Application

Introduction

We have seen how to compute a company's total profits. In this chapter we see how to compute one particular type of a company's profits, namely its Schedule D case I profits.

Schedule D Case I profits are the profits that arise from a company's trade. Your starting point in computing schedule D case I profit is always the net profit in a company's accounts but this must be adjusted to arrive at the taxable schedule D Case I profits. For tax purposes, standard rules on the computation of profits are used instead of individual company accounting policies, so as to ensure fairness.

Learning outcomes covered in this chapter

- **Calculate** the Schedule D Case I profits for tax purposes, showing knowledge of case law and statute

Syllabus content covered in this chapter

- Adjustment of trading profits: statute and case law

1   THE BADGES OF TRADE

1.1   The profits that a company makes from any trade that it carries on in the UK are taxed under schedule D Case I.

> **KEY TERM**
>
> A trade is defined in the legislation only in an unhelpful manner as including every trade, manufacture, adventure or concern in the nature of a trade. It has therefore been left to the courts to provide guidance. This guidance is often summarised in a collection of principles known as the **'badges of trade'**. These are set out below.

The subject matter

1.2 **Whether a person is trading or not may sometimes be decided by examining the subject matter of the transaction.** Some assets are commonly held as investments for their intrinsic value: an individual buying some shares or a painting may do so in order to enjoy the income from the shares or to enjoy the work of art. A subsequent disposal may produce a gain of a capital nature rather than a trading profit. But **where the subject matter of a transaction is such as would not be held as an investment** (for example 34,000,000 yards of aircraft linen (*Martin v Lowry 1927*) or 1,000,000 rolls of toilet paper (*Rutledge v CIR 1929*)), **it is presumed that any profit on resale is a trading profit.**

The frequency of transactions

1.3 Transactions which may, in isolation, be of a capital nature will be interpreted as trading transactions where their **frequency indicates the carrying on of a trade.** It was decided that whereas normally the purchase of a mill-owning company and the subsequent stripping of its assets might be a capital transaction, where the taxpayer was embarking on the same exercise for the fourth time he must be carrying on a trade (*Pickford v Quirke 1927*).

The length of ownership

1.4 The courts may infer adventures in the nature of **trade where items purchased are sold soon afterwards.**

Supplementary work and marketing

1.5 **When work is done to make an asset more marketable,** or steps are taken to find purchasers, the courts will be more ready to ascribe a trading motive. When a group of accountants bought, blended and recasked a quantity of brandy they were held to be taxable on a trading profit when the brandy was later sold (*Cape Brandy Syndicate v CIR 1921*).

A profit motive

1.6 The absence of a profit motive will not necessarily preclude a Schedule D Case I assessment, but its presence is a strong indication that a person is trading. The purchase and resale of £20,000 worth of silver bullion by the comedian Norman Wisdom, as a hedge against devaluation, was held to be a trading transaction (*Wisdom v Chamberlain 1969*).

The way in which the asset sold was acquired

1.7 **If goods are acquired deliberately, trading may be indicated.** If goods are acquired unintentionally, for example by gift or inheritance, their later sale is unlikely to be trading.

The taxpayer's intentions

1.8 Where a transaction is clearly trading on objective criteria, **the taxpayer's intentions are irrelevant.** If, however, a transaction has (objectively) a dual purpose, the taxpayer's intentions may be taken into account. An example of a transaction with a dual purpose is the acquisition of a site partly as premises from which to conduct another trade, and partly with a view to the possible development and resale of the site.

This test is not one of the traditional badges of trade, but it may be just as important.

2 THE ADJUSTMENT OF PROFITS

2.1 Although the net profit before taxation shown in the accounts is the starting point in computing the taxable trading profit, many adjustments may be required to find the profit taxable under Schedule D Case I.

2.2 Here is an illustrative adjustment.

	£	£
Net profit per accounts		140,000
Add: expenditure charged in the accounts which is not deductible under Schedule D Case I		80,000
		220,000
Less: profits included in the accounts but which are not taxable under Schedule D Case I	40,000	
expenditure which is deductible under Schedule D Case I but has not been charged in the accounts	20,000	
		60,000
Profit adjusted for tax purposes		160,000

You may refer to deductible and non-deductible expenditure as allowable and disallowable expenditure respectively. The two sets of terms are interchangeable.

Accounting policies

2.3 **As a rule, accounts drawn up on normal accepted accounting principles are acceptable for tax purposes.** Two special points are worth noting.

- If there is a legal action in progress, the best estimate of the cost should be debited, not the most prudent estimate.

- Under SSAP 9, a loss on a long-term contract is recognised as soon as it is foreseen. Anticipating a loss in this way is not acceptable for tax purposes, so the debit to profit and loss must be added back.

2.4 The taxable profits of a trade, must normally be computed on a basis which gives a true and fair view, subject to adjustments permitted or required by tax law.

Rounding

2.5 Where a single company (not a group of companies) has an annual turnover of at least £5,000,000, and prepares its accounts with figures rounded to at least the nearest £1,000, figures in computations of adjusted profits (including, non-trading profits but excluding capital gains) may generally be rounded to the nearest £1,000.

3 DEDUCTIBLE AND NON-DEDUCTIBLE EXPENDITURE

Payments contrary to public policy and illegal payments

3.1 **Based on case law, fines and penalties are not deductible**. However, the Revenue usually allow employees' parking fines incurred in parking their employer's cars while on their employer's business. Fines relating to directors however, are never allowed.

3.2 A payment is (by statute) not deductible if making it constitutes an offence by the payer. This covers protection money paid to terrorists, and also bribes. Statute also prevents any deduction for payments made in response to blackmail or extortion.

Capital expenditure

3.3 **Capital expenditure is not deductible. The most contentious items of expenditure will often be repairs** (revenue expenditure) **and improvements** (capital expenditure).

- The cost of restoration of an asset by, for instance, replacing a subsidiary part of the asset is revenue expenditure. Expenditure on a new factory chimney replacement was allowable since the chimney was a subsidiary part of the factory (*Samuel Jones & Co (Devondale) Ltd v CIR 1951*). However, in another case a football club demolished a spectators' stand and replaced it with a modern equivalent. This was held not to be repair, since repair is the restoration by renewal or replacement of subsidiary parts of a larger entity, and the stand formed a distinct and *separate* part of the club (*Brown v Burnley Football and Athletic Co Ltd 1980*).

- The cost of initial repairs to improve an asset recently acquired to make it fit to earn profits is disallowable capital expenditure. In *Law Shipping Co Ltd v CIR 1923* the taxpayer failed to obtain relief for expenditure on making a newly bought ship seaworthy prior to using it.

- The cost of initial repairs to remedy normal wear and tear of recently acquired assets is allowable. *Odeon Associated Theatres Ltd v Jones 1971* can be contrasted with the *Law Shipping* judgement. Odeon were allowed to charge expenditure incurred on improving the state of recently acquired cinemas.

3.4 Other examples to note include:

- A one-off payment made by a hotel owner to terminate an agreement for the management of a hotel was held to be revenue rather than capital expenditure in *Croydon Hotel & Leisure Co v Bowen 1996*. The payment did not affect the whole structure of the taxpayer's business; it merely enabled it to be run more efficiently.

- A one-off payment to remove a threat to the taxpayer's business was also held to be revenue rather than capital expenditure in *Lawson v Johnson Matthey plc 1992*.

- An initial payment for a franchise (as opposed to regular fees) is capital and not deductible.

3.5   The costs of **registering patents and trade marks** are specifically allowed as a deduction.

Appropriations

3.6   **Depreciation, amortisation and general provisions are not deductible.** A specific provision against a particular trade debt is deductible if it is a reasonable estimate of the likely loss.

Where payments are made to or on behalf of employees, the full amounts are deductible but the employees may be taxed on benefits in kind if the payment has a private element.

Charges on income

3.7   **Charges on income, such as patent royalties, are added back in the calculation of schedule D Case I profit. They are deducted instead from total profits in computing profits chargeable to corporation tax. The amount added back to the accounts profit (on an accruals basis) and the amount deducted as a charge on income (on a cash basis) may differ.**

Entertaining and gifts

3.8   **Entertaining for and gifts to employees are normally deductible.** Where gifts are made, or the entertainment is excessive, a charge to tax may arise on the employee under the benefits in kind legislation.

3.9   **Gifts to customers not costing more than £50 per donee per year are allowed if they carry a conspicuous advertisement for the business and are not food, drink, tobacco or vouchers exchangeable for goods.** (For corporate accounting periods beginning prior to 1 April 2001, this de minimis limit was £10 per donee.)

3.10   Gifts to charities may be allowed although many will fall foul of the 'wholly and exclusively' rule below. If a gift aid declaration is made in respect of a gift, tax relief will be given as a charge on income under the gift aid scheme, not as a schedule D Case I deduction.

3.11   **Tax relief is available** for certain donations of trading stock and equipment (see below). **All other expenditure on entertaining and gifts is non-deductible.**

Expenditure not wholly and exclusively for the purposes of the trade

3.12   **Expenditure is not deductible if it is not for trade purposes (the remoteness test), or if it reflects more than one purpose (the duality test).**

3.13   **The remoteness test** is illustrated by the following cases.

- *Strong & Co of Romsey Ltd v Woodifield 1906*

   A customer injured by a falling chimney when sleeping in an inn owned by a brewery claimed compensation from the company. The compensation was not deductible: 'the loss sustained by the appellant was not really incidental to their trade as innkeepers and fell upon them in their character not of innkeepers but of householders'.

- *Bamford v ATA Advertising Ltd 1972*

   A director misappropriated £15,000. The loss was not allowable: 'the loss is not, as in the case of a dishonest shop assistant, an incident of the company's trading activities. It arises altogether outside such activities'.

- Expenditure which is wholly and exclusively to benefit the trades of several companies (for example in a group) but is not wholly and exclusively to benefit the trade of one specific company is not deductible *(Vodafone Cellular Ltd and others v Shaw 1995).*

- *McKnight (HMIT) v Sheppard (1999)* concerned expenses incurred by a stockbroker in defending allegations of infringements of Stock Exchange regulations. It was found that the expenditure was incurred to prevent the destruction of the taxpayer's business and that as the expenditure was incurred for business purposes it was deductible. It was also found that although the expenditure had the effect of preserving the taxpayer's reputation, that was not its purpose, so there was no duality of purpose.

3.14 The **duality test** is illustrated by the following case.

- *Mallalieu v Drummond 1983*
  Expenditure by a lady barrister on black clothing to be worn in court (and on its cleaning and repair) was not deductible. The expenditure was for the dual purpose of enabling the barrister to be warmly and properly clad as well as meeting her professional requirements.

Subscriptions and donations

3.15 **The general 'wholly and exclusively' rule determines the deductibility of expenses. Subscriptions and donations are not deductible unless the expenditure is for the benefit of the trade.** The following are the main types of subscriptions and donations you may meet and their correct treatments.

- Trade subscriptions (such as to a professional or trade association) are generally deductible.

- Charitable donations are deductible only if they are small and to local charities. Tax relief may be available for donations under the gift aid scheme. In the latter case they are not a deductible Schedule D Case I expense.

- Political subscriptions and donations are generally not deductible. However, if it can be shown that political expenditure is incurred for the survival of the trade then it may be deducted. This follows a case in which it was held that expenditure incurred in resisting nationalisation was allowable on the grounds that it affected the survival of the business *(Morgan v Tate and Lyle Ltd 1954).*

- When a company makes a gift of equipment manufactured, sold or used in the course of its trade to an educational establishment or for a charitable purpose, nothing need be brought into account as a trading receipt or (if capital allowances had been obtained on the asset - see the next chapter) as disposal proceeds, so full relief is obtained for the cost. The donor company must claim relief within two years of the end of the accounting period of the gift. The value of any benefit to the donor from the gift is taxable.

- Where a donation represents the most effective commercial way of disposing of stock (for example, where it would not be commercially effective to sell surplus perishable food), the donation can be treated as for the benefit of the trade and the disposal proceeds taken as £Nil. In other cases, the amount credited to the accounts in respect of a donation of stock should be its market value.

Legal and professional charges

3.16 **Legal and professional charges relating to capital or non-trading items are not deductible.** These include charges incurred in acquiring new capital assets or legal rights and in issuing shares.

Charges are deductible if they relate directly to trading. Deductible items include:

- legal and professional charges incurred defending a company's title to fixed assets;
- charges connected with an action for breach of contract;
- expenses of the **renewal** (not the original grant) of a lease for less than 50 years;
- charges for trade debt collection;
- normal charges for preparing accounts/assisting with the self assessment of tax.

3.17 Accountancy expenses arising out of an enquiry into the accounts information in a particular period's return are not allowed where the enquiry reveals discrepancies and additional liabilities for the period of enquiry, or any earlier period, which arise as a result of negligent or fraudulent conduct.

Where, however, the enquiry results in no addition to profits, or an adjustment to the profits for the period of enquiry only and that assessment does not arise as a result of negligent or fraudulent conduct, the additional accountancy expenses are allowable.

Bad and doubtful debts

3.18 **Only bad debts incurred in the course of a business are deductible for taxation purposes.** Thus loans to employees written off are not deductible unless the business is that of making loans, or it can be shown that the writing-off of the loan was an emolument laid out for the benefit of the trade. If a trade debt is released as part of a voluntary arrangement under the Insolvency Act 1986, or a compromise or arrangement under s 425 Companies Act 1985, the amount released is deductible as a bad debt.

3.19 **General doubtful debt provisions are not deductible, but specific provisions and write-offs against individual debts are deductible.** The only adjustment needed to the accounts profit is to add back an increase (or deduct a decrease) in the general provision.

Interest

3.20 **Interest paid on a loan taken out for trade purposes (a trading loan relationship) is a deductible schedule D case I expense.** Similarly interest received on a trading loan relationship is included within schedule D Case I profits. This means that no adjustment to the accounts profit is required for such interest.

3.21 Interest paid and received on loans not taken out for trade purposes (non trading loan relationships) is deductible/ taxable under schedule D Case III. This means that the accounts profit must be adjusted to exclude such interest.

3.22 Loan relationships will be looked at in more detail later in this text.

Miscellaneous deductions

3.23 The **costs of seconding employees to charities or educational establishments are deductible.**

3.24 Expenditure incurred before the commencement of trade (**pre-trading expenditure**) is deductible, if it is incurred within seven years of the start of trade and it is of a type that would have been deductible had the trade already started. It is treated as a trading expense incurred on the first day of trading.

3.25 **If emoluments for employees are charged in the accounts but are not paid within nine months of the end of the period of account, the cost is only deductible for the period of account in which the emoluments are paid.** When a tax computation is made within the nine month period, it is initially assumed that unpaid emoluments will not be paid within that period. The computation is adjusted if they are so paid.

Emoluments are treated as paid at the same time as they are treated as received for Schedule E purposes (see later in this text).

3.26 **Redundancy payments made when a trade ends are deductible** on the earlier of the day of payment and the last day of trading. If the trade does not end, they can be deducted as soon as they are provided for, so long as the redundancy was decided on within the period of account, the provision is accurately calculated and the payments are made within nine months of the end of the period of account.

3.27 Here is a list of various other items that you may meet.

Item	Treatment	Comment
Educational courses for staff	Allow	
Removal expenses (to new business premises)	Allow	Only if not an expansionary move
Contribution to expenses of agents under the payroll deduction scheme	Allow	
Redundancy pay in excess of the statutory amount	Allow	If the trade ceases, the limit on allowability is 3 × the statutory amount (in addition to the statutory amount)
Compensation for loss of office and ex gratia payments	Allow	If for benefit of trade: *Mitchell v B W Noble Ltd 1927*
Counselling services for employees leaving employment	Allow	If qualify for exemption from Schedule E charge on employees (see later in this text)
Contributions to any of: local enterprise agencies; training and enterprise councils; local enterprise companies; business link organisations; individual learning accounts (ILA)	Allow	The ILA must qualify for a discount or grant and contributions must be available to all employees generally.
Pension contributions (to schemes for employees and company directors)	Allow	If paid, not if only provided for; special contributions may be spread over the year of payment and future years
Premiums for insurance: against an employee's death or illness to cover locum costs or fixed overheads whilst the policyholder is ill	Allow	Receipts are taxable
Payments to employees for restrictive undertakings	Allow	Taxable on employee
Damages paid	Allow	If not too remote from trade: *Strong and Co v Woodifield 1906*

Item	Treatment	Comment
Preparation and restoration of waste disposal sites	Allow	Spread preparation expenditure over period of use of site. Pre-trading expenditure is treated as incurred on the first day of trading. Allow restoration expenditure in period of expenditure

> ### Exam focus point
>
> In the exam you could be given a profit and loss account and asked to calculate 'taxable profit'. You must look at every expense in the accounts to decide if it is (or isn't) 'tax deductible'. This means that you must become familiar with the many expenses you may see and the correct tax treatment. Look at the above paragraphs again noting what expenses are (and are not) allowable for tax purposes.

4 INCOME NOT TAXABLE UNDER SCHEDULE D CASE I

4.1 **There are three types of receipts which may be found in the accounting profits but which must be excluded from the Schedule D Case I computation.** These are:

(a) **capital receipts;**
(b) **income taxed in another way** (at source or under another case or schedule);
(c) **income specifically exempt from tax.**

Compensation received in one lump sum for the loss of income is likely to be treated as income (*Donald Fisher (Ealing) Ltd v Spencer 1989*).

4.2 Income taxed under another schedule, for example schedule A income is excluded from the computation of schedule D Case I profits but it is brought in again further down in the computation of profits chargeable to corporation tax. Similarly capital receipts are excluded from the computation of schedule D Case I income but they may be included in the computation of chargeable gains.

4.3 In some trades, (eg petrol stations), a wholesaler may pay a lump sum to a retailer in return for the retailer's only supplying that wholesaler's products for several years (an **exclusivity agreement**). If the payment must be used for a specific capital purpose, it is a capital receipt. If that is not the case, it is a revenue receipt. If the sum is repayable to the wholesaler but the requirement to repay is waived in tranches over the term of the agreement, each tranche is a separate revenue receipt when the requirement is waived.

5 DEDUCTIBLE EXPENDITURE NOT CHARGED IN THE ACCOUNTS

5.1 Capital allowances (see the following chapters) **are** an example of **deductible expenditure not charged in the accounts**.

5.2 A second example is **an annual sum** which can be deducted by a company that has paid **a lease premium to a landlord who is taxable on the premium under Schedule A** (see later in this text). Normally, the amortisation of the lease will have been deducted in the accounts and must be added back as an appropriation.

Tax relief for cleaning up contaminated land

5.3   Companies that acquire contaminated land for the purposes of their trade (or Schedule A business) can claim to deduct 150% of their remediation expenditure (ie clean up costs).

5.4   Where the clean up expenditure is capital expenditure, the company can elect for it to be allowed as a deduction in computing profits of the accounting period in which it was incurred. Such an election must be made in writing and is subject to a two year time limit.

5.5   If the deduction gives rise to an unrelieved trading or Schedule A loss (see later in this text), the unrelieved amount can be surrendered to the Inland Revenue in return for a tax payment equal to 16% of the unrelieved amount.

Research and development expenditure

5.6   **Relief for expenditure of a revenue nature on research and development which is related to the company's trade and is undertaken by the company or on its behalf is wholly allowable as a Schedule D Case I deduction.** Similarly, contributions to scientific research associations and universities, colleges and scientific institutes, are allowable, provided they are for research and development relating to the company's trade.

5.7   **Expenditure of a capital nature on research and development related to the company's trade is also wholly allowable as a deduction.** This covers capital expenditure on the provision of laboratories and research equipment. Note, however, that **no deduction is available for expenditure on land. If any proceeds are received from the disposal of the capital assets, the receipt is taxed as a trading receipt.**

Additional R&D tax relief

5.8   Certain companies incurring qualifying research and development (R&D) expenditure after 31 March 2000 can claim additional tax relief.

5.9   The company must be a **small or medium sized enterprise,** as defined by the EU. This means the company should have:

   (a)   **fewer than 250 employees,** and

   (b)   either:

   -    an **annual turnover not exceeding Euro 40 million** (approximately £25m), or

   -    an **annual balance sheet total not exceeding Euro 27 million** (approximately £17m)

5.10   The **company must have spent at least £25,000** on qualifying R&D in the accounting period. This limit is scaled down for short accounting periods and also to reflect the proportion of the accounting period falling after 1 April 2000.

5.11   Qualifying expenditure is **revenue expenditure** which is wholly allowable on:

   (a)   staff costs
   (b)   consumables
   (c)   subcontracted expenditure of the same nature

5.12   The R&D may be undertaken by the company, or directly on its behalf, and any intellectual property resulting must belong to the company. It must be related to the company's trade, or to the medical welfare of workers in that trade. Expenditure for which state aid is received is excluded.

5.13 Staff costs include salaries and benefits, secondary class 1 national insurance (see later in this text) and pension contributions in respect of workers employed in research and development. Staff costs of a director is included if he spends at least 80% of his time on research and development, is excluded if less than 20% of time is so spent, and apportioned if between 20% and 80%. Costs of support staff, such as secretaries, is not included.

5.14 Additional tax relief is given by **increasing the deduction for qualifying R&D from a 100% deduction to a 150% deduction.**

5.15 Where the expenditure was pre-trading expenditure, the company may elect to disapply the pre-trading expenditure rules, and instead claim a **trading loss equal to 150% of the expenditure.** The claim must be made within two years of the end of the accounting period. We will look at trading losses in more detail later in this text.

5.16 Where a company has a '**surrenderable loss' it may claim a R&D tax credit.** A surrenderable loss arises where the company incurs a trading loss, or has claimed a trading loss on the disapplication of the pre-trading expenditure rules. (We will look at trading losses later in this text). The surrenderable loss is the lower of:

(a) the unrelieved trading loss, or

(b) 150% of the qualifying research and development expenditure.

5.17 The unrelieved loss is computed as if a claim had been made under s 393A(1)(a) ICTA 1988 (see later in this text) against other profits, whether or not made, and taking into account any carry back claim made under s 393A(1)(b) ICTA 1988 or group relief claim. Trading losses brought forward or back from other accounting periods are ignored.

5.18 The R&D tax credit is equal to the lower of:

(a) 16% of the surrenderable loss, or

(b) the PAYE and NICs due for tax months ending in the accounting period.

5.19 Where the R&D tax credit is claimed, the trading loss carried forward is reduced correspondingly. If the R&D tax credit is limited under (b) above, there will be a proportionate restriction in the trading loss.

5.20 The R&D tax credit will be paid to the company by the Revenue, or may be set against any corporation tax liabilities due.

Question: Calculation of Sch D Case I profit

Here is the profit and loss account of Pring Ltd.

	£	£
Gross operating profit		30,000
Patent royalty received		860
		30,860
Wages and salaries	7,000	
Rent and rates	2,000	
Depreciation	1,500	
Bad debts written off	150	
Provision against a fall in the price of raw materials	5,000	
Entertainment expenses	750	
Patent royalties	1,200	
Bank interest (paid for trade purposes)	300	
Legal expenses on acquisition of new factory	250	
		(18,150)
Net profit		12,710

(a) No staff were entertained.
(b) The provision of £5,000 is charged because of an anticipated trade recession.
(c) The patent royalties were received and paid net but have been shown gross.

Compute the profit taxable under Schedule D Case I.

Answer

	£	£
Profit per accounts		12,710
Add: depreciation	1,500	
Provision against a fall in raw material prices	5,000	
Entertainment expenses	750	
Patent royalties paid (to treat as a charge)	1,200	
Legal expenses	250	
		8,700
		21,410
Less patent royalty received (to tax as taxed income)		(860)
Adjusted trading profit		20,550

---

6 THE CESSATION OF TRADES

6.1 **Post-cessation receipts** (including any releases of debts incurred by the company) **are taxable under Schedule D Case VI**.

Valuing trading stock on cessation

6.2 **When a trade ceases, the closing stock must be valued.** The higher the value, the higher the profit for the final period of trading will be.

6.3 If the stock is sold to a UK trader who will deduct its cost in computing his taxable profits, it is valued under the following rules.

(a) If the seller and the buyer are unconnected, take the actual price.

(b) If the seller and the buyer are connected, take what would have been the price in an arm's length sale.

(c) However, if the seller and the buyer are connected, the arm's length price exceeds both the original cost of the stock and the actual transfer price, and both the seller and the buyer make an election, then take the greater of the original cost of the stock and the transfer price. The time limit for election is two years after the end of the accounting period of cessation.

6.4 In all cases covered above, the value used for the seller's computation of profit is also used as the buyer's cost.

> **KEY TERM**
>
> Companies are **connected** with anyone controlling them, with other companies under common control and with partnerships under common control.

6.5 If the stock is not transferred to a UK trader who will be able to deduct its cost in computing his profits, then it is valued at its open market value as at the cessation of trade.

Chapter roundup

- The badges of trade can be used to decide whether or not a trade exists. If one does exist, the accounts profits needs to be adjusted in order to establish the taxable profits.

- Disallowable expenditure must be added back to the accounts profit in the computation of schedule D Case I income whilst receipts not taxable under schedule D Case I must be deducted from the accounts profit.

- Expenditure not charged in the accounts that is deductible under schedule D Case I must be deducted when computing Schedule D Case I income.

Quick quiz

1 List the six traditional badges of trade.

2 What are the remoteness test and the duality test?

3 What pre-trading expenditure is deductible?

4 What is the maximum allowable amount of redundancy pay on the cessation of a trade?

5 How much must a qualifying company have spent on research and development expenditure in a twelve month accounting period, if the additional R & D tax relief is to be available?

Answers to quick quiz

1   The subject matter
    The frequency of transactions
    The length of ownership
    Supplementary work and marketing
    A profit motive
    The way in which goods were acquired

2   Expenditure is not deductible if it is not for trade purposes (the remoteness test), or if it reflects more than one purpose (the duality test)

3   Pre-trading expenditure is deductible if it is incurred within seven years of the start of the trade and is of a type that would have been deductible if the trade had already started.

4   3 × statutory amount

5   £25,000

Now try the question below from the Exam Question Bank

Number	Level	Marks	Time
3	Exam	12	22 mins

Chapter 4

CAPITAL ALLOWANCES ON PLANT AND MACHINERY

Topic list		Syllabus reference	Ability required
1	Capital allowances in general	(iii)	Application
2	The definition of plant	(iii)	Application
3	The allowances	(iii)	Application
4	Short-life assets	(iii)	Application
5	Hire purchase and leasing	(iii)	Application
6	Successions	(iii)	Application

Introduction

Depreciation cannot be deducted in computing trading profits. Instead, capital allowances are given. In this and the next chapter, we look at capital allowances, starting with plant and machinery.

Our study of plant and machinery falls into three parts. Firstly, we look at what qualifies for allowances: many business assets get no allowances at all. Secondly, we see how to compute the allowances and lastly, we look at special rules for assets with short lives, for assets which the taxpayer does not buy outright and for transfers of whole businesses.

Learning outcomes covered in this chapter

- **Calculate** the capital allowances entitlement of a company

Syllabus content covered in this chapter

- Capital allowances; plant; short life assets, qualifying expenditure – statute and case law
- Utilisation of surplus ACT existing at 6 April 1999: capital allowances

1   CAPITAL ALLOWANCES IN GENERAL

1.1   **Capital expenditure is not in itself an allowable Schedule D Case I deduction, but it *may* attract capital allowances. Capital allowances are treated as a trading expense and are deducted in arriving at Schedule D Case I profits. Balancing charges, effectively negative allowances, are added in arriving at those profits.**

1.2   Allowances are available on expenditure falling into the following categories:

- plant and machinery;
- industrial buildings;

This chapter deals only with capital allowances on plant and machinery; the next chapter deals with allowances on industrial buildings.

1.3 **Capital allowances are calculated for accounting periods.**

1.4 **For capital allowances purposes, expenditure is generally deemed to be incurred when the obligation to pay becomes unconditional.** This will often be the date of a contract, but if for example payment is due a month after delivery of a machine, it would be the date of delivery. However, amounts due more than four months after the obligation becomes unconditional are deemed to be incurred when they fall due.

2 THE DEFINITION OF PLANT

2.1 **There are two sources of the rules on what qualifies as plant and is therefore eligible for capital allowances.** (Machinery is also eligible, but the word 'machinery' may be taken to have its everyday meaning.) **Statute** lists items which do not qualify, but it does not give a comprehensive list of other items which do qualify. There are several **cases** in which certain items have been accepted as plant. A few items such as thermal insulation and computer software are plant by statute.

The statutory exclusions

Buildings

2.2 **Expenditure on a building and on any asset which is incorporated in a building or is of a kind normally incorporated into buildings does not qualify as expenditure on plant unless the asset falls within the list of exceptions given** below. Even if an asset falls within that list, it does not follow that it is plant (although it probably will be, because the list is based on cases in which assets have been held to be plant and on Revenue practice).

2.3 In addition to complete buildings, **the following assets count as 'buildings', and are therefore not plant.**

- Walls, floors, ceilings, doors, gates, shutters, windows and stairs
- Mains services, and systems, of water, electricity and gas
- Waste disposal, sewerage and drainage systems
- Shafts or other structures for lifts etc

2.4 **The following assets** which would normally count as 'buildings' **can still be plant.**

- Electrical (including lighting), cold water, gas and sewerage systems:

   (i) provided mainly to meet the particular requirements of the trade; or
   (ii) provided mainly to serve particular machinery or plant.

- Space or water heating systems and powered systems of ventilation.

- Manufacturing and display equipment.

- Cookers, washing machines, refrigeration or cooling equipment, sanitary ware and furniture and furnishings.

- Lifts etc.

- Sound insulation provided mainly to meet the particular requirements of the trade.

- Computer, telecommunication and surveillance systems.

- Sprinkler equipment, fire alarm and burglar alarm systems.

- Any machinery.

- Strong rooms in bank or building society premises; safes.

- Partition walls, where movable and intended to be moved.

- Decorative assets in the hotel, restaurant or similar trades; advertising hoardings.

- Glasshouses which have, as an integral part of their structure, devices which control the plant growing environment automatically; swimming pools.

2.5 In addition, the following items may be 'plant'.

- Caravans provided mainly for holiday lettings
- Movable buildings intended to be moved in the course of the trade

2.6 When a building is sold, the vendor and purchaser can make a joint election to determine how the sale proceeds are apportioned between the building and its fixtures. There are anti-avoidance provisions that ensure capital allowances given overall on a fixture do not exceed the original cost of the fixture.

Structures

2.7 **Expenditure on structures** and on works involving the alteration of land **does not qualify as expenditure on plant** unless the asset falls within the list of exceptions given below. Even if an asset falls within that list, it does not follow that it is plant (although it probably will be, because the list is based on cases in which assets have been held to be plant and on Revenue practice).

2.8 A 'structure' is a fixed structure of any kind, other than a building.

2.9 **The following items**, which would normally count as 'structures' **can still be plant**.

- Expenditure on altering land for the purpose only of installing machinery or plant

- Pipelines, and also underground ducts or tunnels with a primary purpose of carrying utility conduits

- Silos provided for temporary storage and storage tanks

- Fish tanks and fish ponds

- A railway or tramway

2.10 In addition, expenditure may qualify as plant despite these rules if the assets bought are items which qualify as plant under the rules in Paragraphs 2.28 and 2.29 below.

Land

2.11 Land or an interest in land does not qualify as plant and machinery. For this purpose 'land' excludes buildings, structures and assets which are installed or fixed to land in such a way as to become part of the land for general legal purposes.

Case law

2.12 The original case law **definition of plant** (applied in this case to a horse) **is 'whatever apparatus is used by a businessman for carrying on his business: not his stock in trade which he buys or makes for sale; but all goods and chattels, fixed or movable, live or**

BPP
PUBLISHING

dead, which he keeps for permanent employment in the business' (*Yarmouth v France 1887*).

2.13 Subsequent cases have refined the original definition and have largely been concerned with the **distinction between plant actively used in the business (qualifying) and the setting in which the business is carried on (non-qualifying). This is the 'functional' test.**

2.14 The cost of excavating and concreting a dry dock was allowed as capital expenditure on plant. The dock played an active part in the operation of the company's trade (*CIR v Barclay Curle & Co 1969*).

2.15 The cost of concrete grain silos has been allowed. Although used to store grain they were more than buildings: they were 'specially constructed for the purpose of rendering more efficient the process of unloading and distribution' (*Schofield v R & H Hall 1975*).

2.16 The whole cost of excavating and installing a swimming pool was allowed to the owners of a caravan park. *CIR v Barclay Curle & Co 1969* was followed: the pool performed the function of giving 'buoyancy and enjoyment' to the persons using the pool (*Cooke v Beach Station Caravans Ltd 1974*).

2.17 A barrister succeeded in his claim for his law library: 'Plant includes a man's tools of his trade. It extends to what he uses day by day in the course of his profession. It is not confined to physical things like the dentist's chair or the architect's table' (*Munby v Furlong 1977*).

2.18 Office partitioning was allowed. Because it was movable it was not regarded as part of the setting in which the business was carried on (*Jarrold v John Good and Sons Ltd 1963*).

2.19 A ship used as a floating restaurant was regarded as a 'structure in which the business was carried on rather than apparatus employed ... ' (Buckley LJ). No capital allowances could be obtained (*Benson v Yard Arm Club 1978*). The same decision was made in relation to a football club's spectator stand. The stand performed no function in the actual carrying out of the club's trade (*Brown v Burnley Football and Athletic Co Ltd 1980*).

2.20 At a motorway service station, false ceilings contained conduits, ducts and lighting apparatus. They did not qualify because they did not perform a function in the business. They were merely part of the setting in which the business was conducted (*Hampton v Fortes Autogrill Ltd 1979*).

2.21 Light fittings, decor and murals can be plant. A company carried on business as hoteliers and operators of licensed premises. The function of the items was the creation of an atmosphere conducive to the comfort and well being of its customers (*CIR v Scottish and Newcastle Breweries Ltd 1982*).

2.22 On the other hand, it has been held that when an attractive floor is provided in a restaurant, the fact that the floor performs the function of making the restaurant attractive to customers is not enough to make it plant. It functions as premises, and the cost therefore does not qualify for capital allowances (*Wimpy International Ltd v Warland 1988*).

2.23 General lighting in a department store is not plant, as it is merely setting. Special display lighting, however, can be plant (*Cole Brothers Ltd v Phillips 1982*).

2.24 Free-standing decorative screens installed in the windows of a branch of a building society qualified as plant. Their function was not to act a part of the setting in which the society's business was carried on; it was to attract local custom, and accordingly the screens formed part of the apparatus with which the society carried on its business (*Leeds Permanent Building Society v Proctor 1982*).

2.25 In *Bradley v London Electricity plc 1996* an electricity substation was held not to be plant because it functioned as premises in which London Electricity carried on a trading activity rather than apparatus with which the activity was carried out.

2.26 A building holding car wash equipment is not plant, even if the design of the building is a key element in the car wash system (*Attwood v Anduff Car Wash Ltd 1995*).

2.27 A special greenhouse, constructed with a particular type of glass and with manually operated ventilation panels, is not plant (*Gray v Seymours Garden Centre (Horticulture) 1995*).

Expenditure deemed to be on plant and machinery

2.28 Plant and machinery capital allowances are also available on:

- expenditure incurred by a company in complying with fire regulations for a building which it occupies;

- expenditure by a company on thermal insulation of an industrial building;

- expenditure by a company in meeting statutory safety requirements for sports ground.

On disposal, the sale proceeds for the above are deemed to be zero, so no balancing charge (see below) can arise.

Computer software

2.29 **Capital expenditure on computer software** (both programs and data) **qualifies as** expenditure on **plant and machinery**:

(a) regardless of whether the software is supplied in a tangible form (such as a disk) or transmitted electronically; and

(b) regardless of whether the purchaser acquires the software or only a licence to use it.

Disposal proceeds are brought into account in the normal way, except that if the fee for the grant of a licence is taxed as income of the licensor, no disposal proceeds are taken into account in computing the licensee's capital allowances.

2.30 Where someone has incurred expenditure qualifying for capital allowances on computer software (or the right to use software), and receives a capital sum in exchange for allowing someone else to use the software, that sum is brought into account as disposal proceeds. However, the cumulative total of disposal proceeds is not allowed to exceed the original cost of the software, and any proceeds above this limit are ignored for capital allowances purposes (although they may lead to chargeable gains).

2.31 If software is expected to have a useful economic life of less than two years, its cost may be treated as revenue expenditure.

BPP PUBLISHING

3 THE ALLOWANCES

Writing down allowances

> ### KEY TERM
>
> A **writing down allowance (WDA)** is given on expenditure incurred on most plant and machinery **at the rate of 25% a year** (on a reducing balance basis). The WDA is calculated on the written down value (WDV) on all plant on a 'pool' basis, after adding the current period's additions and taking out the current period's disposals.

3.1 It is unnecessary to keep track of individual written down values.

3.2 Allowances are claimed in the tax return. Any company can claim less than the full allowances. This may be to its advantage, if, for example, the company wants to avoid making such a large loss claim as to lose the benefit of non trade charges on income (losses are covered later in this text). Alternatively it may be of advantage if the company wants to maximise PCTCT so as to maximise the use of surplus ACT b/f at 6.4.99.

3.3 If less than the full allowances are claimed, higher capital allowances will then be available in later years because the WDV carried forward will be higher.

3.4 When plant is sold the proceeds (but limited to a maximum of the original cost) are taken out of the pool of qualifying expenditure. Provided that the trade is still being carried on, the balance remaining is written down in the future by writing down allowances, even if there are no assets left.

3.5 **Writing down allowances are 25% × months/12** where the accounting period is shorter than 12 months (a company's accounting period for tax purposes is never longer than 12 months), or where the trade concerned started in the accounting period and was therefore carried on for fewer than 12 months.

3.6 Expenditure on plant and machinery by a company about to begin a trade is treated as incurred on the first day of trading. Assets previously owned by an individual and then brought into the trade (at the start of trading or later) are treated as bought for their market values at the times when they are brought in.

First year allowances

Spending by small and medium sized enterprises

3.7 **Expenditure incurred on plant and machinery** (other than leased assets, cars, sea going ships or railway assets) after 2 July 1998 **by small and medium sized enterprises qualifies for a first year allowance** (FYA) of 40%.

3.8 The above expenditure qualified for a FYA of 50% if it was incurred in the year to 1 July 1998.

> **Exam focus point**
> The rates of FYAs will be given to you on the exam paper.

KEY TERM

A **small or medium sized enterprise,** is a company that either satisfies at least two of the following conditions in the financial year in which the expenditure is incurred.

(a) **Turnover not more than £11.2 million**
(b) **Assets not more than £5.6 million**
(c) **Not more than 250 employees**

or which was small or medium sized in the previous year. A company must not be a member of a large group when the expenditure is incurred.

Spending by small enterprises on information and communication technology

3.9   Expenditure by **small enterprises on information and communication technology equipment** (computers, software and internet enabled mobile phones) **in the three year period from 1 April 2000 to 31 March 2003 qualifies for a 100% FYA.**

3.10   Equipment acquired for leasing does not qualify for the 100% FYA.

KEY TERM

A **small enterprise** is a company, which satisfies at least two of the following conditions in the financial year in which the expenditure is incurred:

(a) **Turnover not more than £2.8 million**
(b) **Assets not more than £1.4 million**
(c) **Not more than 50 employees**

or which was small in the previous year. If a company is a member of a group, the group must also be small when the expenditure is incurred

Energy saving plant and machinery

3.11   A 100% FYA is available for expenditure incurred after 31 March 2001 on certain energy saving plant and machinery. This is known as an **enhanced capital allowance (ECA).** ECAs may be claimed by companies of any size.

ECAs may only be claimed on new (as distinct from second hand) equipment. They cannot be claimed on buildings or structures, or on assets acquired for leasing or letting.

ECAs may only be claimed on qualifying expenditure. This includes major installations such as combined heat and power systems, small items such as boiler controls, insulation to reduce heat loss from pipes and low energy lighting. Detailed information about qualifying products is available from the Department of Environment, Transport and the Regions website www.eca.gov.uk.

100% FYAs for flats above shops

3.12   From the date of Royal Assent of Finance Act 2001 (11 May 2001), a 100% FYA was introduced to allow property owners and occupiers to obtain tax relief on the costs of converting space above shops and other commercial properties into flats for rent.

Qualifying properties

(a)   The property must have been built before 1980

(b)   The property must not have more than five floors (including the ground floor)

(c)   The ground floor must have been used for a business purpose when the work commenced

(d)   The upper floors must have been unoccupied or used for storage for at least one year before the work started.

The new flats

(a)   Must be self contained with external access separate from the ground floor premises. They must contain no more than four rooms (excluding bathroom and kitchen)

(b)   Must be within the boundaries of the existing building (but an extension to provide access to the flats will be permitted)

(c)   Must not be a 'high value' flat (eg rental more than £480 pw for four room flat in London).

The allowances

(a)   Allowances will follow the IBA rules (see the next chapter) with some simplifications. If a FYA of 100% is not claimed, a WDA of 25% (calculated on the reducing balance basis) is available for subsequent chargeable periods.

(b)   Allowances will not be clawed back unless the freehold is sold or long lease is granted within seven years.

(c)   Allowances are not transferable to a new owner.

Calculation of first year allowances

3.13   For FYA purposes, the provisions which treat capital expenditure incurred prior to the commencement of trading as incurred on the first day of trading do not apply.

3.14   **First year allowances are given in the place of writing down allowances.** For subsequent years a WDA is given on the balance of expenditure at the normal rate. You should therefore transfer the balance of the expenditure to the pool at the end of the first period.

3.15   FYAs are given for incurring expenditure. It is irrelevant whether the accounting period of expenditure is twelve months or not. FYAs are not scaled up or down by reference to the length of the period.

Question: Calculation of schedule D case I profits

Walton Ltd starts a trade on 1 March 1998, and has the following results (before capital allowances).

Period of account	Profits £
1.3.98 - 31.7.99	42,500
1.8.99 - 31.7.00	36,800
1.8.00 - 31.7.01	32,000

Plant (none of which qualifies for a 100% FYA) is bought as follows.

Date	Cost
	£
1.3.98	13,000
1.6.98	8,000
1.6.00	5,000
31.7.01	2,000

On 1 May 2000, plant which cost £7,000 is sold for £4,000.

Walton Ltd's business is a small or medium sized enterprise for FYA purposes.

Show the Schedule D Case I profits arising as a result of the above.

Answer

The seventeen month period of account must be split into two accounting periods for corporation tax purposes. The first period is the twelve months to 28.2.99 and the second period is the five months to 31.7.99.

The capital allowances are as follows.

	FYA	Pool	Allowances
	£	£	£
1.3.98 – 28.2.99			
Additions	21,000		
FYA @ 50%	(10,500)		5,250 10,500
1.3.99 – 31.7.99		10,500	
WDA 25% × 5/12		(1,094)	1,094
		9,406	
1.8.99 – 31.7.00			
Disposals		(4,000)	
		5,406	
WDA 25%		(1,352)	1,352
		4,054	
Addition (1.6.00)	5,000		
FYA 40%	(2,000)		2,000
		3,000	3,352
		7,054	
1.8.00 – 31.7.01			
WDA 25%		(1,764)	1,764
		5,290	
Addition (31.7.01)	2,000		
FYA 40%	(800)		800
		1,200	
TWDV c/f		6,490	
			2,564

The profits of the accounting periods are as follows.

Period of account	Working	Profits
		£
1.3.98 – 28.2.99	£(42,500 × 12/17 – 10,500)	19,500
1.3.99 – 31.7.99	£(42,500 × 5/17 – 1,094)	11,406
1.8.99 – 31.7.00	£(36,800 – 3,352)	33,448
1.8.00 – 31.7.01	£(32,000 – 2,564)	29,436

BPP PUBLISHING

> ### Exam focus point
>
> Note the tax planning opportunities available. It may be important to buy plant just before an accounting date, so that allowances become available as soon as possible. On the other hand, it may be worthwhile to claim less than the maximum allowances so as to increase profits chargeable to corporation tax and maximise the set off of surplus ACT b/f on 6.4.99.

The disposal value of assets

3.16 **The most common disposal value at which assets are entered in a capital allowances computation is the sale proceeds**. But there are a number of less common situations.

3.17 **Where the asset is sold at below market value** (or is given away) **the market value is used instead of the actual sale proceeds**. This general rule has two exceptions. The actual proceeds of sale are used:

(a) where the buyer will be able to claim capital allowances on the expenditure;

(b) where an employee acquires an asset from his employer at undervalue (or as a gift) and so faces a charge under the Schedule E benefit-in-kind rules.

If the asset is demolished, destroyed or otherwise lost, the disposal value is taken to be the actual sale proceeds from any resulting scrap, plus any insurance or other compensation moneys.

3.18 With all these rules, there is an overriding rule that the capital allowances **disposal value cannot exceed the original purchase price**.

Balancing charges and allowances

3.19 **Balancing charges occur when the disposal value deducted exceeds the balance remaining in the pool. The charge equals the excess and is effectively a negative capital allowance**, increasing profits. Most commonly this happens when the trade ceases and the remaining assets are sold. It may also occur, however, whilst the trade is still in progress.

3.20 In certain circumstances it may be worthwhile to not claim first year allowances on expenditure, but instead to include the expenditure in the general pool and thus avoid (or reduce) a balancing charge that would otherwise arise.

3.21 **Balancing allowances on the capital allowance pools of expenditure arise only when the trade ceases**. The balancing allowance is equal to the remaining unrelieved expenditure after deducting the disposal value of all the assets. Balancing allowances also arise on items which are not pooled (see below) whenever those items are disposed of.

Cars

3.22 **Cars** (but not lorries, vans, short-term hire cars, taxis and vehicles unsuitable for private use) **have a special capital allowance treatment**. There are two categories of cars. **Cars costing more than £12,000 are dealt with on an individual basis (see below). Cars costing £12,000 or less are pooled.**

3.23 **Prior to Finance Act 2000 the car pool was a separate one to that used for general plant and machinery.** However, the separate pool for cars costing £12,000 or less is abolished for companies for accounting periods ending after 31 March 2000. The balance that was brought forward on the separate pool at the end of the last period before the abolition is transferred to the main pool.

3.24 Companies can choose to delay the abolition of the separate car pool until the first accounting period ending after 31 March 2001.

3.25 FYAs are not available on cars.

Assets which are not pooled

3.26 Some items are not pooled. A separate record of allowances and WDV must be kept for each such asset and when it is sold a balancing allowance or charge emerges. The items are:

(a) **motor cars costing more than £12,000** where the maximum WDA is £3,000 a year. The limit is £3,000 × months/12 for accounting periods of less than twelve months.

(b) **short-life assets** for which an election has been made (see below).

Assets not wholly used for business purposes

3.27 An asset with some private use by an employee of a company, suffers no restriction in capital allowances. The employee may be taxed on a benefit in kind **so the company gets capital allowances on the full cost of the asset**.

3.28 An employee who provides plant and machinery necessarily for use in the performance of his duties may claim capital allowances, to set against his employment income (see later in this text). If there is any private use of the asset concerned the capital allowances given are restricted to the proportion of the allowances that reflects the business use of the asset. In the case of cars and bicycles, the provision of the car need not be necessary for the employment. Capital allowances will not be available on cars and bicycles from 6 April 2002.

The cessation of a trade

3.29 **When a company ceases to trade no FYAs or WDAs are given in the final accounting period.** Each asset is deemed to be disposed of on the date the trade ceased (usually at the then market value). Additions in the relevant period are brought in and then the disposal proceeds (limited to cost) are deducted from the balance of qualifying expenditure. If the proceeds exceed the balance then a balancing charge arises. If the balance of qualifying expenditure exceeds the proceeds then a balancing allowance is given.

4 SHORT-LIFE ASSETS

4.1 **A company can elect that specific items of plant be kept separately from the general pool. The election is irrevocable and must be made within** two years of the end of the accounting period of the expenditure. **Any asset subject to this election is known as a 'short-life asset'**, and the election is known as a 'de-pooling election'.

> ### KEY TERM
>
> Provided that the asset is disposed of within four years of the end of the accounting period in which it was bought, it is a **short life asset** and a balancing charge or allowance is made on its disposal.

4.2 The receipt of a capital sum in return for the right to use computer software does not count as a disposal for this purpose. If the asset is not disposed of in the correct time period, its tax written down value is added to the general pool at the end of that time.

4.3 The election should be made for assets likely to be sold within four years for less than their tax written down values. It should not be made for assets likely to be sold within four years for more than their tax written down values. (These are, of course, only general guidelines based on the assumption that a company will want to obtain allowances as quickly as possible. There may be other considerations, such as a desire to utilise surplus ACT b/f at 6.4.99.)

4.4 An election should not necessarily be made if including the expenditure in the general pool would reduce a balancing charge that would otherwise arise.

Question: Short life assets

Caithin Ltd bought an asset on 1 July 1997 for £12,000 and elected for de-pooling. The accounting period end is 31 March. Calculate the capital allowances due if:

(a) the asset is scrapped for £300 in August 2001;
(b) the asset is scrapped for £200 in August 2002.

Answer

(a)	*Year to 31.3.98*	£
	Cost	12,000
	WDA 25%	(3,000)
		9,000
	Year to 31.3.99	
	WDA 25%	(2,250)
		6,750
	Year to 31.3.00	
	WDA 25%	(1,688)
		5,062
	Year to 31.3.01	
	WDA 25%	(1,266)
		3,796
	Year to 31.3.02	
	Disposal proceeds	(300)
	Balancing allowance	3,496

(b) If the asset is still in use at 31 March 2002, a WDA of 25% × £3,796 = £949 would be claimable in the year to 31 March 2002. The tax written down value of £3,796 - £949 = £2,847 would be added to the general pool at the beginning of the next accounting period. The disposal proceeds of £200 would be deducted from the general pool in that period's capital allowances computation.

4.5 Short-life asset treatment cannot be claimed for:

• motor cars;
• plant used partly for non-trade purposes;
• plant received by way of gift;
• plant in respect of which a subsidy is received;

4.6 **Where a short-life asset is disposed of within the four year period to a connected person (see below):**

(a) the original owner receives a balancing allowance calculated as normal and the new owner receives WDAs on the cost to him; but

(b) **if both parties so elect, the asset is treated as being sold for its tax written down value at the start of the chargeable period in which the transfer takes place, so there is no balancing charge or allowance for the vendor.**

In both situations, the acquiring party will continue to 'de-pool' the asset up to the same date as the original owner would have done.

4.7 **Companies are connected with anyone controlling them, with other companies under common control and with partnerships under common control.**

5 HIRE PURCHASE AND LEASING

Assets on hire purchase

5.1 **Any asset (including a car) bought on hire purchase (HP) is treated as if purchased outright for the cash price.** Therefore:

(a) the buyer normally obtains **capital allowances on the cash price** when the agreement begins;

(b) he may write off the **finance charge as a trade expense** over the term of the HP contract.

Leased assets

5.2 **Under a lease, the lessee merely hires the asset over a period.** The hire charge can normally be deducted in computing Schedule D Case I profits.

5.3 An expensive car (one costing over £12,000) will attract WDAs limited to £3,000 a year if bought. If it is leased instead, the maximum allowable deduction from trading profits for lease rentals is

$$\frac{£12,000 + P}{2P} \times R$$

where   P = the purchase price (if bought outright)
              R = the annual rental

5.4 This restriction does not apply to the finance charges in hire purchase payments (which could be regarded as payment for the hire of the car), provided the amount payable to acquire the car at the end of the hire period is no more than 1% of the car's retail price when new.

5.5 EXAMPLE: LEASED CARS

A car is used by a business under a lease. The purchase price would have been £20,000. The annual rental is £5,000. The rental allowed for tax purposes is

$$\frac{£12,000 + £20,000}{2 \times £20,000} \times £5,000 = £4,000$$

Since £5,000 is deducted in the profit and loss account, £5,000 - £4,000 = £1,000 is added back in computing taxable profits.

5.6 A lessor of plant normally obtains the benefit of capital allowances although there are anti-avoidance provisions which deny or restrict capital allowances on certain finance leases. Leasing is thus an activity which attracts tax allowances and which can be used to defer tax liabilities where the capital allowances given exceed the rental income.

6 SUCCESSIONS

6.1 **Balancing adjustments arise on the cessation of a business.** No writing down allowances are given, but the final proceeds (limited to cost) on sales of plant are compared with the tax WDV to calculate balancing allowances or charges.

6.2 **Balancing charges may be avoided where the trade passes from one connected person (see paragraph 4.7 above) to another.** If a succession occurs both parties must elect if the avoidance of the balancing adjustments is required. **An election will result in the plant being transferred at its tax written down value for capital allowances purposes.** The predecessor can write down the plant for the period prior to cessation and the successor can write it down from the date of commencement. The election must be made within two years of the date of the succession.

6.3 If no election is made on a transfer of business to a connected person, assets are deemed to be sold at their market values. If an election is made the limit on proceeds to be brought into account on a later sale of an asset is the original cost of the asset, not the deemed transfer price.

Chapter roundup

- Statutory rules generally exclude specified items from treatment as plant, rather than include specified items as plant.

- There are several cases on the definition of plant. To help you to absorb them, try to see the function/setting theme running through them.

- With capital allowances computations, the main thing is to get the layout right. Having done that, you will find that the figures tend to drop into place.

- Most expenditure on plant and machinery qualifies for a WDA at 25% every 12 months.

- First year allowances (FYA) may be available for certain expenditure.

- Short life asset elections can bring forward the allowances due on an asset.

Quick quiz

1 For what periods are a company's capital allowances calculated?

2 Are writing down allowances pro-rated in a six month accounting period?

3 Are first year allowances pro-rated in a six month accounting period?

4 When may balancing allowances arise?

5 Within what period must an asset be disposed of if it is to be treated as a short life asset?

6 What is the formula which gives the allowable lease payments for expensive cars?

Answers to quick quiz

1   Accounting periods

2   Yes. In a six month period, writing down allowance are pro-rated by multiplying by 6/12.

3   No. First year allowances are given in full in a short period.

4   Balancing allowances may arise in respect of pooled expenditure only when the trade ceases. Balancing allowances may arise on non-pooled items whenever those items are disposed of.

5   Within four years of the end of the accounting period in which it was bought

6   $\dfrac{£12,000 + P}{2P} \times R$

   P = Purchase price
   R = Annual lease rental payments

Now try the question below from the Exam Question Bank

Number	Level	Marks	Time
4	Exam	10	18 mins

Chapter 5

INDUSTRIAL BUILDINGS ALLOWANCES

Topic list		Syllabus reference	Ability required
1	Industrial buildings	(iii)	Application
2	Industrial buildings allowances	(iii)	Application

Introduction

We now conclude our study of capital allowances. This chapter deals with industrial buildings allowances. Industrial buildings generally get an allowance of 4% a year on a straight-line basis. Hotels can also get this allowance, but there is no allowance for office buildings unless they are in enterprise zones (where the government wants to encourage economic activity).

Learning outcomes covered in this chapter

- **Calculate** the capital allowances entitlement of a company

Syllabus content covered in this chapter

- Capital allowances: industrial buildings

1   INDUSTRIAL BUILDINGS

Types of building

1.1   A special type of capital allowance (an **industrial buildings allowance** or IBA) is available in respect of **expenditure on certain types of building**. The types of building are:

- general industrial buildings;
- hotels;
- buildings in enterprise zones.

1.2   The allowance is available to:

- trading companies (taxable under Schedule D Case I);
- companies that let qualifying buildings to traders.

General industrial buildings

> **KEY TERM**
>
> **Industrial buildings** include:
>
> (a) all factories and ancillary premises used in:
>
>   (i)   a manufacturing business;
>   (ii) a trade in which goods and materials are subject to any process;
>   (iii) a trade in which goods or raw materials are stored;
>
> (b) staff welfare buildings (such as workplace nurseries and canteens, but not directors' restaurants) where the trade is qualifying;
>
> (c) sports pavilions in any trade;
>
> (d) buildings in use for a transport undertaking, agricultural contracting, mining or fishing;
>
> (e) roads operated under highway concessions. The operation of such roads is treated as a trade for capital allowances purposes. The operator is treated as occupying the roads.

1.3   The key term in (a) (ii) above is 'the subjection of goods to any process'.

  *   The unpacking, repacking and relabelling of goods in a wholesale cash and carry supermarket did not amount to a 'process' but was a mere preliminary to sale (*Bestway Holdings Ltd v Luff 1998*).

  *   The mechanical processing of cheques and other banking documents was a process but pieces of paper carrying information were not 'goods' and thus the building housing the machinery did not qualify (*Girobank plc v Clarke 1998*).

1.4   Estate roads on industrial estates qualify, provided that the estate buildings are used wholly or mainly for a qualifying purpose.

1.5   Dwelling houses, retail shops, showrooms and offices are not industrial buildings.

1.6   Warehouses used for storage often cause problems in practice. A warehouse used for storage which is merely a transitory and necessary incident of the conduct of the business is not an industrial building. Storage is only a qualifying purpose if it is an end in itself.

1.7   Any building is an industrial building if it is constructed for the welfare of employees of a company whose trade is a qualifying one (that is, the premises in which the trade is carried on are industrial buildings).

1.8   Sports pavilions provided for the welfare of employees qualify as industrial buildings. In this case, it does not matter whether the taxpayer is carrying on a trade in a qualifying building or not. Thus a retailer's sports pavilion would qualify for IBAs.

1.9   Drawing offices which serve an industrial building are regarded as industrial buildings themselves (*CIR v Lambhill Ironworks Ltd 1950*).

Hotels

1.10   Allowances on hotels are given as though they were industrial buildings.

> **KEY TERM**
>
> For a building to qualify as a '**hotel**' for industrial buildings allowance purposes:
>
> (a)   it must have at least ten letting bedrooms;
>
> (b)   it must have letting bedrooms as the whole or main part of the sleeping accommodation;
>
> (c)   it must offer ancillary services including at least:
>
> > (i)   breakfast;
> > (ii)   evening meals;
> > (iii) the cleaning of rooms; and
> > (iv)   the making of beds; and
>
> (d)   it must be open for at least four months during the April to October season.

Buildings in enterprise zones

1.11   **Any commercial building** or hotel **built in an enterprise zone qualifies for industrial buildings allowances,** provided that the construction expenditure is contracted for within 10 years, and actually incurred within 20 years, of the zone's designation.

A commercial building is any building that is used for trading purposes or as offices. Dwelling houses are not commercial buildings.

Eligible expenditure

1.12   **Capital allowances are computed on the amount of eligible expenditure incurred on qualifying buildings**. The eligible expenditure is:

- the original cost of a building if built by the trader; or
- the purchase price if the building was acquired from a person trading as a builder.

If the building was acquired other than from a person trading as a builder, the eligible expenditure is the lower of the purchase price and the original cost incurred by the person incurring the construction expenditure.

If a building is sold more than once before being brought into use, the last buyer before the building is brought into use obtains the allowances. If, in such cases, the building was first sold by someone trading as a builder, the eligible expenditure is the lower of the price paid by the first buyer and the price paid by the last buyer.

In all cases where a building is sold before use and artificial arrangements have increased the purchase price, it is reduced to what it would have been without those arrangements.

1.13   **Where part of a building qualifies as an industrial building and part does not, the whole cost qualifies for IBAs, provided that the cost of the non-qualifying part is not more than 25% of the total expenditure.** If the non-qualifying part of the building does cost more than 25% of the total, its cost must be excluded from the capital allowances computation.

1.14 Difficulties arise where non-qualifying buildings (particularly offices and administration blocks) are joined to manufacturing areas. In *Abbott Laboratories Ltd v Carmody 1968* a covered walkway linking manufacturing and administrative areas was not regarded as creating a single building. The administrative area was treated as a separate, non-qualifying building.

1.15 The cost of land is disallowed but expenditure incurred in preparing land for building does qualify. The cost of items which would not be included in a normal commercial lease (such as rental guarantees) also does not qualify.

1.16 Professional fees, for example architects' fees, incurred in connection with the construction of an industrial building qualify. The cost of repairs to industrial buildings also qualifies, provided that the expenditure is not deductible as a trading expense.

2   INDUSTRIAL BUILDINGS ALLOWANCES

Writing down allowances

2.1 **A writing down allowance (WDA) is given to the person holding the 'relevant interest'.** Broadly, the relevant interest is the interest of the first acquirer of the industrial building and may be a freehold or leasehold interest.

2.2 Where a long lease (more than 50 years) has been granted on an industrial building, the grant may be treated as a sale so that allowances may be claimed by the lessee rather than the lessor. A claim must be made by the lessor and lessee jointly, within two years of the start of the lease. The election allows allowances to be claimed on industrial buildings where the lessor is not subject to tax (as with local authorities).

2.3 **The WDA is given for a period provided that the industrial building was in use as such on the last day of the accounting period concerned.**

2.4 **If the building was not in use as an industrial building at the end of the relevant period it may have been:**

- **unused** for any purpose; or
- **used for a non-industrial purpose.**

The distinction is important in ascertaining whether WDAs are due to the company. **If any disuse is temporary and previously the building had been in industrial use, WDAs may be claimed in exactly the same way as if the building were in industrial use.** The legislation does not define 'temporary' but in practice, any subsequent qualifying use of the building will usually enable the period of disuse to be regarded as temporary.

Non-industrial use has different consequences. **If this occurs a notional WDA is deducted from the balance of unrelieved expenditure but no WDA may be claimed by the company.**

2.5 **The WDA is 4%** of the eligible expenditure incurred by the company. For expenditure before 6 November 1962, the rate is 2%.

The allowance is calculated on a straight line basis (in contrast to WDAs on plant and machinery which are calculated on the reducing balance), starting when the building is brought into use.

2.6 **The WDA is 4%** (or 2%) $\times$ **months/12 if the accounting period is not 12 months long.**

2.7 **Buildings in enterprise zones qualify for a 100% allowance** when built, without waiting for them to be brought into use (unlike other buildings). However, not all the allowance need be taken, and any expenditure not so allowed is written off straight line, at 25% of the full cost each year, over a period of up to four years starting when the building is brought into use.

2.8 If a building in an enterprise zone is sold (one or more times) before being brought into use, the allowances are given not to the person incurring the construction expenditure but to the last buyer before the building is brought into use. The rules in Paragraph 1.13 above determine the eligible expenditure.

2.9 If a building in an enterprise zone is brought into use, and is then sold (for the first time after being brought into use) within two years, the seller suffers a balancing charge or obtains a balancing allowance, but the buyer obtains allowances as if he were buying the building unused, and so obtains 100% initial allowances and 25% straight line writing down allowances.

2.10 Buildings always have a **separate computation for each building**. They are never pooled.

Initial allowances

2.11 Where **expenditure is incurred** on an industrial building or a hotel under a contract entered into **between 1 November 1992 and 31 October 1993 inclusive**, the building is brought into use by 31 December 1994 and the 100% allowance for buildings in enterprise zones is not available, **an initial allowance (IA) of 20%** of the cost is given. The 4% WDA is also given, on the full cost (not on the remaining 80% of the cost), each year once the building has been brought into use. The IA and the WDA can be given in the same year. The buyer of a building which has already been used cannot get an IA.

Question: Industrial buildings allowances

Y Ltd makes up accounts for calendar years. On 1 March 1993 it bought a new factory for £500,000. The factory was brought into use on 1 August 1993. Show the industrial buildings allowances available.

Answer

	£	£
Y/e 31.12.93		
Initial allowance 20%	100,000	
WDA 4%	20,000	
Total for y/e 31.12.93		120,000
Y/e 31.12.94 to y/e 31.12.12 inclusive		
£20,000 a year for 19 years		380,000
		500,000

Balancing adjustments on sale

The tax life

2.12 **The 'tax life' of an industrial building is 25 years** (hence the 4% straight line WDA) after it is first used, or 50 years if constructed before 6 November 1962. The 25 year life applies even if an initial allowance applies. (In such cases, allowances will stop when all the expenditure has been allowed, even if the tax life has not yet ended.) Balancing adjustments apply *only* if a building is sold within its tax life of 25 or 50 years.

2.13 On a sale between connected persons, the parties may jointly elect that the transfer price for IBAs purposes should be the lower of the market value and the residue of unallowed expenditure before the sale. This avoids a balancing charge unless there has been non-industrial use.

2.14 If someone who has obtained allowances on a building in an enterprise zone realises a capital sum by granting a lease, and the sum is paid (or an agreement to pay it is made) within seven years of the agreement for him to incur the expenditure or buy the building, the payment is taken into account like a receipt on a sale, so that a balancing charge arises based on the amount received (less any amount treated as income under the Schedule A '2% $\times$ (n − 1)' rule on premiums, see later in this text). This treatment does not entitle the grantee to IBAs, and cannot lead to a balancing allowance for the grantor of the lease. If the original acquisition of the building was on terms making the grant of a lease likely, the seven year period is extended to 25 years.

Sales without non-industrial use

2.15 **The seller's calculation is quite straightforward providing the building has not been put to non-industrial use at any time during his ownership.** It takes the following form.

	£
Cost	X
Less allowances previously given	(X)
Residue before sale	X
Less proceeds (limited to cost)	(X)
Balancing (charge)/allowance	(X)

2.16 **The buyer obtains annual straight line WDAs for the remainder of the building's tax life** (25 years if constructed after 5 November 1962). This life is calculated to the nearest month. The allowances are granted on the residue after sale which is computed thus.

	£
Residue before sale	X
Plus balancing charge or less balancing allowance	X
Residue after sale	X

This means that **the second owner will write off the lower of his cost or the original cost.**

Question - Calculation of IBAs

Frankie Ltd, which started to trade in 1996 preparing accounts to 31 December, bought an industrial building for £100,000 (excluding land) on 1 October 1997. The company brought the building into use as a factory immediately. On 1 September 2001 it sold the building for £120,000 to Holly Ltd. Holly Ltd's accounting date is 30 September and it brought the building into industrial use immediately. Show the IBAs available to Frankie Ltd and to Holly Ltd.

Answer

	£
Frankie Ltd	
Cost 1.10.97	100,000
Y/e 31.12.97 to y/e 31.12.00 WDA 4 × 4%	(16,000)
Residue before sale	84,000
Y/e 31.12.01 Proceeds (limited to cost)	(100,000)
Balancing charge	(16,000)

	£
Holly Ltd	
Residue before sale	84,000
Balancing charge	16,000
Residue after sale	100,000

The tax life of the building ends on 1.10.97 + 25 years = 30.9.2022
The date of Holly Ltd's purchase is 1.9.01
The unexpired life is therefore 21 years 1 month

	£
Y/e 30.9.01 WDA £100,000/21.083333	4,743
Next 20 accounting periods at £4,743 a year	94,860
Y/e 30.9.22 (balance)	397
	100,000

Exam focus point

The Inland Revenue allow IBA's equal to the fall in value of a building over the company's use of that building. As a general rule if an industrial building is sold for more than its original cost a balancing charge equal to the allowances given to date will arise. This is because there was no fall in value so no allowances are actually due.

If it is sold for less than original cost we could calculate the fall in value of the building and that would equal the allowances available for this building. If we compare this to the allowances already given, the difference would be the balancing adjustment due on the sale.

In the above question if Frankie Ltd sold the building Holly Ltd for £90,000:

	£
Fall in value (£100,000 – £90,000) = allowances due	10,000
Less: allowances already given to Frankie Ltd	16,000
Balancing adjustment = Balancing charge	6,000

Over the use of the building by Frankie Ltd £16,000 of IBA's were claimed. On the sale of the building the fall in value is calculated as £10,000. Thus Frankie Ltd should only have received £10,000 of allowances not £16,000. So £6,000 is paid back as a balancing charge.

Sales after non-industrial use

2.17 If at the end of a period, an industrial building was in non-industrial use, then the owner will not have been able to claim WDAs, but the building will have been written down by notional WDAs.

2.18 **If, following a period of non-industrial use, an industrial building is sold for more than its original cost, the balancing charge is the actual allowances given. The residue after sale is the original cost minus the notional allowances.**

Question - Non-industrial use

The facts are as in the above question except that on 1 October 1998 Frankie Ltd ceases manufacturing in the building, letting it out as a theatrical rehearsal studio. On 1 June 2000 he recommences manufacturing in the building and, as before, sells it to Holly Ltd for £120,000 on 1 September 2001. Show the IBAs available to Frankie Ltd and to Holly Ltd.

Answer

	£
Frankie Ltd	
Cost 1.10.97	100,000
Y/e 31.12.97 WDA 4%	(4,000)
	96,000
Y/e 31.12.98 and y/e 31.12.99 No WDA since not in industrial use at the ends of the accounting periods, but deduct notional allowances 2 × 4%	(8,000)
	88,000
Y/e 31.12.00 WDA 4%	(4,000)
Residue before sale	84,000
Balancing charge for y/e 31.12.01: real (not notional) allowances £(4,000 + 4,000)	£(8,000)

	£
Holly Ltd	
Residue before sale	84,000
Add: balancing charge	8,000
Residue after sale	92,000

	£
Y/e 30.9.01 WDA £92,000/21.083333	4,364
Next 20 account periods at £4,364 a year	87,280
Y/e 30.9.22 (balance)	356
	92,000

2.19 If, after a period of non-industrial use, a building is sold for less than original cost the balancing adjustment is calculated as follows.

	£
Cost	X
Less proceeds	(X)
Net cost	X
Less proportion of net cost for period(s) in non-industrial use	(X)
Adjusted net cost	X
Less actual allowances given	(X)
Balancing (charge)/allowance	(X)

The buyer gets allowances on the lower of:

(a) the residue after sale;

(b) the amount paid.

Question: Non-industrial use

The facts are as in the above question except that the building is sold to Holly Ltd for £60,000. Calculate Frankie Ltd's balancing allowance or charge and the figure on which Holly Ltd will obtain allowances.

Answer

	£
Frankie Ltd	
Cost	100,000
Less proceeds	(60,000)
Net cost	40,000
Less: net cost × $\dfrac{\text{period of non} - \text{industrial use}}{\text{total period from first use to sale}}$	
$\dfrac{20 \text{ months}}{47 \text{ months}} \times £40,000$	(17,021)
Adjusted net cost	22,979
Less allowances actually given (as before)	(8,000)
Balancing allowance	14,979

	£
Holly Ltd	
Residue before sale (as before)	84,000
Less balancing allowance	(14,979)
Residue after sale	69,021
Limited to cost	£60,000

Holly Ltd will get allowances totalling £60,000, spread over the remaining tax life of the building.

Exam focus point

If an industrial building is sold for more than original cost a balancing charge equal to the allowances given (ie actual allowances not notional allowances) to date will arise. This rule applies where there has been industrial or non-industrial use.

If a building is sold for less than cost the fall in value equals the allowances due. This is compared with the allowances claimed to calculate a balancing adjustment. However, this rule only applies where there has only been industrial use.

Where there has been non-industrial use and the building is sold for less than its cost a balancing adjustment will arise. This time the fall in value must be time apportioned to find the **industrial use element** before the normal comparison with actual allowances given can be made.

In the above example.

	£

$$\text{Fall in value} \times \frac{\text{Industrial use } (47-20)}{\text{Total use } (47)} = \text{allowances due}$$

	£
(£100,000 – 60,000) × $^{27}/_{47}$ months	22,979
Less: actual allowances given to Frankie Ltd	(8,000)
Balancing adjustment = balancing allowance	14,979

Note: Effectively the £22,979 is the fall in value (and hence allowances available) of the building whilst it was being used for an industrial purpose. Since only £8,000 of real allowance was claimed this means that a further £14,979 is due now as a balancing allowance.

Chapter roundup

- The computations for industrial buildings are a little more complicated than those for plant and machinery, but there is less case law to learn.

- Basically allowances equal to the fall in value of the building whilst it was being used industrially are available to the company.

- Try to see the rationale of the computation when an industrial building which has had some non-industrial use is sold: compare a fair proportion of the fall in value of the building with the actual allowances given to calculate a balancing adjustment.

Quick quiz

1 List four types of building which do not usually qualify for industrial buildings allowance.

2 When are drawing offices industrial buildings?

3 What are the conditions for a hotel to qualify for allowances?

4 When must a 'notional allowance' be deducted from the qualifying cost of an industrial building?

5 What is the amount of the balancing charge on a sale where there been non-industrial use?

Answers to quick quiz

1 Dwelling houses, retail shops, showrooms and offices.

2 Drawing offices which serve an industrial building are industrial buildings.

3 (a) It must have ten letting bedrooms

    (b) It must have letting bedrooms as the whole or main part of the sleeping accommodation

    (c) It must offer ancillary services including at least

        (i) Breakfast
        (ii) Evening meals
        (iii) The cleaning of rooms
        (iv) The making of beds

    (d) It must be open for at least four months during the April to October letting season.

4 A notional allowance will be given if a building was in non-industrial use at the end of the accounting period concerned.

5 The balancing charge is equal to the industrial buildings allowances actually given.

Now try the questions below from the Exam Question Bank

Number	Level	Marks	Time
5	Exam	20	36 mins
6	Exam	25	45 mins

BPP PUBLISHING

Chapter 6

COMPANY FUNDING AND INVESTMENTS

Topic list	Syllabus reference	Ability required
1 Loan relationships (borrowing and lending)	(iii)	Comprehension
2 Schedule A income	(iii)	Application
3 Other investment income	(iii)	Application
4 The Corporate venturing scheme	(iii)	Analysis
5 The Enterprise investment scheme (EIS)	(vii)	Analysis
6 Venture capital trusts (VCTS)	(vii)	Analysis
7 Financial structure (gearing) of a company	(vii)	Analysis

Introduction

When a company borrows or lends money it has a loan relationship. In this chapter we see how loan relationships effect a company's CT liability. We also see how to compute various other types of investment income that we must include in calculating a company's profits chargeable to corporation tax.

Companies can raise equity finance through corporate venturing, the enterprise investment scheme (EIS) and through venture capital trusts. These schemes offer tax incentives to the investors. We look at the schemes in this chapter.

We end the chapter by considering the tax implications of the financial structure of a company.

Learning outcomes covered in this chapter

- **Explain** the effect of the loan relationship rules on a company's CT liability
- **Calculate** the total profits of a company for CT purposes
- **Calculate** the CT liability of a company
- **Contrast** the tax implications of financing a company by debt or equity

Syllabus content covered in this chapter

- Loan relationships rules – all aspects including the reliefs for non trading deficits

- Tax implications of alternative financial structures. Balance between debt and equity. The impact of EIS and VCT

- Calculation of total profits and CT liability

1   LOAN RELATIONSHIPS (BORROWING AND LENDING)

1.1 **If a company borrows or lends money, including issuing or investing in debentures or buying gilts, it has a loan relationship. This can be a creditor relationship** (where the company lends or invests money) **or a debtor relationship** (where the company borrows money or issues securities).

Treatment of trading loan relationships

1.2 If the company is a party to a **loan relationship for trade purposes, any expenses ('debits')** – **ie interest paid or other debt costs** – **charged through its accounts are allowed as a trading expense** and are therefore deductible in computing Schedule D Case I profits. Debentures are an example of a loan relationship which is usually issued for trade purposes. If debentures are issued for trade purposes any interest which the company pays on them is deductible in computing Schedule D Case I profits.

1.3 Similarly **if any income ('credits') – ie interest income or other debt returns – arise on a trading loan these are treated as a trading receipt and are taxable under Schedule D Case I.** This is not likely to arise unless the trade is one of money lending.

Treatment of non-trading loan relationships

1.4 **If a loan relationship is not one to which the company is a party for trade purposes any income and expenses must be pooled. Examples of non-trading loan relationships are bank and building society accounts held for investment (ie non-trade) purposes.**

1.5 **A net credit on the pool of non-trading loan relationships is chargeable as income under Schedule D Case III. A net deficit on the pool may be:**

(a) **set against other income of the same accounting period**

(b) **surrendered as group relief** (covered later in this text)

(c) **carried back and set against any surpluses on non-trading loan relationships** (taxed under Schedule D Case III) **for the previous twelve months**

(d) **carried forward and set against future non-trading profits**

Any deficit remaining after the above claims is automatically carried forward as an opening DIII debit of the next accounting period.

These methods of relief are discussed in more detail later in this text.

Accounting methods

1.6 The following bases are acceptable for recognising debits or credits.

(a) the accruals basis; or
(b) the mark to market basis.

The mark to market basis places a fair value on the loan relationship for each accounting period and determines the credit or debit on the change in the value.

If neither the accruals or mark to market method is used in the accounts, the accruals basis must be used for tax purposes. In this study text, we assume that the accruals basis applies. The mark to market basis is only likely to be used by companies in the financial sector such as banks.

Incidental costs of loan finance

1.7 Under the loan relationship rules expenses ('debits') are allowed if incurred directly:

BPP
PUBLISHING

(a) in bringing a loan relationship into existence;

(b) entering into or giving effect to any related transactions;

(c) making payment under a loan relationship or related transactions; or

(d) taking steps to ensure the receipt of payments under the loan relationship or related transaction.

A related transaction means 'any disposal or acquisition (in whole or in part) of rights or liabilities under the relationship, including any arising from a security issue in relation to the money debt in question'.

The above categories of incidental costs are also allowable even if the company does not enter into the loan relationship (ie abortive costs). Cost directly incurred in varying the terms of a loan relationship are also allowed.

Other matters

1.8 It is not only the interest costs of borrowing that are allowable or taxable. The capital costs are treated similarly. Thus if a company issues a loan at a discount and repays it eventually at par, the capital cost is allowed either on redemption (if the accruals basis is adopted) or period by period (if it is accounted for on a mark to market basis).

1.9 Relief for pre-trading expenditure extends to expenses incurred on trading relationships in accounting periods ending within seven years of the company starting to trade. An expense that would have been a trading debit if it was incurred after the trade had commenced, is treated as a trading debit of the first trading period. An election has to be made within two years of the end of the first trading period.

1.10 **Short interest** (ie interest which is not paid annually) or **interest to a UK bank is payable gross**. In addition since 1 April 2001 all payments of interest to UK corporate recipients has been paid gross. 'Yearly' interest (such as debenture interest) payable to individuals is paid net of 20% tax. Any tax withheld must be dealt with under the CT61 quarterly accounting system. (See earlier in this text.)

1.11 Interest charged on underpaid tax is allowable and interest received on overpaid tax is assessable under the loan relationship rules.

2 SCHEDULE A INCOME

2.1 **Income from land and buildings in the UK, including caravans and houseboats which are not moved, is taxed under Schedule A.**

2.2 **A company with rental income is treated as running a 'Schedule A business'. All the rents and expenses for all properties are pooled, to give a single profit or loss. Profits and losses are computed in the same way as trading profits are computed for Schedule D Case I purposes,** on an accruals basis (see earlier in this text).

2.3 **Interest paid on a loan taken out to buy a property is dealt with under the loan relationship rules (see above).** It is not deducted in computing schedule A income.

2.4 **Capital allowances are given on plant and machinery used in the Schedule A business and on industrial buildings, in the same way as they are given for a Schedule D Case I business.** Capital allowances are not normally available on plant or machinery used in a dwelling (although in certain cases, they may exceptionally be available on radiators and boilers). A company that lets property furnished cannot claim capital allowances on the furniture. However, it can choose instead between the renewals basis and the 10% wear and tear allowance.

- Under the *renewals* basis, there is no deduction for the cost of the first furniture provided, but the cost of replacement furniture is treated as a revenue expense. However, the part of the cost attributable to improvement, as opposed to simple replacement, is not deductible.

- Under the *10% wear and tear* basis, the actual cost of furniture is ignored. Instead, an annual deduction is given of 10% of rents. The rents are first reduced by amounts which are paid by the landlord but are normally a tenant's burden. These amounts include any water rates and council tax paid by the landlord.

2.5 If plant and machinery is used partly in a dwelling house and partly for other purposes a just and reasonable apportionment of the expenditure can be made.

2.6 Rent for furniture supplied with premises is taxed as part of the rent for the premises, unless there is a separate trade of renting furniture.

Loss relief

2.7 Schedule A losses are first set off against non-Schedule A income and gains of the company for the current period and any excess is:

(a) carried forward as a Schedule A loss of the following accounting period provided (except for investment companies) that the Schedule A business has not ceased; or

(b) available for surrender as group relief (see later in this text).

Premiums on leases

2.8 **When a premium or similar consideration is received on the grant** (that is, by a landlord to a tenant) **of a short lease (50 years or less), part of the premium is treated as rent received in the year of grant**. A lease is considered to end on the date when it is most likely to terminate. This could be, for instance, the date from which the rent is to be substantially increased.

The premium taxed under Schedule A is the whole premium, less 2% of the premium for each complete year of the lease, except the first year.

This rule does not apply on the *assignment* of a lease (one tenant selling his entire interest in the property to another).

Premiums paid

2.9 **Where a trading company (taxed under Schedule D Case I) pays a premium for a lease it may deduct an amount from its taxable profits in each year of the lease. The amount deductible is the figure treated as rent received by the landlord divided by the number of years of the lease.** For example, suppose that B Ltd, pays A Ltd a premium of £30,000 for a ten year lease. A Ltd is treated as receiving £30,000 − (£30,000 × (10 − 1) × 2%) = £24,600. B Ltd can therefore deduct £24,600/10 = £2,460 in each of the ten years. The company starts with the accounting period in which the lease starts and apportions the relief to the nearest month.

Premiums for granting subleases

2.10 **A tenant may decide to sublet property and to charge a premium on the grant of a lease to the subtenant. This premium is treated as rent received in the normal way** (because this is a grant and not an assignment, the original tenant retaining an interest in the property). **Where the tenant originally paid a premium on the grant of his own head lease, this deemed rent is reduced by:**

$$\text{Rent part of premium for head lease} \times \frac{\text{duration of sub} - \text{lease}}{\text{duration of head lease}}$$

If the relief exceeds the part of the premium for the sub-lease treated as rent (including cases where there is a sub-lease with no premium), the balance of the relief is treated as rent payable by the head tenant, spread evenly over the period of the sub-lease. This rent payable is an expense, reducing the overall Schedule A profit.

Question: Taxable premium received

C Ltd granted a lease to D Ltd on 1 March 1991 for a period of 40 years. D Ltd paid a premium of £16,000. On 1 June 2001 D Ltd granted a sublease to E Ltd for a period of ten years. E Ltd paid a premium of £30,000. Calculate the amount treated as rent out of the premium received by D Ltd.

Answer

	£
Premium received by D Ltd	30,000
Less £30,000 × 2% × (10-1)	(5,400)
	24,600
Less allowance for premium paid	
(£16,000 - (£16,000 × 39 × 2%)) × 10/40	(880)
Premium treated as rent	23,720

Furnished holiday lettings

2.11 **There are special rules for furnished holiday lettings. The income from such lettings is taxed under Schedule A but Schedule D Case I rules apply for all purposes** as follows.

(a) Relief for losses is available as if they were trading losses (see later in this text), including the facility to set losses against other income. The usual Schedule A loss reliefs do not apply.

(b) Capital allowances are available on furniture: the renewals basis and the 10% wear and tear basis do not apply if capital allowances are claimed.

(c) Capital gains tax rollover relief is available (see later in this text).

2.12 The letting must be of furnished accommodation made on a commercial basis with a view to the realisation of profit. The property must satisfy the following conditions.

(a) It is available for commercial letting to the public for not less than 140 days in an accounting period, and is so let for at least 70 days in that 140 day period. If two or more properties each pass the 140 day test separately, then they need only pass the 70 day test on average. That is, the test becomes [(sum of numbers of days let)/(number of properties)] must be at least 70. A landlord may choose to leave particular properties out of the averaging computation if they would pull the average down to below 70 days.

(b) For at least seven months (including the 70 days) it is not normally in the same occupation for more than 31 days.

2.13   If a company has furnished holiday lettings and other lettings, draw up two profit and loss accounts as if they had two separate Schedule A businesses. This is so that the profits and losses treated as trade profits and losses can be identified.

3   OTHER INVESTMENT INCOME

Interest income

3.1   **Interest received on non-trading loan relationships is taxed under Schedule D Case III on an accruals basis** (see above). This includes interest received on bank and building society accounts held for investment (rather than trade) purposes.

3.2   **UK companies receive interest gross from banks and building societies. Interest received from other companies is also received gross** (with effect from 1 April 2001).

3.3   **Interest on most gilt edged securities** is received gross but in certain limited circumstances it is received net of tax at 20%. Gilt edged securities will normally be held for non-trade purposes and are, therefore, an example of a non trading loan relationship.

3.4   Interest received from another UK company (such as debenture or loan stock interest) was received net of tax at 20% prior to 1 April 2001. Income tax suffered at source was dealt with through the quarterly accounting system (see earlier in this text). **Interest received from an individual or partnership will continue to be received net of tax after 1 April 2001.** The gross amount of interest received must be included in the company's profits chargeable to corporation tax even where interest is received net.

3.5   Interest received on trading loan relationships (eg debentures issued for trade purposes) is dealt with under Schedule D Case I.

Unit trusts

3.6   A unit trust allocates units to investors in return for money they pay in. The sums paid in are then invested in shares and securities. The dividends and interest arising on those shares and securities are passed on to the investors. When an investor wishes to withdraw an investment, it sells units back to the unit trust managers. The price of units varies with the market values of the shares and securities, so investors may make gains or losses.

3.7   If a company holds units in a unit trust, then in general it is in the same position as if it held shares in a company. Dividends from the trust are, like dividends on shares, not taxable income for a company. There are the following exceptions to this rule.

   (a)   If more than 60% (by market value) of the unit trust's investments are interest-bearing investments, then the units are treated as a creditor loan relationship for the company. The accruals basis cannot be used: the mark to market basis must be used instead and distributions out of the unit trust's interest income are treated as interest received.

   (b)   In other cases, a proportion of a dividend paid by the unit trust is treated as interest. This is called the unfranked part of the distribution: it corresponds to the proportion of the unit trust's income which is not dividend income.

4   THE CORPORATE VENTURING SCHEME

4.1   **The corporate venturing scheme allows an investing company to obtain corporation tax relief at 20% on amounts invested in ordinary shares held for at least 3 years.**

4.2 The investment must be in new ordinary shares of an unquoted 'small high risk trading company'. As long as the company is unquoted at the time the shares are issued and there are no arrangements in place (or planned) at that time for seeking a listing, relief will not be withdrawn if the company subsequently becomes quoted during the three year period for which the shares must be held.

4.3 The investing company can defer any chargeable gains made on corporate venturing investments that it reinvests in another shareholding under the scheme.

4.4 Any capital loss (net of corporation tax relief) arising on a disposal of the shares can be set against the company's income.

4.5 Tax relief is withdrawn if the shares are not held for three years.

4.6 A corporate venturer cannot obtain tax relief under the scheme if it controls the small company in which it has invested.

The investing company

4.7 The investing company must either be:

   (a) A trading company which is neither engaged in a financial trade nor a member of a group whose business consists of financial trades or non-trading activities, or

   (b) An investment company which is a member of a non-financial trading group.

4.8 The investing company must not hold more than 30% of the:

   (a) Ordinary share capital, or
   (b) The combined share and loan capital which can be converted into ordinary share capital

   of the company in which the investment is made (the issuing company).

The issuing company

4.9 The issuing company must not have gross assets of more than £15 million before the investment and not more than £16 million immediately after it.

4.10 For a period of three years from the later of the issue of shares and the start of trading:

   (a) The issuing company must carry on a qualifying trade or be a parent company whose business does not consist to a substantial extent of excluded activities and which has at least one group member carrying on a qualifying trade. If the issuing company is a parent company, each of the other group members must be at least 75% owned by the company or another of its subsidiaries.

   (b) The issuing company must not be under the control of any other company.

   (c) The issuing company must not be involved in a partnership or joint venture with another company which is owned by the same person as owns the issuing company.

   (d) At least 20% of the issuing company's ordinary share capital must be owned by individuals who are not employees or directors of the investing company.

Qualifying trade

4.11 A trade must be carried on on a commercial basis and must not consist to a substantial extent of certain excluded activities (as defined for EIS purposes; see below).

4.12 Research and development which is intended to lead to or benefit a qualifying trade is treated as a qualifying trade.

Anti-avoidance rules

4.13 There are extensive anti-avoidance rules designed to ensure that money invested is genuinely put at risk. These rules mirror the EIS anti avoidance rules.

Clearance

4.14 The issuing company can apply for advance clearance from the Revenue that an issue will meet the qualifying conditions.

5 THE ENTERPRISE INVESTMENT SCHEME (EIS)

> **KEY TERM**
>
> The **EIS** is a scheme designed to promote enterprise and investment by helping high-risk, unlisted trading companies raise finance by the issue of ordinary shares to individual investors who are unconnected with that company.

5.1 Individuals who subscribe for EIS shares are entitled to both income tax and capital gains tax reliefs.

Income tax relief

5.2 Broadly, an individual can reduce his income tax liability by 20% of any qualifying EIS investment.

5.3 To be eligible for relief the minimum subscription of shares in any company is £500. The maximum EIS investments qualifying for income tax relief is £150,000, but individuals can invest in excess of this amount if they wish.

5.4 If an investor subscribes for different EIS issues, or full relief is not available in a tax year because the £150,000 limit is exceeded, tax relief is attributed to the various shares according to the amounts subscribed. For different issues, the relief attributed to each issue is apportioned equally between the shares in that issue and any bonus shares subsequently added to the holding. Attribution rules are needed in case the relief is subsequently withdrawn.

5.5 A tax year for an individual runs from 6 April in one year to 5 April in the next year. If shares are issued in the first six months of the tax year (ie before 6 October), the investor may claim to have up half of the shares treated as issued in the previous tax year. This is subject to a maximum carry back of £25,000 if £50,000 or more shares are issued in the first six months.

5.6 When carrying back relief, relief given in the previous year must not exceed overall EIS limits for that year.

5.7 **EIS relief can be claimed by an individual who subscribes wholly in cash for new ordinary shares in a qualifying company.** All the shares issued must be issued to finance a qualifying business activity. The shares must be subscribed, and issued, for bona fide commercial purposes and not as part of a scheme to avoid tax.

5.8   For three years after the later of, the issue of the shares and, the commencement of trade the shares must have no right to redemption, nor preferential right to dividends or to the company's assets in a winding up. For issues prior to 6.4.00 this condition applied for five years rather than three years.

5.9   A company must issue a certificate stating that an investment qualifies for relief to the individual taxpayer before any tax relief claim can be made.

Qualifying individual

5.10   **The investor must not be 'connected with' the company** during the **'designated period'** starting two years prior to the share issue (or from incorporation if later) and ending three years after the share issue (or commencement of trade, if later). This means, neither the investor, nor any associate of his, may be:

(a)   an employee, director or partner of the company or its 51% subsidiaries (but see below)

(b)   an employee or director of a partner of the company or its 51% subsidiaries

(c)   in possession of, or entitled to acquire, more than 30% of the company's (or any 51% subsidiary's) issued share capital, loan capital or voting power. For this purpose loan capital includes any debt incurred by the company for any money borrowed or capital assets acquired, but not a bank overdraft which arises in the ordinary course of business.

(d)   able to control the company (or any 51% subsidiary), eg. by virtue of powers conferred in the Articles of Association.

For issues prior to 6 April 2000 the 'designated period' extends to five years after the share issue.

5.11   An exception to the above allows investors (or their associates) to be unpaid directors of the company or even paid directors provided the remuneration paid is:

(a)   reasonable for the services rendered; and

(b)   the investor was never connected to the company before the share issue, or employed by a person who previously carried on the trade which is now being carried on by the company. (This stops the relief being of benefit to existing management hoping to organise a management buy-out).

5.12   For these purposes **associates** include husband, wife, parent, grandparent, child, grandchild. Brothers, sisters, uncles, aunts and in-laws are not associates.

Conditions to be satisfied by the company

5.13   In outline, a qualifying company is an unquoted trading company which exists wholly to carry on a qualifying business activity for a minimum of three years. The company must not be a subsidiary of, or be controlled by, any other company or any other company and a connected person. Any subsidiary must be at least 90% owned and the group taken as a whole must qualify in respect of its business activities.

5.14   As long as the company is unquoted at the time the shares are issued and there are no arrangements in place (or planned) at that time for seeking a listing, EIS relief is not withdrawn if the company subsequently becomes quoted.

Qualifying business activity

5.15 The shares must be issued to finance a qualifying business activity. The following are a 'qualifying business activity':

(a) a qualifying trade

(b) research and development or oil exploration from which it is intended to derive a qualifying trade

(c) activities preparatory to carrying on a qualifying trade, providing the trade commences within two years after the share issue.

The company must carry on the qualifying business activity wholly or mainly (more than 50%) **in the UK for a period of three years from the date of the share issue.**

Qualifying trades

5.16 **The company must exist wholly to carry on qualifying trades or to act as a holding or financing company for qualifying subsidiaries.** The trade must be conducted on a commercial basis with a view to making profits. Most trades are qualifying trades. However, the following are prohibited:

(a) dealing in commodities, shares, securities, land and futures

(b) dealing in goods otherwise than in the course of an ordinary trade of wholesale or retail distribution

(c) banking, insurance, money lending, debt factoring, HP financing or other financial activities

(d) oil extraction (without exploration) activities

(e) leasing (other than short-term leasing of ships), including letting assets on hire, or receiving royalties or licence fees (subject to certain limited exceptions)

(f) providing legal or accountancy services

(g) property development

(h) farming or market gardening

(i) holding or managing woodlands or any other forestry activity

(j) operating or managing hotels, nursing homes or residential care homes

(k) providing services or facilities for the above trades carried on by another person if the company and the other person are under common control, eg a service company for a firm of accountants where the partners in the firm control the company. This prohibition does not extend to supplies to a parent company by its subsidiary.

Companies in liquidation or receivership may continue to be treated as carrying on a qualifying trade.

5.17 The company must use 80% the money from the share subscription for its qualifying business activity generally within twelve months of the share issue. Where the company intends to carry on a qualifying trade and that trade is commenced up to two years after the subscription date, 80% of the money must be used within twelve months from the commencement of trade. Any remaining money must be used within the following twelve month period.

5.18   A company does not have to be incorporated and resident in the UK (although it must of course still carry on its qualifying trade etc. wholly or mainly (in practice 50%) in the UK.

5.19   The assets of the company (including assets of group companies) must not exceed £15 million immediately before the share issue and must not exceed £16 million immediately afterwards.

Withdrawal of relief

5.20   Shares issued before 6 April 2000 must be held by an investor for at least five years for the maximum available tax relief to be given. This minimum holding period is reduced to three years for EIS shares issued on or after this date by a company that is carrying on a qualifying trade at the time of issue. For companies which are preparing to trade at the time of issue, the minimum holding period ends when the company has been carrying on a qualifying trade for three years.

5.21   The main reason for the withdrawal of relief will be the sale of the shares by the investor within the five/three year period mentioned above. The consequences depend on whether the disposal is at arms length or not:

(a)   If the disposal is not a bargain at arms length the full amount of relief originally obtained is withdrawn.

(b)   If the disposal is a bargain at arms length there is a withdrawal of relief on the consideration received.

5.22   EIS relief is also withdrawn:

(a)   in respect of shares in a company which takes over a trade in which the investor previously had an interest

(b)   by reference to any value received from the company (or a 51% subsidiary) if it is received during the period starting one year prior to the share issue and ending three years after the issue (or incorporation if later). Value received will include the receipt of rent. However, reasonable director's remuneration insignificant amounts and receipts of value which are returned without unreasonable delay are disregarded.

5.23   Relief is reduced where, during the designated period, there is a repayment of capital by the company or its 51% subsidiary to the other shareholders.

5.24   A transfer of shares between spouses does not give rise to a withdrawal of relief.

Miscellaneous provisions

5.25   Relief is not available if the investor takes out a loan linked to the investment during the designated period. Any relief given must be repaid to the Revenue.

5.26   EIS relief is not available if 'relevant arrangements' exist at or before the time shares are issued. Relevant arrangements are defined as those that protect or guarantee the individual's investment or provide for the investor to dispose of the shares.

Capital gains tax reliefs

5.27   Where shares qualify for income tax relief under the EIS there are also special rules that apply to those shares for capital gains purposes.

(a) Where an investor disposes of shares after the five/three year period any gain is exempt from capital gains tax. If the shares are disposed of within five/three years no capital gains relief is available.

(b) If EIS shares are disposed of at a loss at any time, the loss is allowable for chargeable gains purposes but the acquisition cost of the shares is reduced by the amount of EIS tax relief attributable to the shares.

Note that in your exam you will not be expected to compute chargeable gains or allowable losses for individuals.

5.28 EIS reinvestment relief may be available to defer chargeable gains if an individual invests in EIS shares in the period commencing one year before and ending three years after the disposal of the asset. For further details of this relief see Chapter 11.

6 VENTURE CAPITAL TRUSTS (VCTs)

> **KEY TERM**
>
> **Venture capital trusts (VCTs)** are listed companies which invest in unquoted trading companies and meet certain conditions.

6.1 The VCT scheme differs from EIS in that the individual investor may spread his risk over a number of higher-risk, unquoted companies. **An individual investing in a VCT obtains the following tax benefits.**

- Income tax relief of 20% of the amount invested, in the year of making the investment.

- Dividends received are tax-free income.

- Capital gains on the sale of shares in the VCT are exempt from capital gains tax (and losses are not allowable).

In addition, capital gains which the VCT itself makes on its investments are not chargeable gains, and so are not subject to corporation tax.

6.2 The above reliefs are not available if shares were acquired other than for bona fide commercial purposes of for the purpose of tax avoidance.

Conditions to qualify as a VCT

6.3 A VCT must be approved by the Inland Revenue. Approval is withdrawn if a VCT fails any of the following detailed conditions.

6.4 The VCT must not be a close company. A close company is, broadly, one which is under the control of its shareholder-directors or of five or fewer shareholders.

6.5 The VCT's income must be wholly or mainly derived from shares or securities.

6.6 (a) At least 70% by value of the VCT's investments must normally be in shares or securities which are **qualifying holdings** (see below). Loans, loan stock and debentures only count as securities if no-one can require their repayment or redemption within five years of their being made or issued (except in cases of default by the borrower). Loans and securities must not be guaranteed by a third party.

(b) At least 30% by value of the VCT's qualifying holdings must be in the form of **eligible shares**. These are ordinary shares carrying no preferential rights in respect of dividends, assets or redemption. At least 10% of the total investment in any company must be held in ordinary, non-preferential shares.

(c) No holding in any company (other than another VCT) may exceed 15% by value of the VCT's investments.

Holdings are valued when they are acquired, or when they were last added to or further money was spent on them (for example in paying a call on shares). Thus holdings do not need to be sold merely because their market values have changed.

6.7 All of the VCT's ordinary shares must be listed on the Stock Exchange (this would not include AIM shares).

6.8 The VCT must not retain more than 15% of the income it derives from shares and securities.

Qualifying holdings

6.9 Shares and securities are qualifying holdings if:

(a) they were issued to the VCT (that is, the VCT did not acquire them secondhand); and

(b) all of the conditions set out below are satisfied.

6.10 The issuing company must be unquoted. The shares may be AIM shares. However, if it becomes quoted after the issue of the shares or securities, at a time when the VCT still qualifies as a VCT, the holding continues to be qualifying for five years from that time.

6.11 The company (or its group, which must only include 75% subsidiaries) must exist wholly to carry on qualifying trades, or research and development intended to lead to qualifying trades. Trades are qualifying if they would qualify for the purposes of the EIS (see Section above). However, the EIS exclusions of leasing and of oil extraction do not apply, so such trades are permitted.

6.12 At the time of issue of the shares or securities and at all times since, the issuing company (or its subsidiary) must have been carrying on a qualifying trade (or research and development for one) wholly or mainly in the UK, or have been preparing to do so. However, preparing to do so ceases to be enough to make the holding qualifying two years after the time of issue. It will only stay qualifying if the company or subsidiary actually started to carry on the trade, research or development within two years of the time of issue, and has done so wholly or mainly in the UK continuously since the end of that two year period. The holding will also cease to qualify as soon as the issuing company or its subsidiary abandons its intention to carry on a qualifying trade, research or development wholly or mainly in the UK.

6.13 A company that is carrying on a trade at the time of issue of shares to the VCT must use at least 80% of the money raised for the purposes of its trade within twelve months. The remainder must be so used within 24 months of the issue. Where a company is preparing to carry on a trade, these time periods run from the date of commencement of the trade.

6.14 The value of the trading company's assets must not have exceeded £15m immediately before the issue of shares or securities or £16m immediately afterwards. Where there is a group of companies, the limits apply to the group's assets.

Tax relief on investment in a VCT

6.15 An individual who is at least 18 years of age and subscribes for new VCT can claim income tax relief of up to 20% of the amount subscribed.

6.16 The shares issued must be new ordinary shares, which for at least three years from issue carry no preferential rights to dividends, assets or redemption. For issues prior to 6 April 2000 this period was a five year rather than a three year period.

6.17 The investment which can qualify for tax relief is broadly, limited to £100,000 per individual per tax year. More can be invested in VCTs, but the excess will not qualify for tax relief.

6.18 If a loan is made to the individual, within the period from incorporation of the VCT (or two years before the issue, if later) to three years after the issue (or five years for issues before 6.4.00), and the loan is linked to the investment in the VCT, any tax relief previously given must be repaid to the Revenue.

6.19 **If the shares in the VCT are disposed of within three years of issue (five years for shares issued before 6 April 2000), the tax reliefs given may be wholly or partly withdrawn.**

- If the shares are not disposed of under a bargain made at arm's length, all the tax relief is withdrawn.

- If the shares are disposed of under a bargain made at arm's length, the tax relief is withdrawn, up to the disposal proceeds × 20%.

6.20 Relief is not withdrawn on a disposal between spouses living together.

6.21 When shares are disposed of, we assume that shares acquired on an earlier day are disposed of before shares acquired on a later day. If shares were acquired on the same day, we assume that shares which did not generate a tax relief are disposed of before those which did. This could happen, for example, if an individual subscribed £150,000 to a VCT on one day.

6.22 If a VCT's approval is withdrawn within three years of issue (five years for issues before 6 April 2000) any tax relief given is withdrawn.

Tax-free dividends

6.23 **Dividends received on ordinary shares in VCTs are tax-free income,** for individuals.

6.24 The shareholder must be aged at least 18, and must have acquired the shares at a time when the company qualified as a VCT.

6.25 The profits in respect of which the dividend is paid must have arisen in an accounting period, at the end of which the company qualified as a VCT.

The CGT exemption

6.26 **If an individual disposes of ordinary shares in a company which was a VCT when he acquired the shares and is still a VCT at the time of disposal, there is no chargeable gain and no allowable loss.**

6.27 The shareholder must be aged at least 18 at the time of the disposal.

6.28   If a VCT loses its approval, anybody who holds shares in it which would (ignoring the age 18 requirement) qualify for the CGT exemption is deemed to sell those shares and buy them back for their market value. The deemed sale is exempt, and the newly non-exempt shares are treated as if they were bought at the time withdrawal of approval takes effect for their then market value. The only time when this rule does not apply is when approval was given before all the conditions to be a VCT were satisfied, and that approval was then declared void from the beginning. In that case, the shares are treated for CGT purposes as bought when they were actually bought for their actual price.

6.29   VCT reinvestment relief may be available to defer an individual's chargeable gains when he invests in VCT shares (see chapter 11).

7   FINANCIAL STRUCTURE (GEARING) OF A COMPANY

7.1   **Companies with a high debt to equity ratio are often referred to as highly geared companies.** They are identified for tax purposes as having **thin capitalisation**. They are treated favourably by the UK CT system.

Debt finance

7.2   We saw at the start of this chapter how both interest and capital costs of loan relationships can be deducted in arriving at PCTCT. This makes debt a very attractive method of raising finance.

7.3   In addition a deduction is allowed under the loan relationship rules for the incidental costs of obtaining medium or long term business loans and for issuing loan stock. Allowable costs include professional fees and commissions, also advertising and printing costs even if the exercise is abortive.

7.4   There is anti-avoidance legislation under which the Revenue can prevent a thinly capitalised company from deducting all of its debt costs if the financial structure of the company has been chosen for the purpose of tax avoidance.

Equity finance

7.5   **Companies can raise finance by issuing shares to shareholders. Capital can be raised in this way for trading and non-trading purposes.**

7.6   **Companies can distribute profits to shareholders in a variety of ways,** of which the payment of dividends is the most common. The payments made are collectively referred to as 'distributions'.

7.7   **The cost of making distributions to shareholders is not an allowable expense when calculating the taxable profits of a company.**

7.8   **Legal and professional expenses incurred in issuing share capital are also disallowable.**

7.9   The above two points mean that equity finance is, in general, less attractive than debt finance. The enterprise investment scheme, venture capital trusts and the corporate venturing scheme have all been introduced to promote equity investment.

Investors

7.10   **Interest income received from a company on loan stock etc is taxable income for the recipient.** From 1 April 2001 interest is paid gross to corporate recipients but net of 20% tax when paid to individuals or partnerships.

7.11 **Dividend income received from a shareholding in a company is taxable on an individual investor only to the extent he has taxable income above £29,400.** Such income is not taxable on a company investor.

7.12 There is a 10% tax credit on dividend income which can never be repaid to non taxpaying individuals. The tax suffered on interest income must be repaid.

Chapter roundup

- Interest arising on a non-trading loan relationship is taxable, normally on an accruals basis, under Schedule D Case III

- Interest on trading loan relationships is dealt with under Schedule D Case I.

- Income from land is taxed under Schedule A. Schedule A profits are computed on an accruals basis in the same way as Schedule D Case I profits

- Companies can obtain tax relief on certain investments they make

- The enterprise investment scheme and venture capital trusts are schemes that help unlisted companies to raise finance by giving individual investors tax relief for their investments.

- A company with a high debt/equity ratio is known as a highly geared (or thinly capitalised company).

Quick quiz

1 Against what future profits can a net deficit on a non-trading loan relationship be set in future periods?

2 How much of a premium received on the grant of a short lease is taxed under Schedule A?

3 From what date is interest always received gross by a company when received from another UK company?

4 What tax relief is available when investments are made under the corporate venturing scheme?

5 What type of companies may raise finance under the enterprise investment scheme?

6 What is a highly geared company?

Answers to quick quiz

1 It can be set against future non-trading profits.

2 Premium – 2% × Premium × (n – 1), where n = number of years of the lease.

3 1 April 2001.

4 20% of amounts invested in ordinary shares.

5 Unlisted trading companies.

6 A company with a high debt to equity ratio.

Now try the question below from the Exam Question Bank

Number	Level	Marks	Time
7	Exam	11	20 mins

Chapter 7

LOSSES AND DEFICITS ON NON-TRADING LOAN RELATIONSHIPS

Topic list	Syllabus reference	Ability required
1 Reliefs for losses	(iii)	Comprehension
2 Loss relief against future trading income: s 393 (1) ICTA 1988	(iii)	Comprehension
3 Loss relief against total profits: s 393A(1) ICTA 1988	(iii)	Comprehension
4 Reliefs for deficits on non-trading loan relationships	(iii)	Comprehension
5 Restrictions on loss relief	(iii)	Comprehension
6 The choice between loss reliefs	(iii)	Application

Introduction

In this chapter we see how a company may obtain relief for both losses and for deficits on non-trading loan relationships.

Learning outcomes covered in this chapter

- **Identify** the effect of all forms of loss relief on a company's CT liability
- **Explain** the effect of the loan relationship rules on a company's CT liability
- **Calculate** the form of loss relief which will minimise the CT liability in a single company

Syllabus content covered in this chapter

- All forms of relief for trading losses and charges in a single company
- Loan relationships rule: all aspects including reliefs for non trading deficits

1 RELIEFS FOR LOSSES

Trading losses

1.1 **In summary, the following reliefs are available for trading losses incurred by a single company.**

(a) **Set-off against current profits**
(b) **Carry back against earlier profits**
(c) **Carry forward against future trading profits**

Reliefs (a) and (b) must be claimed, and are given in the order shown. Relief (c) is given for any loss for which the other reliefs are not claimed.

Non-trading deficits

1.2 Non-trading deficits on loan relationships can be relieved in the same ways as trading losses, but against different profits.

Capital losses

1.3 **Capital losses can only be set against capital gains in the same or future accounting periods,** never against income (except losses suffered by an investment company on shares in a qualifying trading company). Capital losses must be set against the first available gains.

Schedule D Case V losses

1.4 In the case of a trade which is controlled outside the UK **any loss made in an accounting period can only be set against trading income from the same trade in later accounting periods.**

Schedule D Case VI losses

1.5 Where in an accounting period a company makes a loss in a transaction taxable under Schedule D Case VI, **the company can set the loss against any income from other transactions taxable under Case VI in the same or later accounting periods.** The loss must be set against the earliest income available.

Schedule A losses

1.6 Schedule A losses are first set off against non-Schedule A income and gains of the company for the current period. Any excess is then:

(a) carried forward as if a Schedule A loss arising in the later accounting period for offset against future income (of all descriptions); or

(b) available for surrender as group relief (in a similar fashion to management expenses - see later in this text).

2 LOSS RELIEF AGAINST FUTURE TRADING INCOME: S 393(1) ICTA 1988

2.1 **A company must set off a trading loss, not otherwise relieved, against income from the same trade in future accounting periods. Relief is against the first available profits.**

2.2 Further relief (under s 393(9) ICTA 1988) is available for trade charges which are unrelieved in an accounting period. These **unrelieved trade charges are carried forward and set off against future trading profits in the same way** as a s 393(1) loss. In practice, such unrelieved trade charges are added to any trading losses being carried forward under s 393(1). Computations can then include a single line for 's 393(1)(9) relief'.

2.3 Relief under s 393(9) is only available in respect of payments made wholly and exclusively for the purposes of the trade (such as patent royalties). Payments not made wholly and exclusively for trading purposes (such as gift aid payments) are set against current year profits before trade charges in the first instance, but if a loss is brought back under s 393A(1) (see below) and trade charges have already been set against profits, those trade charges are not set free to carry forward.

Question: Carrying forward losses

A Ltd has the following results for the three years to 31 March 2002

	Year ended		
	31.3.00	*31.3.01*	*31.3.02*
	£	£	£
Trading profit/(loss)	(8,000)	3,000	6,000
Non-trade charges	300	400	700
Trade charges	400	150	200

Calculate the profits chargeable to corporation tax for all three years showing any losses available to carry forward at 1 April 2002.

Answer

	Year ended		
	31.3.00	*31.3.01*	*31.3.02*
	£	£	£
Schedule D Case I	0	3,000	6,000
Less: s 393(1) loss relief		(3,000)	(5,550)
non-trade charges			(450)
PCTCT	0	0	0
Unrelieved non-trade charges	300	400	250

In the year to 31.3.02, non-trade charges are offset before trade charges leaving the trade charges available to carry forward.

Loss memorandum

	£
Loss for y/e 31.3.00	8,000
Unrelieved trade charges y/e 31.3.00	400
Loss carried forward at 1.4.00	8,400
Less s 393(1)(9) relief y/e 31.3.01	(3,000)
	5,400
Unrelieved trade charges y/e 31.3.01	150
Loss carried forward at 1.4.01	5,550
Less s 393(1)(9) relief y/e 31.3.02	(5,550)
	0
Unrelieved trade charges y/e 31.3.02	200
Loss carried forward at 1.4.02	200

3 LOSS RELIEF AGAINST TOTAL PROFITS: S 393A(1) ICTA 1988

3.1 **A company may claim to set a trading loss** (arising in a Schedule D Case I trade, not a Schedule D Case V trade controlled abroad) **incurred in an accounting period against total profits (before deducting any charges) of the same accounting period.** The result may be that trade charges become unrelieved, and available to carry forward.

3.2 **Such a loss may then be carried back and set against total profits (after deducting trade charges but before deducting non-trade charges) of an accounting period falling wholly or partly within the 12 months of the start of the period in which the loss was incurred.**

In each such period, enough profits must be left to match against trade charges, so that trade charges do not become unrelieved and available to carry forward.

If a period falls partly outside the 12 months, loss relief is limited to the proportion of the period's profits (before all charges) equal to the proportion of the period which falls within the 12 months.

3.3 **The 12 month carry back period is extended to 36 months where the trading loss arose in the 12 months immediately before the company ceased to trade.**

3.4 Any possible s 393A(1) claim for the period of the loss must be made before any excess loss can be carried back to a previous period.

Any carry-back is to more recent periods before earlier periods. Relief for earlier losses is given before relief for later losses.

3.5 A claim for relief against current or prior period profits must be made within two years of the end of the accounting period in which the loss arose. Any claim must be for the *whole* loss (to the extent that profits are available to relieve it). The loss can however be reduced by not claiming full capital allowances, so that higher capital allowances are given (on higher tax written down values) in future years. Any loss remaining unrelieved may be carried forward under s 393(1) to set against future profits of the same trade.

Question: S 393A loss relief

Helix Ltd has the following results.

	Year ended			
	30.9.99	30.9.00	30.9.01	30.9.02
	£	£	£	£
Trading profit/(loss)	2,000	11,500	10,000	(35,000)
Bank interest	400	500	500	500
Chargeable gains	800	0	0	4,000
Charges on income:				
trade charges	0	1,000	1,000	1,000
non-trade charges	250	250	250	250

Show the PCTCT for all the years affected assuming that s 393A(1) loss relief is claimed. Assume the provisions of FA 2001 continue to apply.

Answer

The loss of the year to 30.9.02 is relieved under s 393A ICTA 1988 against current year profits and against profits of the previous twelve months.

	Year ended			
	30.9.99	30.9.00	30.9.01	30.9.02
	£	£	£	£
Schedule D Case I	2,000	11,500	10,000	0
Schedule D Case III	400	500	500	500
Chargeable gains	800	0	0	4,000
	3,200	12,000	10,500	4,500
Less s 393A current period relief	0	0	0	(4,500)
	3,200	12,000	10,500	0
Less: trade charges	0	(1,000)	(1,000)	0
	3,200	11,000	9,500	0
Less s 393A carryback relief	0	0	(9,500)	0
	3,200	11,000	0	0
Less: Non-trade charges	(250)	(250)	0	0
PCTCT	2,950	10,750	0	0
Unrelieved non-trade charges			250	250

S 393A (1) loss memorandum	£
Loss incurred in y/e 30.9.02	35,000
Less s 393A (1): y/e 30.9.02	(4,500)
y/e 30.9.01	(9,500)
Remaining loss	21,000
Unrelieved trade charges y/e 30.9.02	1,000
Loss available to carry forward under s 393(1)(9)	22,000

3.6 If, in the accounting period in which a trade ceases, there are unrelieved trade charges which could (if the trade had continued) have been carried forward, they are added to a loss to be claimed under s 393A(1). Don't forget that when a company ceases to trade the loss for the final 12 months of trading can be carried back for up to three years.

Question: Ceasing to trade

Loser Ltd had always made up accounts to 31 December, but ceased to trade on 31 December 2001. Results had been as follows.

	Year ended			
	31.12.98	31.12.99	31.12.00	31.12.01
	£	£	£	£
Schedule D Case I/(loss)	25,000	30,000	27,000	(60,000)
Trade charges	2,000	2,000	2,000	1,200
Non-trade charges	170	170	170	80

Show the profits chargeable to corporation tax for all years after relief for the loss.

Answer

	Year ended			
	31.12.98	31.12.99	31.12.00	31.12.01
	£	£	£	£
Schedule D Case I	25,000	30,000	27,000	0
Less trade charges	(2,000)	(2,000)	(2,000)	0
	23,000	28,000	25,000	0
Less: s 393A carryback	(8,200)	(28,000)	(25,000)	0
	14,800	0	0	0
Less: non-trade charges	(170)	0	0	0
	14,630	0	0	0
Unrelieved non-trade charges		170	170	80

The loss available is £(60,000 + 1,200) = £61,200

4 RELIEFS FOR DEFICITS ON NON-TRADING LOAN RELATIONSHIPS

4.1 **A deficit on a non-trading loan relationship may be set, in whole or part, against any profit of the same accounting period. Relief is given after relief for any trading loss brought forward but before relief is given for a trading loss of the same or future period.**

Question: Relief for deficit on non-trading loan relationship

Witherspoon Ltd has the following results for the two years ended 31 December 2001:

	2000	2001
	£	£
Trading profit/(loss)	40,000	(12,000)
Trading losses brought forward	(20,000)	-
Bank interest receivable	2,000	
Interest payable on a loan for non-trading purposes	(11,000)	

Show how relief may be given for the deficit on the non-trading loan relationship in the year ended 31.12.00.

Answer

	2000 £
Schedule D Case I	40,000
s 393(1) losses brought forward	(20,000)
	20,000
Less: non-trading deficit £(11,000 – 2,000)	(9,000)
	11,000
Losses carried back s 393A	(11,000)
Chargeable profits	Nil

4.2   A deficit is eligible for group relief (see later in this text).

4.3   A deficit may be set against non-trading income arising from loan relationships in the previous twelve months provided the income has not been reduced by:

(a)   loss relief in respect of a period prior to the deficit period

(b)   trade charges

(c)   management expenses of an investment company

4.4   A deficit may be set against the non-trading profits of the company in the following accounting period. Non-trade profits represent PCTCT less Schedule D Case I.

4.5   Any deficits unrelieved after claiming the above reliefs are automatically carried forward and treated as a deficit for the next accounting period.

4.6   A claim under 4.1 to 4.3 above must be made within two years of the deficit period. A claim under 4.4 above must be made within two years of the accounting period in which the deficit is used.

4.7   A company can choose how much deficit to relieve in the current period, how much to carry back and how much to carry forward: unlike s 393A relief, these are not all or nothing claims, and the company can choose to carry back a deficit even if it does not claim current period relief.

5   RESTRICTIONS ON LOSS RELIEF

The continuity of trades

5.1   **Relief under s 393(1) and (9) is only available against future profits arising from the same trade as that in which the loss arose.**

5.2   The continuity of trade for this purpose was considered in a case involving a company trading as brewers: *Gordon & Blair Ltd v CIR 1962*. It ceased brewing but continued to bottle and sell beer. The company claimed that it carried on the same trade throughout so that its losses from brewing could be set off against profits from the bottling trade. The company lost their case and were prevented from obtaining any further relief for losses in the brewing trade under s 393(1)(9).

The disallowance of loss relief following a change in ownership

5.3 **No relief is available for trading losses in accounting periods on one side of (before or after) a change in ownership of a company if the loss making accounting period is on the other side of (after or before) the change in ownership and either:**

- **there is a major change in the nature or conduct of the trade within three years before or three years after the change in ownership; or**

- **after the change in ownership there is a considerable revival of the company's trading activities which at the time of the change had become small or negligible.**

5.4 Examples of a major change in the nature or conduct of a trade include changes in:

- the type of property dealt in (for example a company operating a dealership in saloon cars switching to a dealership in tractors);

- the services or facilities provided (for example a company operating a public house changing to operating a discotheque);

- customers;

- outlets or markets.

However, changes to keep up to date with technology or to rationalise existing ranges of products are unlikely to be regarded as major. The Revenue consider both qualitative and quantitative issues in deciding if a change is major.

5.5 If the change in ownership occurs in (and not at the end of) an accounting period, that period is notionally divided into two periods, one up to and one after the change, for the purposes of this rule, with profits and losses being time-apportioned.

5.6 A change in ownership is disregarded for this purpose if both immediately before and immediately after the change the company is a 75% subsidiary of the same company.

Uncommercial trades

5.7 **A loss made in a trade which is not conducted on a commercial basis and with a view to the realisation of gain cannot be set off against the company's profits in the same or previous accounting periods under s 393A(1). Such losses are only available to carry forward under s 393(1) and (9) against future profits of the same trade.**

Farming and market gardening

5.8 A company carrying on the trade of farming or market gardening is treated in the same way as one that trades on an uncommercial basis in any accounting period if, in the five successive years immediately before that accounting period, the trade made a loss (before capital allowances).

6 THE CHOICE BETWEEN LOSS RELIEFS

6.1 **Several alternative loss reliefs may be available. In making a choice consider:**

(a) **The rate at which relief will be obtained:**

    (i)   30% at the full rate (FY 2001);

    (ii)   20% at the small companies' rate (FY 2001);

    (iii)   10% at the starting rate (FY 2001)

    (iv)   22.5% if the starting rate marginal relief applies (FY 2001)

(v) 32.5% if small companies marginal relief applies (FY 2001);

Remember that the rates of corporation tax were different in earlier financial years.

(b) **How quickly relief will be obtained**: s 393A(1) relief is quicker than s 393(1) relief.

(c) **The extent to which relief for non-trade charges might be lost.**

Exam focus point

When choosing between loss relief claims ALWAYS consider the rate of tax 'saved' by the loss first.

If in the current period the loss 'saves' 20% tax but if carried forward saves 30% tax then a carry forward is the better choice (even though the timing of loss relief is later).

If the tax saved now is 20% and in the future is the same (20%) THEN consider timing (in this example a current claim is better timing wise).

So, first - rate of tax saved, second - timing.

Question: The choice between loss reliefs

M Ltd has had the following results.

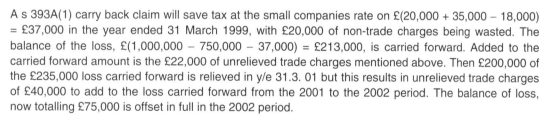

	1998	*1999*	*2000*	*2001*	*2002*
	£	£	£	£	£
Schedule D Case I/(loss)	5,000,000	20,000	(1,000,000)	200,000	200,000
Chargeable gains	0	35,000	750,000	0	0
Trade charges	30,000	18,000	22,000	40,000	40,000
Non-trade charges	20,000	20,000	20,000	20,000	20,000

Recommend appropriate loss relief claims, and compute the mainstream corporation tax for all years based on your recommendations. Assume that future years' profits will be similar to those of the year ended 31 March 2002 and that future rates of tax remain at FY 2001 levels.

Answer

A s 393A(1) claim for the year ended 31 March 2000 will save tax partly in the small companies' marginal relief band and partly at the small companies rate, and will waste non-trade charges of £20,000. The trade charges of £22,000 will save tax at the small companies rate in future accounts since it is carried forward.

A s 393A(1) carry back claim will save tax at the small companies rate on £(20,000 + 35,000 − 18,000) = £37,000 in the year ended 31 March 1999, with £20,000 of non-trade charges being wasted. The balance of the loss, £(1,000,000 − 750,000 − 37,000) = £213,000, is carried forward. Added to the carried forward amount is the £22,000 of unrelieved trade charges mentioned above. Then £200,000 of the £235,000 loss carried forward is relieved in y/e 31.3. 01 but this results in unrelieved trade charges of £40,000 to add to the loss carried forward from the 2001 to the 2002 period. The balance of loss, now totalling £75,000 is offset in full in the 2002 period.

If no s 393A(1) claim is made, £200,000 of the loss will save tax at the small companies rate and at the starting rate in the year ended 31 March 2001, with £20,000 of non-trade charges being wasted. The remaining £800,000 of the loss, together with £40,000 of trade charges, would be carried forward to the year ended 31 March 2002 and later years to save tax at the small companies rate and at the starting rate.

So to conclude S 393A(1) claims should be made for both the year of the loss and previous year. £40,000 of non-trade charges would be wasted, but much of the loss would save tax at the small companies' marginal corporation tax rate and relief would be obtained quickly.

The final computations are as follows.

	1998 £	1999 £	2000 £	2001 £	2002 £
Schedule D Case I	5,000,000	20,000	0	200,000	200,000
Less s 393(1)(9) relief	0	0	0	(200,000)	(75,000)
	5,000,000	20,000	0	0	125,000
Chargeable gains	0	35,000	750,000	0	0
	5,000,000	55,000	750,000	0	125,000
Less: s 393A current relief		0	(750,000)	0	0
	5,000,000	55,000	0	0	125,000
Less: trade charges	(30,000)	(18,000)	0	0	(40,000)
	4,970,000	37,000	0	0	85,000
Less: s 393A c/b		(37,000)			
	4,970,000	0	0	0	85,000
Less: non-trade charges	(20,000)	0	0	0	(20,000)
Profits chargeable to corporation tax	4,950,000	0	0		65,000
MCT at 31%/20%	1,534,500	0	0	0	13,000
Unrelieved non-trade charges	0	20,000	20,000	20,000	0

Year ended 31 March

Chapter roundup

- Trading losses may be relieved against current total profits, against total profits of earlier periods or against future trading income.

- Non-trading deficits may also be relieved in the current, previous or future periods but relief is given against different profits.

- There are several restrictions on loss relief and there are many factors to consider when selecting a loss relief.

Quick quiz

1 Against what profits may trading losses carried forward be set?

2 What charges may be carried forward?

3 To what extent may losses in a continuing trade be carried back?

4 What relief is available in the current AP for a non-trading deficit incurred by a single company?

5 Why might a company make a reduced capital allowances claim?

Answers to quick quiz

1   Profits from the same trade.

2   Unrelieved trade charges may be carried forward. Trade charges are payments made wholly and exclusively for the purposes of the trade (eg patent royalties).

3   A loss may be carried back and set against total profits (after deducting trade charges) of the prior 12 months. The loss carried back is the trading loss left unrelieved after a claim against total profits (before deducting any charges) of the loss making AP has been made.

4   A deficit on a non-trading loan relationship may be set against profit of the same AP. Relief is given after relief for any trading loss brought forward but before relief is given for a current or future trading loss.

5   Reducing capital allowances in the current AP reduces the loss available for relief under s 393A. Section 393A demands that all of the available loss is utilised. Reducing capital allowances reduces the size of the available loss.

Now try the question below from the Exam Question Bank

Number	Level	Marks	Time
8	Exam	10	18 mins

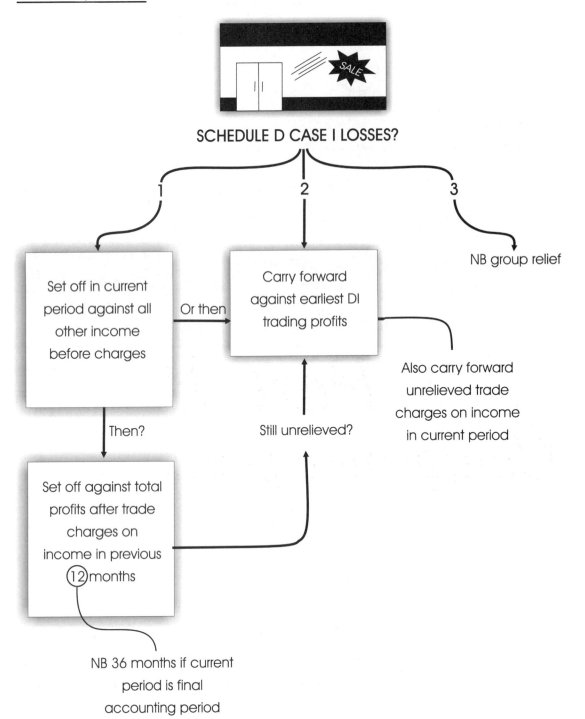

SCHEDULE D CASE I LOSSES?

1

2

3

Set off in current period against all other income before charges

Or then

Carry forward against earliest DI trading profits

NB group relief

Then?

Still unrelieved?

Also carry forward unrelieved trade charges on income in current period

Set off against total profits after trade charges on income in previous ⑫months

NB 36 months if current period is final accounting period

Part B
Chargeable gains

Chapter 8

CHARGEABLE GAINS : AN OUTLINE

Topic list		Syllabus reference	Ability required
1	Taxing a company's chargeable gains	(iii), (vii)	Application
2	Chargeable persons, disposals and assets	(v)	Comprehension
3	Computing a gain or loss	(v)	Application
4	The indexation allowance	(v)	Application
5	Assets held on 31 March 1982	(v)	Application
6	Valuing assets	(v)	Application
7	Connected persons	(v)	Application
8	Disposals on a no gain/no loss basis	(v)	Application
9	Part disposals	(v)	Application

Introduction

Companies can have both income and capital gains. If, for example, a company buys a factory for £10,000, uses the factory for 20 years and then sells it for £200,000, it will have a capital gain.

In this chapter we see when a chargeable gain will arise, how to compute a chargeable gain and how a company is taxed on its net chargeable gains.

Learning outcomes covered in this chapter

- **Identify** chargeable assets for taxation as chargeable gains
- **Calculate** a gain
- **Calculate** the CT liability of a company (including that of small and intermediate companies)

Syllabus content covered in this chapter

- Scope, exemptions, chattels
- Reliefs for losses
- Computation of total income and CT liability
- Integration of tax planning into the budgeting process

1 TAXING A COMPANY'S CHARGEABLE GAINS

1.1 Since its introduction by the Finance Act 1965, the taxation of chargeable gains has undergone significant amendment. As some knowledge of the history of taxing gains may help you understand the present rules, we summarise the main changes below:

BPP PUBLISHING

1965	The taxation of chargeable gains was introduced.
1982	An indexation allowance was introduced to give some relief in respect of gains due to inflation.
1985	There were major amendments to the calculation of the indexation allowance.
1988	The base date for taxing gains was generally moved from 1965 to 1982, the tax charge being confined to gains accruing from 31 March 1982.
1992	Legislation concerning the taxation of gains was consolidated into the Taxation of Chargeable Gains Act 1992 (TCGA 1992).
1993	The use of the indexation allowance to create or increase a loss ended.

1.2 **A company's net chargeable gains for an accounting period are included within the computation of profits chargeable to corporation tax.** A company, therefore, pays CT on its net chargeable gains. Any overall allowable loss in an accounting period is carried forward to set against the first chargeable gains arising in future accounting periods.

1.3 From a tax planning point of view it is important to realise that a badly timed disposal (near the end of the accounting period) can raise the 'profits' of a company into a higher rate band of CT. In addition, from a cash flow point of view, by delaying a disposal into the next accounting period the payment date for CT on the gain is delayed for twelve months.

2 CHARGEABLE PERSONS, DISPOSALS AND ASSETS

Exam focus point

For a chargeable gain to arise there must be:

- a chargeable person; and
- a chargeable disposal; and
- a chargeable asset

otherwise no charge to tax occurs.

Chargeable persons

2.1 A company is a chargeable person.

Chargeable disposals

2.2 The following are chargeable disposals.

- Sales of assets or parts of assets
- Gifts of assets or parts of assets
- Receipts of capital sums following the surrender of rights to assets
- The loss or destruction of assets
- The appropriation of assets as trading stock

2.3 **A chargeable disposal occurs on the date of the contract** (where there is one, whether written or oral), or the date of a conditional contract becoming unconditional. This may differ from the date of transfer of the asset. However, when a capital sum is received on a surrender of rights or the loss or destruction of an asset, the disposal takes place on the day the sum is received.

Where a disposal involves an acquisition by someone else, the date of acquisition is the same as the date of disposal.

Transfers to and from trading stock

2.4 When a company acquires an asset other than as trading stock and then uses it as trading stock, the appropriation to trading stock normally leads to an immediate chargeable gain or allowable loss, based on the asset's market value at the date of appropriation. The asset's cost for Schedule D Case I purposes is that market value.

2.5 Alternatively, the company can elect to have no chargeable gain or allowable loss: if it does so, the cost for Schedule D Case I purposes is reduced by the gain or increased by the loss. The time limit for the election is two years after the end of the accounting period of appropriation.

2.6 When an asset which is trading stock is appropriated to other purposes, the company is treated for Schedule D Case I purposes as selling it for its market value, and for those other purposes as having bought it at the time of the appropriation for the same value.

Chargeable assets

2.7 **All forms of property, wherever in the world they are situated, are chargeable assets unless they are specifically designated as exempt.**

2.8 The following are exempt assets (thus gains are not taxable and losses on their disposal are not in general allowable losses: the few exceptions are explained in this text).

- Motor vehicles suitable for private use
- Certain chattels (eg racehorses)
- Debts (except debts on a security)

3 COMPUTING A GAIN OR LOSS

3.1 **A chargeable gain (or an allowable loss) is generally calculated as follows.**

	£
Disposal consideration (or market value)	45,000
Less incidental costs of disposal	(400)
Net proceeds	44,600
Less allowable costs	((21,000)
Unindexed gain	23,600
Less indexation allowance	(8,500)
Indexed gain	15,100

3.2 **Incidental costs of disposal** may include:

- valuation fees (but not the cost of an appeal against the Revenue's valuation);
- estate agency fees;
- advertising costs;
- legal costs.

These costs should be deducted separately from any other allowable costs (because they do not qualify for any indexation allowance if it was available on that disposal).

3.3   **Allowable costs** include:

- the original cost of acquisition;
- incidental costs of acquisition;
- capital expenditure incurred in enhancing the asset.

Incidental costs of acquisition may include the types of cost listed above as incidental costs of disposal, but acquisition costs do qualify for indexation allowance (from the month of acquisition) if it is available on the disposal.

3.4   **Enhancement expenditure** is capital expenditure which enhances the value of the asset and is reflected in the state or nature of the asset at the time of disposal, or expenditure incurred in establishing, preserving or defending title to, or a right over, the asset. Excluded from this category are:

- costs of repairs and maintenance;
- costs of insurance;
- any expenditure deductible for Schedule D Case I purposes;
- any expenditure met by public funds (for example council grants).

Enhancement expenditure may qualify for indexation allowance from the month in which it becomes due and payable.

The consideration for a disposal

3.5   **Usually the disposal consideration is the proceeds of sale of the asset, but a disposal is deemed to take place at market value:**

(a)   where the disposal is **not a bargain at arm's length**;

(b)   where the disposal is made for a **consideration which cannot be valued**;

(c)   where the disposal is by way of a **gift**.

3.6   Sometimes an asset is sold for a fixed sum plus a possible addition depending on some contingency. For example, land might be sold without planning permission, and with an extra payment to be made to the vendor if planning permission is obtained. In such cases, the contingent right to additional proceeds must be valued, and that value must be added to the known proceeds. If additional proceeds are in fact received, that receipt is treated as proceeds of the disposal of the contingent right. A chargeable gain or allowable loss will then arise: the allowable cost is the value of the right brought into account in the initial computation of the capital gain (*Marren v Ingles 1980*).

4   THE INDEXATION ALLOWANCE

4.1   Indexation was introduced in 1982. The purpose of having an indexation allowance is to remove the inflationary element of a gain from taxation.

4.2   **Companies are entitled to an indexation allowance from the date of acquisition (or March 1982, if later) until the date of disposal of an asset.**

4.3   EXAMPLE: INDEXATION ALLOWANCE

J Ltd bought a painting on 2 January 1987 and sold it on 19 November 2001.

Indexation allowance is available from January 1987 until November 2001.

EXAM FORMULA

The indexation factor is:

$$\frac{\text{RPI for month of disposal} - \text{RPI for month of acquisition (or March 1982)}}{\text{RPI for month of acquisition (or March 1982)}}$$

The calculation is expressed as a decimal and is rounded to three decimal places.

The indexation factor is multiplied by the cost of the asset to calculate the indexation allowance. If the RPI has fallen, the indexation allowance is zero: it is not negative.

RPI values are given in the Rates and Allowances Tables in this text, including estimated values for January 2001 onwards.

Question: The indexation allowance

An asset is acquired by a company on 15 February 1983 (RPI = 83.0) at a cost of £5,000. Enhancement expenditure of £2,000 is incurred on 10 April 1984 (RPI = 88.6). The asset is sold for £20,500 on 20 December 2001 (RPI 178.0). Incidental costs of sale are £500. Calculate the chargeable gain arising.

Answer

The indexation allowance is available until December 2001 and is computed as follows.

	£
$\frac{178.0 - 83.0}{83.0} = 1.145 \times £5,000$	5,725
$\frac{178.0 - 88.6}{88.6} = 1.009 \times £2,000$	2,018
	7,743

The computation of the chargeable gain is as follows.

	£
Proceeds	20,500
Less incidental costs of sale	(500)
Net proceeds	20,000
Less allowable costs £(5,000 + 2,000)	(7,000)
Unindexed gain	13,000
Less indexation allowance (see above)	(7,743)
Chargeable gain	5,257

Exam focus point

In your examination you will not be expected to calculate the indexation allowance decimal. Instead you will be given the rise in the RPI between two dates. Thus in the above question you would be told that the indexation factor for the period from February 1983 to December 2001 is 1.145 and that for the period from April 1984 to December 2001 it is 1.009.

In our text we have shown you how the factor is derived to aid your understanding of how indexation allowance works. You do not need to do such workings in your own answers to questions.

Indexation and losses

4.4 **The indexation allowance cannot create or increase an allowable loss.** If there is a gain before the indexation allowance, the allowance can reduce that gain to zero, but no further. If there is a loss before the indexation allowance, there is no indexation allowance.

5 ASSETS HELD ON 31 MARCH 1982

5.1 **On the disposal of an asset owned on 31 March 1982, we do two calculations. One uses actual cost and the other uses the market value on 31 March 1982. In *both* calculations we base the indexation allowance on the higher of the two.** The final gain or loss is then:

- if both calculations produce gains, the lower gain;

- if both calculations produce losses, the lower loss (so if one produces a loss of £1,000 and the other a loss of £2,000, the allowable loss is £1,000);

- if one calculation produces a gain and the other a loss, or if either produces a result of £nil, no gain and no loss.

5.2 In the computation based on the 31 March 1982 value, that value replaces cost plus all enhancement expenditure up to that date. However, we still use that cost and enhancement expenditure to compute the indexation allowance if they add up to more than the 31 March 1982 value.

Question: assets held on 31 March 1982

A Ltd acquired a property as an investment in 1977 at a cost of £28,500. The company installed central heating for £1,500 in 1981. The market value of the property on 31 March 1982 had dropped to £20,000 owing to land subsidence. The property was eventually sold to a property developer in May 2001 for £150,000, the subsidence problem having been rectified at a cost of £15,000 in March 1984.

Compute the chargeable gain.

Answer

	Cost £	31.3.82 value £
Proceeds	150,000	150,000
Less: cost 1977	(28,500)	
enhancement cost 1981	(1,500)	
31.3.82 value (includes 1981 improvement)		(20,000)
enhancement cost 1984	(15,000)	(15,000)
Unindexed gain	105,000	115,000
Less indexation allowance		
On original cost (March 1982 to May 2001):		
$\frac{174.5 - 79.4}{79.4} = 1.198 \times £28,500$	(34,143)	(34,143)
On enhancement cost 1981 (March 1982 to May 2001):		
$\times £1,500$	(1,797)	(1,797)
On enhancement cost 1984 (March 1984 to May 2001):		
$\frac{174.5 - 87.5}{87.5} = 0.994 \times £15,000$	(14,910)	(14,910)
	54,150	64,150

The chargeable gain is the lower gain of £54,150.

At 31 March 1982 the cost of the house was £30,000 (£28,500 + £1,500) compared to the equivalent March 1982 market value of £20,000. Thus the indexation allowance available from March 1982 is based on the cost values in this question.

Question: Calculation of gain or loss

B Ltd acquired a freehold farm in 1978 for £20,000. The market value of the farm on 31 March 1982 was £150,000. The company sold the farm in June 2001 for £250,000. Compute the chargeable gain or allowable loss.

Answer

	Cost	31.3.82 value
	£	£
Proceeds	250,000	250,000
Less: cost	(20,000)	
31.3.82 value		(150,000)
Unindexed gain	230,000	100,000
Less indexation allowance (March 1982 to June 2001)		
$\dfrac{175.0 - 79.4}{79.4} = 1.204 \times £150,000$	(180,600)	(100,000)
Indexed gain (indexation cannot create or increase a loss)	49,400	0

There is no chargeable gain and no allowable loss.

5.3 **Companies can elect that gains/losses arising on all assets held at 31 March 1982 should be computed using their 31 March 1982 values only.** Indexation allowance can then only be based on 31 March 1982 value and later enhancement expenditure. The election must be made within two years of the end of the accounting period of the first disposal after 5 April 1988. In working out the time limit for the election, the Revenue ignore disposals to charities. An election once made is irrevocable.

5.4 Before making the election, the company should consider the net effect on all its assets owned at 31 March 1982. The effect might be to increase the gain or decrease the loss on some assets.

5.5 Special rules apply to assets acquired before 6 April 1965. These rules will not be examined.

5.6 For disposals before 6 April 1988, the 31 March 1982 value *could not* be used in place of cost, but for disposals after 5 April 1985 it *could* be used in computing the indexation allowance. As we shall see later, we occasionally need to work out gains arising some time ago in order to work out gains on assets sold more recently.

6 VALUING ASSETS

6.1 **Where market value is used in a chargeable gains computation** (see Section 3 above), **the value to be used is the price which the assets in question might reasonably be expected to fetch on a sale in the open market.**

Shares and securities

6.2 **Quoted shares and securities are valued using prices in The Stock Exchange Daily Official List,** taking the lower of:

- lower quoted price + 0.25 × (higher quoted price - lower quoted price);

- the average of the highest and lowest marked bargains (ignoring bargains marked at special prices).

Question: Calculation of CGT value

Shares in A plc are quoted at 100-110p. The highest and lowest marked bargains were 99p and 110p. What would be the market value for CGT purposes?

Answer

The value will be the lower of:
(a) $100 + 0.25 \times (110 - 100) = 102.5$;
(b) $\dfrac{110 + 99}{2} = 104.5$.

The market value for CGT purposes will therefore be 102.5p per share.

6.3   Unquoted shares are harder to value than quoted shares. The Revenue have a special office, the Shares Valuation Division, to deal with the valuation of unquoted shares.

Negligible value claims

6.4   **If a chargeable asset's value becomes negligible a claim may be made to treat the asset as though it were sold, and then immediately reacquired at its current market value.** This will probably give rise to an allowable loss.

The sale and reacquisition are treated as taking place when the claim is made, or at a specified earlier time. The earlier time can be as far back as the start of the earliest accounting period which ends within two years of the date of claim. The asset must have been of negligible value at the specified earlier time.

On a subsequent actual disposal, any gain is computed using the negligible value as the acquisition cost.

7   CONNECTED PERSONS

7.1   **A transaction between 'connected persons' is treated as one between parties to a transaction otherwise than by way of a bargain made at arm's length. This means that the acquisition and disposal are deemed to take place for a consideration equal to the market value of the asset, rather than the actual price paid.** In addition, if a loss results, it can be set only against gains arising in the same or future years from disposals to the same connected person and the loss can only be set off if that person is still connected with the person sustaining the loss.

> **KEY TERM**
> **Connected person.**
>
> A company is connected with:
>
> - a person who (alone or with persons connected with him) controls it;
> - another company under common control.

8   DISPOSALS ON A NO GAIN/NO LOSS BASIS

8.1   **If a company owns 75% or more of the ordinary share capital of one or more subsidiaries, then transfers of chargeable assets made between two group companies do not give rise to chargeable gains or allowable losses, provided that the assets stay within**

the charge to UK corporation tax on chargeable gains. Full details are given in later in this text.

8.2 Special rules apply to the indexation allowance on no gain/no loss disposals. To illustrate the rules, we assume that company H Ltd buys an asset and later transfers it to company W Ltd in the same group. W Ltd sells the asset to an outsider.

H Ltd buys the asset before 1 April 1982

8.3 On W Ltd's sale to the outsider treat W Ltd as having bought the asset when H Ltd bought it and for the price it paid. Thus W Ltd can use the 31 March 1982 value, and can get indexation from March 1982.

H Ltd buys the asset after 31 March 1982

8.4 W Ltd is deemed to have bought the asset at the time when H Ltd transferred it. W Ltd's cost is H Ltd's cost plus indexation allowance up to the time of the transfer. When W Ltd sells the asset, it computes indexation allowance from the time of the transfer.

9 PART DISPOSALS

9.1 **The disposal of part of a chargeable asset is a chargeable event. The chargeable gain (or allowable loss) is computed by deducting from the disposal value a fraction of the original cost of the whole asset.**

EXAM FORMULA

The fraction is:

$$\frac{A}{A+B} = \frac{\text{value of the part disposed of}}{\text{value of the part disposed of} + \text{market value of the remainder}}$$

In this fraction, A is the proceeds (for arm's length disposals) *before* deducting incidental costs of disposal.

9.2 The part disposal fraction should not be applied indiscriminately. Any expenditure incurred wholly in respect of a particular part of an asset should be treated as an allowable deduction in full for that part and not apportioned. An example of this is incidental selling expenses, which are wholly attributable to the part disposed of.

Question: Part disposals

Heal Ltd owns land which originally cost £27,000 in March 1994. It sold a quarter interest in the land in July 2001 for £29,700. The market value of the three-quarter share remaining is estimated to be £59,400. What is the chargeable gain?

Answer

The amount of the original cost attributable to the part sold is

$$\frac{29,700}{29,700 + 59,400} \times £27,000 = £9,000$$

	£
Proceeds	29,700
Less cost (see above)	(9,000)
Unindexed gain	20,700
Less indexation allowance (March 1994 to July 2001)	
$\dfrac{175.5 - 142.5}{142.5} = 0.232 \times £9,000$	(2,088)
Gain	18,612

Small part disposals of land

9.3 Two special reliefs apply to small part disposals of land. They are only available if the land is freehold or on a lease with at least 50 years to run.

9.4 If the disposal is the result of a compulsory purchase order and the value of the consideration is 'small', the company may claim to have the consideration received deducted from the base cost of the asset retained, instead of doing a part disposal computation. **'Small' means either 5% or less of the total value of the land immediately before the part disposal; or £3,000 or less.**

9.5 If, however, the above relief is not available, an alternative relief may be claimed. If the value of the consideration is 20% or less of the total value of the land immediately before the part disposed and the total consideration in that accounting period from all disposals of land (excluding disposals under compulsory purchase orders where the consideration is small) does not exceed £20,000, then the company may claim to deduct the consideration from the base cost of the remaining land instead of doing a part disposal computation.

9.6 The time limit for claims for companies is two years after the end of the accounting period of disposal.

9.7 When a subsequent disposal of the remaining land occurs, indexation is calculated on the initial allowable expenditure, before adjusting for the part disposal. A negative indexation allowance is then deducted from this indexation allowance: it is calculated on the sale proceeds received for the part disposal, from the date of receipt of the part disposal proceeds to the date of sale of the remaining land.

Chapter roundup

- A chargeable gain is computed by taking the proceeds and deducting both the costs and the indexation allowance.

- An asset owned on 31 March 1982 needs two computations, one based on its cost and the other based on its value on that date.

- There are special rules for disposals between connected persons and disposals within groups of companies.

- On a part disposal, the cost must be apportioned between the part disposed of and the part retained.

Quick quiz

1   What enhancement expenditure is allowable?

2   How is the chargeable gain/allowable loss on assets held on 31 March 1982 computed?

3   Shares in A plc are quoted at 410 – 414, with bargains at 408, 410 and 416. What is the value for CGT?

4   With whom is a company connected?

5   10 acres of land are sold for £15,000 out of 25 acres. Original cost in 1996 £9,000. Costs of sale £2,000. Rest of land valued at £30,000. What is the allowable expenditure?

Answers to quick quiz

1   Enhancement expenditure reflected in the state and nature of the asset on the date of disposal.

2   Two computations required – one on cost, one on 31.3.82 MV. IA always on higher of cost and 31.3.82 MV. If two gains – take lower gain. If two losses – take lower loss. If one gain, one loss – no gain/no loss.

3   Lower of:

$410 + \frac{1}{4}(414 - 410) = 411$

$$\frac{416 + 408}{2} = 412$$

ie <u>411</u>

4   A company is connected with:

(a)   any person who (alone or with persons connected with him) controls it
(b)   another company under common control

5    $\dfrac{15{,}000}{15{,}000 + 30{,}000} \times £9{,}000 = £3{,}000 + £2{,}000 \text{ (costs of disposal)} = \underline{£5{,}000}$

Now try the questions below from the Exam Question Bank

Number	Level	Marks	Time
9	Introductory	5	9 mins
10	Exam	15	27 mins

BPP PUBLISHING

Chapter 9

SHARES AND SECURITIES

Topic list	Syllabus reference	Ability required
1 Share matching rules for companies	(v)	Application
2 The FA 1985 pool	(v)	Application
3 The 1982 holding	(v)	Application
4 Alterations of share capital	(v)	Application

Introduction

So far we have considered assets in general. In this chapter, we look at shares and securities. Shares and securities need a special treatment because a company may hold several shares or securities in the same company, bought at different times for different prices but otherwise identical.

When a company issues new shares in exchange for old shares, or one company takes over another and issues its own shares to shareholders in the target company, shareholders dispose of their old shares but get no cash with which to pay tax. We will see how the gain on the old shares is deferred until a sale of the new shares. We will also look at bonus issues and rights issues.

Learning outcomes covered in this chapter

* **Calculate** the gain arising on the disposal of quoted securities using the pooling system

Syllabus content covered in this chapter

* Shares and securities, including pooling, bonus issues and rights issues

1 SHARE MATCHING RULES FOR COMPANIES

1.1 Quoted and unquoted shares and securities and units in a unit trust present special problems when attempting to compute gains or losses on disposal. For instance, suppose that a company buys some quoted shares in X plc as follows.

Date	Number of shares	Cost £
5 May 1973	100	150
17 January 1985	100	375

On 15 June 2001, it sells 120 of its shares for £1,450. To determine its chargeable gain, we need to be able to work out which shares out of the two original holdings were actually sold.

1.2 We therefore need **matching rules**. These **allow us to decide which shares have been sold and so work out what the allowable cost on disposal should be.**

112

1.3 **At any one time, we will only be concerned with shares or securities of the same class in the same company.** If a company owns both ordinary shares and preference shares in X plc, we will deal with the two classes of share entirely separately, because they are distinguishable.

1.4 In what follows, we will use 'shares' to refer to both shares and securities.

1.5 **For companies the matching of shares** sold is in the following order.

   (a) Shares acquired on the **same day**
   (b) Shares acquired in the **previous nine days**, taking earlier acquisitions first
   (c) Shares from the **FA 1985 pool**
   (d) Shares from the **1982 holding**
   (e) Shares purchased before 6 April 1965, taking later acquisitions first (not examinable)

   If a company owns 2% or more of another company, disposals are matched (after same day acquisitions) with shares acquired within one month before or after the disposal (for Stock Exchange transactions) or six months (in other cases) before being matched with shares from the FA 1985 pool.

1.6 Where shares are disposed of within nine days of acquisition, **no indexation allowance is available** even if the acquisition and the disposal fall in different months. Acquisitions matched with disposals under the nine day rule never enter the FA 1985 pool.

1.7 The composition of the FA 1985 pool and the 1982 holding is explained below.

> ### Exam focus point
>
> Learn the 'matching rules' because a crucial first step to getting a shares question right is to correctly match the shares sold to the original shares purchased.

2 THE FA 1985 POOL

2.1 For companies we treat shares as a 'pool' which grows as new shares are acquired and shrinks as they are sold. **The FA 1985 pool** (so called because it was introduced by rules in the Finance Act 1985) **comprises the following shares of the same class in the same company.**

   • **Shares held by a company on 1 April 1985 and acquired by that company on or after 1 April 1982.**

   • **Shares acquired by that company on or after 1 April 1985.**

2.2 In making computations which use the FA 1985 pool, we must keep track of:

   (a) the **number** of shares;
   (b) the **cost** of the shares ignoring indexation;
   (b) the **indexed cost** of the shares.

2.3 Each FA 1985 **pool is started by aggregating the cost and number of shares acquired between 1 April 1982 and 1 April 1985** inclusive. In order to calculate the indexed cost of these shares, an indexation allowance, computed from the relevant date of acquisition of the shares to April 1985, is added to the cost.

2.4 EXAMPLE: THE FA 1985 POOL

Oliver Ltd bought 1,000 shares in Judith plc for £2,750 in August 1984 and another 1,000 for £3,250 in December 1984. The FA 1985 pool at 1 April 1985 is as follows.

2.5 SOLUTION

	No of shares	Cost £	Indexed cost £
August 1984 (a)	1,000	2,750	2,750
December 1984 (b)	1,000	3,250	3,250
	2,000	6,000	6,000
Indexation allowance			
$\dfrac{94.8 - 89.9}{89.9} = 0.055 \times £2,750$			151
$\dfrac{94.8 - 90.9}{90.9} = 0.043 \times £3,250$			140
Indexed cost of the pool at 1 April 1985			6,291

2.6 Disposals and acquisitions of shares which affect the indexed value of the FA 1985 pool are termed 'operative events'. **Prior to reflecting each such operative event within the FA 1985 share pool, a further indexation allowance (described as an indexed rise) must be computed up to the date of the operative event concerned from the date of the last such operative event** (or from the later of the first acquisition and April 1985 if the operative event in question is the first one).

2.7 **Indexation calculations within the FA 1985 pool** (after its April 1985 value has been calculated) **are not rounded to three decimal places.** This is because rounding errors would accumulate and have a serious effect after several operative events.

If there are several operative events between 1 April 1985 and the date of a disposal, the indexation procedure described above will have to be performed several times over.

Question: Value of FA 1985 pool

Following on from the above example, assume that Oliver Ltd acquired 2,000 more shares on 10 July 1986 at a cost of £4,000. Recalculate the value of the FA 1985 pool on 10 July 1986 following the acquisition.

Answer

	No of shares	Cost £	Indexed cost £
Value at 1.4.85	2,000	6,000	6,291
Indexed rise			
$\dfrac{97.5 - 94.8}{94.8} \times £6,291$			179
	2,000	6,000	6,470
Acquisition	2,000	4,000	4,000
Value at 10.7.86	4,000	10,000	10,470

2.8 **In the case of a disposal, following the calculation of the indexed rise to the date of disposal, the cost and the indexed cost attributable to the shares disposed of are deducted from the amounts within the FA 1985 pool. The proportions of the cost and indexed cost to take out of the pool should be computed using the A/(A + B) fraction**

that is used for any other part disposal. However, we are not usually given the value of the remaining shares (B in the fraction). We then just use numbers of shares.

2.9 The indexation allowance is the indexed cost taken out of the pool minus the cost taken out. As usual, the indexation allowance cannot create or increase a loss.

Question: the FA 1985 pool

Continuing the above exercise, suppose that Oliver Ltd sold 3,000 shares on 10 July 2001 for £17,000. Compute the gain, and the value of the FA 1985 pool following the disposal.

Answer

	No of shares	Cost £	Indexed cost £
Value at 10.7.86	4,000	10,000	10,470
Indexed rise			
$\dfrac{175.5 - 97.5}{97.5} \times £10,470$			8,376
	4,000	10,000	18,846
Disposal	(3,000)		
Cost and indexed cost $\dfrac{3,000}{4,000} \times £10,000$ and £18,846		(7,500)	(14,135)
Value at 10.7.01	1,000	2,500	4,712

The gain is computed as follows:

	£
Proceeds	17,000
Less cost	(7,500)
	9,500
Less indexation allowance £(14,135 – 7,500)	(6,635)
Chargeable gain	2,865

2.10 When shares are transferred on a no gain no/loss basis between group companies, thereby creating or adding to an FA 1985 pool belonging to the acquiring company, the usual rules on no gain/no loss disposals and later disposals set out in the previous chapter do not apply. The disposing company still has no gain and no loss, but the acquiring company takes the shares into their FA 1985 pool at original cost to the disposing company plus (in the indexed cost column) indexation up to the date of transfer.

Exam focus point

In your examination you will be given an indexed cost for the FA 1985 pool at a specified date along with indexation factors to be used for time since that date. In the above question we illustrated how the FA 1985 pool is constructed from scratch using the RPI so that you could see how the indexed cost is calculated. You will not need to do such workings in your own answers. You should use the (rounded) indexation factors supplied.

3   THE 1982 HOLDING

3.1 Shares (of the same class in the same company) acquired in the period from 6 April 1965 to 31 March 1982 inclusive are pooled as a '1982 holding'. Indexation is dealt with separately on each disposal, outside the holding. The usual rule that the indexation allowance cannot create or increase a loss applies.

3.2 As with the FA 1985 pool, compute the cost to take out of the pool using A/(A + B) if values are given, but using numbers of shares if they are not given.

3.3 EXAMPLE: THE 1982 HOLDING

J plc acquired 2,000 shares in V plc for £3,750 on 1 March 1976 and a further 2,500 shares in V plc for £2,000 on 30 June 1980. The market value per share on 31 March 1982 was £1.20. J plc sold 2,400 shares on 3 June 2001 for £16,000.

3.4 SOLUTION

	No of shares	Cost £
1.3.76	2,000	3,750
30.6.80	2,500	2,000
Value of 1982 holding	4,500	5,750

	Pool cost £	31.3.82 value £
Proceeds	16,000	16,000
Less: pool cost		
$\dfrac{2,400}{4,500} \times £5,750$	((3,067)	
31.3.82 value		
$2,400 \times £1.20$		(2,880)
Unindexed gain	12,933	13,120
Less indexation allowance		
$\dfrac{175.0-79.4}{79.4} = 1.204 \times £3,067$	(3,693)	(3,693)
Indexed gain	9,240	9,427

The chargeable gain is £9,240, the lower gain.

4 ALTERATIONS OF SHARE CAPITAL

4.1 On a reorganisation we must apportion the original base cost of whatever the shareholder had beforehand between the elements of whatever the shareholder has afterwards.

Capital distributions

4.2 **Normally a capital distribution is treated as a part disposal of an asset. If, however, the distribution is small then any gain can be deferred by treating the distribution as a deduction from the cost of the shares for the purposes of calculating any gains or losses on future disposals.** A distribution is normally taken to be small if it is not more than the higher of 5% of the value of the shares and £3,000. If the company wants a part disposal the Revenue will allow this even if the proceeds are small.

4.3 Where receipts are not treated as disposals but are deducted from allowable cost under the above rule and the original shares are in the FA 1985 pool, we simply compute the indexed rise up to the time of receipt and then deduct the receipt from the cost and from the indexed cost. If the original shares are not in the FA 1985 pool, the indexation allowance on a subsequent disposal is computed by first applying the relevant increase in the Retail Prices Index to all expenditure (ignoring the deduction occasioned by the small disposal) and then deducting from that figure the proceeds of small disposal × the percentage increase in the RPI from the date of the small disposal to the date of the subsequent disposal.

Question: Capital distributions

Barr Ltd holds 1,000 shares in Woodleigh plc that cost £3,000 in 1980. Woodleigh plc is now in liquidation and in June 1997 the liquidator made a distribution of 35p per share. The market value of the shares after the distribution was £7,000. In November 2001 Barr Ltd received a final distribution of £7,200.

Because of the company's poor trading record the value of the shares at 31 March 1982 was only £1,000.

Show any chargeable gains arising, assuming that there is no part disposal in June 1997.

Answer

No gain arises in June 1997 as the distribution in June 1997 is not more than the higher of £3,000 and 5% of the value of the shares: £(350 + 7,000) × 5% = £368. The November 2001, distribution is treated as follows.

	Cost £	31.3.82 value £
Proceeds	7,200	7,200
Less: cost less £350	(2,650)	
31.3.82 value less £350		(650)
Unindexed gain	4,550	6,550
Less indexation allowance (March 1982 to November 2001)		
$\dfrac{177.5 - 79.4}{79.4} = 1.236 \times £3,000$	(3,708)	(3,708)
Add $\dfrac{177.5 - 157.5}{157.5} = 0.127 \times £350$ (June 1997 to November 2001)	44	44
	886	2,886

The chargeable gain on the November 2001 distribution is £798.

Bonus issues (scrip issues)

4.4 **When a company issues bonus shares all that happens is that the size of the original holding is increased. Since bonus shares are issued at no cost there is no need to adjust the original cost. Instead the numbers purchased at particular times are increased by the bonus.** The normal matching rules will then be applied.

4.5 EXAMPLE: BONUS ISSUES

The following transactions in the ordinary shares of X plc would be matched as shown below:

6.4.66	Purchase of 600 shares
6.4.70	Purchase of 600 shares
6.4.83	Purchase of 1,000 shares
6.10.86	Bonus issue of one for four
6.5.01	Sale of 2,250 shares

(a) *The FA 1985 pool*

		No of shares
6.4.83		1,000
6.10.86 Bonus issue one for four		250
		1,250
Disposal 6.5.01		(1,250)

(b) *The 1982 holding*

		No of shares
6.4.66		600
6.4.70		600
		1,200
6.10.86 Bonus issue one for four		300
		1,500
Disposal 6.5.01		(1,000)
Remaining shares		500

Rights issues

4.6 **The difference between a bonus issue and a rights issue is that in a rights issue the new shares are paid for and this results in an adjustment to the original cost. For the purposes of calculating the indexation allowance, expenditure on a rights issue is taken as being incurred on the date of the issue and not on the date of acquisition of the original holding.**

As with bonus issues, rights shares derived from shares in the 1982 holding go into that holding those derived from the 1985 pool shares go into that pool.

4.7 In an **open offer** shareholders have a right to subscribe for a minimum number of shares based on their existing holdings and may buy additional shares. Subscriptions up to the minimum entitlement are treated as a rights issue. Additional subscriptions are treated as new purchases of shares.

Question: Rights issues

J Ltd had the following transactions in the shares of T plc.

July 1980	Purchased 1,500 shares for £2,000
July 1985	Purchased 1,000 shares for £3,000
May 1986	Took up one for four rights issue at £4.20 per share
October 2001	Sold 3,000 shares for £24,000

The value of the shares on 31 March 1982 was £2.50 per share.

Compute the chargeable gain or allowable loss arising on the sale in October 2001.

Answer

(a) *The FA 1985 pool*

	No of shares	Cost £	Indexed cost £
July 1985	1,000	3,000	3,000
Indexed rise to May 1986			
$\dfrac{97.8 - 95.2}{95.2} \times £3,000$			82
May 1986 one for four rights	250	1,050	1,050
	1,250	4,050	4,132
Indexed rise to October 2001			
$\dfrac{177.0 - 97.8}{97.8} \times £4,132$			3,346
	1,250	4,050	7,478
Disposal in October 2001	(1,250)	(4,050)	(7,478)

(b)   *The 1982 holding*

	No of shares	Cost £	31.3.82 value £
July 1980	1,500	2,000	3,750
May 1986 one for four rights	375	1,575	1,575
	1,875	3,575	5,325

(c)   *The chargeable gain*

(i)   *FA 1985 pool shares*

	£
Proceeds: $£24,000 \times \dfrac{1,250}{3,000}$	10,000
Less cost	(4,050)
	5,950
Less indexation allowance £(7,478 – 4,050)	(3,428)
Chargeable gain	2,522

(ii)   *1982 holding shares*

	Cost £	31.3.82 value £
Proceeds: $£24,000 \times \dfrac{1,750}{3,000}$	14,000	14,000
Less: cost $\dfrac{1,750}{1,875} \times £3,575$	(3,337)	
31.3.82 value $\dfrac{1,750}{1,875} \times £5,325$		(4,970)
Unindexed gain	10,663	9,030

Less indexation allowance
On original shares (March 1982 to October 2001)

$\dfrac{177.0 - 79.4}{79.4} = 1.229 \times \dfrac{1,750}{1,875} \times £3,750$ (ie 31.3.82 value)	(4,302)	(4,302)

On rights issue shares (May 1986 to October 2001)

$\dfrac{177.0 - 97.8}{97.8} = 0.810 \times \dfrac{1,750}{1,875} \times £1,575$	(1,191)	(1,191)
	5,170	3,537

The chargeable gain is £3,537.

Note: The cost of £3,575 is made up of the £2,000 original cost plus the rights cost of £1,575 (1,500/4 x £4.20).

The 31 March 1982 value of £5,325 is made up of the £3,750 (1,500 x £2.50) original 31 March 1982 value plus the rights cost of £1,575.

(iii)   The total chargeable gain is £2,522 + £3,537 = £6,059.

Sales of rights nil paid

4.8   **Where the shareholder does not take up his rights but sells them to a third party without paying the company for the rights shares, the proceeds are treated as a capital distribution** (see above) **and will be dealt with either under the part disposal rules or, if not more than the higher of £3,000 and 5% of the value of the shareholding giving rise to the disposal, as a reduction of original cost** (unless the company wants a part disposal), with the same consequences for indexation as were mentioned in Paragraph 4.3 above.

Stock dividends

4.9 A stock dividend is the receipt of a dividend by the issue of additional shares rather than cash. For shareholders which are companies, **a stock dividend is treated as a rights issue taken up**. The shares are treated as bought for the value of the (net) stock dividend.

Reorganisations

4.10 **A reorganisation takes place where new shares or a mixture of new shares and debentures are issued in exchange for the original shareholdings. The new shares take the place of the old shares.** The problem is how to apportion the original cost between the different types of capital issued on the reorganisation.

4.11 If the new shares and securities are quoted, then the cost is apportioned by reference to the market values of the new types of capital on the first day of quotation after the reorganisation. No amendment to the indexation process occurs unless further consideration is contributed, when indexation will be computed as for rights issues: indexation on new consideration will run from the time when it is contributed.

Question: Reorganisations

An original quoted shareholding is made up of ordinary shares purchased as follows.

1980   2,000 shares costing £1,750
1985   3,000 shares costing £13,250

In 2001 there is a reorganisation whereby each ordinary share is exchanged for two 'A' ordinary shares (quoted at £2 each) and one preference share (quoted at £1 each). Show how the original costs will be apportioned.

Answer

The new holding will be as follows.

	Value
	£
10,000 ordinary shares at £2	20,000
5,000 preference shares at £1	5,000
	25,000

The costs will be apportioned between the new 'A' ordinary shares and the preference shares in the ratio of 20,000:5,000 = 4:1 as follows.

1982 holdings	£
4,000 ($^2/_5 \times 10,000$) new 'A' ordinary shares, deemed acquired in 1980 ($^4/_5 \times £1,750$)	1,400
2,000 ($^2/_5 \times 5,000$) preference shares, deemed acquired in 1980 ($^1/_5 \times £1,750$)	350
	1,750

FA 1985 pools	£
6,000 ($^3/_5 \times 10,000$) new 'A' ordinary shares, deemed acquired in 1985 ($^4/_5 \times £13,250$)	10,600
3,000 ($^3/_5 \times 5,000$) preference shares, deemed acquired in 1985 ($^1/_5 \times £13,250$)	2,650
	13,250

4.12 Where a reorganisation takes place and the new shares and securities are unquoted, the cost of the original holding is apportioned using the values of the new shares and securities when they come to be disposed of. Further consideration is treated in the same way as for quoted shares.

4.13 For both quoted and unquoted shares and securities, any incidental costs (such as professional fees) are treated as additional consideration for the new shares and securities.

Takeovers

4.14 **A chargeable gain does not arise on a 'paper for paper' takeover. The cost** (or 31 March 1982 value if applicable) **of the original holding is passed on to the new holding** which takes the place of the original holding. **If part of the takeover consideration is cash then a gain must be computed**: the normal part disposal rules will apply. If the cash received is not more than the higher of 5% of the total value on the takeover, and £3,000, then the small distribution rules apply and the cash received will be deducted from cost for the purpose of further disposals.

The takeover rules apply where the company issuing the new shares ends up with more than 25% of the ordinary share capital of the old company or the majority of the voting power in the old company, or the company issuing the new shares makes a general offer to shareholders in the other company which is initially made subject to a condition which, if satisfied, would give the first company control of the second company.

Question: Takeovers

Le Bon Ltd held 20,000 £1 shares out of a total number of issued shares of one million bought for £2 each in Duran plc. In 2001 the board of Duran plc agreed to a takeover bid by Spandau plc under which shareholders in Duran received three Spandau shares plus 90p cash for every four shares held in Duran plc. Immediately following the takeover, the shares in Spandau plc were quoted at £5 each. What gain has Le Bon Ltd made? The RPI rose by 18% from the acquisition date to the date of the takeover

Answer

The total value due to Le Bon Ltd on the takeover is as follows.

		£
Shares	20,000 × 3/4 × £5	75,000
Cash	20,000 × 1/4 × 90p	4,500
		79,500

Since the cash (£4,500) exceeds both £3,000 and 5% of £79,500 it cannot be rolled over by deducting it from the acquisition cost. There is a part disposal.

	£
Disposal proceeds	4,500

Apportioned cost:

$$\frac{\text{Value of disposal}}{\text{Value of disposal} + \text{value of part retained}} \times \text{cost}$$

	£
$\dfrac{£4,500}{£4,500 + £75,000} \times 20,000 \times £2$	(2,264)
	2,236
Less indexation allowance £2,264 × 0.180	(408)
Indexed gain	1,828

4.15 Part of the takeover consideration may include the right to receive deferred consideration in the form of shares or debentures in the new company. The amount of the deferred consideration may be unascertainable at the date of the takeover, perhaps because it is dependent on the future profits of the company whose shares are acquired. The right is valued and treated as a security. This means the takeover rules apply and there is no need to calculate a gain in respect of the right. The issue of shares or debentures as a result of the right is treated as a conversion of the right and, again, no gain arises.

Chapter roundup

- When dealing with shares held by companies, we usually need to construct both a FA 1985 pool and a 1982 holding.

- On an alteration of share capital, the general principle is only to tax gains immediately if cash is paid to the investors.

Quick quiz

1   In what order are acquisitions of shares matched with disposals for companies?

2   What shares are included in the FA 1985 pool held by a company?

3   What shares are included in the 1982 holding of a company?

Answers to quick quiz

1   For companies the matching of shares sold is in the following order.

    (a)   Shares acquired on the same day
    (b)   Shares acquired in the previous nine days, taking earlier acquisitions first
    (c)   Shares from the FA 1985 pool
    (d)   Shares from the 1982 holding
    (e)   Shares purchased before 6 April 1965, taking later acquisitions first (not examinable)

If a company owns 2% or more of another company, disposals are matched (after same day acquisitions) with shares acquired within one month before or after the disposal (for Stock Exchange transactions) or six months (in other cases) before being matched with shares from the FA 1985 pool.

2   Shares held on 1 April 1985 and acquired after 31.3.82 and shares acquired after 31.3.1985.

3   Shares acquired from 1 April 1965 to 31 March 1982.

Now try the question below from the Exam Question Bank

Number	Level	Marks	Time
11	Exam	10	18 mins

Chapter 10

CHATTELS, WASTING ASSETS, LEASES AND COMPENSATION

Topic list	Syllabus reference	Ability required
1 Chattels	(v)	Application
2 Wasting assets	(v)	Application
3 Leases	(v)	Application
4 Compensation and insurance proceeds	(v)	Application

Introduction

Some gains are too small, and arise too often, to be worth taxing. These are gains on movable physical property (such as books or furniture) which are sold for £6,000 or less. These gains are exempt, as we will see in Section 1.

Other movable physical assets, such as computers, tend to fall in value over their lives, so that losses are more likely than gains. These assets are generally exempt, so that the losses are not allowable. The Revenue are happy to miss out on a few gains in exchange for ruling out a lot of losses.

Leases of land also fall in value over their lives: a lease with ten years left to run is worth less than one with thirty years left to run. Rather than making a lease exempt, the Revenue run down its cost so that the cost falls as the value falls. This makes losses unlikely.

Finally we will look at what happens if an asset is damaged or destroyed.

Learning outcomes covered in this chapter

- **Identify** chargeable assets for taxation as chargeable gains
- **Calculate** the total profits of a company for CT purposes

Syllabus content covered in this chapter

- Scope, exemptions, chattels
- Computation of total income

1 CHATTELS

> **KEY TERMS**
>
> A **chattel** is tangible movable property.
>
> A **wasting asset** is an asset with an estimated remaining useful life of 50 years or less.

1.1 **Plant and machinery, whose predictable useful life is always deemed to be less than 50 years, is an example of a wasting chattel (unless it is immovable, in which case it will be wasting but not a chattel).** Machinery includes, in addition to its ordinary meaning, motor vehicles (unless exempt as cars), railway and traction engines, engine-powered boats and clocks.

1.2 **Wasting chattels are exempt** (so that there are no chargeable gains and no allowable losses). There is one exception to this: assets used for the purpose of a trade in respect of which capital allowances have been or could have been claimed. This means that items of plant and machinery used in a trade are not exempt merely on the ground that they are wasting. (However, cars are always exempt.)

1.3 **If a chattel is not exempt under the wasting chattels rule, any gain arising on its disposal will still be exempt if the asset is sold for gross proceeds of £6,000 or less**, even if capital allowances were claimed on it.

1.4 **If sale proceeds exceed £6,000, any gain is limited** to a maximum of $5/3 \times$ (gross proceeds – £6,000).

Question: Gains on chattels

A Ltd purchased a Chippendale chair on 1 June 1984 for £800. On 10 October 2001 the company sold the chair at auction for £6,300 (which was net of the auctioneer's 10% commission). What was the chargeable gain?

Answer

Proceeds	7,000
Less incidental costs of sale	(700)
Net proceeds	6,300
Less cost	(800)
Unindexed gain	5,500
Less indexation allowance (June 1984 to October 2001)	
$\dfrac{177.0 - 89.2}{89.2} = 0.984 \times £800$	(787)
Indexed gain	4,713

The maximum gain is $5/3 \times £(7,000 - 6,000) = £1,667$

The chargeable gain is the lower of £4,713 and £1,667, so it is £1,667.

Losses

1.5 **Where a chattel, not exempt under the wasting chattels rule is sold for less than £6,000 and a loss arises, the allowable loss is restricted by assuming that the chattel was sold for £6,000.** This rule cannot turn a loss into a gain, only reduce the loss, perhaps to zero.

Question: Computation of gain or loss

E Ltd purchased a rare first edition on 1 July 1982 for £8,000 which was sold in October 2001 at auction for £2,700 (which was net of 10% commission). Compute the gain or loss.

Answer

	£
Proceeds (assumed)	6,000
Less incidental costs of disposal (£2,700 x 10/90)	(300)
	5,700
Less cost	(8,000)
Allowable loss (indexation allowance cannot increase a loss)	(2,300)

Sets

1.6 The £6,000 chattel exemption cannot be exploited by selling separately each of a number of items which make up a set, unless the purchasers are unconnected with each other. **If two or more assets which have formed part of a set all owned by the same person** (for example a set of Chippendale chairs) **are disposed of separately to the same person or to persons either acting in concert or connected with one another, then the separate disposals are treated as a single transaction.** Gains will only be wholly exempt if the aggregate proceeds do not exceed £6,000. Otherwise the maximum total gain on all the disposals will be 5/3 × (total proceeds – £6,000).

1.7 Where losses arise and total proceeds are less than £6,000, deemed total proceeds of £6,000 are compared with the total of all actual costs and indexation allowances to determine the maximum total loss.

A part disposal by way of disposal of a right or interest

1.8 Where there is a disposal of a right or interest in or over tangible movable property, the chattel exemption is applied only if the sum of the consideration and the value of what remains undisposed of does not exceed £6,000. Where the aggregate value exceeds £6,000, the limit on the gain is

$$5/3 \times (\text{aggregate value} - £6,000) \times \frac{\text{consideration}}{\text{aggregate value}}$$

1.9 If a loss arises, it is restricted (but cannot be either increased or turned into a gain) by using

$$\text{deemed proceeds of } £6,000 \times \frac{\text{consideration}}{\text{aggregate value}}$$

2 WASTING ASSETS

2.1 As we have seen, a wasting asset is one which has an estimated remaining useful life of 50 years or less and whose original value will depreciate over time. **Freehold land is never a wasting asset,** and there are special rules for leases of land, given below.

2.2 **Wasting chattels are exempt except for those on which capital allowances have been** (or could have been) **claimed.** Where capital allowances were available (on any asset, not just a chattel) and a loss would arise, the base cost is reduced by the net capital allowances obtained: the result is no gain and no loss, except in the case of industrial buildings with periods of non-industrial use. Gains on such assets may still be exempted or restricted under the chattels rules based on £6,000 as long as the assets are not fixed. Items of fixed plant and machinery are not movable and so are not chattels.

2.3 EXAMPLE: WASTING CHATTEL

X Ltd bought a computer for £17,000 in January 1992. The computer was sold for £8,000 in December 2001. Capital allowances were claimed on the computer which will have equalled £9,000 (£17,000 cost less £8,000 disposal proceeds) in total over the life of the computer.

	£	£
Sale proceeds		8,000
Cost	17,000	
Less net capital allowances claimed	(9,000)	
		(8,000)
Gain on disposal		NIL

Options

2.4 **An option** (for example an option to buy shares) **is a wasting asset,** because after a certain time it can no longer be exercised.

2.5 We must distinguish between traded options (or 'quoted' options) with dealings on an exchange and other options.

Traded options

2.6 **If a traded option is exercised, the grantor's position varies, depending on whether it is a put option** (the grantee's right to sell the underlying asset) **or a call option** (the grantee's right to buy the underlying asset). In the case of a call option, the grantor must add the consideration received for the sale of the option to the sale proceeds of the assets covered by the option. In the case of a put option, the grantor must deduct the consideration received from the acquisition cost of the assets covered. The grantee's position is the same in either case: it increases the allowable cost by the cost of the option. The cost of the option is not written down over time, either here or on abandonment or sale of an option.

2.7 When a traded option is abandoned, the abandonment is regarded as a disposal for chargeable gains purposes and so an allowable loss will arise.

2.8 When a traded option is sold, there is a normal chargeable gains computation. Where it is designed to be settled and is in fact settled by a cash payment by the grantor to the grantee, the grantor has a chargeable gain (or allowable loss) of the amount received for the option – the amount paid to the grantee; the grantee has a normal chargeable gains computation based on proceeds of the receipt from the grantor, a cost of the option's cost and indexation from grant to settlement.

2.9 When a person sells (grants) a traded option and then effectively cancels his obligations under it by buying an identical option, the cost of the purchase is treated as an incidental expense of the original sale.

Other options

2.10 Other options can also be exercised or abandoned. If a non-traded option is exercised, the position is the same as with traded options, but the cost is progressively written down over the life of the option (as described below). If a non-traded option is abandoned, no deemed disposal arises and so there is no allowable loss.

Other wasting assets

2.11 The cost is written down on a straight line basis before calculating the indexation allowance. Thus, if a company acquires such an asset with a remaining life of 40 years and disposes of it after 15 years (with 25 years remaining) only 25/40 of the cost is deducted from the disposal consideration. Indexation allowance is computed on the written down cost rather than the full original cost.

2.12 Examples of such assets are copyrights (with 50 years or less to run) and registered designs.

2.13 Where the asset has an estimated residual value at the end of its predictable life, it is the cost less residual value which is written off on a straight line basis over the asset's life. Where additional expenditure is incurred on a wasting asset the additional cost is written off over the life remaining when it was incurred.

2.14 Assets eligible for capital allowances and used throughout the period of ownership in a trade, do not have their allowable expenditure written down.

3 LEASES

Types of disposal

3.1 The gain that arises on the disposal of a lease will be chargeable according to the terms of the lease disposed of. We must consider:

(a) the assignment of a lease or sub-lease with 50 years or more to run;
(b) the assignment of a lease or sub-lease with less than 50 years to run;
(c) the grant of a lease or sub-lease for 50 years or more;
(d) the grant of a lease or sublease for less than 50 years.

3.2 **There is an assignment when a lessee sells the whole of his interest. There is a grant when a new lease or sub-lease is created out of a freehold or existing leasehold, the grantor retaining an interest.**

3.3 The duration of the lease will normally be determined by the contract terms. The expiry date, however, will be taken as the first date on which the landlord has an option to terminate the lease or the date beyond which the lease is unlikely to continue because of, for example, the likelihood that the rent will be substantially increased at that date.

The assignment of a lease with 50 years or more to run

3.4 An **ordinary disposal computation** is made and the whole of any gain on disposal will be chargeable.

The assignment of a lease with less than 50 years less to run

3.5 In calculating the gain on the disposal of a lease with less than 50 years to run only a certain proportion of the original expenditure counts as an allowable deduction from the disposal proceeds. This is because a lease is losing value anyway as its life runs out: only the cost

BPP
PUBLISHING

related to the tail end of the lease being sold is deductible. The proportion is determined by a table of percentages, which is reproduced in the Rates and Allowances Tables in this text.

3.6 **The allowable cost is given by original cost × X/Y, where X is the percentage for the number of years left for the lease to run at the date of the assignment, and Y is the percentage for the number of years the lease had to run when first acquired by the seller.**

3.7 The table only provides percentages for exact numbers of years. Where the duration is not an exact number of years the relevant percentage should be found by adding 1/12 of the difference between the two years on either side of the actual duration for each extra month. Fourteen or more odd days count as a month.

Question: The assignment of a short lease

A Ltd acquired a 20 year lease on a block of flats which it rents out on 1 August 1995 for £15,000. The company assigned the lease on 1 August 2001 for £19,000. Compute the chargeable gain arising.

Answer

	£
Proceeds	19,000
Less cost £15,000 × $\dfrac{58.971}{72.770}$	(12,156)
Unindexed gain	6,844
Less indexation allowance (August 1995 to August 2001)	
$\dfrac{176.0 - 149.9}{149.9} = 0.174 \times £12,156$	(2,115)
Indexed gain	4,729

58.971 = percentage for 14 years (life from 1.8.01)
72.770 = percentage for 20 years (life from 1.8.95)

3.8 If a lease was acquired before 31 March 1982, then in the calculation based on 31 March 1982 value, 31 March 1982 is treated as the date of acquisition of the lease.

Question: Calculation of gain arising

B Ltd acquired a 30 year lease on an investment property on 1 January 1981 for £20,000. It assigned the lease on 1 July 2001 for £28,000. The lease was valued at £15,000 on 31 March 1982. Compute any chargeable gain arising. The indexation factor from March 1982 to July 2001 is 1.210.

Answer

	Cost £	31.3.82 value £
Proceeds	28,000	28,000
Less: cost		
£20,000 × $\dfrac{44.925}{87.330}$	(10,289)	
31.3.82 value		
£15,000 × $\dfrac{44.925}{85.933}$		(7,842)
Unindexed gain	17,711	20,158
Less indexation allowance (March 1982 to July 2001)		
1.210 × £10,289	(12,450)	(12,450)
	5,261	7,708

The chargeable gain is £5,261.

Percentages are as follows.

1.7.2001:	9½ years:	$43.154 + (46.695 - 43.154) \times {}^{6}/_{12} = 44.925$
31.3.1982:	28¾ years:	$85.053 + (86.226 - 85.053) \times {}^{9}/_{12} = 85.933$
1.1.1981:	30 years:	87.330

The grant of a long lease or long sub-lease out of a freehold or a long lease

3.9 If the company grants a lease out of its existing interest this is treated as a part disposal. Where the lease granted is for 50 years or more, the gain on the part disposal is calculated in accordance with the usual part disposal rules. The gain will therefore be calculated by deducting from the proceeds the following proportion of the original cost.

$$\text{Original cost} \times \frac{\text{Value of part disposed of}}{\text{Value of part disposed of } + \text{ Value of remainder}}$$

3.10 The value of the part disposed of will simply be the premium paid for the lease. The value of the remainder includes the value of the right to receive the rents under the lease as well as the discounted capital value of the reversion of the property on the expiry of the lease. This overall value is known as the **reversionary interest.**

Question: the grant of a long lease

C Ltd acquired a freehold property for £12,000 on 1 January 1975. On 1 July 2001 it granted a 60 year lease for a premium of £26,000. At the time of the granting the value of the rent receivable under the lease was £10,000 and the discounted capital value of the right to re-occupy the property after 60 years was £15,000. The market value of the property on 31 March 1982 was £18,000. Compute any chargeable gain arising. The indexation factor from March 1982 to July 2001 is 1.210.

Answer

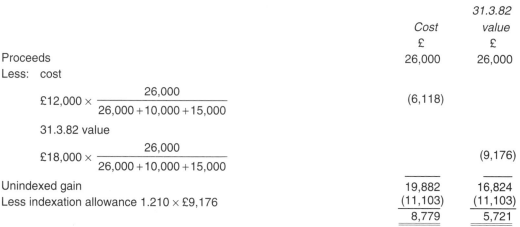

	Cost £	31.3.82 value £
Proceeds	26,000	26,000
Less: cost		
$£12,000 \times \dfrac{26,000}{26,000 + 10,000 + 15,000}$	(6,118)	
31.3.82 value		
$£18,000 \times \dfrac{26,000}{26,000 + 10,000 + 15,000}$		(9,176)
Unindexed gain	19,882	16,824
Less indexation allowance 1.210 × £9,176	(11,103)	(11,103)
	8,779	5,721

The chargeable gain is £5,721

The grant of a short lease or a short sub-lease out of a freehold or a long lease

3.11 If a short lease or a short sub-lease is granted, part of the premium will be income under Schedule A and must therefore be excluded from the chargeable gains computation.

Question: the grant of a short lease out of a freehold or a long lease

The facts are as in the previous example, except that the sub-lease is for 30 years rather than 60 years. Compute any chargeable gain arising.

Answer

The Schedule A income from the premium will be as follows.

	£
Premium	26,000
Less 2% × £26,000 × (30 − 1)	(15,080)
Schedule A	10,920

	Cost £	31.3.82 value £
Reduced premium		
£(26,000 − 10,920)	15,080	15,080
Less: cost		
$£12,000 \times \dfrac{15,080}{26,000 + 10,000 + 15,000}$	(3,548)	
31.3.82 value		
$£18,000 \times \dfrac{15,080}{26,000 + 10,000 + 15,000}$		(5,322)
Unindexed gain	11,532	9,758
Less indexation allowance		
1.210 × £5,322	(6,440)	(6,440)
	5,092	3,318

The chargeable gain is £3,318.

Note that the numerator of the part disposal fraction is the premium as reduced by the Schedule A income, whilst the denominator remains unadjusted.

The grant of a sub-lease out of a short lease

3.12 Where a sub-lease is granted out of a head lease which has less than 50 years unexpired duration:

(a) the head lease is treated as a wasting asset; and

(b) part of the premium paid for the sub-lease will be income under Schedule A.

3.13 The fact that the head lease is a wasting asset is dealt with by using a similar formula to that used for the assignment of short leases. The formula used in this case for calculating the allowable proportion of the original cost is

$$\frac{X - Y}{Z} \times \text{original cost}$$

where:

(a) X is the percentage obtained from the table for the number of unexpired years of the head lease at the time the sub-lease is granted;

(b) Y is the percentage for the number of unexpired years of the head lease at the date of the expiry of the sub-lease;

(c)   Z is the percentage for the number of unexpired years of the head lease on the date of its acquisition by the owner (or in a calculation based on 31 March 1982 value, on 31 March 1982).

3.14   To deal with the Schedule A part of the premium we just calculate the chargeable gain using the formula and the full premium and then reduce the final figure by the amount of the Schedule A element. However, this final reduction cannot be used to create or increase an allowable loss: if the Schedule A element exceeds the calculated gain then the chargeable gain is zero, and if the chargeable gains calculation gives a loss, then that is the allowable loss and the Schedule A adjustment is ignored for chargeable gains purposes (although it is still taxable income).

Question: the grant of a short lease out of a short lease

D Ltd was granted a 40 year lease on 30 April 1987 for £14,000. On 30 April 2001 it granted a ten year sub-lease for £11,000. Compute any chargeable gain arising. The indexation factor from April 1987 to April 2001 is 0.709.

Answer

The Schedule A element is as follows.

	£	£	£
Premium		11,000	
Less 2% × £11,000 × (10 − 1)		(1,980)	
			9,020
Less relief for premium paid to superior landlord			
Premium	14,000		
Less 2% × £14,000 × (40 − 1)	(10,920)		
	3,080		
£3,080 × 10/40			(770)
Schedule A			8,250

The chargeable gain is computed as follows.

	£
Proceeds (in full)	11,000
Less cost	
$£14,000 \times \dfrac{82.496 - 64.116}{95.457}$	(2,696)
Unindexed gain	8,304
Less indexation allowance 0.709 × £2,696	(1,911)
	6,393
Indexed gain	6,393
Less Schedule A	(8,250)
Chargeable gain	0

The Schedule A deduction cannot create an allowable loss.

Percentages are as follows.

16 years:	64.116
26 years:	82.496
40 years:	95.457

4 COMPENSATION AND INSURANCE PROCEEDS

Damaged assets

4.1 **If an asset is damaged and compensation or insurance money is received as a result, then this will normally be treated as a part disposal. By election, however, a company can avoid a part disposal computation. A capital sum received can be deducted from the cost of the asset rather than being treated as a part disposal if:**

(a) the amount not spent in restoring the asset is small; or

(b) the capital sum is small.

4.2 The Revenue accept a sum as 'small' if it is either less than 5% of the value of the asset or is less than £3,000. There are special restrictions if the asset is wasting (that is, it has a remaining useful life of 50 years or less).

(a) The *whole* capital sum must be spent on restoration.

(b) The capital sum can only be deducted from what would have been the allowable expenditure on a sale immediately after its application. This will be less than the full cost of the asset, because the cost of a wasting asset is run down over its life.

4.3 If the amount not used in restoring the asset is not small, then the company can elect for the amount used in restoration to be deducted from the cost; the balance will continue to be treated as a part disposal.

Question: Damaged assets

J Ltd bought an office block for renting out which cost £18,000 on 15 August 1985. On 10 September 2001 the office block was damaged in a fire and, as a result, £27,000 insurance proceeds were received in December 2001. £20,000 was spent to restore the building in October 2001; the market value of the building immediately after restoration was £62,000. What gain arose and what will be the base cost of the building in future computations? Assume that J Ltd elects for the amount used in restoration to be deducted from the base cost of the building.

Assume indexation	August 1985 to December 2001	0.864
	October 2001 to December 2001	0.006

Answer

	£	£
The part disposal in December 2001		
Capital sum not used for restoration		
£(27,000 - 20,000)		7,000
Less: part of original cost (incurred August 1985)		
$£18,000 \times \dfrac{7,000}{7,000 + 62,000}$	1,826	
part of restoration cost (incurred October 2001)		
$£20,000 \times \dfrac{7,000}{7,000 + 62,000}$	2,029	
		(3,855)
Unindexed gain		3,145
Less indexation allowance		
0.864 × £1,826		(1,578)
0.006 × £2,029		(12)
Chargeable gain		1,555

The base cost of the restored building	£	£
Original cost		18,000
Restoration expenditure		20,000
		38,000
Less: costs used in part disposal	3,855	
restoration expenditure rolled over	20,000	
		(23,855)
Base cost		14,145

The date of the part disposal is the date of receipt of the insurance monies (December 2001). J Ltd purchased the asset in August 1985 and also spent £20,000 in restoring the building in October 2001.

Destroyed assets

4.4 **If an asset is destroyed (as opposed to merely being damaged) any compensation or insurance monies received will normally be brought into an ordinary disposal computation as proceeds. But if all the proceeds from a non-wasting asset are applied for the replacement of the asset within 12 months, any gain can be deducted from the cost of the replacement asset.** If only part of the proceeds are used, the gain immediately chargeable can be limited to the amount not used. The rest of the gain is then deducted from the cost of the replacement.

Question: Destroyed assets

Fion Ltd bought an asset for £25,000 in June 2001. It was destroyed three years later. Insurance proceeds were £34,000, and Fion Ltd spent £32,500 on a replacement asset. Compute the chargeable gain and the base cost of the new asset. Ignore indexation.

Answer

	£
Proceeds	34,000
Less cost	(25,000)
	9,000
Gain immediately chargeable £(34,000 – 32,500)	(1,500)
Deduction from base cost	7,500

The base cost of the new asset is £(32,500 – 7,500) = £25,000

Chapter roundup

- When a chattel is sold for up to £6,000, any gain is exempt and any loss is restricted. Gains on most wasting chattels sold for any amount are exempt, and losses on them are not allowable.

- Other wasting assets generally have their cost written down over time. For leases of land, a special table of percentages is used.

- When an asset is damaged or destroyed there is usually a part disposal computation but in certain circumstances a company may elect to avoid this computation.

Quick quiz

1   How are gains on non-wasting chattels sold for more than £6,000 restricted?

2   How are losses on non-wasting chattels sold for less than £6,000 restricted?

3   What is the general treatment of intangible wasting assets (eg a copyright)?

4   Distinguish between the grant and the assignment of a lease.

5   When a lease with less than 50 years to run is assigned, what proportion of the cost is allowable?

6   When may a part disposal computation be avoided on the receipt of insurance proceeds?

Answers to quick quiz

1   Gain restricted to 5/3 × (gross proceeds – £6,000)

2   Allowable loss restricted by deeming proceeds to be £6,000

3   The cost is written down on a straight line basis

4   Grant of lease – creating of new lease or sub-lease
    Assignment of lease – disposal of existing lease

5   Allowable cost is original cost × X/Y where X is the % for the years left of the lease to run at assignment and Y is the % for the years the lease had to run when first acquired by the seller.

6   No part disposal on receipt of compensation if

    - any amount not spent in restoring the asset is 'small'
    - the capital sum received is 'small'

Now try the question below from the Exam Question Bank

Number	Level	Marks	Time
12	Exam	8	14 mins

Chapter 11

DEFERRAL RELIEFS

Topic list	Syllabus reference	Ability required
1 Rollover relief	(v)	Application
2 Holdover relief	(v)	Application
3 The choice of assets for claims	(v)	Application
4 EIS and VCT reinvestment relief	(v), (vii)	Analysis

Introduction

An obvious problem for companies is that if an asset, such as a factory, is sold at a gain and replaced, the gain on the old asset could cost so much in tax that the company might not have enough money left to buy a replacement. In this chapter we look at reliefs which solve this problem by allowing the gain to be deferred.

An individual can defer his chargeable gains when he invests in enterprise investment scheme shares or in a venture capital trust. We end this chapter by looking at these reliefs.

Learning outcomes covered in this chapter

- **Apply** rollover and holdover reliefs for business assets
- **Identify** chargeable assets for taxation as chargeable gains

Syllabus content covered in this chapter

- Rollover relief; holdover relief
- EIS and VCTs

1   ROLLOVER RELIEF

1.1   **A gain may be 'rolled over' (deferred) where it arises on the disposal of a business asset which is replaced.** This is **rollover relief**. A claim cannot specify that only part of a gain is to be rolled over.

1.2   All the following conditions must be met.

(a)   **The old asset sold and the new asset bought are both used only in the trade** or trades carried on **by the company claiming rollover relief.** Where part of a building is in non-trade use for all or a substantial part of the period of ownership, the building (and the land on which it stands) can be treated as two separate assets, the trade part (qualifying) and the non-trade part (non-qualifying). This split cannot be made for other assets.

(b)   **The old asset and the new asset both fall within one** (but not necessarily the same one) **of the following classes.**

(i) Land and buildings (including parts of buildings) occupied as well as used only for the purpose of the trade

(ii) Fixed (that is, immovable) plant and machinery

(iii) Ships, aircraft and hovercraft

(iv) Goodwill

(v) Satellites, space stations and spacecraft

(vi) Milk quotas, potato quotas and ewe and suckler cow premium quotas

(vii) Fish quota

(c) **Reinvestment of the proceeds of the old asset takes place in a period beginning one year before and ending three years after the date of the disposal.**

(d) **The new asset is brought into use in the trade on its acquisition** (not necessarily immediately, but not after any significant and unnecessary delay).

1.3 The new asset can be for use in a different trade from the old asset.

1.4 A rollover claim is not allowed when a company buys premises, sells part of the premises at a profit and then claims to roll over the gain into the part retained. However, a rollover claim is allowed (by concession) when the proceeds of the old asset are spent on improving a qualifying asset which the company already owns. The improved asset must already be in use for a trade, or be brought into trade use immediately the improvement work is finished.

1.5 **Deferral is obtained by deducting the chargeable gain from the cost of the new asset. For full relief, the whole of the consideration for the disposal must be reinvested. Where only part is reinvested, a part of the gain equal to the lower of the full gain and the amount not reinvested will be liable to tax immediately.**

1.6 The new asset will have a base 'cost' for chargeable gains purposes, of its purchase price less the gain rolled over into its acquisition.

1.7 If a company expects to buy new assets, it can make a provisional rollover claim on its tax return which includes the gain on the old asset. The gain is reduced accordingly. If new assets are not actually acquired, the Revenue collect the tax saved by the provisional claim.

Question: Rollover relief

A freehold factory was purchased by X Ltd in August 1995. It was sold in December 2001 for £70,000, giving rise to an indexed gain of £17,950. A replacement factory was purchased in June 2002 for £60,000. Compute the base cost of the replacement factory, taking into account any possible rollover gain from the disposal in December 2001.

Answer

	£
Total gain	17,950
Less: amount not reinvested, immediately chargeable £(70,000 – 60,000)	(10,000)
Rollover gain	7,950
Cost of new factory	60,000
Less rolled over gain	(7,950)
Base cost of new factory	52,050

1.8 Where an old asset has not been used in the trade for a fraction of its period of ownership (ignoring periods before 1 April 1982), the amount of the gain that can be rolled over is reduced by the same fraction. If the proceeds are not fully reinvested the restriction on rollover by the amount not reinvested is also calculated by considering only the proportion of proceeds relating to the part of the asset used in the trade or the proportion relating to the period of trade use.

Question: Assets with non-business use

Y Ltd bought a factory in July 1990 for £100,000. It sold the factory in November 2001 for £215,000. The company let out a quarter of the factory on commercial terms for the entire period of ownership. Y Ltd bought a replacement factory in August 2001 for £165,000, which was used wholly for its trade.

Calculate the chargeable gain in the first factory and the base cost of the second factory.

Answer

Gain on 1st factory

	Business (75%) £	Non business (25%) £
Proceeds	161,250	53,750
Less: cost	(75,000)	(25,000)
	86,250	28,750
Less: indexation allowance		
$\frac{177.5 - 126.8}{126.8}$ (= 0.400) × £75,000/25,000	(30,000)	(10,000)
Indexed gain	56,250	18,750

The gain of £19,750 is chargeable.

Base cost of 2nd factory

All of business proceeds are reinvested so full relief is available.

	£
Cost	165,000
Less: rolled over gain	(56,250)
Base cost	108,750

Claims for rollover relief between 31 March 1982 and 6 April 1988

1.9 **A special rule applies** when:

(a) a new asset is disposed of after 5 April 1988; and

(b) that new asset had been acquired after 31 March 1982; and

(c) a gain on an old asset acquired before 31 March 1982 and disposed of before 6 April 1988 had been rolled over against that new asset.

1.10 The rebasing provisions cannot be applied on the sale of the new asset since it was not owned on 31 March 1982, so **the rolled over gain is halved when computing the gain on the sale of the new asset.**

1.11 Similarly, only half of any gain crystallising in respect of a depreciating asset (see below) is chargeable.

New assets acquired before 1 April 1982

1.12 If a new asset was acquired before 1 April 1982 and a gain was rolled over into it, then on the disposal of the new asset the usual two computations of the gain or loss use:

(a) the cost minus the gain rolled over;

(b) the value on 31 March 1982 with *no* deduction for the gain rolled over. This is because the asset is deemed to have been re-acquired on 31 March 1982 for its then market value.

Indexation allowance is based on the higher of (a) and (b) in both computations.

We then take the lower gain, the lower loss, or no gain and no loss as usual.

2 HOLDOVER RELIEF

2.1 **Where the replacement asset is a depreciating asset, the gain is not rolled over by reducing the cost of the replacement asset. Rather it is 'held over' (simply deferred) until it crystallises on the earliest of:**

(a) the disposal of the replacement asset;
(b) ten years after the acquisition of the replacement asset;
(c) the date the replacement asset ceases to be used in the trade.

KEY TERM

An asset is a **depreciating asset** if it is, or within the next ten years will become, a wasting asset. Thus, any asset with an expected life of 60 years or less is covered by this definition. Plant and machinery (including ships, aircraft, hovercraft, satellites, space stations and spacecraft) is always treated as depreciating unless it becomes part of a building: in that case, it will only be depreciating if the building is held on a lease with 60 years or less to run.

Question: Deferred gain on investment into depreciating asset

N Ltd bought a factory for use in its business in June 1999 for £125,000. The factory was sold it for £140,000 on 1 August 2001. On 10 July 2001, N Ltd bought some fixed plant and machinery for use in its business, costing £150,000. The company sold the plant and machinery for £167,000 on 19 November 2002. Show N Ltd's chargeable gains position.

Answer

Gain deferred

	£
Proceeds of factory	140,000
Less cost	(125,000)
Gain	15,000
Less indexation $\frac{176.0-165.6}{165.6} = 0.063 \times £125,000$	(7,875)
	7,125

This gain is deferred in relation to the purchase of the plant and machinery.

Sale of plant and machinery

	£
Proceeds	167,000
Less cost	(150,000)
Gain	17,000
Less indexation $\frac{183.5 - 175.5}{175.5} = 0.046 \times £150,000$	(6,900)
	10,100
Total gain chargeable on sale (gain on plant and machinery plus deferred gain) £(10,100 + 7,125)	£17,225

2.2 Where a gain on disposal is held over against a replacement depreciating asset it is possible to transfer the held over gain to a non-depreciating asset provided the non-depreciating asset is bought before the held-over gain has crystallised.

Question: Transfer of 'held over' gain into non-depreciating asset

In July 1991, Julius Ltd sold a warehouse used in its trade, realising a gain of £30,000. The company invested the whole of the proceeds of sale of £95,000 into fixed plant and machinery in January 1992 and made a claim to 'hold over' the gain on the warehouse.

In August 2001, Julius Ltd bought a freehold shop for use in its business costing £100,000. Julius Ltd has not bought any other assets for use in the business and wishes to minimise chargeable gains arising in its accounting period to 31.3.02. What advice would you give Julius Ltd?

Answer

Julius Ltd should claim to transfer the deferred gain of £30,000 to the purchase of the shop. If it does not do so, the deferred gain will be chargeable in January 2002, at the latest (10 years after the acquisition of the plant and machinery).

The effect of the claim will be to reduce the base cost of the shop to £(100,000 - 30,000) = £70,000.

3 THE CHOICE OF ASSETS FOR CLAIMS

3.1 Sometimes more than one eligible asset will be sold, but acquisitions will not allow all the gains to be rolled over or held over. A choice must then be made, and the choice may affect the total gains deferred and thus the total immediately chargeable.

Question: The choice of assets

Asset A was bought for £98 and is sold for £108, giving a gain of £10.

Asset B was bought for £45 and is sold for £50, giving a gain of £5.

Asset C is bought for £100, and gains on assets A and B could be rolled over against this purchase. Compute the gains chargeable immediately under the possible claims.

Answer

If a claim is made for asset A, the gains chargeable immediately will be £8 (proceeds not reinvested) + £5 (asset B) = £13.

If a claim is made for asset B, the gain chargeable immediately will be £10 (asset A). Note that an additional claim for asset A would have no effect, because the balance of cost of asset C after claiming for asset B would be £(100 – 50) = £50, and the proceeds of asset A not reinvested would be £(108 – 50) = £58, which exceeds the gain on asset A.

3.2 The reverse problem may arise when there are plenty of acquisitions, but not enough disposals to make full use of the capacity to defer gains. In choosing which assets to use in claims, the following points should be considered.

(a) Rollover claims against non-depreciating assets allow gains to be deferred indefinitely, whereas gains held over against depreciating assets will crystallise within ten years (unless rollover claims are substituted).

(b) If two alternative rollover claims or two alternative holdover claims are possible, it is probably better to choose the new assets which are likely to be retained for longer, so as to maximise the period of deferral.

4 EIS AND VCT REINVESTMENT RELIEF

4.1 A company may raise finance by issuing shares under the enterprise investment scheme or through a venture capital trust (see earlier in this text).

EIS investment relief

4.2 The attraction of this means of raising finance is that it gives individual investors tax reliefs. In addition to the income and capital gains tax reliefs discussed earlier in this text an individual may defer a gain arising on the disposal of any type of asset if he invests in qualifying Enterprise Investment Scheme (EIS) shares. This is a deferral relief because the deferred gain will become chargeable, for example when the shares are disposed of (subject to a further claim for the relief being made).

4.3 For EIS deferral relief, it is not necessary for the shares acquired to be subject to the EIS income tax relief. For example, there is no upper limit for investment into shares nor do the conditions restricting relief where the investor is connected with the company apply.

4.4 The amount of the gain that can be deferred is the lower of:

(a) the amount subscribed by the investor for his shares, which has not previously been matched under this relief or the similar relief for investment into Venture Capital Trust shares; and

(b) the amount specified by the investor in the claim. This means that the investor can choose the amount of relief that is most efficient from a tax point of view.

The investor

4.5 The investor must either be an individual or trustees of trusts for individuals. The investor must be UK resident or ordinarily resident (see later in this text) at the time the gain to be deferred was made and at the time the investment was made in the shares.

The company

4.6 The company must be a qualifying company under the EIS rules (basically an unquoted company carrying on a qualifying trade) (see earlier in this text).

The shares

4.7 The shares must be subscribed for wholly in cash by the investor. The shares must be new ordinary shares, fully paid up. The shares must not be redeemable broadly within three years of their issue, nor must they have preferential rights to dividends or assets on a winding up within that period.

4.8   The shares must be subscribed and issued for bona fide commercial purposes (not for the avoidance of tax) and for the purpose of raising money for a qualifying business activity. At least 80% of the money must be used for this purpose within twelve months of the issue of the shares (or within twelve months of the commencement of the trade). All of the money must be used for this purpose within twelve months of the end of the first twelve month period (ie within twenty-four months). If this condition is not satisfied the shares cease to be eligible shares (see below).

Time for investment

4.9   The shares must be issued to the investor within the period of one year before and three years after the gain to be deferred accrues (or such longer period as the Board of Inland Revenue may allow). If the gain accrues after the issue of the shares, the shares must still be held by the investor at the time that the gain arises.

Gain coming back into charge

4.10   The gain deferred will come back into charge on the following events:

(a)   the investor disposing of the shares except by an inter-spouse disposal;

(b)   the spouse of an investor disposing of the shares, if the spouse acquired the shares from the investor;

(c)   the investor becoming non resident (see the next chapter), broadly within three years of the issue of the shares (except if employed full time abroad for up to three years and retaining the shares until his return to the UK);

(d)   the spouse of an investor becoming non resident, broadly within three years of the issue of the shares (except if employed full time abroad for up to three years and retaining the shares until his return to the UK), if the spouse acquired the shares from the investor;

(e)   the shares ceasing to be eligible shares eg. the company ceases to be a qualifying company, the money subscribed not being used for a qualifying business activity. However, relief is not withdrawn if the company becomes a quoted company. This is provided that there were no arrangements in existence at the time of the issue of the shares for the company to cease to be unquoted.

Note that the gain becomes chargeable in the year of the event, not the year when the original gain was made (if different). It will be charged on the holder of the shares at the date of the event eg. on the investor if he/she still holds the shares or the spouse if the shares have been passed to her/him.

Reorganisations and amalgamations

4.11   There are rules relating to reorganisations and amalgamations which are similar to the rules for EIS income tax relief. In general, their purpose is to enable the identification of the original EIS shares (and any associated relief) with replacement shares and to stop the dilution of the relief into rights issue shares. In certain circumstances a reorganisation or amalgamation may result in a chargeable event, for example, if the replacement shares are not new ordinary shares or on a takeover if the new company does not satisfy the rules for EIS qualifying companies.

Anti-avoidance

4.12 There are a number of provisions designed to prevent abuse of the relief. Relief is usually not given if any of these provisions apply before the investment is made or is withdrawn if the rule is broken. The provisions include:

(a) shares disposed of in a company and investment made in the same company or member of the same group of companies;

(b) there is a pre-arranged exit from the investment;

(c) the shares are subject to options to buy or sell;

(d) value is received from the company by the investor or other persons (subject to similar rules as for income tax eg to ignore receipts of insignificant value (see earlier in this text)).

(e) there is an investment-linked loan.

VCT reinvestment relief

4.13 There is a similar deferral relief in respect of investment into VCT shares. The main differences between the EIS relief and the VCT relief are:

(a) the shares must qualify for the VCT income tax relief. Therefore the investment relief limit for income tax also applies for the VCT reinvestment relief;

(b) the time for investment into the shares is 12 months before and 12 months after the gain to be deferred arises.

Chapter roundup

- When assets falling within certain classes are sold and other such assets are bought, it is possible to 'rollover' the gains on the assets sold.

- A rolled over gain is deducted from the base cost of the asset acquired.

- When the replacement asset is a depreciating asset, the gain on the old asset is 'held over' rather than rolled over.

- Individuals may be able to defer chargeable gains when they acquire EIS or VCT shares.

Quick quiz

1   What assets are eligible for rollover relief on the replacement of business assets?

2   What deferral of a gain is available when a business asset is replaced with a depreciating business asset?

3   When is EIS reinvestment relief available?

4   When will a gain come back into charge under EIS reinvestment relief?

Answers to quick quiz

1   Assets eligible for rollover relief are:

- land and buildings occupied as well as used only for the purposes of trade
- fixed plant and machinery
- ships, aircraft and hovercraft
- goodwill
- satellites, space stations and spacecraft
- milk quota, potato quota, ewe and suckler cow premium quota
- fish quota

2   Where a depreciating asset is acquired, the gain is 'held over' (deferred) until it crystallises on the earliest of the replacement of the replacement asset, ten years after the acquisition of the replacement asset and the date the replacement asset ceases to be used in the trade.

3   EIS reinvestment relief is available where an individual makes a gain (on any type of asset) and invests in EIS shares.

4   A gain will come back into charge under EIS reinvestment relief where:

- investor disposes of the shares (except inter-spouse)

- investor's spouse disposes of shares (if acquired from investor)

- investor (or investor's spouse who acquires shares from investor) becomes non-resident within 3 years of issue of shares, unless employed full-time abroad for up to 3 years

- shares cease to be eligible shares (does not generally include becoming quoted)

Now try the question below from the Exam Question Bank

Number	Level	Marks	Time
13	Exam	25	45 mins

BPP PUBLISHING

PROFITS CHARGEABLE TO CORPORATION TAX | **?**

1 SCHEDULE D CASE I • Adjust accounts for disallowables +/- • Depreciation etc Non trade etc • Remove items not taxed under DI • Work out capital allowances and deduct • Plant & machinery • Industrial buildings	**TRADING PROFITS**	**+**
SCHEDULE A Compute Schedule A profit on an accruals basis Deductible vs non deductible expenses	**RENT INCOME**	**+**
SCHEDULE D CASE III Compute <u>net</u> interest from <u>non-trading</u> loans or investments on accruals basis NB interest received/paid for trading purposes is Schedule D Case I	**% INTEREST FROM NON-TRADING LOAN**	**+**
SCHEDULE D CASE V Payments ⟶ gross up for ⟨ witholding ↓ underlying ⟩ tax	**FOREIGN INCOME**	**+**
TAXED INCOME Gross up patent royalties received from individuals	**%**	**+**
CHARGEABLE GAINS Proceeds - cost - indexation allowance ⟶ then consider ⟨ roll over / hold over	- Sales of assets eg copyrights buildings etc	**+**
CHARGES ON INCOME Trade: patent royalties Non trade: Gift aid	NB Remember difference between trade and non-trade charges	**£** —

PROFITS CHARGEABLE TO CORPORATION TAX | **=**

Part C
Employee taxation

Chapter 12

EMPLOYEE TAXATION

Topic list	Syllabus reference	Ability required
1 The Schedule E charge	(ii)	Evaluate
2 Allowable deductions	(ii)	Evaluate
3 Occupational pension schemes	(ii)	Evaluate
4 Personal pension schemes	(ii)	Evaluate
5 Payments on the termination of employment	(ii)	Evaluate
6 Shares and share options made available to employees	(ii)	Evaluate
7 Overseas aspects	(ii)	Evaluate

Introduction

In this chapter we start to look at the taxation of employees. Although personal tax computations do not feature in the business tax syllabus, all aspects of the taxation of employees are examinable.

We look at several tax efficient methods of rewarding employees in this chapter, namely, pensions, tax exempt termination payments and share incentive schemes. We also look at several overseas aspects relating to the taxation of employees.

Learning outcomes covered in this chapter

- **Evaluate** the tax efficiency of different methods of rewarding employees

Syllabus content covered in this chapter

- Schedule E; emoluments; expenses; share options
- Status issues
- Personal pension plans (PPP) and approved occupational pension schemes
- Tax efficient methods of rewarding employees
- Returns required from employers in connection with all aspects of employee tax

1   THE SCHEDULE E CHARGE

Taxable income

> **KEY TERM**
>
> 'Emoluments' from an office or employment are taxed under Schedule E. The term 'emoluments' includes 'all salaries, fees, wages, perquisites and profits whatsoever'.

1.1 Emoluments include tips from customers and benefits in kind. Benefits in kind are converted into their cash equivalent using the rules set out in the next chapter. Employees must pay income tax on their total schedule E emoluments.

1.2 **Earnings (or 'emoluments') are taxed in the year of receipt.** There is a general definition of 'receipt' and a wider one for directors (who are in a position to manipulate the timing of payments). **The general rule is that emoluments are treated as received on the earlier of:**

- **the time payment is made;**
- **the time entitlement to payment arises.**

1.3 The time of receipt for directors' earnings is the earliest of:

(a) the earlier of the two alternatives given in the general rule (above);

(b) when the amount is credited in the company's accounting records;

(c) the end of the company's period of account (if the amount was determined by then);

(d) when the amount is determined (if after the end of the company's period of account).

1.4 The receipts basis does not apply to benefits in kind. Benefits are taxable when provided.

1.5 Pensions and taxable state benefits (such as the jobseeker's allowance) are also taxable under Schedule E. Unlike normal salary, however, the taxable amount is the amount accruing during the tax year, irrespective of whether or not it has actually been received in the tax year.

1.6 **An income tax year is the year that runs from 6 April in one year to 5 April in the next year.** (Note that this is different to a financial year for CT purposes). **The 2001/02 income tax year is the year that starts on 6 April 2001 and ends on 5 April 2002.**

Employment and self employment

1.7 **A taxpayer who has a choice between being employed and being self-employed, on similar gross incomes, should consider the following points.**

(a) An employee must pay **income tax and National Insurance Contributions (NICs) as salary is received, under the PAYE** system (see later in this text) and on a current year basis. A self-employed person pays **some NICs during the year, but income tax and some NICs are at least partly payable after all of the profits concerned have been earned.** There is thus a cash flow advantage in self-employment.

(b) **An employee is likely to suffer significantly higher NICs in total than a self-employed person,** although the employee's entitlement to state benefits will also be higher.

(c) An **employee may receive benefits in kind as well as salary.** Taxable values of benefits may be less than their actual value to the employee and benefits do not attract employee NICs (this is however only relevant if salary does not exceed the upper NIC limit) (see later in this text). Most benefits attract Employer's Class 1A NIC.

(d) The **rules on the deductibility of expenses are much stricter for employees** (incurred wholly, exclusively and necessarily in the performance of duties) than for the self-employed (normally incurred wholly and exclusively for the purposes of the trade).

1.8 **The distinction between employment (Schedule E) and self employment (Schedule D) is a fine one. Employment involves a contract of service, whereas self employment involves a contract for services.**

1.9   Factors which may be of importance include:

- the degree of control exercised over the person doing the work;
- whether he must accept further work;
- whether the other party must provide further work;
- whether he provides his own equipment;
- whether he hires his own helpers;
- what degree of financial risk he takes;
- what degree of responsibility for investment and management he has;
- whether he can profit from sound management;
- whether he can work when he chooses;
- the wording used in any agreement between the parties.

1.10   Relevant cases include:

(a)   *Mitchell & Edon v Ross 1961*

A doctor with a private practice (assessable under Schedule D) also held a part-time appointment with a regional hospital board.

Held: the income from the part-time appointment was taxable under Schedule E.

(b)   *Edwards v Clinch 1981*

A civil engineer acted occasionally as an inspector on temporary ad hoc appointments.

Held: there was no ongoing office which could be vacated by one person and held by another so the fees received were taxable under Schedule D and not under Schedule E.

(c)   *Hall v Lorimer 1994*

A vision mixer was engaged under a series of short-term contracts.

Held: the vision mixer was self employed, not because of any one detail of the case but because the overall picture was one of self-employment.

(d)   *Barnett v Brabyn 1996*

Mr Barnett worked under an oral agreement for a partnership. The parties agreed that Mr Barnett was self-employed and free to exploit other opportunities.

Held: Although a number of factors indicated employment, the deciding factors indicated self employment. The deciding factors were the agreement between the parties and that Mr Barnett could decide how much time he spent working for the partnership.

(e)   *Carmichael and Anor v National Power plc 1999*

Individuals engaged as visitor guides on a casual 'as required' basis were not employees. An exchange of correspondence between the company and the individuals was not a contract of employment as there was no provision as to the frequency of work and there was flexibility to accept work or turn it down as it arose. Sickness, holiday and pension arrangements did not apply and neither did grievance and disciplinary procedures.

2   ALLOWABLE DEDUCTIONS

2.1   **Certain types of expenditure are specifically deductible against Schedule E income:**

(a)   **contributions to approved occupational pension schemes (see below)**

(b)   **subscriptions to professional bodies** on the list of bodies issued by the Inland Revenue (which includes most UK professional bodies), if relevant to the duties of the employment

(c)   payments for certain liabilities and for insurance against them

(d) Payments to charity made under the payroll deduction scheme operated by an employer

2.2 Otherwise, **Schedule E deductions are notoriously hard to obtain. They are limited to**:

- **qualifying travel expenses** (see below);

- **other expenses incurred wholly, exclusively and necessarily in the performance of the duties of the employment**;

- **capital allowances on plant and machinery necessarily provided for use in the performance of those duties. Capital allowances may currently be claimed in respect of an employee's car or bicycle used for business purposes without having to satisfy the necessarily test. From 2002/03 employees will be entitled to claim statutory authorised mileage relief (see below) in respect of a vehicle used for qualifying business travel but they will no longer be able to claim capital allowances.**

Liabilities and insurance

2.3 If a director or employee incurs a qualifying liability or pays for insurance against such a liability, the cost is a deductible expense. If the employer pays such amounts, there is no taxable benefit in kind.

2.4 A qualifying liability is one which is imposed in respect of the director's or employee's acts or omissions as director or employee. Thus, for example, liability for negligence would be covered. Related costs, for example the costs of legal proceedings, are included.

Payments after employment ceases

2.5 The deduction is normally made from the emoluments of the directorship or employment. It cannot be made from other income, except as follows.

2.6 Payments made after the directorship or employment ceases, but which would have been deductible if it had continued, are deductible in computing statutory total income (STI) for the year in which the payments are made.

2.7 Payments are only deductible if they are made in the last tax year of the directorship or employment or in the following six tax years.

2.8 Amounts taken out of retirement or other post-employment benefits are deductible (so that only the remaining payments to the employee are taxable). Payments borne by the ex-employer are not deductible, but they are not taxable on the ex-director or employee.

2.9 If the amount deductible in a tax year exceeds total income, the excess cannot be carried back or forward to any other year. However, the employee can claim to set the excess against his chargeable gains for the year.

Travelling expenses

2.10 **Tax relief is not available for an employee's normal commuting costs**. This means relief is not available for any costs an employee incurs in getting from home to his normal place of work. However **employees are entitled to relief for 'qualifying travelling expenses' which basically are the full costs that they are obliged to incur in travelling in the performance of their duties or travelling to or from a place which they have to attend in the performance of their duties (other than the normal place of work).**

2.11 EXAMPLE: TRAVEL IN THE PERFORMANCE OF DUTIES

Judi is an accountant. She often travels to meetings at the firm's offices in the North of England returning to her office in Leeds after the meetings. Relief is available for the full cost of these journeys as the travel is undertaken in the performance of her duties.

Question: Relief for travelling costs

Zoe lives in Wycombe and normally works in Chiswick. Occasionally she visits a client in Wimbledon and travels direct from home. Distances are shown in the diagram below:

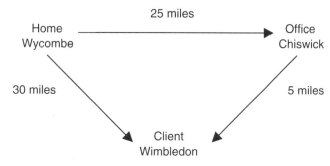

What tax relief is available for Zoe's travel costs?

Answer

Zoe is not entitled to tax relief for the costs incurred in travelling between Wycombe and Chiswick since these are normal commuting costs. However, relief is available for all costs that Zoe incurs when she travels from Wycombe to Wimbledon to visit her client.

2.12 To prevent manipulation of the basic rule normal commuting will not become a business journey just because the employee stops en-route to perform a business task (eg make a 'phone call'). Nor will relief be available if the journey is essentially the same as the employee's normal journey to work.

2.13 EXAMPLE: NORMAL COMMUTING

Judi is based at her office in Leeds City Centre. One day she is required to attend a 9.00 am meeting with a client whose premises are around the corner from her Leeds office. Judi travels from home directly to the meeting. As the journey is substantially the same as her ordinary journey to work relief is not available.

2.14 Site based employees (eg construction workers, management consultants etc) who do not have a permanent work place, are entitled to relief for the costs of all journeys made from home to wherever they are working. This is because these employees do not have an ordinary commuting journey or any normal commuting costs. However there is a caveat that the employee does not spend more than 24 months of continuous work at any one site.

2.15 Tax relief is available for travel, accommodation and subsistence expenses incurred by an employee who is working at a temporary location on a secondment expected to last up to 24 months. If a secondment is initially expected not to exceed 24 months, but it is extended, relief ceases to be due from the date the employee becomes aware of the change. When looking at how long a secondment is expected to last, the Revenue will consider not only the terms of the written contract but also any verbal agreement by the employer and other factors such as whether the employee buys a house etc.

Question: Temporary workplace

Philip works for Vastbank at its Newcastle City Centre branch. Philip is sent to work full-time at another branch in Morpeth for 20 months at the end of which he will return to the Newcastle branch. Morpeth is about 20 miles north of Newcastle.

What travel costs is Philip entitled to claim as a deduction?

Answer

Although Philip is spending all of his time at the Morpeth branch it will not be treated as his normal work place because his period of attendance will be less than 24 months. Thus Philip can claim relief in full for the costs of travel from his home to the Morpeth branch.

Other expenses

2.16 **The word 'exclusively' strictly implies that the expenditure must give no private benefit at all. If it does, none of it is deductible. In practice inspectors may ignore a small element of private benefit or make an apportionment between business and private use.**

2.17 **Whether an expense is 'necessary' is not determined by what the employer requires. The test is whether the duties of the employment could not be performed without the outlay.**

- *Sanderson v Durbridge 1955*

  The cost of evening meals taken when attending late meetings was not deductible because it was not incurred in the performance of the duties.

- *Nolder v Walters 1930*

  An airline pilot was liable to be called for duty at any time. He claimed a deduction for:

  (i)   travel to the airport;
  (ii)   telephone costs;
  (iii)   subsistence in excess of his employer's allowance.

  Held: (i) and (ii) were not deductible because they were not necessarily incurred in the performance of the duties. (iii) was deductible.

- *Blackwell v Mills 1945*

  As a condition of his employment, an employee was required to attend evening classes. The cost of his textbooks and travel was not deductible because it was not incurred in the performance of the duties.

- *Lupton v Potts 1969*

  Examination fees incurred by a solicitor's articled clerk were not deductible because they were incurred neither wholly nor exclusively in the performance of the duties, but in furthering the clerk's ambition to become a solicitor.

- *Brown v Bullock 1961*

  The expense of joining a club that was virtually a requisite of an employment was not deductible because it would have been possible to carry on the employment without the club membership, so the expense was not necessary.

- *Elwood v Utitz 1965*

  A managing director's subscriptions to two residential London clubs were claimed by him as an expense on the grounds that they were cheaper than hotels.

  The expenditure was deductible as it was necessary in that it would be impossible for the employee to carry out his London duties without being provided with first class accommodation. The residential facilities (which were cheaper than hotel accommodation) were given to club members only.

2.18 The cost of business telephone calls on a private telephone is deductible, but **no part of the line or telephone rental charges is deductible** (*Lucas v Cattell 1972*).

2.19 **The cost of clothes for work is not deductible,** except that for certain trades requiring protective clothing there are annual deductions on a set scale.

2.20 Journalists cannot claim a deduction for the cost of buying newspapers which they read to keep themselves informed, since they are merely preparing themselves to perform their duties (*Fitzpatrick v IRC 1994; Smith v Abbott 1994*).

2.21 **An employee required to work at home may be able to claim a deduction for an appropriate proportion of his or her expenditure on lighting, heating and** (if a room is used exclusively for work purposes) **the council tax.**

3 OCCUPATIONAL PENSION SCHEMES

> **KEY TERM**
>
> Employers may set up an **occupational pension scheme**. Such schemes may either require contributions from employees or be non-contributory. The employer may use the services of an insurance company (an insured scheme) or may set up a totally self administered pension fund.

3.1 There are two kinds of occupational pension scheme - earnings-related (**final salary schemes**) and investment-related (**money purchase schemes**).

> **KEY TERM**
>
> In a **final salary scheme** - also known as a **defined benefits scheme** - the pension is generally based on employees' earnings at retirement and linked to the number of years they have worked for the firm.

3.2 For example, the basis might be a pension of 1/80th of earnings at retirement multiplied by the number of years they have been with the firm. If, therefore, earnings at retirement are £16,000 a year and they have worked for the firm for 20 years, the pension will be:

$$£16,000 \times 1/80\text{th} \times 20 \text{ years} = £4,000 \text{ per annum.}$$

The advantage of this type of pension is that it gives a **guarantee** of a pension linked to earnings at retirement.

> **KEY TERM**
>
> In a **money purchase pension** - also known as a **defined contribution scheme** - there is no guarantee regarding the level of pension which will be available. Whilst an individual is earning, contributions are paid to a fund. The total fund is built up by the contributions and the returns on the investment of the contributions. At retirement the fund is used to buy an annuity, which is then payable as a pension for the remainder of the individual's life.

Maximum benefits available under an occupational pension scheme

Retirement benefits

3.3 On retirement an individual can take a **tax free lump sum** and a retirement pension from an occupational pension scheme. The retirement pension is taxable under Schedule E.

3.4 There is a limit on the retirement pension of **two-thirds of an employee's remuneration at retirement**. Thus, in the case of our office manager, if her final salary is £16,000 pa she will be allowed to have a **maximum pension** of two-thirds of £16,000, ie £10,667.

3.5 There is a limit on the tax free lump sum of **1½ times an employee's earnings at retirement**. For our office manager the maximum tax free lump sum is £16,000 × 1½ = £24,000.

3.6 Maximum benefits can be provided subject to completion of **20 years service**. In the case of the office manager, if her employment begins at the age of 40 and she retires at the age of 60 she will achieve this qualifying period. Benefits are reduced below the maximum if an employee has less than 20 years service.

3.7 There is a limit on the amount of earnings on which a pension and the tax free lump sum can be based. This limit - known as **the earnings cap** - is £95,400 for the tax year 2001/02.

The maximum benefits for 2001/2002 are therefore as follows.
Lump sum   1.5 × £95,400   = £143,100
Pension   2/3 × £95,400   = £63,600

Death in service

3.8 A tax free lump sum may be payable on the occurrence of a death in service. The **maximum lump sum** is **four times an employee's remuneration at that time** or £5,000 if greater. If the employee has contributed to the scheme then the employee's contributions may be added to this lump sum together with interest on them. In addition, dependants may become entitled to a pension.

Contributions limits

3.9 Employees' contributions to an occupational pension scheme are limited to **15% of their earnings**. These earnings are subject to the earnings cap of £95,400 (2001/02). In the case of a final salary scheme, there is no specific limit on the **employer's** contributions. However the contributions must not be so great that they are likely to produce benefits in excess of the maximum limits.

Tax relief

3.10 Provided a scheme is an exempt 'approved' scheme, **employer contributions are a deductible expense for the employer** but they **are not a benefit in kind for an employee**. Consequently, amking pension contributions is a tax efficient method of rewarding employees. **Any employee contributions can be deducted from Schedule E income.**

Additional voluntary contributions (AVCs)

3.11 An employee may be entitled, under an occupational pension scheme, to benefits which are **less than the maximum allowed by the Inland Revenue**. In this case, an employee may make **additional voluntary contributions** (AVCs) (in **addition** to any compulsory contributions) in order to improve the his pension position.

3.12 There are three ways of maturing AVCs:

(a) Via the employer by in-house AVCs. Employers must provide AVC schemes if employees wish to contribute voluntarily.

(b) Independently by FSAVCs (free standing AVCs). An employee can arrange to pay voluntary contributions to a provider quite independently of the employer.

(c) From 6 April 2001, certain individuals who are members of an occupational pension scheme may also contribute to a **personal pension scheme under the concurrent membership rules**. Such individuals are broadly those **earning £30,000 or less who are not controlling directors of the employing company**. The limit on contributions is **£3,600 for 2001/02.** This is in addition to any AVCs or FSAVCs that the individual may be paying. Personal pensions are discussed below.

3.13 An employee may contribute to **both** an in house **and** an FSAVC scheme. However, **the limit on the benefits does not change.** The benefits from the main scheme, plus those from an in house AVC scheme plus those from an FSAVC scheme, must not exceed in **total** the limits set by the Revenue. In addition the total employee contributions to the schemes must not exceed 15% of earnings (limited to the earning cap).

4 PERSONAL PENSION SCHEMES

4.1 The rules relating to personal pensions were substantially revised with effect from 6 April 2001. This section deals with the rules for personal pensions in existence before and after 6 April 2001 and also the new 'stakeholder' pensions available from 6 April 2001.

> **KEY TERM**
>
> **Personal pensions** are money purchase schemes.

Eligibility

4.2 **An individual who is below the age of** 75 may contribute to a personal pension scheme in a tax year if he satisfies one of the following conditions:

(a) he has **no actual net relevant earnings** (see below) in the year and is not in an occupational pension scheme, but is **resident and ordinarily resident in the UK at some time in the tax year** (see below). An individual may also continue contributing to pension arrangements made whilst he was resident and ordinarily resident in the UK for up to five tax years after he ceases to satisfy the residency condition, or

(b) **he is in an occupational pension scheme** and is entitled to join a personal pension scheme under '**concurrent membership**' (see below), or

(c) he has **actual net relevant earnings** in the year.

4.3 **It is possible for a personal pension scheme to accept payments from a person other than the scheme member where that member satisfies condition (a).** Thus a parent may make contributions for his child (even under the age of 18) or a working spouse could contribute on behalf of a housewife/husband. **If a scheme member is employed (ie falls**

under condition (b) or (c)), his employer may make contributions to the personal pension scheme.

4.4 **Concurrent membership** (ie. membership of both an occupational scheme and a personal pension scheme) is available to an individual who satisfies the following conditions:

(a) **the individual is not a controlling director** of a company at any time in the tax year or in any tax year in the last five tax years (counting from 2000/01 onwards only), and

(b) **in at least one out of the last five tax years (counting from 2000/01 onwards only) his earnings were below the remuneration limit.** This is set as £30,000 for 2001/02.

(c) he is resident and ordinarily resident in the UK at sometime in the tax year (or was so resident and ordinarily resident at the time the arrangements were made and at some time in the last five tax ears).

A 'controlling director' is broadly an individual who owns or controls (by himself or with his family or business associates) more than 20% of the company which employs him.

Limits

Time of retirement

4.5 **Normal Retirement Age** can be at any time between 50 and 75. Early retirement can normally take place before age 50 on the grounds of serious ill health. Some occupations are allowed to have normal retirement ages earlier than 50.

Benefits

4.6 There are **no limits** on the **amount of the pension**. At retirement the fund can be used to buy the highest annuity available at the time.

4.7 It is also possible to take a **tax-free cash lump sum** on retirement. There is **no restriction** on the **amount** of tax-free cash but it is limited to 25% of the size of the fund at the time. The individual effectively takes a reduced pension in order to obtain tax free cash because only the balance (75%) of the fund remains for an annuity purchase (ie buying a pension).

Contributions

4.8 **There is a restriction placed on contributions.**

4.9 For individuals within 4.2(a) and (b) above (ie those with no net relevant earnings or with concurrent membership), **annual contributions (by the scheme member and anyone else, eg employer, parent) to the personal pension scheme cannot in total exceed the contributions threshold.** The contributions threshold is £3,600 for 2001/02. £3,600 is the gross amount – payments are actually paid net of basic rate tax (see below).

4.10 For individuals within 4.2(c) (those with net relevant earnings), gross **annual contributions (by the scheme member and anyone else, eg employer) to the personal pension scheme cannot in total exceed the greater of:**

(a) the **contributions threshold,** and
(b) the **relevant percentage of net relevant earnings** of the **basis year** (see further below).

Net relevant earnings in a tax year cannot exceed the earnings cap (£95,400 for 2001/02).

4.11 Net relevant earnings (NRE) is calculated thus.

	£	£
Earnings from self employment		X
Schedule E emoluments not providing occupational pension scheme rights		X
Schedule A income from furnished holiday lettings		X
		X
Less: the excess of trade charges over other income	X	
loss relief*	X	
Schedule E deductions	X	
		(X)
Net relevant earnings		X

* If, in any tax year for which an individual claims relief for a premium payment, a deduction for loss relief is made from income *other* than relevant earnings but that loss relates to activities any income from which *would* be relevant earnings, then the individual's NRE for the *next* tax year are treated as reduced by the loss. Any balance is carried forward to the third year and so on.

4.12 Non-trading charges are not deducted in arriving at NRE even if there is insufficient other income to deduct them from.

4.13 **In any tax year in which he has actual NRE, an individual may choose a basis year for his deemed NRE on which contributions are based.** This can be the **current tax year or one of the previous five tax years**. Therefore, for 2001/02 the basis year may be any year from 1996/97 to 2001/02. If a basis year is not chosen, only contributions up to the contributions threshold can be made.

4.14 The basis year need not be a tax year in which the individual was a member of the personal pension scheme. Evidence of NRE in the basis year (eg. P60 for employees) must be given to the scheme provider by the individual.

4.15 Once a basis year is chosen, NRE are presumed to be the same in that year and the next five tax years. Therefore, if 2001/02 is chosen as the basis year NRE will be deemed to be the same for 2001/02 to 2006/07 and no further evidence of earnings need be given. It is, however possible to choose a new basis year with higher earnings within this time frame in order to make increased contributions.

4.16 Having determined the basis year, the next stage is to determine the relevant percentage for the tax year of the contribution. The maximum gross contributions are:

Age at start *of tax year of contribution*	*% of NRE of the basis year*
Up to 35	17.5
36 - 45	20
46 - 50	25
51 - 55	30
56 - 60	35
61 - 74	40

Question: Basis years and relevant percentages

An individual (born 13 January 1956) first has net relevant earnings for 2001/02 and wishes to make maximum personal pension contributions in that year and all following years. He expects to have the following net relevant earnings:

2001/02	£30,000
2002/03	£25,000
2003/04	£20,000
2004/05	£28,000
2005/06	£27,500
2006/07	£24,000
2007/08	£20,000
2008/09	£34,000

Show the maximum amount of pension contributions he can pay for 2001/02 up to 2008/09, assuming the rules in 2001/02 stay the same in later years.

Answer

Tax year	Age at start of yr	% of NRE	Basis year	Maximum contribution
2001/02	45	20	2001/02(N1)	£30,000 × 20% = £6,000
2002/03	46	25(N2)	2001/02	£30,000 × 25% = £7,500
2003/04	47	25	2001/02	£30,000 × 25% = £7,500
2004/05	48	25	2001/02	£30,000 × 25% = £7,500
2005/06	49	25	2001/02	£30,000 × 25% = £7,500
2006/07	50	25	2001/02	£30,000 × 25% = £7,500
2007/08	51	30	2004/05(N3)	£28,000 × 30% = £8,400
2008/09	52	30	2008/09(N4)	£34,000 × 30% = £10,200

Notes

1. The basis year for 2001/02 will apply for 2001/02 to 2006/07 (maximum).

2. The relevant percentage is determined by the age of the individual at the start of the *contribution* year. The basis year used is irrelevant.

3. In 2007/08, any year from 2002/03 to 2007/08 inclusive can be chosen as the basis year. 2004/05 has been chosen as it gives the highest NRE. This does not affect the contributions made in 2004/05 to 2006/7 because the basis year for those years (2001/02) has higher NRE.

4. In 2008/09, any year from 2003/04 to 2008/09 inclusive can be chosen as the basis year. 2008/09 has been chosen as it gives the highest NRE.

4.17 If an individual ceases to have NRE, contributions can be made above the contributions threshold in the five tax years following the cessation.

The first year in which the individual has no NRE is known as '**the break year**'. The year in which NRE cease is known as the '**cessation year**'. The cessation year and the five previous years are known as the '**reference years**'.

4.18 An individual may continue to make contributions based on NRE in the five tax years following the cessation year or, if earlier, until he has NRE again or becomes a member of an occupational pension scheme.

4.19 In determining the basis year for such contributions, **the individual may nominate any one of the reference years to be the basis year.**

Question: Cessation

Sharon (born 7 March 1970) gives up work on 7 August 2001, prior to the birth of her first child. She intends to take a career break to stay at home with her small child(ren). Her NRE is:

1996/97	£40,000
1997/98	£38,000
1998/99	£35,000
1999/00	£37,000
2000/01	£30,000
2001/02	£10,000

What are the maximum contributions that Sharon may make for 2001/02 to 2007/08 inclusive? What would be the effect if Sharon returned to work in January 2004 and earns £8,000 in the tax year to 5 April 2004?

Assume the rules for 2001/02 also apply in later years.

Answer

Tax year	Age at start of yr	% of NRE	Basis year	Maximum contribution
2001/02	31	17.5	1996/97 (N1)	£40,000 × 17.5% = £7,000
2002/03	32	17.5	1996/97 (N2)	£40,000 × 17.5% = £7,000
2003/04	33	17.5	1996/97 (N2)	£40,000 × 17.5% = £7,000
2004/05	34	17.5	1996/97 (N2)	£40,000 × 17.5% = £7,000
2005/06	35	17.5	1996/97 (N2)	£40,000 × 17.5% = £7,000
2006/07	36	20	1996/97 (N2)	£40,000 × 20% = £8,000
2007/08	37	20	n/a (N3)	£3,600 (contributions threshold)

Notes

1. 2001/02 is the cessation year. Sharon can make 1996/97 her basis year for 2001/02 under the normal rules.

2. 2002/03 is the break year. The reference years are the preceding six tax years ie. 1996/97 to 2001/02. Therefore, Sharon can again chose 1996/97 as her basis years for post cessation contributions. These can be made for 2002/03 to 2006/07 inclusive.

3. No contributions can be made above the contributions threshold in 2007/08.

If Sharon goes back to work in 2003/04, the post cessation rules cease to apply for that year. Sharon can then chose a new basis year between 1998/99 and 2001/02 (she had no NRE in 2002/03 so this cannot be a basis year). She should choose 1999/00 to give a maximum contribution of £37,000 x 17.5% = £6,475.

4.20 Some of the premium paid can be used to secure a lump sum or an annuity for a spouse or dependants in the event of death prior to retirement age. The limit (which forms part of the overall limit) for such premiums is 10% of the total contribution (5% of NRE for schemes set up before 6 April 2001).

Carrying back premiums

4.21 It is possible in certain circumstances to treat a contribution as if it were paid in the previous tax year. This is useful to self employed people who wish to maximise contributions, but cannot determine their NRE until after the end of the tax year.

4.22 An irrevocable election must be made at or before the time the contribution is paid and the contribution must be paid by 31 January following the end of the tax year in which it is to be treated has having been paid. So, if a contribution is to be treated as paid in 2001/02 it must be paid by 31 January 2003.

4.23 It is possible to carry back a contribution paid by 31 January 2002 to 2000/01. This means that the contribution is subject to the old rules on carry forward of unused relief (see below).

Tax treatment of contributions

4.24 All contributions to a personal pension scheme are treated as amounts paid net of basic rate tax. This applies whether the member is an employee, self employed or not employed at all. The Inland Revenue then pays the basic rate tax to the pension provider. For example, if the permitted contributions were £5,000, a net payment of £3,900 could be made on which tax relief of £1,100 would be given by the Inland Revenue to the pension provider, resulting in a total payment of £5,000 into the personal pension fund.

4.25 Further tax relief is given if the scheme member is a higher rate taxpayer. The relief is given through the individual's personal tax computation. (Not examinable)

Unused relief – rules up to 2000/01

4.26 **Unused relief was the amount by which premiums paid were less than the maximum calculated as a percentage of NRE of the year. It could be carried forward for six years.** For example, in 2000/01 unused relief from 1994/95 (six years earlier) to 1999/00 could be taken into account to increase the maximum allowable premium. Any unused relief at 6 April 2001 cannot be carried forward to 2001/02 (although it is possible to carry back a contribution made up to 31 January 2002 to 2000/01).

The relief available for a particular tax year must have been used before unused relief brought forward, and relief brought forward was used on a FIFO basis.

Question: Relief for premiums paid

An individual born in 1976 who took out a PPS on 1 July 1997 has the following NRE and paid the following gross premiums.

	NRE	17½% of NRE	Gross premiums
	£	£	£
1997/98	35,000	6,125	5,800
1998/99	33,000	5,775	5,700
1999/00	38,000	6,650	6,850
2000/01	43,000	7,525	8,000

Show the relief available for premiums paid.

Answer

1997/98	£
17½% of NRE	6,125
Less premium paid	(5,800)
Unused relief	325

1998/99	£
17½% of NRE	5,775
Less premium paid	(5,700)
Unused relief	75

1999/00	£
17½% of NRE	6,650
Unused relief 1997/98	200
	6,850
Less premium paid	(6,850)
Unused relief	0

2000/01	£
17½% of NRE	7,525
Unused relief: 1997/98 (balance)	125
1998/99	75
	7,725
Less premium paid	(8,000)
Unrelieved premium (must be repaid)	275

Excess contributions

4.27 Any contributions in excess of the amount eligible for relief must be repaid to the taxpayer.

5 PAYMENTS ON THE TERMINATION OF EMPLOYMENT

5.1 **Termination payments may be entirely exempt, partly exempt or entirely chargeable.**

5.2 The following payments on the termination of employment are exempt.

- Payments on accidental death

- Payments on account of injury or disability

- Lump sum payments from approved pension schemes

- Legal costs recovered by the employee from the employer following legal action to recover compensation for loss of employment, where the costs are ordered by the court or (for out-of-court settlements) are paid directly to the employee's solicitor as part of the settlement.

5.3 **Payments to which the employee is contractually entitled are, in general, taxable in full** (*Thorn EMI Electronics Ltd v Coldicott 1999*). Payments for work done (terminal bonuses), for doing extra work during a period of notice, payments in lieu of notice where stated in the original contract, or for extending a period of notice are therefore taxable in full. A payment by one employer to induce an employee to take up employment with another employer is also taxable in full (*Shilton v Wilmshurst 1991*).

5.4 **Other payments on termination (such as compensation for loss of office and including statutory redundancy pay), which are not taxable under the normal Schedule E rules** because they are not in return for services, are nevertheless brought under the Schedule E regime by statute. Such payments **are partly exempt: the first £30,000 is exempt; any excess is taxable.**

5.5 Payments and other benefits provided in connection with termination of employment (or a change in terms of employment) are taxable in the year in which they are received.

5.6 **Employers have an obligation to report termination settlements which include benefits in kind to the Revenue by 6 July following the tax year end.** No report is required if the package consists wholly of cash. Employers must also notify the Revenue by this date of settlements which (over their lifetime) may exceed £30,000.

5.7 The Inland Revenue regard payments notionally made as compensation for loss of office but which are made on retirement or death (other than accidental death) as lump sum payments under unapproved pension schemes, and therefore taxable in full. It may be possible to obtain approval for such a deemed pension scheme so as to make the whole payment tax exempt, provided that the employee is not already a member of an approved pension scheme and the payment is within the statutory limits on lump sum payments from approved schemes (see above). If the employee is not a member of an approved scheme and the payment is no more than 1/12 of the pensions earnings cap (£95,400/12 = £7,950 for 2001/02), the payment will be tax free and approval need not be obtained. Also, payments in circumstances which amount to unfair dismissal are treated as eligible for the £30,000 exemption.

5.8 The provision of counselling for unemployment or to help an employee leaving to find new employment or self-employment is not a taxable benefit, nor is the reimbursement of the cost of such counselling taxable, provided that the employee has been in full time employment for at least two years and similar provision is made for other employees generally or other employees of the same class.

5.9 An employee may, either on leaving an employment or at some other time, accept a limitation on his future conduct or activities in return for a payment. Such payments are taxable. However, a payment accepted in full and final settlement of any claims the employee may have against the employer is not automatically taxable under this rule.

5.10 A payment to an employee as compensation for the loss of rights under a redundancy scheme has been held not to be taxable (*Mairs v Haughey 1993*). A payment to compensate for loss of rights under a share option scheme, following a management buyout of the subsidiary which the employee worked for, has also been held not to be taxable (*Wilcock v Eve 1994*).

5.11 All payments to an employee on termination in cash and in kind should be considered. Non-cash benefits are taxed by reference to their cash equivalent (using the normal rules set out in the next chapter). Thus if a company car continues to be made available to an ex-employee say for a further year after redundancy he will be taxed on the same benefit value as if he had remained in employment.

5.12 If the termination package is a partially exempt one and exceeds £30,000 then the £30,000 exempt limit is allocated to earlier benefits and payments. In any particular year the exemption is allocated to cash payments before non-cash benefits.

5.13 EXAMPLE: REDUNDANCY PACKAGE

Jonah is made redundant on 31 December 2001. He receives (not under a contractual obligation) the following redundancy package:

- cash in total of £40,000 payable as £20,000 in January 2002 and £20,000 in January 2003
- use of company car for period to 5 April 2003 (benefit in kind value per annum £5,000)

In 2001/02 Jonah receives as redundancy:

	£
Cash	20,000
Car (£5,000 × $^3/_{12}$)	1,250
	21,250

Wholly exempt (allocate £21,250 of £30,000 exemption to cash first then benefit).

In 2002/03 Jonah receives:

	£
Cash	20,000
Car	5,000
	25,000
Exemption (remaining)	(8,750)
Taxable	16,250

Thus of the cash payment £11,250 (£20,000 less £8,750) is taxable and PAYE at the basic rate should have been applied to this by Jonah's former employer (see below).

6 SHARES AND SHARE OPTIONS MADE AVAILABLE TO EMPLOYEES

Shares

6.1 **If a director or an employee is given shares, or is sold shares for less than their market value, there is a Schedule E charge on the difference between the market value and the amount (if any) which the director or employee pays for the shares.**

6.2 If, while the director or employee still has a beneficial interest in the shares, a 'chargeable event' occurs, there is a Schedule E charge on the increase in the value of the interest caused by the chargeable event.

6.3 A chargeable event is a change of rights or restrictions attaching to either the shares in question or to other shares which leads to the value of the shares in question increasing, and which takes place while the person concerned is still a director or an employee (of the company or of an associated company) or within seven years of his last ceasing to be one.

However, where the change applies to all shares of the same class there is not in general a chargeable event.

6.4 If a director or employee, having obtained shares by reason of his being a director or employee, receives any special benefit because of his owning the shares, he is taxable under Schedule E on the benefit unless:

(a) The benefit is available to at least 90% of persons holding shares of the same class, and

(b) (i) The majority of the shares of the same class are not held by directors or employees, or

(ii) The company is employee-controlled by virtue of holdings of the same class of shares.

6.5 If an employee or director receives shares which may later be forfeited, there is no income tax charge when the shares are acquired. There is an income tax charge when the risk of forfeiture is lifted or when the shares are sold, if sooner. The Schedule E amount will be the difference between the market value of the shares less the cost of the shares.

6.6 If shares received as a result of employment are subsequently converted to shares of another class, there is an income tax charge on conversion on the difference between the market value and cost of the shares.

6.7 In the above situations when the base cost of the shares is being calculated for capital gains purposes any amount charged to income tax is added to the acquisition cost of the shares.

Share options

6.8 **If a director or an employee is granted an option to acquire shares, then when he exercises it there is a Schedule E charge on the market value of the shares minus the sum of what he paid for the option and what he paid for the shares.** If he assigns or releases the option for money, or agrees (for money) not to exercise it or to grant someone else a right to acquire the shares, he is likewise taxable on the amount he gets minus the amount he paid for the option.

6.9 **If an option could be exercised more than ten years after its grant, then there is also a Schedule E charge at the time of grant,** on the market value at that time of the shares which could be acquired minus the sum of what the director or employee pays for the option and what he would have to pay for the shares (taking the lowest price at which he could acquire the shares if the price can vary). Thus there will be no income tax charge on the grant of a share option if that option cannot be exercised later than ten years after the grant.

Any tax paid under this rule is deducted from the tax due on any later Schedule E charge in relation to the same option.

6.10 National insurance contributions (NICs – see later in this Text) are payable by both an employee and employer when gains are realised on the exercise of an unapproved share option and where the shares are readily convertible into cash. The employer and employee may agree that the employee should bear the employer 's NICs, as well as his own. In this case the amount of employer NIC paid by the employee can be deducted from the taxable gain arising on the exercise of the option.

Special schemes

6.11 Successive governments have recognised the need to encourage schemes that broaden share ownership among employees or reward personnel. A number of tax efficient schemes exist.

Profit sharing schemes

6.12 This type of scheme was designed to enable employees to obtain shares in their company with no income tax payable on the receipt of the shares. The scheme is being replaced by the all employee share scheme (see below). Since 6 April 2001 no new applications for approval of schemes have been allowed and from 6 April 2002 no further tax free awards will be allowed under existing schemes.

6.13 **The scheme must be set up in the form of a trust administered by trustees. Payments by the company to the trustees will be deductible for corporation tax purposes** until 5 April 2002 provided the trustees use the contribution to acquire shares and those shares are awarded to employees within 9 months of the end of the accounting period in which the contribution is made, or by 5 April 2002, if earlier.

6.14 **The shares falling under the scheme are immediately allocated to employees but must then be held by the trustees for at least two years** or until the employee reaches an age specified in the scheme (which must be between 60 and 75). Once this initial period of retention is up, employees are free to dispose of shares allocated to them.

6.15 **Provided that the individual does not ask the trustees to sell his shares until at least three years after they were allocated to him, no charge to income tax arises.** If they are sold within that period, however, there is a charge to income tax on the lower of:

(a) The shares' market value when appropriated to the employee

(b) The sale proceeds

6.16 However, if the employee has reached the age specified in the scheme mentioned in Paragraph 6.14 above, or has ceased to be a director or employee, the charge is only on half of the market value or proceeds.

6.17 Despite the fact that the legal owners of the shares are the scheme trustees, beneficial ownership passes to the employee once shares have been appropriated to him. Consequently, any dividends are taxable on the employee in the normal way.

6.18 The normal capital gains tax rules apply to all disposals of scheme shares no matter when they take place. A disposal within three years normally gives rise to both an income tax and a capital gains tax charge. A disposal outside the three year limit will give rise only to capital gains tax. No deduction is allowed for any amount charged to income tax, but the allowable cost for capital gains tax purposes is the market value of the shares when they were allocated to the employee.

Conditions for profit sharing schemes

6.19 The total of the initial market values of the shares allocated to any participant in a tax year must not exceed £3,000 or, if greater, 10% of an employee's salary, up to a maximum of £8,000. Salary is defined as emoluments subject to PAYE, excluding benefits in kind.

6.20 All employees and full-time directors must be eligible for the scheme. The company can, however, impose a minimum period of employment before an individual becomes eligible but this must not exceed five years. Individuals must remain eligible for 18 months after employment ceases.

6.21 Anyone who has within the preceding 12 months held over 25% of the shares of a close company which is the company whose shares may be acquired under the scheme, or which controls that company either alone or as part of a consortium, must be excluded from the scheme. A close company is (broadly) a company controlled by five or fewer shareholders or by shareholder-directors.

6.22 All employees must participate on similar terms. The scheme can, however, allocate shares unequally depending, for example, on length of service or on salary.

The costs of setting up profit sharing schemes

6.23 Where a company incurs expenditure in setting up a profit sharing scheme and no shares are allocated before the Revenue approve the scheme, the costs are deductible in computing trading profits. If, however, the scheme is approved more than nine months after the end of the period of account in which the expenditure is incurred, it is treated as incurred in the period of account in which approval is given.

Employee share ownership trusts (ESOTs)

Exam focus point
ESOTs may also be called employee share ownership plans (ESOPs).

6.24 **Under ESOTs shares may be distributed to employees through a specially established trust. This scheme is similar to the profit sharing scheme** outlined above but is wider in scope and does not have a restriction on the value of shares that may be distributed. Shares must be distributed to employees within a maximum of 20 years of their acquisition by the trust. Broadly, all employees (except part-time directors, who must be excluded) must be eligible on similar terms.

6.25 The trust established by the ESOT can receive funds to buy shares from a number of sources, principally from the company establishing the ESOT (the founding company), from subsidiaries of the founding company and by borrowing.

The shares can be transferred to employees exercising options under savings-related share option schemes (see below). The shares can also be transferred by the trustees to an all employee share plan (see below) without a chargeable event occurring.

Savings-related schemes

6.26 **An employer can set up a scheme, under which employees can choose to make regular monthly investments in special bank or building society accounts called sharesave accounts. Employees can save a fixed monthly amount of between £5 and £250. The investments are made for three or five years, and a tax-free bonus is then added to the account by way of interest.** The employee may either withdraw the money or leave it for another two years. If he leaves it in the account, another tax-free bonus is added.

6.27 **At the withdrawal date, the employee may take the money in cash. Alternatively, he may use it to buy ordinary shares in his employer company or its holding company. The price of these shares is fixed when the employee starts to save in the account, by granting the employee options to buy shares.** The option price must be at least 80% of the market value at the date the options are granted.

6.28 **The only tax charge is to capital gains tax, on the gain on the shares when they are finally sold.** This gain is computed as if the employee bought the shares for the price he actually paid for them.

6.29 A scheme must be open to all employees and full-time directors, and on similar terms. Part-time directors may be included, but can be excluded. However, a minimum qualifying period of employment (of up to five years) may be imposed, and there may be differences based on remuneration or length of service.

6.30 Anyone who has within the preceding 12 months held over 25% of the shares of a close company which is the company whose shares may be acquired under the scheme, or which controls that company either alone or as part of a consortium, must be excluded from the scheme.

Company share option plans (CSOP)

6.31 **An employee can be granted options on shares under a CSOP. There is no income tax on the grant of an option, on the profit arising from the exercise of an option between three and ten years after the grant or on the disposal of the shares. Capital gains tax will, however, arise on the gain made when an employee eventually sells his shares.**

6.32 **To obtain Revenue approval schemes must satisfy** the following **conditions**.

(a) The shares must be fully paid ordinary shares.

(b) The price of the shares must not be less than their market value at the time of the grant of the option.

(c) Participation in the scheme must be limited to employees and full-time directors. Options must not be transferable. However, ex-employees and the personal representatives of deceased employees may exercise options; personal representatives must do so within one year after the death. The scheme need not be open to all employees and full-time directors.

(d) No options may be granted which take the total market value of shares for which an employee holds options above £30,000. Shares are valued as at the times when the options on them are granted.

(e) If the issuing company has more than one class of shares, the majority of shares in the class for which the scheme operates must be held other than by:

(i) Persons acquiring them through their positions as directors or employees (unless the company is an employee controlled company)

(ii) A holding company (unless the scheme shares are quoted)

(f) Anyone who has within the preceding 12 months held over 10% of the shares of a close company which is the company whose shares may be acquired under the scheme, or which controls that company either alone or as part of a consortium, must be excluded from the scheme.

6.33 The tax exemption is lost in respect of an option if it is exercised earlier than three years or later than ten years after grant, or within three years after the employee last exercised an option on which the tax exemption was obtained. However, neither of these three year waiting periods need be observed when personal representatives exercise the options of a deceased employee (but the ten year rule still applies).

6.34 Schemes may be altered so that in the event of the company concerned being taken over, employees may exchange their existing options for equivalent options over shares in the acquiring company.

6.35 The costs of setting up approved share option schemes (both savings related and company share option plans) are deductible in the same way as the costs of setting up profit sharing schemes, and with the same nine month rule (see above).

Enterprise Management Incentives (EMI)

6.36 This scheme is intended to encourage people to 'take the plunge' and leave established careers in large companies for riskier jobs in smaller, start-up or developing firms.

6.37 **A qualifying company can grant each of its employees options over shares worth up to £100,000 at the time of grant, subject to a maximum of £3m in total.**

6.38 **No income tax or national insurance is chargeable on either the grant or exercise of the options provided the exercise takes place within 10 years of the grant and the exercise price is the market value of the shares at the date of the grant.** If options are granted at a discount, the discount is taxed at the date of exercise as normal.

6.39   An employing company may set a target to be achieved before an option can be exercised. The target must clearly be defined at the time the option is granted.

6.40   **When the shares are sold, the gain is subject to CGT.**

Qualifying company

6.41   The company, which can be quoted or unquoted, must meet certain conditions when the options are granted. In particular, **the company's gross assets must not exceed £15m. The company must not be under the control of any other company.**

6.42   The company must carry out one of a number of qualifying trades.

Eligible employees

6.43   **Employees must be employed by the company or group for at least 25 hours a week, or, if less, for at least 75% of their working time** (including self-employment). **Employees who own 30% or more of the ordinary shares in the company** (disregarding unexercised options shares) **are excluded. Employees who participate in EMI cannot hold options under a CSOP although they can participate in savings related schemes.**

Qualifying shares

6.44   The share must be **fully paid up irredeemable ordinary shares.** The rules permit restrictions on sale, forfeiture conditions and performance conditions.

Limit

6.45   At any one time, an employee may hold EMI options over shares with a value of up to £100,000 at the date of grant. Restrictions and conditions attaching to the shares may not be taken into account when valuing shares. Where options are granted above the £100,000 limit, relief is given on options up to the limit. Once the employee has reached the limit, no more EMI options may be granted for 3 years.

Disqualifying events

6.46   There are a number of disqualifying events including an employee ceasing to spend at least 75% of his working time with the company. EMI relief is available to the date of an event.

Relief for costs

6.47   The costs of setting up a scheme and on-going administration are deductible in computing profits.

Approval

6.48   It is not necessary to submit schemes to the Revenue for approval. Instead, the Revenue must be notified of the grant of options within 92 days. The Revenue then has 12 months to check whether the grants satisfy the EMI rules.

6.49   A company may submit details in writing to the Small Company Enterprise Centre before the options are granted. The Inspector will then confirm in writing whether he is satisfied that the company will be a qualifying company on the basis of information supplied.

Advance approval is not possible in respect of any other aspect of EMI such as whether an employee is an eligible employee.

All-employee share ownership plans (AESOPs)

6.50   **Employers can give up to £3,000 of 'free shares' a year to employees with no tax or NICs.**

6.51   Employees can buy **'partnership shares' with their pre-tax salary up to:**

(a)   Maximum of 10% of gross earnings, subject to an upper limit of £1,500 per tax year

(b)   Maximum monthly contributions of £125

(c)   Any minimum monthly contributions as specified in the plan but this minimum cannot be more than £10

Purchases do not affect pension contribution limits. **Employers can give up to 2 free 'matching shares' for each partnership share purchased.** The matching shares, up to a maximum of £3,000 are in addition to the £3,000 of free shares and must be provided on the same basis for all employees.

6.52   Employers offering free shares must offer a minimum amount to each employee on 'similar terms'. Between the minimum and the maximum of £3,000, the employer can offer shares in different amounts and on different bases to different employees. This means that employers can reward either individual or team performance. Employers can set performance targets subject to the overriding requirement that a plan must not contain any features that concentrate rewards on directors and more highly paid employees.

6.53   **Free and matching shares must normally be held in a plan for at least three years. If shares are withdrawn within three years** (because the employee leaves) **there is a charge to income tax and NIC on the market value of the shares at the time of withdrawal. If shares are taken out of the plan after three years but before five years, there is charge to income tax and NIC based on the lower of the initial value of the shares** - and their value at the date of withdrawal so any increase in value is free of income tax and NIC. If one of the specified reasons applies eg redundancy or retirement, there is no tax or NIC charge. **Once the shares have been held for five years there is no income tax or NIC.**

6.54   **Partnership shares can be taken out at any time. If the shares are held for less than three years, there is a charge to income tax and NIC on the market value at the time the shares are removed. If the share are removed after three years but before five years, the charge to income tax and NIC is based on the lesser of salary used to buy the shares and the market value at the date of removal. Once the shares have been held for five years there is no income tax or NICs.**

6.55   **Dividends of up to £1,500 on shares in the plan are tax-free provided the dividends are used to acquire additional shares in the company, which are then held in the plan for three years. These 'dividend' shares do not affect entitlement to partnership or matching shares.**

6.56   A plan may provide for free and matching shares to be forfeited if the employee leaves within three years, unless the employee leaves for specified reasons such as retirement or redundancy. All shares have to come out of a plan if an employee leaves his job.

6.57 Provided they were held in the plan for at least 3 years, there is no charge to CGT on shares taken out of a plan and sold immediately. A charge to CGT will arise on sale to the extent that the shares increase in value after they are withdrawn from the plan.

6.58 The plan must be operated through a UK resident trust. The trustees acquire the shares from the company or – if the plan incorporates partnership shares – from the employees. The existence of arrangements to enable employees to sell shares held in a new plan trust will not of itself make those shares readily convertible into cash and require employers, for example, to operate national insurance. There is also a form of 'roll over' relief for individuals who dispose of shares to the trustees - this is discussed later in the text.

6.59 Stamp duty is not payable when an employee purchases shares from an AESOP trust. The trust must pay stamp duty when it acquires the shares. No taxable benefit arises on an employee as a result of an AESOP trust or an employer paying either stamp duty or the incidental costs of operating the plan.

6.60 A deduction in computing profits is given for:

- The costs of setting up and administering the plan.

- The gross salary allocated by employees to buy partnership shares.

- The costs of providing shares to the extent that the costs exceed the employees contributions.

- The market value of free and matching shares when they are acquired by the trustees.

- Interest paid by the trustees on borrowing to acquire shares where the company meets the trustees' costs.

6.61 Shares used in the plan must be fully paid up irredeemable ordinary shares in a company either:

(a) Listed on a recognised stock exchange (or in its subsidiary), or
(b) Not controlled by another company.

6.62 A plan established by a company that controls other companies, may be extended to any or all of these other companies. Such a plan is called a group plan.

6.63 A plan need not include all the components – it is possible to have a plan with only free shares.

6.64 Companies must offer all full and part-time employees the opportunity to participate in the plan. A minimum qualifying period of employment may be specified, but not more than 18 months. If a minimum period is specified it can be satisfied by working for any company within a group.

7   OVERSEAS ASPECTS

Residence, ordinary residence and domicile

7.1 A taxpayer's **residence, ordinary residence** and **domicile** have important consequences in establishing the treatment of employment income.

7.2 An individual is resident in the UK for a given tax year if, in that tax year, he satisfies either of the following criteria.

(a) **He is present in the UK for 183 days or more** (days of arrival and departure are excluded).

(b) **He makes substantial annual visits to the UK.** Visits averaging 91 days or more a year for each of four or more consecutive years will make the person resident for each of these tax years (for someone emigrating from the UK, the four years are reduced to three).

If days are spent in the UK because of exceptional circumstances beyond the individual's control (such as illness), those days are ignored for the purposes of the 91 day rule (but not for the 183 day rule above).

7.3 **A person who is resident in the UK will be ordinarily resident where his residence is of a habitual nature.** Ordinary residence implies a greater degree of permanence than residence. A person who is ordinarily resident in the UK and who goes abroad for a period which does not include a complete tax year, is regarded as remaining resident and ordinarily resident throughout.

7.4 Strictly, each tax year must be looked at as a whole. A person is resident and/or ordinarily resident either for no part of, or for all of, the tax year. It is the practice for income tax purposes by concession, however, to split the tax year if the person:

(a) is a new permanent resident or comes to stay in the UK for at least two years, provided he has not been ordinarily resident;

(b) has left the UK for permanent residence abroad provided that he becomes not ordinarily resident in the UK; or

(c) is going abroad to take up employment for at least a whole tax year (see below).

7.5 A spouse's residence and ordinary residence is not governed by the other spouse's status but is determined independently.

Domicile

7.6 A person is domiciled in the country in which he has his permanent home. Domicile is distinct from nationality or residence. A person may be resident in more than one country, but he can be domiciled in only one country at a time. **A person acquires a domicile of origin at birth**; this is normally the domicile of his father (or that of his mother if his father died before he was born or his parents were unmarried at his birth) and therefore not necessarily the country where he was born. **A person retains this domicile until he acquires a different domicile of dependency (if, while he is under 16, his father's domicile changes) or domicile of choice. A domicile of choice can be acquired only by individuals aged 16 or over.**

7.7 **To acquire a domicile of choice a person must sever his ties with the country of his former domicile and settle in another country with the clear intention of making his permanent home there.** Long residence in another country is not in itself enough to prove that a person has acquired a domicile of choice: there has to be evidence that he firmly intends to live there permanently.

The cases of Schedule E

7.8 **Schedule E is divided into three Cases. The Case under which a taxpayer is taxed depends on the taxpayer's residence status and the place where he performs his duties.**

BPP PUBLISHING

Status	*Duties wholly or partly in the UK*		*Duties wholly outside the UK*
	Emoluments for UK duties	*Emoluments for non-UK duties*	
Resident and ordinarily resident	I	I	I★
Resident but not ordinarily resident	II	III	III
Not resident	II	Not taxable	Not taxable

★ Case III for foreign emoluments. These are emoluments earned by a non-domiciled individual employed by a non-resident employer.

7.9 **If a taxpayer is taxable under Schedule E Cases I or II, then he will be taxed on all emoluments received during the tax year (wherever they are received). If, on the other hand, he is taxable under Case III, he will be taxed only on amounts actually remitted to the UK from abroad.**

7.10 If an employee is either non-resident or not ordinarily resident, and some of his duties are performed abroad, not all of his pay will be subject to UK income tax. In such cases, PAYE (see later in this text) must be applied to the proportion of pay estimated to be liable to UK income tax. If an estimate is not agreed with the Revenue, PAYE must be applied to all pay.

Is an employee works for someone in the UK but is employed and paid by someone overseas, the person in the UK for whom the work is done must operate PAYE in respect of any taxable income in the form of an asset which can be readily converted to cash.

7.11 If the person is absent for a complete tax year then he becomes non-resident for the period of the contract of employment. There will be no UK tax on the overseas income.

Travel expenses for work abroad

7.12 **If an individual who is resident and ordinarily resident in the UK has an employment the duties of which are performed wholly abroad, he may deduct the cost of certain items from his emoluments** (so long as they are not foreign emoluments). **If his employer pays for these items, the employee can obtain a deduction equal to the Schedule E benefit on the amount involved.** The items are as follows.

- **Travel** from any place in the UK to take up the overseas employment, and travel back to any place in the UK on its termination

- **Board and lodging outside the UK** provided for the purpose of enabling the employee to perform the duties of the overseas employment

When either item is provided partly for the purposes of the overseas employment and partly for other purposes, only the cost of the part attributable to the purposes of the employment is deductible.

7.13 Where an individual resident and ordinarily resident in the UK has two or more employments and the duties of at least one of them are performed wholly or partly outside the UK, and he performs the duties of one employment at one place then travels to another place to perform the duties of another employment, he may deduct the cost of the journey from the emoluments of the second employment provided that:

- at least one end of the journey is outside the UK; and
- the emoluments of the second employment are not foreign emoluments.

If the journey is made partly to perform the duties of the second employment and partly for other purposes, only part of the cost is deductible.

7.14 If the duties of an employment are performed partly outside the UK, and the employer either pays or reimburses to the employee the cost of a journey from any place in the UK to the place of performance of the duties outside the UK, or back from there to any place in the UK, the employee can obtain a deduction equal to the Schedule E benefit on the amount involved provided that:

- the duties in question can only be performed outside the UK; and

- the journey is made wholly and exclusively for the purposes of performing those duties or of returning to the UK after performing them.

No deduction is available under this rule when the employee bears the cost of travel himself, without reimbursement by the employer (although a deduction could be obtained if the employee could show that the expense had been incurred necessarily in the performance of his duties).

7.15 Where an employee not domiciled in the UK receives emoluments for duties performed in the UK, and the employer either pays or reimburses to the employee the cost of a journey from the place (outside the UK) where he usually lives to any place in the UK in order to perform his duties, or back again after performing his duties, then the employee can obtain a deduction equal to the Schedule E benefit on the amount involved, so long as both of the following conditions are satisfied.

(a) There is a date on which the employee came to the UK to perform the duties of the employment and:

   (i) he was not resident in the UK for either of the two tax years preceding the year which includes that date; or

   (ii) he had not been in the UK at all in the 24 months immediately preceding that date.

(b) Not more than five years have passed since the date in (a).

If a journey is made partly for the purpose of performing the duties or returning home, and partly for other purposes, the part attributable to other purposes is not deductible.

Travel costs of family to join a taxpayer abroad

7.16 **When an employee works abroad and is absent from the UK for a continuous period of at least 60 days he can claim a deduction equal to the benefit in kind if his employer pays for, or reimburses the cost of, up to two return journeys per tax year for his spouse and children (aged under 18 at the start of the outward journey) to visit him.** However, no Schedule E deduction is given where the employee actually bears the cost himself without reimbursement.

7.17 The same deduction, with exactly the same rules, is available for family visits where a non-domiciled employee is in the UK for at least 60 days continuously, but the employee must satisfy the conditions set out in Paragraph 7.15(a) and (b) above.

Chapter roundup

- The Schedule E charge has a very wide scope.

- Deductions for expenses are extremely limited.

- Individuals maybe members of occupational pension schemes and/or personal pension schemes.

- There are tax concessions in relation to schemes designed to give employees a stake in their employers' profitability.

- Individuals working abroad may claim certain deductions for travelling expenses.

Quick quiz

1   On what basis are earnings taxed?

2   What are the two types of occupational pension scheme?

3   What is the maximum pension available under an occupational pension scheme?

4   What is the limit on employee contributions to an occupational pension scheme?

5   When can a member of a personal pension plan retire?

6   Which termination payments are partly exempt?

7   What is the maximum amount of EMI scheme options that an employee can hold?

8   How may 'free shares' can an employee receive under the all employee share plan without suffering income tax or NIC?

Answers to quick quiz

1   Earnings are taxed on a receipts basis.

2   Occupational pension schemes may be final salary schemes or money purchase schemes.

3   $2/3^{rd}$ of the employee's remuneration (subject to the earnings cap) at retirement.

4   15% of earnings. (Earnings are subject to the earnings cap).

5   Between the ages of 50 and 75, unless retirement is because of ill-health or some occupations.

6   The first £30,000 of genuinely ex-gratia termination payments

7   An employee may hold options over shares worth up to £100,000 at the date of grant.

8   Up to £3,000 worth

Now try the question below from the Exam Question Bank

Number	Level	Marks	Time
14	Exam	11	20 mins

Chapter 13

BENEFITS IN KIND

Topic list	Syllabus Reference	Ability required
1 Benefits in kind: all employees	(ii)	Application
2 Benefits in kind: P11D employees	(ii)	Application

Introduction

An employee's Schedule E income includes the taxable value of benefits on kind provided by his employer. In this chapter we see how to compute the taxable value of benefits in kind.

Learning outcomes covered in this chapter

- **Apply** knowledge of the benefits in kind system for employees
- **Identify** the rules for different types of employee
- **Calculate** the total assessable benefits of an employee

Syllabus content covered in this chapter

- Benefits in kind
- Returns required from employers in connection with all aspects of employee tax
- Current issues and proposals

1   BENEFITS IN KIND: ALL EMPLOYEES

1.1   **Generally, benefits in kind are taxable at the cost of providing them** (but only the marginal cost, where the benefit is also sold to non-employees). So if an employer spent £200 on a suit and gave it to an employee earning £9,000 a year, the taxable benefit would be £200.

1.2   **The above does not apply to employees who are not directors and earn less than £8,500 a year. For them benefits are taxed on their 'cash equivalent', the amount they would fetch if the employee were to dispose of them to a third party.** If, the employee above earned £7,000 a year, the benefit of the suit would be the secondhand value, which might be only £10.

1.3   **Several rules override the cost or secondhand value rule,** as follows:

Vouchers

1.4   If an employee:

    (a)   receives cash vouchers (vouchers exchangeable for cash)

    (b)   uses a credit token (such as a credit card) to obtain money, goods or services, or

(c)   receives exchangeable vouchers (such as book tokens), also called non-cash vouchers

he is taxed on the cost of providing the benefit, less any amount made good.

1.5   **The first 15p per working day of luncheon vouchers is not taxed.**

Entertainment

1.6   No benefit in kind arises on entertainment received by employees from third parties, even if it is provided by giving the employee a voucher. The exemption is intended to cover hospitality such as seats at sporting and cultural events. The exemption applies provided:

(a)   Neither the employer nor a connected person either bears the cost or procured the entertainment, and

(b)   The entertainment is not provided in recognition of services which have been or are to be performed.

The exemption also covers gifts of goods (or vouchers exchangeable for goods) if the total cost (including VAT) of all gifts by the same donor to the same employee in the tax year is £150 or less. If the £150 limit is exceeded, the full amount is taxable, not just the excess.

Long service awards

1.7   Awards for long service are in general taxable. However non-cash awards are exempt if the period of service was at least 20 years, no similar award was made to the employee in the past 10 years and the cost is not more than £20 per year of service.

Suggestion schemes

1.8   Awards to employees under suggestion schemes are in general taxable, but an extra-statutory concession exempts awards when all the following conditions are satisfied.

(a)   There is a formal scheme, open to all employees on equal terms.

(b)   The suggestion is outside the scope of the employee's normal duties.

(c)   Either the award is not more than £25, or the award is only made after a decision is taken to implement the suggestion.

(d)   Awards over £25 reflect the financial importance of the suggestion to the business, and either do not exceed 50% of the expected net financial benefit during the first year of implementation or do not exceed 10% of the expected net financial benefit over a period of up to five years.

(e)   Awards of over £25 are shared on a reasonable basis between two or more employees putting forward the same suggestion.

1.9   If an award exceeds £5,000, the excess is always taxable.

Accommodation

1.10 **The taxable value of accommodation provided to any employee or director is the rent that would have been payable if the premises had been let at their annual value** (taken to be their **rateable value,** despite the abolition of domestic rates). **If the premises are rented** rather than owned by the employer, then **the taxable benefit is the higher of the rent**

actually paid and the annual value. If property does not have a rateable value the Revenue estimate a value.

1.11 **Where the cost of any one property exceeds £75,000, an additional benefit in kind is chargeable upon the employee or director.** The additional benefit is

(Cost of providing the living accommodation - £75,000) × the official rate of interest.

Thus with an official rate of 10%, the total benefit for accommodation costing £90,000 and with an annual value of £2,000 would be £2,000 + £(90,000 − 75,000) × 10% = £3,500.

The 'cost of providing' the living accommodation is the aggregate of the cost of purchase and the cost of any improvements made before the start of the tax year for which the benefit is being computed. It is therefore not possible to avoid the charge by buying an inexpensive property requiring substantial repairs and improving it.

Where the property was acquired more than six years before first being provided to the employee, the market value when first so provided plus the cost of subsequent improvements is used as the cost of providing the living accommodation. However, unless the actual cost plus improvements up to the start of the tax year in question exceeds £75,000, the additional charge cannot be imposed, however high the market value.

> **Exam focus point**
> The 'official rate' of interest will be given to you in the exam.

1.12 **There is no taxable benefit in respect of job related accommodation.** Accommodation is job related if:

(a) Residence in the accommodation is necessary for the proper performance of the employee's duties (as with a caretaker), or

(b) The accommodation is provided for the better performance of the employee's duties and the employment is of a kind in which it is customary for accommodation to be provided (as with a policeman), or

(c) The accommodation is provided as part of arrangements in force because of a special threat to the employee's security.

Directors can only claim exemptions (a) or (b) if:

(i) They have no material interest ('material' means over 5%) in the company, and

(ii) Either they are full time working directors or the company is non-profit making or is a charity.

1.13 Any contribution paid by the employee is deducted from the annual value of the property and then from the additional benefit.

1.14 If there is some other way of taxing the benefit (for example taking the amount of salary which the employee could have had instead of the accommodation), ignore it and apply the above rules. Next tax the amount under the other way minus the amount already taxed (so we tax the higher figure).

1.15 **If an employer pays an employee's council tax, the amount paid is always a taxable benefit, unless the tax arises in connection with job-related accommodation.**

Removal expenses and benefits

1.16 **There is no taxable benefit in respect of the first £8,000** of removal expenses paid by an employer for an employee and his family. For this purpose, benefits are valued under the normal benefits rules for the employee concerned. The £8,000 exemption is in addition to any deduction which may be available under the rules for overseas travel (see the previous chapter). **Payments above the £8,000 limit are taxable**, but PAYE need not be applied to them.

1.17 This exemption applies only if:

(a) The employee does not already live within a reasonable daily travelling distance of his new place of employment, but will do so after moving.

(b) The expenses are incurred or the benefits provided by the end of the tax year following the tax year of the start of employment at the new location.

Work related benefits

1.18 **If an employer runs a workplace nursery the cost is not a taxable benefit for the employees.** However, cash or vouchers given so that employees can obtain nursery facilities, are taxable.

1.19 **Sporting or recreational facilities available to employees generally and not to the general public do not give rise to taxable benefits**, unless they are provided on domestic premises, or they consist in an interest in or the use of any mechanically propelled vehicle or any overnight accommodation. Vouchers only exchangeable for such facilities also do not give rise to taxable benefits, but membership fees for sports clubs are taxable benefits.

1.20 Subject to certain exemptions for potentially high value benefits (eg cars and living accommodation), no taxable benefit arises on assets or services used in performing the duties of employment provided any private use of the item concerned is insignificant. This exempts, for example, the benefit arising on the private use of employer-provided tools.

1.21 Welfare counselling and other similar minor benefits are exempt if the benefit concerned is available to employees generally.

Authorised mileage rates

1.22 If an employee uses his own car, pedal cycle or motor cycle on his employer's business, he will normally be paid a mileage allowance. Strictly, this **mileage allowance is subject to both tax and National Insurance contributions (NICs) (see later in this text). The employee is entitled to make a claim under s 198 ICTA 1988 to deduct any expenses incurred wholly, exclusively and necessarily in the performance of his duties.**

1.23 To facilitate the above employers must return details to tax offices of amounts paid to individual employees. Employees than have to make detailed claims for relief based on their actual expenditure. These reporting and record keeping requirements can be avoided by using **Inland Revenue Authorised Mileage Rates (AMRs)** (previously known as the fixed profit car scheme). If an employer pays amounts at or below the AMRs he may apply to his tax office for a dispensation which will relieve him of the obligation to report expense payments.

1.24 AMRs are the levels of mileage allowances that may be paid free of income tax and NICs to employees who use their own cars, pedal cycles and motorcycles for business travel. Any excess allowance received is a taxable benefit. In general, the employee cannot also make a s 198 ICTA 1988 claim in respect of any business expenses actually incurred but exceptionally, a deduction for the business proportion of any interest paid on a loan taken out to buy a car, pedal cycle of motorcycle may be claimed.

1.25 AMRs for 2001/02 are set out in the Rates and Allowances Tables in this text.

Question: Authorised mileage rates

Anita travels 9,000 business miles in her own 1800cc car during 2001/02. Her employer pays a mileage allowance of 35p per mile for cars with up to 2000cc engines. What taxable benefit arises on Anita?

Answer

	£
Mileage allowance paid (9,000 × 35p)	3,150
Authorised mileage rates tax free amount	
4,000 miles @ 45p	(1,800)
5,000 miles @ 25p	(1,250)
Taxable benefit	100

1.26 AMRs can be used as a basis for an expense claim if the employee does not receive a mileage allowance or receives less than the tax free amount. So, if Anita in the above example had received total mileage allowances of £2,000, the amount received would have been tax free and she could also have made a claim to deduct £1,050 (3,050 – 2,000).

Current issues and proposals

1.27 From 6 April 2002, a single authorised mileage rate for business journey's in an employee's own vehicle will apply to all cars and vans (irrespective of engine size). There will be no income tax on NICs on payments up to this rate. As employers will not have to report mileage allowances up to this amount, reporting dispensations will no longer be relevant.

Bicycles and motorcycles

1.28 **There is no taxable benefit in respect of bicycles or cycling safety equipment provided to enable employees to get to and from work or to travel between one workplace and another.** The equipment must be available to the employer's employees generally. Also, it must be used mainly for the aforementioned journeys.

1.29 There is **no taxable benefit in respect of workplace parking**.

Scholarship and apprenticeship schemes

1.30 If an employer allows an employee to go on a full-time course lasting at least a year, with average full-time attendance of at least 20 weeks a year, then the employer may pay the employee up to £7,000 a year tax free. However, if the £7,000 limit is exceeded, the whole amount paid is taxable income of the employee.

Work related training and Individual Learning Accounts

1.31 **No taxable benefit arises in respect of work related training or any related cost.**

1.32 Work related training is training that is likely to be useful to an employee performing his duties and training that better qualifies the employee for the employment or for any charitable or voluntary activity associated with the employment.

1.33 Similarly, **no taxable benefit arises** on:

(a) **Contributions paid directly to an individual learning account (ILA).** The ILA must be eligible for a grant or discount and contributions must be available to all employees on similar terms.

(b) **Any related costs whether paid directly or reimbursed to the employee.**

1.34 For these purposes, related costs include incidental costs incurred wholly and exclusively as a result of the employee undertaking the training (eg the cost of additional child-care), assessment or examination fees and the costs of any qualification, registration or award arising as a result of the training. Related costs also include travel and subsistence costs to the extent that such costs incurred by the employee would have been deductible if he had undertaken the training in the performance of his duties (see below).

1.35 **No taxable benefit normally arises in respect of training material, or any asset either made during training or incorporated into something so made.**

Air miles and car fuel coupons

1.36 If an employee flies on business, uses a company credit card or buys fuel for business travel, and thereby earns air miles or car fuel coupons which he uses for private purposes, there is no taxable benefit.

Travel

1.37 There is no taxable benefit in respect of work buses and minibuses or subsidies to public bus services provided employees pay the same fare as the public.

A works bus must have a seating capacity of 12 or more and a works minibus a seating capacity of 9 or more but not more than 12 and be available generally to employees of the employer concerned. The bus or minibus must mainly be used by employees for journeys to and from work and for journeys between workplaces.

1.38 The following amounts paid by an employer are exempt benefits.

(a) Transport/overnight costs where public transport is disrupted by industrial action.

(b) Late night taxis.

(c) Travel costs exceptionally incurred where car sharing arrangements unavoidably breakdown.

2 BENEFITS IN KIND: P11D EMPLOYEES

2.1 **The benefit in kind rules discussed in this section apply to directors and employees whose 'emoluments' are at the rate of £8,500 a year or more.** Such individuals are sometimes referred to as 'P11D employees'. A P11D is the form on which the employer must report the benefits available to these individuals to the Inland Revenue.

2.2 **'Emoluments' for this purpose include salary, commissions, fees, reimbursed expenses and also benefits in kind taxable on such employees.** In other words, assume that an employee falls into this category in order to determine whether or not he really does. In seeing whether he does, we ignore any deductible expenses.

2.3 Where a car is provided but the employee could have chosen an alternative benefit, the benefit to use for the £8,500 test is the sum of:

(a) The higher of the car benefit plus any fuel benefit and the value of the alternative

(b) Any expense payments in relation to the car or benefits relating to it obtained by non-cash vouchers or credit tokens

2.4 **The term 'director' refers to any person who acts as a director or any person in accordance with whose instructions the directors are accustomed to act** (other than a professional adviser). An individual is not, however, subject to the special benefit in kind rules solely because he is a director, if he has no material interest in the company ('material' means more than 5%) and either:

(a) He is a full time working director, or
(b) The company is either non-profit making or is established for charitable purposes.

But such a person will be subject to the special rules if he earns £8,500 or more a year.

2.5 A benefit is taxable if it arises 'by reason of the employment' and is provided either to the employee or to a member of his family or household. There is no need for the employer to provide it directly.

General business expenses

2.6 **If business expenses on such items as travel or hotel stays, are reimbursed by an employer, the reimbursed amount is a taxable benefit.** To avoid being taxed on this amount, **an employee must then make a claim to deduct it as an expense** under the usual rules (see previous chapter). **In practice**, however, **many such expense payments are not reported to the Inland Revenue and can be ignored because it is agreed in advance that a claim to deduct them would be possible (a P11D dispensation)**.

2.7 When an individual has to spend one or more nights away from home, his employer may reimburse expenses on items incidental to his absence (for example meals and private telephone calls). Such incidental expenses are not taxable if:

(a) The expenses of travelling to each place where the individual stays overnight, throughout the trip, are incurred necessarily in the performance of the duties of the employment (or would have been, if there had been any expenses).

(b) The total (for the whole trip) of incidental expenses not deductible under the usual rules is no more than £5 for each night spent wholly in the UK and £10 for each other night. If this limit is exceeded, all of the expenses are taxable, not just the excess. The expenses include any VAT.

2.8 This incidental expenses exemption applies to expenses reimbursed, and to benefits obtained using credit tokens and non-cash vouchers.

Expenses connected with living accommodation

2.9 In addition to the benefit of living accommodation itself, which is taxable on all employees, **employees earning £8,500 or more a year and directors are taxed on related expenses paid by the employer**, such as:

    (a) **Heating, lighting or cleaning the premises**

    (b) **Repairing, maintaining or decorating the premises**

    (c) **The provision of furniture** (the annual value is 20% of the cost)

2.10 Unless the accommodation qualifies as 'job related' (as defined above) **the full cost of ancillary services** (excluding structural repairs) **is taxable. If the accommodation is 'job related'**, however, **taxable ancillary services are restricted to a maximum of 10% of the employee's 'net emoluments'**. For this purpose, net emoluments are all amounts taxable under Schedule E (excluding the ancillary benefits (a) - (c) above) less any allowable expenses, contributions to approved occupational pension schemes (but not personal pension schemes) and capital allowances. If there are ancillary benefits other than those falling within (a) - (c) above (such as a telephone) they are taxable in full.

Question: Expenses connected with living accommodation

Mr Quinton has a gross salary in 2001/02 of £28,850. He normally lives and works in London, but he is required to live in a company house in Scotland which cost £70,000 three years ago, so that he can carry out a two year review of his company's operations in Scotland. The annual value of the house is £650. In 2001/02 the company pays an electricity bill of £550, a gas bill of £400, a gardener's bill of £750 and redecoration costs of £1,800. Mr Quinton makes a monthly contribution of £50 for his accommodation. He also pays £1,450 occupational pension contributions.

Calculate the Schedule E income for 2001/02.

Answer

	£	£
Salary		28,850
Less occupational pension scheme contributions		(1,450)
Net emoluments		27,400
Accommodation benefits		
Annual value: exempt (job related)		
Ancillary services		
Electricity	550	
Gas	400	
Gardener	750	
Redecorations	1,800	
	3,500	
Restricted to 10% of £27,400	2,740	
Less employee's contribution	(600)	
		2,140
Schedule E income		29,540

Cars

2.11 **For employees earning £8,500 or more a year and directors, a car provided by reason of the employment gives rise to a taxable benefit.**

    (a) A tax charge arises whether the car is provided by the employer or by some other person. The benefit is computed as shown below, even if the car is taken as an alternative to another benefit of a different value.

    (b) **The benefit chargeable to tax each year is found as follows.**

       (Price of car – capital contributions) × % × age factor

    (c) The price of the car is the sum of the following items.

(i)   The list price of the car for a single retail sale at the time of first registration, including charges for delivery and standard accessories. The manufacturer's, importer's or distributor's list price must be used, even if the retailer offered a discount. A notional list price is estimated if no list price was published.

(ii) The price (including fitting) of all optional accessories provided when the car was first provided to the employee, excluding mobile telephones and equipment needed by a disabled employee. The extra cost of adapting or manufacturing a car to run on road fuel gases is not included.

(iii) The price (including fitting) of all optional accessories fitted later and costing at least £100 each, excluding mobile telephones and equipment needed by a disabled employee. Such accessories affect the taxable benefit from and including the tax year in which they are fitted. However, accessories which are merely replacing existing accessories and are not superior to the ones replaced are ignored. Replacement accessories which *are* superior are taken into account, but the cost of the old accessory is then ignored.

(d)   There is a special rule for classic cars. If the car is at least 15 years old (from the time of first registration) at the end of the tax year, and its market value at the end of the year (or, if earlier, when it ceased to be available to the employee) is over £15,000 and greater than the price found under (c), that market value is used instead of the price. The market value takes account of all accessories (except mobile telephones and equipment needed by a disabled employee).

(e)   If the price or value found under (c) or (d) exceeds £80,000, then £80,000 is used instead of the price or value.

(f)   Capital contributions are payments by the employee in respect of the price of the car or accessories. In any tax year, we take account of capital contributions made in that year and previous years (for the same car). The maximum deductible capital contributions is £5,000: contributions beyond that total are ignored.

(g)   If the car is at least four years old (from the date of first registration) at the end of the tax year, then the age factor is ¾. Otherwise it is 1.

(h)   The 'percentage' for 2001/02 depends on the **business** mileage in the tax year:

Business mileage	First car	Other cars
Less than 2,500	35%	35%
At least 2,500, less than 18,000	25%	35%
At least 18,000	15%	25%

The 'other cars' percentages apply when two or more cars are provided simultaneously. The car with the greatest business mileage is the first car, and the 'first car' percentages are used for that car only.

(i)   In *Henwood (HMIT) v Clarke 1997* a car was made available to the taxpayer for private and business use throughout the year but the first car was replaced by another car during the year. The taxpayer's total business mileage exceeded 2,500 miles in the tax year but the proportion of business miles travelled in each car differed. It was held that the mileage threshold applied to each car separately rather than to the driver.

(j)   The benefit is reduced on a time basis where a car is first made available or ceases to be made available during the tax year or is incapable of being used for a continuous period of not less than 30 days (for example because it is being repaired). The mileage factor limits of 2,500 and 18,000 miles are also reduced on a time basis in such cases. If a car is unavailable for less than 30 days and a replacement car of similar quality is provided, the replacement car is ignored and business mileage in it counts as business mileage in the usual car.

(k) The benefit is reduced by any payment the user must make for the private use of the car (as distinct from a capital contribution to the cost of the car). Payments for insuring the car do not count *(IRC v Quigley 1995)*. The benefit cannot become negative to create a deduction from the employee's income.

(l) Pool cars are exempt. A car is a pool car if **all** the following conditions are satisfied.

- It is used by more than one director or employee and is not ordinarily used by any one of them to the exclusion of the others.

- Any private use is merely incidental to business use.

- It is not normally kept overnight at or near the residence of a director or employee.

2.12 Employers must make quarterly returns in respect of changes to cars provided to employees on form P46 (car). These returns must be made within 28 days of the end of each income tax quarter (quarters end on 5 July, 5 October, 5 January and 5 April).

Current issues and proposals

2.13 From 2002/03 the way in which taxable car benefits are calculated will change. The starting point for calculating a car benefit will continue to be the list price of the car (plus accessories) but the percentage of the list price that is taxable will depend on the car's CO_2 emissions.

Fuel for cars

2.14 **Where fuel is provided there is a further benefit on a set scale in addition to the car benefit.** The fuel benefits are given in the Rates and Allowances Tables in this text.

No taxable benefit arises where either

(a) All the fuel provided was made available only for business travel, or

(b) The employee is required to make good, and has made good, the whole of the cost of any fuel provided for his private use.

Unlike most benefits, a reimbursement of only part of the cost of the fuel available for private use does not reduce the scale charge.

The benefit is reduced in the same way as the car benefit if the car is not available for 30 days or more, but it is not adjusted for business mileage.

2.15 There are many ancillary benefits associated with the provision of cars, such as insurance, repairs, vehicle licences and a parking space at or near work. No extra taxable benefit arises as a result of these, with the exception of the cost of providing a driver.

Question: Car and Fuel benefit

An employee was provided with a new car (2,500 cc) costing £15,000. During 2001/02 the employer spent £900 on insurance, repairs and a vehicle licence. The employee did 20,000 miles of which 15,000 were on business. The firm paid for all petrol, costing £1,500, without reimbursement. The employee paid the firm £270 for the private use of the car. Calculate the taxable benefit.

Answer

	£
Car benefit £15,000 × 25%	3,750
Fuel benefit	3,620
	7,370
Less contribution towards use of car	(270)
	7,100

If the contribution of £270 had been towards the petrol the benefit would have been £7,370.

Vans and heavier commercial vehicles

2.16 **If a van** (of normal maximum laden weight up to 3,500 kg) **is made available for an employee's private use, there is an annual scale charge of £500, or £350 if the van is at least four years old at the end of the tax year.** The scale charge covers ancillary benefits such as insurance and servicing (but not van telephones). Paragraphs 2.11 (a), (i), (j) and (k) above apply to vans as they do to cars, but there is no adjustment for mileage.

2.17 If a commercial vehicle of normal maximum laden weight over 3,500 kg is made available for an employee's private use, but the employee's use of the vehicle is not wholly or mainly private, no taxable benefit arises except in respect of the provision of a driver.

Mobile telephones

2.18 **No taxable benefit arises in respect of a mobile telephone** made available to an employee or a member of his family (**the employer retaining ownership of the telephone**).

Other assets made available for private use

2.19 **Assets made available to employees earning £8,500 or more a year and directors are taxable on an annual value of 20% of the market value when first provided as a benefit to any employee, or on the rent paid by the employer if higher.** The 20% charge is time-apportioned when the asset is provided for only part of the year. The charge after any time apportionment is reduced by any contribution made by the employee.

2.20 If an asset made available is subsequently acquired by the employee, **the taxable benefit on the acquisition is the** *greater* **of:**

- The **current market value minus the price paid by the employee.**

- The **market value when first provided minus any amounts already taxed (ignoring contributions by the employee) minus the price paid by the employee.**

This rule prevents tax free benefits arising on rapidly depreciating items through the employee purchasing them at their low secondhand value.

2.21 EXAMPLE: ASSETS MADE AVAILABLE FOR PRIVATE USE

A suit costing £400 is purchased by an employer for use by an employee on 6 April 2000. On 6 April 2001 the suit is purchased by the employee for £30, its market value then being £50.

The benefit in 2000/01 is £400 × 20%   £80

The benefit in 2001/02 is £290, being the *greater* of:

		£
(a)	Market value at acquisition by employee	50

Less price paid	(30)
	20

	£
	400
(b) Original market value	(80)
Less taxed in respect of use	320
	(30)
Less price paid	290

Computer equipment

2.22 **The first £500 of any benefit which arises under the above rules in respect of computer equipment** made available for the private use of an employee or a member of his family household is **exempt.** If the benefit exceeds £500, the excess is taxable.

Assets sold to employers

2.23 If an employee sells an asset to his employer (for example his house when he is being relocated), **there is a taxable benefit of the amount paid minus the market value of the asset.** If the employer pays his own transaction costs (for example solicitors' fees), they do not count as a taxable benefit. However, if the employer pays the employee's transaction costs, there is a taxable benefit unless a specific exemption (for example the removal expenses exemption) applies.

Scholarships

2.24 If scholarships are given to members of a director's or employee's family, the director or **employee is taxable on the cost** unless the scholarship fund's or scheme's payments by reason of people's employments are not more than 25% of its total payments.

PAYE tax liabilities

2.25 **If a company pays any PAYE tax** on behalf of a director (not an employee), **any amount not made good by the director is a taxable benefit.** Directors with no material interest in the company (that is, not more than 5%) who are full time working directors or who work for non profit making or charitable companies are excluded from this rule.

Beneficial loans

2.26 **Loans to employees, directors and their families give rise to a benefit equal to:**

(a) **Any amounts written off** (unless the employee has died), and

(b) **The excess of the interest based on an official rate prescribed by the Treasury, over any interest actually charged.** Interest payable during the tax year but paid after the end of the tax year is taken into account, but if the benefit is determined before such interest is paid a claim must be made to take it into account.

2.27 The following loans are normally ignored altogether for the purposes of computing taxable income because of low interest (but not for the purposes of the charge on loans written off).

(a) A loan on normal commercial terms made in the ordinary course of the employer's money-lending business.

(b) A loan made by an individual in the ordinary course of the lender's domestic, family or personal arrangements.

Calculating the interest benefit

2.28 There are two alternative methods of calculating the taxable benefit. The simpler '**average**' **method** automatically applies unless the taxpayer or the Revenue elect for the alternative '**strict**' **method**. (The Revenue normally only make the election where it appears that the 'average' method is being deliberately exploited.) In both methods, the benefit is the interest at the official rate minus the interest payable.

2.29 The 'average' method averages the balances at the beginning and end of the tax year (or the dates on which the loan was made and discharged if it was not in existence throughout the tax year) and applies the official rate of interest to this average. If the loan was not in existence throughout the tax year only the number of complete tax months (from the 6th of the month) for which it existed are taken into account.

2.30 The 'strict' method is to compute interest at the official rate on the actual amount outstanding on a daily basis.

Question: Loan benefit

At 6 April 2001 a low interest loan of £30,000 was outstanding to an employee earning £12,000 a year, who repaid £20,000 on 7 December 2001. The remaining balance of £10,000 was outstanding at 5 April 2002. Interest paid during the year was £250. What was the benefit under both methods for 2001/02, assuming that the official rate of interest was 6.25%?

Answer

Average method

	£
$6.25\% \times \dfrac{30,000 + 10,000}{2}$	1,250
Less interest paid	(250)
Benefit	1,000

Alternative method (strict method)

	£
$£30,000 \times \dfrac{245}{365}$ (6 April - 6 December) $\times 6.25\%$	1,259
$£10,000 \times \dfrac{120}{365}$ (7 December - 5 April) $\times 6.25\%$	205
	1,464
Less interest paid	(250)
Benefit	1,214

The Revenue might opt for the alternative method.

The de minimis test

2.31 **The benefit is not taxable if:**

(a) The **total of all loans to the employee did not exceed £5,000** at any time in the tax year, or

(b) **The loan is not a qualifying loan and the total of all non-qualifying loans to the employee did not exceed £5,000** at any time in the tax year.

2.32 **A qualifying loan is one on which any interest paid would qualify for tax relief.** Qualifying loans include those taken out to buy shares in an employee controlled company and those taken to buy shares in a partnerhsip.

2.33 In applying the £5,000 test, ignore any loans which are to be ignored under the rules above.

2.34 When the £5,000 threshold is exceeded, a benefit arises on interest on the whole loan, not just on the excess of the loan over £5,000.

2.35 When a loan is written off and a benefit arises, there is no £5,000 threshold: writing off a loan of £1 gives rise to a £1 benefit.

2.36 If interest on a loan qualifies for tax relief in full, the loan does not have to be reported on Form P11D. In addition, no Class 1A NICs will be due (see the next chapter).

Question: Beneficial loans

Anna, who is single, has an annual salary of £30,000, and two loans from her employer.

(a)   A season ticket loan of £2,300 at no interest
(b)   A loan to buy shares in her employee-controlled company of £54,000 at 3% interest

The loan to buy shares in the employee controlled company is a qualifying loan. The season ticket loan is non-qualifying.

The official rate of interest is to be taken as 6.25%.

What is Anna's Schedule E income for 2001/02?

Answer

	£
Salary	30,000
Season ticket loan: not over £5,000	0
Loan to buy shares £54,000 × (6.25 - 3 = 3.25%)	1,755
Schedule E	31,755

Medical services and insurance

2.37 The cost of medical diagnosis and treatment provided by an employer is a taxable benefit, except for the cost of routine check-ups. **Private medical insurance premiums are also taxable benefits,** except for premiums or extra premiums to cover treatment when the employee is outside the UK in the performance of his duties.

Staff parties

2.38 The **cost of staff parties is taxable, except** when the parties are open to staff generally and the **cost per staff member per year (including VAT) is £75 or less.** The £75 limit may be split between several parties. If it is exceeded, the full amount is taxable, not just the excess over £75.

Uniforms

2.39 No taxable benefit arises in respect of employer provided uniforms which employees must wear as part of their duties.

Chapter roundup

- Generally benefits in kind are taxable on the cost of providing them, but employees earning at the rate of less than £8,500 per annum who are not directors are taxed on the 'cash equivalent' value.

- There are special rules for taxing many benefits in kind. Some rules apply to all employees. Other rules apply only to P11D employees.

Quick quiz

1   What accommodation does not give rise to a taxable benefit?

2   To what extent are removal expenses paid for by an employer taxable?

3   How may an employee who is provided with a fuel by his employer avoid a fuel scale charge?

Answers to quick quiz

1   Job related accommodation

2   The first £8,000 of removal expenses are exempt. Any excess is taxable.

3   There is no fuel scale charge if:

   (a)   All the fuel provided was made available only for business travel, or

   (b)   the full cost of any fuel provided for private use was completely reimbursed by the employee

Now try the question below from the Exam Question Bank

Number	Level	Marks	Time
15	Exam	10	18 mins

Chapter 14

PAYE, NICs AND TAX EFFICIENT REMUNERATION

Topic list	Syllabus reference	Ability required
1 The PAYE system	(i), (ii)	Comprehension
2 National insurance contributions (NICs)	(ii), (vii)	Comprehension
3 Status issues	(ii)	Analysis
4 Remuneration packages	(ii)	Evaluate
5 Directors and shareholders	(ii)	Evaluate

Introduction

Employers must deduct income tax and national insurance contributions (NICs) from employees pay under the PAYE system. We start this chapter by looking in detail, at the PAYE system. We then look at NICs and identify methods of minimising NICs.

We also look at the anti-avoidance rules that aim to prevent individuals from avoiding PAYE by providing their services through an intermediary.

Finally, we consider how tax efficient remuneration packages can be structured.

Learning outcomes covered in this chapter

- **Explain** the effect of assessable benefits on code numbers
- **Identify** the compliance requirements imposed on employers in relation to employee taxation
- **Identify** methods of minimising employer's national insurance contributions (NICs)
- **Evaluate** the relative tax efficiency of different methods of rewarding employees

Syllabus content

- Returns required from employers in connection with all aspects of employee taxation
- Schedule E; pay as you earn (PAYE), employer's and employee's NICs
- National insurance contribution planning
- Status issues - IR 35
- Contrasting salary with dividends
- Tax efficient methods of rewarding employees

1   THE PAYE SYSTEM

1.1   The objective of the PAYE system is to deduct the correct amount of tax over the year. Its scope is very wide. It applies to most cash payments, other than reimbursed business expenses, and to certain non cash payments.

1.2 In addition to wages and salaries, PAYE applies to taxable lump sum payments on leaving most lump sum payments on joining, round sum expense allowances and payments instead of benefits in kind. It also applies to statutory sick pay, statutory maternity pay and any readily convertible asset.

1.3 A readily convertible asset is any asset which can effectively be exchanged for cash. The amount subject to PAYE is the amount taxable under Schedule E. This is usually the cost to the employer of providing the asset. Shares or rights over shares (eg options), in the employing company (or in a company controlling it) are not readily convertible assets if they are provided under Revenue approved schemes (see earlier in this text), or if they are not marketable.

1.4 Tips paid direct to an employee are normally outside the PAYE system (although still assessable under Schedule E). An exception may apply in the catering trades where tips are often pooled. Here the PAYE position depends on whether a 'tronc', administered other than by the employer, exists.

1.5 **It is the employer's duty to deduct income tax from the pay of his employees,** whether or not he has been directed to do so by the Revenue. **If he fails to do this he** (or sometimes the employee) **must pay over the tax which he should have deducted and the employer may be subject to penalties.** Interest will also run from 14 days after the end of the tax year concerned on any underpaid PAYE. Officers of the Inland Revenue can inspect employer's records in order to satisfy themselves that the correct amounts of tax are being deducted and paid over to the Revenue.

Benefits in kind

1.6 **PAYE is not normally operated on benefits in kind; instead the employee's PAYE code is restricted** (see below).

1.7 However, PAYE must be applied to remuneration in the form of a taxable non-cash voucher if at the time it is provided:

(a) the voucher is capable of being exchanged for readily convertible assets; or
(b) the voucher can itself be sold, realised or traded.

1.8 PAYE must be normally operated on cash vouchers and on each occasion when a director/employee uses a credit-token (eg a credit card) to obtain money or goods which are readily convertible assets. However, a cash voucher or credit token which is used to defray expenses is not subject to PAYE.

How PAYE works

1.9 To operate PAYE the employer needs:

(a) deductions working sheets;
(b) codes for employees that reflect the tax allowances to which the employees are entitled;
(c) tax tables.

1.10 **The employer works out the amount of PAYE tax to deduct on any particular pay day by using the employees code number (see below) in conjunction with the PAYE tables. The tables are designed so that tax is normally worked out on a cumulative basis.** This means that with each payment of emoluments the running total of tax paid is compared with tax due on total emoluments to that date. The difference between the tax due and the tax paid is the tax to be deducted on that particular payday.

1.11 National insurance tables are used to work out the national insurance due on any payday.

1.12 Although PAYE is normally operated on a cumulative basis, an employee may have a week 1/month 1 code (see below). In this case the figures for pay and tax deducted are not cumulated, and the tax on each payday is worked out on the pay on that payday as if it were the first payday in the tax year (using week1/month 1 table).

1.13 If a K code applies there is a restriction on the amount of tax that can be deducted (see below). On a cumulative basis, this restriction will be recouped on a later payday (subject to the overriding limit on the later pay day). On a week 1/month 1 basis the restriction cannot be recouped, and will be dealt with by the Revenue after the end of the tax year.

Records

1.14 **The employer must keep records of each employee's pay and tax at each pay day**. The records must also contain details of National Insurance. The employer has a choice of three ways of recording and returning these figures:

(a) he may use the official deductions working sheet (P11);
(b) he may incorporate the figures in his own pay records using a substitute document;
(c) he may retain the figures on a computer.

These records will be used to make a return at the end of the tax year.

Payment under the PAYE system

1.15 **Under PAYE income tax and national insurance is normally paid over to the Inland Revenue monthly, 14 days after the end of each tax month.**

1.16 The PAYE system is also used to collect student loan repayments. An employer must deduct repayments from an employee's pay if the Revenue notify him that he must do so or if the employee gives him a P45 with a Y in the student loan box. Student loan deduction tables are used to ascertain the amount to deduct on any payday and this amount is paid to the Revenue together with the employer's PAYE and NIC.

1.17 Employers may have to pay the working families tax credit (WFTC) and the disabled persons tax credit (DPTC) to employees through the PAYE system. Any amounts paid can be set against the employer's PAYE liabilities.

1.18 **If an employer's average monthly payments under the PAYE system are less than £1,500, the employer may choose to pay quarterly, within 14 days of the end of each tax quarter.** Tax quarters end on 5 July, 5 October, 5 January and 5 April. Payments can continue to be made quarterly during a tax year even if the monthly average reaches or exceeds £1,500, but a new estimate must be made and a new decision taken to pay quarterly at the start of each tax year. Average monthly payments are the average net monthly payments due to the Inland Revenue for income tax, NICs and recovered student loans after taking into account the WFTC and DPTC.

PAYE codes

1.19 **An employee is normally entitled to various allowances. Under the PAYE system an amount reflecting the effect of a proportion of these allowances is set against his pay each pay day. To determine the amount to set against his pay the allowances are expressed in the form of a code which is used in conjunction with the Pay Adjustment Tables** (Tables A).

1.20 An employee's code may be any one of the following:

(a) a code of one, two or three numbers followed by a single suffix letter (a suffix code): for example 453L. The letter allows the Revenue to tell the employer how the code should be adjusted each year to take account of Budget changes. The letter L indicates that an individual is entitled to the personal allowance but other allowance.

(b) the prefix D is usually followed by the number 0; these codes apply on a one-off basis and require the use of higher rate tax tables D.

(c) code BR, which means that tax will be deducted at the basic rate with no tax free allowances;

(d) code NT, which means that no tax is to be deducted;

(e) a code with a K prefix, followed by one to four numbers.

(f) a code with a P suffix means that the individual is entitled to an age allowance

(g) a code with a Y suffix means that the individual is entitled to additional age allowances

1.21 **Generally, a tax code number is arrived at by deleting the last digit in the sum representing the employee's tax free allowances.** Every individual is entitled to a personal tax free allowance of £4,535. The code number for an individual who is entitled to this but no other allowance is 453L.

The code number may also reflect other items. For example, **it will be restricted to reflect benefits in kind, small amounts of untaxed income** and **unpaid Schedule E tax from earlier years**. If an amount of tax is in point, it is necessary to gross up the tax in the code using the taxpayers estimated marginal rate of income tax.

Question: PAYE codes

Adrian is a 40 year old single man (suffix letter L) who earns £15,000 pa. He has benefits in kind of £560 and his unpaid Schedule E tax for 2000/01 was £57.50. As Adrian is single he is entitled to a tax free personal allowance of £4,535 in 2001/02.

Adrian pays income tax at the marginal rate of 22%.

What is Adrian's PAYE code for 2001/02?

Answer

	£
Personal allowance	4,535
Benefits in kind	(560)
Unpaid tax £57.50 × 100/22	(261)
Available allowances	3,714

Adrian's PAYE code is 371L

1.22 Codes are determined and amended by the Revenue. They are normally notified to the employer on a code list (Form P6). The employer must act on the code notified to him until amended instructions are received from the Revenue, even if the employee has appealed against the code.

1.23 **By using the code number in conjunction with the tax tables, an employee is generally given 1/52nd or 1/12th of his tax free allowances against each week's/month's pay.** However because of the cumulative nature of PAYE, if an employee is first paid in, say, September, that month he will receive six months' allowances against his gross pay. In cases where the employee's previous PAYE history is not known, this could lead to under-deduction of tax. To avoid this, codes for the employees concerned have to be operated on a 'week 1/month1' basis, so that only 1/52nd or 1/12th of the employee's allowances are available each week/month.

1.24 **'K' codes increase taxable pay instead of reducing it.** This means benefits exceed allowances. The PAYE deducted under a K code could remove all of an employee's actual remuneration for a pay period. As this could cause hardship, **the PAYE deduced on any payday is not to exceed 50% of the amount of actual remuneration on that pay day.** (This overriding limit does not restrict the tax on non cash payments).

Employer's responsibilities: year end returns and employees leaving or joining

1.25 **At the end of each tax year, the employer must provide each employee with a form P60.** This shows total taxable emoluments for the year, tax deducted, code number, NI number and the employer's name and address. **The P60 must be provided by 31 May following the year of assessment.**

1.26 **Following the end of each tax year, the employer must send the Revenue:**

(a) **by 19 May;**

 (i) **End of year Returns P14** (showing the same details as the P60);
 (ii) **Form P35** (summary of tax and NI deducted).

(b) **by 6 July:**

 (i) **Forms P11D** (benefits in kind etc for directors and employees paid £8,500+ pa);
 (ii) **Forms P11D(b)** (return of Class 1A NICs (see below));
 (iii) **Forms P9D** (benefits in kind etc for other employees).

1.27 **A copy of the form P11D (or P9D) must also be provided to the employee by 6 July.** The details shown on the P11D include the full cash equivalent of all benefits, so that the employee may enter the details on his self-assessment tax return. Specific reference numbers for the entries on the P11D are also used on the employee's self assessment tax return.

1.28 The full value of any assessable benefits must usually be entered on Form P11D. Employees must then make a separate s 198 claim in respect of any expenses incurred wholly, exclusively and necessarily for the purposes of the employment. Alternatively, employers sometimes reach an agreement with the Revenue that certain expenses reimbursed to employees are tax deductible and do not need to be entered on form P11D. The company is then said to have a **'P11D Dispensation'** covering these items.

1.29 **When an employee leaves, a certificate on form P45 (particulars of Employee Leaving) must be prepared. This form shows the employee's code and details of his income and tax paid to date and is a four part form. One part is sent to the Revenue, and three parts handed to the employee. One of the parts (part 1A) is the employee's personal copy. If**

the employee takes up a new employment, he must hand the other two parts of the form P45 to the new employer. **The new employer will fill in details of the new employment and send one part to the Revenue, retaining the other.** The details on the form are used by the new employer to calculate the PAYE due on the next payday. If the employee dies a P45 should be completed, and the whole form sent to the Revenue.

1.30 If an employee joins with a form P45, the new employer can operate PAYE. If there is no P45 the employer still needs to operate PAYE. The employee is required to complete a form P46. If he declares that the employment is his first job since leaving education, or his only or main job and that he not in receipt of a pension, the emergency code (453L for 2001/02) applies, on a cumulative basis or week 1/month 1 basis respectively. Otherwise the employer must use code BR. The P46 is sent to the Revenue, unless the pay is below the PAYE and NIC thresholds, and the emergency code applies. In this case no PAYE is deductible until the pay exceeds the threshold.

Penalties

1.31 A form P35 is due on 19 May after the end of the tax year. In practice, a 7 day extension to the due date of 19 May is allowed.

1.32 **Where a form P35 is late, a penalty of £100 per month per 50 employees may be imposed.** This penalty cannot be mitigated. **This penalty ceases 12 months after the due date and a further penalty of up to 100% of the tax (and NIC) for the year which remains unpaid** at 19 April may be imposed. This penalty can be mitigated. The Revenue automatically reduce the penalty by concession to the greater of £100 and the total PAYE/NIC which should be reported on the return.

1.33 Where a person has fraudulently or negligently submitted an incorrect form P35 the penalty is 100% of the tax (and NIC) attributable to the error. This penalty can be mitigated.

PAYE settlement agreements

1.34 **PAYE settlement agreements (PSAs) are arrangements under which employers can make single payments to settle their employees' income tax liabilities on expense payments and certain benefits in kind.** Benefits may be included in a PSA if the Inspector considers them to be minor (eg small gifts), irregular (eg, relocation payments of over £8,000) or benefits in respect of which it is impractical to apply PAYE or identify the amount attributable to a particular employee (eg free dental care). Items covered by a PSA do not have to be included on either Forms P9D or P11D or on the employee's tax return.

1.35 PSAs cannot be used to settle tax on:

(a) cash payments of salaries, wages or bonuses

(b) major benefits provided regularly for the sole use of individual employees (for example, company cars)

(c) round sum allowances

1.36 **Tax due under a PSA must be paid by 19 October following the end of the tax year.**

Charitable donations under the payroll deduction scheme

1.37 Employees can make tax deductible donations under the payroll deduction scheme to an approved charity of their choice by asking their employer to deduct the donation from their gross earnings prior to calculating PAYE due thereon. The government will pay a 10% supplement on all donations made under the scheme before 6 April 2003.

2   NATIONAL INSURANCE CONTRIBUTIONS (NICS)

2.1   Four classes of contribution exist, as set out below.

(a)   **Class 1.** This is divided into:

(i)   **primary,** paid by employees;

(ii)   **secondary, Class 1A and Class 1B** paid by employers

(b)   **Class 2.** Paid by the self-employed

(c)   **Class 3.** Voluntary contributions (paid to maintain rights to certain state benefits)

(d)   **Class 4** Paid by the self-employed

Knowledge of Class 1, Class 1A and Class 1B contributions is required for exam purposes. The other contributions are outside the scope of your syllabus.

2.2   The Contributions Agency, which is part of the Inland Revenue, examines employers' records and procedures to ensure that the correct amounts of NICs are collected.

2.3   Employers' contributions are deductible Schedule D Case I expenses.

2.4   Employers pay secondary NIC's related to an employee's earnings. 'Earnings' broadly comprise gross pay, excluding benefits in kind which cannot be turned into cash by surrender (eg holidays). No deduction is made for superannuation contributions or contributions under the payroll giving scheme.

2.5   An employer's contribution to an employee's approved personal pension or an approved occupational pension scheme is excluded from the definition of 'earnings'. However, NICs are due on employer contributions to funded unapproved retirement benefit schemes.

2.6   In general income tax and NIC exemptions mirror one another. For example, payment of personal incidental expenses covered by the £5/£10 a night income tax de minimis exemption are excluded from NIC earnings. Relocation expenses of a type exempt from income tax are also excluded from NIC earnings but without the income tax £8,000 upper limit (although expenses exceeding £8,000 are subject to class 1A NICs as described below).

2.7   An expense with a business purpose is not treated as earnings. For example, if an employee is reimbursed for business travel or for staying in a hotel on the employer's business this is not normally 'earnings'. However, if an employee is reimbursed for his own home telephone charges the reimbursed cost of private calls (and all reimbursed rental) is earnings.

2.8   Where an employer reimburses an employee using his own car for business mileage, the earnings element is the excess of the mileage rate paid over the Inland Revenue 'up to 4,000 business miles' Authorised Mileage Rate appropriate to the engine size. This applies even where business mileage exceeds 4,000 pa.

2.9   In general, non cash vouchers are subject to NICs. However, the following are exempt.

- Childcare vouchers for children up to 16 years old
- Vouchers for the use of sports and recreational facilities (where tax exempt)
- Vouchers for meals on the employer's premises
- Other luncheon vouchers to a maximum of 15p per day

- Transport vouchers where the employee earns less than £8,500 a year.

2.10 Non-contracted out employees pay contributions of 10% of earnings between the primary threshold of £4,535 and the upper earnings limit of £29,900.

Employers normally pay secondary contributions of 11.9% on earnings above the earnings threshold of £4,535.

2.11 If an employee is in a contracted out occupational pension scheme, reduced contributions are payable.

2.12 **Employers must pay Class 1A NIC at 11.9% in respect of most taxable benefits for example, private medical insurance. However, benefits are exempt if they are:**

- within class 1; or
- covered by a PAYE dispensation; or
- provided for employees earning at a rate of less than £8,500 a year; or
- included in a PAYE settlement agreement; or
- otherwise not required to be reported on P11Ds

In addition, all kinds of childcare provision in kind, for example, where the employer contracts for places in commercial nurseries, are exempt from Class 1A NICs. However, if an employer provides cash to meet or reimburse childcare expenses the cash is 'earnings' for employer and employee Class 1 NIC purposes. There is also exemption for certain other minor benefits already noted in the text (eg small private use of employer's assets) **and for certain travel and subsistence benefits for employees seconded to the UK or abroad and certain personal security items supplied by an employer to employee.**

2.13 **Employee contributions are not charged on benefits in kind. Employees may, however, agree to pay employer's contributions.**

2.14 Class 1A contributions are collected annually in arrears, and are due by 19 July following the tax year.

2.15 The provision by an employer of fuel for use in an employee's own car does not lead to a Class 1A charge. However, mileage allowances in excess of the Authorised Mileage Rates lead to Class 1 (primary and secondary) contributions on the excess (subject to the usual upper limit for primary contributions).

2.16 If Class 1 contributions for a year are not paid to the Revenue by 19 April following the year, or Class 1A contributions due in a year are not paid over by 19 April following the year, interest is charged from the relevant 19 April onwards. Interest is paid to employers on excessive payments refunded to them, but only from the end of the year of payment and never from earlier than 12 months after the end of the year for which the contributions were paid.

2.17 Employers who pay their employee's income tax liabilities via a PAYE settlement agreement (PSA) (see above) must pay Class 1B contributions. Class 1B NICs are payable at 11.9% on both the emoluments subject to NIC included within the PSA and on the tax paid by the employer.

2.18 Class 1B is only relevant to the second and subsequent years of a PSA operation. Class 1 liability applies to the first year. The Class 1B rate is 11.9% and is payable on the 19 October following the tax year covered by the PSA.

National insurance contribution planning

2.19 NIC is payable on 'earnings'. This means that remuneration packages structured to include the following items which are not 'earnings' would reduce the NIC burden;

(a) **Dividends** - director/shareholders could take remuneration in the form of dividends. Dividend waivers and adjustments to bonuses would probably be required. There are CT implications as salary and NIC costs are allowable business expenses whereas dividends are not.

Provided the starting rate or small companies rate of CT applies dividends are an efficient way of avoiding NICs. However dividend income is not earnings for pension purposes. There is also a cash flow impact since PAYE would not apply to remuneration in the form of dividends.

(b) **Rents** - a director owning a property used by a company could be paid rent instead of remuneration. Again the rental expense is a deductible business expense for the company. The income is not earnings for pension contribution purposes for the individual and it is not subject to tax under the PAYE system.

2.20 Employers must pay Class 1A NIC on benefits in kind. This means that, in general, the substitution of benefits for salary is not an NIC - efficient planning point from the employer's point of view. Employees do not pay NICs on benefits in kind so from an employee's viewpoint benefits could be NIC efficient but the usefulness of this planning point is limited as employees do not pay NICs on salary above the upper limit of £29,900.

2.21 Certain benefits in kind are specifically NIC efficient as NICs are not due on them, eg childcare provision in kind.

3 STATUS ISSUES

3.1 We looked at the distinction between employment and self employment earlier in this text. Taxpayers normally prefer to avoid being classified as employees. Here we will look at the anti-avoidance rules that apply when a worker provides services through an intermediary.

Provision of services through an intermediary (IR 35)

3.2 If a worker provides services through an intermediary, the intermediary's receipts from the worker's engagement may be deemed to be Schedule E earnings. These earnings are then subject to income tax (on the worker) and employer's Class 1 (NICs).

3.3 An intermediary can be a company, a partnership or an individual. A worker providing services through an intermediary may be within the scope of these rules if the intermediary:

(a) is a company in which the worker either has a material interest (broadly more than 5%) or from which he receives non-Schedule E remuneration (eg dividends) that can reasonably be taken to represent payment for a relevant engagement;

(b) is a partnership and either the worker who is a partner is entitled to more than sixty per cent of the partnership's profits or there is a direct relationship between any profit share and income from relevant engagements; or

(c) is a partnership or an individual and the worker, being an employee, receives payments from the intermediary that can reasonably be taken to represent payment for a relevant engagement.

3.4   Only engagements performed by the worker that would be treated as an employment if undertaken directly for the client are within the scope of these rules. The services must also be performed for a client's business.

3.5   The income and expenses relating to the 'relevant engagements' must be identified and, if necessary, apportioned to allow a computation of the deemed Schedule E amount, and the deemed NIC earnings. The computation requires all the receipts in respect of a worker's relevant engagements for a tax year to be brought into account. The following deductions are then permitted:

(a)   A general, flat rate deduction of five per cent of the receipts brought into account.

(b)   Expenses that would have been allowable deductions if incurred by the worker in the performance of the duties of an employment consisting of the worker's relevant engagements.

(c)   Capital allowances that could have been claimed by the worker in the performance of the duties of an employment consisting of the worker's relevant engagements.

(d)   Any pension scheme contributions paid by the intermediary on behalf of the worker.

(e)   Any employer's national insurance contributions paid in respect of the worker.

(f)   The amount of any actual Schedule E taxable emoluments paid or made available to the worker.

3.6   The result of the computation is a figure which represents a gross amount comprising the deemed Schedule E payment and the employer's NIC thereon. The deemed payment is treated for income tax purposes as if it were paid on 5 April of the year concerned.

3.7   The deemed payment and the employer's NIC is allowed as a deduction in computing Schedule DI Case I profits when it is deemed paid (ie normally on the relevant 5 April in the accounting period). If the worker leaves the intermediary during the tax year, the date of leaving is used as the deemed payment date.

3.8   The payment of employer's NIC and accounting for the worker's Schedule E tax via PAYE will need to be done by 19 April following the relevant tax year. The details will need to be included on the employer's end of year PAYE returns due in May following the year concerned.

3.9   Where the intermediary is a company and the worker is entitled to receive a dividend from the company, relief is available to prevent double taxation occurring in respect of the deemed Schedule E payment and the distribution.

3.10   Intermediaries that are based overseas are brought within the scope of these rules if the worker is UK-resident, the client carries on a UK-based business and the services comprising the relevant engagements are performed in the UK.

3.11   Where an intermediary fails to account for income tax and NIC on relevant engagements, the Revenue have the power to transfer the liability to the worker (employee) for collection.

4   REMUNERATION PACKAGES

4.1   **An employee will usually be rewarded largely by salary, but several other elements can be included in a remuneration package. Some of them bring tax benefits to the employee only, and some will also benefit the employer.**

4.2 **Bonuses** are treated like salary, except that if a bonus is accrued in the employer's accounts but is paid more than nine months after the end of the period of account, its deductibility for Schedule D Case I purposes will be delayed.

4.3 The general position for benefits in kind is that they are subject to income tax and employer Class 1A NICs. The cost of providing benefits is generally deductible in computing Schedule D Case I profit for the employer (but if a car costing over £12,000 is provided, the employer's capital allowances (or deductions for lease payments) are restricted).

However, there are a large number of tax and NI free benefits in kind and there is a great deal of planning that can be done to ensure a tax and NIC efficient benefits package for directors and employees. The optimum is to ensure that the company receives a Schedule DI deduction for the expenditure whilst creating tax and NI free remuneration for employees. The main tax free benefits ones are listed below:

- (i) Grant, growth in value and exercise in shares in approved share option schemes
- (ii) Free car parking at/near place of work
- (iii) Contributions to approved occupational or personal pension scheme
- (iv) Mileage paid at Revenue Approved rates
- (v) Training courses provided
- (vi) Air miles obtained through business travel
- (vii) Beneficial loans under £5,000
- (viii) Long service awards (20 years, max £20 pa)
- (ix) Staff suggestion schemes
- (x) Free or subsidised canteens available to all staff
- (xi) Sports facilities provided on the employer's premises
- (xii) Crèche facilities provided on the employer's premises
- (xiii) Staff uniforms
- (xiv) Provision of goods or services at marginal cost only
- (xv) Gifts from third parties up to £150 per source
- (xvi) Removal expenses up to £8,000
- (xvii) Health checks, screening and eye tests
- (xviii) Mobile phones
- (xix) Computer equipment worth less than £2,500
- (xx) The first £30,000 of an ex gratia termination payment

For further details of benefits in kind see earlier in this text.

Question: Comparison of two remuneration packages

Employee A receives a salary of £20,000.

Employee B receives a salary of £15,000, the use of a video camera which cost £800 in January 2001 and the use of a car which cost £17,732 on 1.1.01. The Schedule E benefit for this car is £4,433. No fuel is supplied.

Employee B is also in an occupational pension scheme (not contracted out) to which he contributes 5% of his gross salary (excluding benefits) and his employer company contributes 10% of his gross salary (excluding benefits).

A and B are both single and have no other income.

Compute the Schedule E earnings of each employee and show the NIC effects of the two remuneration packages on both the employees and their employers. Use 2001/02 tax rates and allowances and assume that the employer prepares accounts to 31 March each year.

Show the amount that the employer will be able to deduct in its corporation tax computation in respect of each employee.

Answer

A's Schedule E earnings and NIC computations are as follows.

	£
Schedule E	20,000

NICs

£(20,000 − 4,535) × 10%	£1,547

A's employer must pay NICs of £20,000 − £4,535 × 11.9% = £1,840, and can deduct £(20,000 + 1,840) = £21,840 in computing trading profits.

B's Schedule E and NIC computations are as follows.

	£
Salary	15,000
Use of video camera £800 × 20%	160
Car	4,433
	19,593
Less pension contribution £15,000 × 5%	(750)
Schedule E	18,843

NICs

£(15,000 − 4,535) × 10%	1,047

B's employer must pay NICs as follows.

Class 1 NICs

£15,000 − £4,535 × 11.9%	1,245

Class 1A NICs

£(4,433 + 160) × 11.9%	547
	1,792

B's employer will have the following deductions in computing profits.

	£	£
Salary		15,000
Pension contribution £15,000 × 10%		1,500
NICs		1,792
Capital allowances		
Car (WDV b/f £14,732)	3,000	
Video camera £800 × 75% × 25%	150	
		3,150
		21,442

5 DIRECTORS AND SHAREHOLDERS

The decision whether to pay dividends or remuneration

5.1 Payments of dividends or remuneration will reduce a company's retained profits which means a reduction in net asset value and hence the value of the shares, ultimately reducing any chargeable gain on the disposal of those shares. However, the immediate tax cost of paying dividends or remuneration must be weighed against this advantage.

5.2 **Remuneration and the cost of benefits will be allowed as deductions in computing the company's profits chargeable to corporation tax.** The decision whether or not to make such payments could affect the rate of corporation tax by reducing the level of profits.

5.3 Conversely, dividends are not deductible Schedule D Case I expenses. They are paid out of post tax profits.

5.4 Remuneration and benefits give rise to an entitlement to pay personal pension premiums, whereas dividends do not.

5.5 Remuneration and benefits may be subject to NICs. Dividends are not subject to NICs.

5.6 Tax must be withheld on remuneration by an employer under the PAYE system. Conversely, dividend income does not fall within the PAYE system. Dividend income is paid net of a 10% tax credit and taxpayers with a taxable income of below £29,400 do not have any additional tax to pay. Other taxpayer's may have additional tax to pay. Non-taxpayers cannot reclaim the 10% tax credit attaching to dividend income.

5.7 If dividends are paid, timing can be important. The tax year in which a dividend is paid affects the due date for any additional tax that may have to be paid, and if a shareholder's other income fluctuates it may determine whether or not there is any additional tax to pay.

Liquidation

5.8 **An alternative to both dividends and remuneration is to retain profits in a company and then liquidate it. The company itself may have capital gains on the sale of its assets, and the shareholders will have capital gains on the liquidation, which will be treated as a disposal of their shares for the amounts paid to them.** The relative tax advantage of this alternative will have to be considered carefully.

5.9 This route may be worth considering when a company is set up to undertake a single project which will be completed within a few years.

Chapter roundup

- It is an employer's responsibility to deduct income tax and national insurance from amounts paid to employees.
- Numerous compliance requirements in relation to employee tax are imposed on employers.
- Both employers and employees must pay national insurance contributions.
- For director/shareholders the decision whether to pay dividends or remuneration is a major planning consideration.

Quick quiz

1 Give an example of a PAYE code.

2 What National insurance contributions are payable by employers?

Answers to quick quiz

1 453L

2 Class 1, Class 1A and Class 1B contributions

Now try the question below from the Exam Question Bank

Number	Level	Marks	Time
16	Exam	20	36 mins

Part D
Advanced corporate tax matters

Chapter 15

GROUPS AND CONSORTIA. REORGANISATIONS

Topic list	Syllabus reference	Ability required
1 Types of group	(iii), (v), (vii)	Comprehension
2 Group relief	(iii), (vii)	Application
3 Chargeable gains	(v) (vii)	Application
4 Reorganisations and liquidations	(iii), (vii)	Evaluation
5 Purchase or sale of business	(vii)	Evaluation

Introduction

In this chapter we consider the extent to which tax law recognises group relationships between companies. Companies in a group are still separate entities with their own tax liabilities, but tax law recognises the close relationship between group companies. They can, if they meet certain conditions, share their losses and pass assets between each other without chargeable gains.

We also look at some of the consequences of changes in the composition of a group, and at other changes in a company's capital. Finally we consider the tax implications of the alternative methods of acquiring other businesses.

Learning outcomes covered in this chapter

- **Identify** the effect of all kinds of loss relief on a company's, group's or consortium's CT liability

- **Identify** the CGT reliefs available in a group situation and the anti-avoidance rules relating to pre-entry assets

- **Demonstrate** the most efficient method of disposing of assets to third parties by a group of companies

- **Calculate** the form of loss relief which will minimise the CT liability in either a single company or in a group of companies

- **Evaluate** the efficiency of alternative methods of acquiring other businesses

Syllabus content covered in this chapter

- Group structures: group relief; group capital gains, including the rules for pre-entry losses and gains

- Loss strategy: maximisation of group and consortia relief; intragroup transfers of assets

- Company takeovers: changes in ownership: methods of acquisition – assets or shares

- Integration of tax planning into the budgeting process

1 TYPES OF GROUP

1.1 A group exists for taxation purposes where one company is a subsidiary of another. The percentage shareholding involved determines the taxation consequences of the fact that there is a group.

1.2 The four types of relationship for tax purposes are:

- **associated companies;**
- **75% subsidiaries;**
- **consortia;**
- **groups for chargeable gains purposes (capital gains groups).**

Associated companies

1.3 **Two companies are associated with each other for taxation purposes if one is under the control of the other, or both are under the control of a third party.** Control for these purposes means entitlement to more than 50% of any one of:

- the share capital;
- the votes;
- the income;
- the net assets on a winding up.

1.4 **The number of associated companies determines the limits for the starting rate of corporation tax, the small companies rate and marginal relief.**

2 GROUP RELIEF

2.1 **The group relief provisions enable companies within a 75% group to transfer trading losses to other companies within the group,** in order to set these against taxable profits and reduce the group's overall corporation tax liability.

> **KEY TERM**
>
> For one company to be a **75% subsidiary** of another, the holding company must have:
>
> - At least 75% of the ordinary share capital of the subsidiary
> - A right to at least 75% of the distributable income of the subsidiary, and
> - A right to at least 75% of the net assets of the subsidiary were it to be wound up.
>
> Two companies are members of a group for group relief purposes where one is a 75% subsidiary of the other, or both are 75% subsidiaries of a third company. Ordinary share capital is any share capital other than fixed dividend preference shares.

2.2 Two companies are in a group only if there is a 75% effective interest. Thus an 80% subsidiary (T) of an 80% subsidiary (S) is not in a group with the holding company (H), because the effective interest is only 80% × 80% = 64%. However, S and T are in a group and can claim group relief from each other. S *cannot* claim group relief from T and pass it on to H; it can only claim group relief for its own use.

2.3 A group relief group may include non-UK resident companies. **However, losses may generally only be surrendered between UK resident companies although in certain circumstances group relief is available to UK branches of overseas companies.**

The relief

2.4 A **claimant company** is assumed to use its own current year losses or losses brought forward in working out the profits against which it may claim group relief, even if it does not in fact claim s 393A relief for current losses. Furthermore, **group relief is against profits after all other reliefs for the current period or brought forward from earlier periods**, including non-trading deficits on loan relationships and charges. Group relief is given before relief for any amounts brought back from later periods.

2.5 **A surrendering company may group relieve a loss before setting it against its own profits for the period of the loss, and may specify any amount to be surrendered.** This is important for **tax planning as it enables the surrendering company to leave profits in its own computation to be charged to corporation tax at the small companies rate or starting rate, while surrendering its losses to other companies to cover profits which would otherwise fall into a marginal relief band or be taxed at the full rate.** Note that profits in the small companies marginal relief band are taxed at the marginal rate of 32.5%. Profits in the starting rate marginal relief band are taxed at the marginal rate of 22.5%.

Question: Group relief of losses

In a group of four companies, the results for the year ended 31 March 2002 are as follows.

	Profit/(loss) £
A Ltd	2,000
B Ltd	212,500
C Ltd	1,000,000
D Ltd	(400,000)

How should the loss be allocated to save as much tax as possible? How much tax is saved?

Answer

The upper and lower limits for small companies' marginal relief are £1,500,000/4 = £375,000 and £300,000/4 = £75,000 respectively. The upper and lower limits for starting rate marginal relief are £50,000/4 = £12,500 and £10,000/4 = £2,500 respectively.

	A Ltd £	B Ltd £	C Ltd £
Profits before group relief	2,000	212,500	1,000,000
Less group relief (note)	0	(137,500)	(262,500)
PCTCT	2,000	75,000	737,500

Tax saved
£137,500 × 32.5%	44,688	
£262,500 × 30%		78,750

Total £(44,688 + 78,750) = £123,438

Note: We wish to save the most tax possible for the group.

Since A Ltd is in the starting rate band any loss given to it will only save 10% tax.

B Ltd is in the marginal relief for small companies rate band. Therefore, any loss given to B saves the effective marginal rate of 32.5% until the profits fall to £75,000 (the small companies lower limit). After this only 20% is saved.

C Ltd is in the full rate band of 30% until profits fall to £375,000 (the small companies upper limit).

So to conclude it is best to give B Ltd £137,500 of loss and save 32.5% tax on the profits in the marginal relief band. The balance of the loss is then given to C Ltd to save 30% tax.

2.6 **A company may surrender to other group companies trading losses, excess Schedule A losses, non-trading deficits on loan relationships and excess charges on income, including non-trading charges.** Charges can only be group-relieved to the extent that they exceed profits before taking account of losses brought forward or back from other accounting periods. **Excess management expenses of investment companies may also be surrendered.** If there are excess charges, Schedule A losses and management expenses available for surrender then they are surrendered in that order.

2.7 Capital losses cannot be group relieved. However, see paragraph 3.9 below for details of how a group may net off its gains and losses.

2.8 **Only current period losses are available for group relief. Furthermore, they must be set against profits of a corresponding accounting period.** If the accounting periods of a surrendering company and a claimant company are not the same this means that both the profits and losses must be apportioned so that only the results of the period of overlap may be set off. Apportionment is on a time basis. However, in the period when a company joins or leaves a group, an alternative method may be used if the result given by time-apportionment would be unjust or unreasonable.

Question: corresponding accounting periods

	£
S Ltd incurs a trading loss for the year to 30 September 2001	(15,000)
H Ltd makes taxable profits:	
for the year to 31 December 2000	20,000
for the year to 31 December 2001	10,000

What group relief can H Ltd claim from S Ltd?

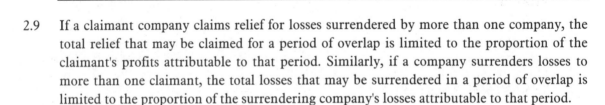

Answer

	£
H Ltd can claim group relief as follows.	
For the year ended 31 December 2000 profits of the corresponding accounting period (1.10.00 - 31.12.00) are £20,000 × 3/12	5,000
Losses of the corresponding accounting period are £15,000 × 3/12	3,750
A claim for £3,750 of group relief may be made against H Ltd's profits	
For the year ended 31 December 2001 profits of the corresponding accounting period (1.1.01 - 30.9.01) are £10,000 × 9/12	7,500
Losses of the corresponding accounting period are £15,000 × 9/12	11,250
A claim for £7,500 of group relief may be made against H Ltd's profits	

2.9 If a claimant company claims relief for losses surrendered by more than one company, the total relief that may be claimed for a period of overlap is limited to the proportion of the claimant's profits attributable to that period. Similarly, if a company surrenders losses to more than one claimant, the total losses that may be surrendered in a period of overlap is limited to the proportion of the surrendering company's losses attributable to that period.

2.10 **A claim for group relief is normally made on the claimant company's tax return** It is ineffective unless a notice of consent is also given by the surrendering company.

2.11 A claimant company may not amend a group relief claim but it may withdraw it and replace it with a new claim. The time limit for making or withdrawing a claim is the latest of:

(a) The first anniversary of the filing date for the CT return.

(b) 30 days after the completion of an enquiry into a return.

(c) 30 days after the amendment of a self assessment by the Revenue following the completion of an enquiry.

(d) 30 days after the settlement of an appeal against an amendment to the self assessment made by the Revenue following an enquiry.

The Revenue has discretion to accept a late claim/withdrawal.

2.12 Group wide claims/surrenders can be made as one person can act for two or more companies at once.

2.13 Any payment by the claimant company for group relief, up to the amount of the loss surrendered, is ignored for all corporation tax purposes.

Anti-avoidance rules

2.14 **If arrangements exist for a company to leave a group, then group relief is not available in respect of losses incurred after such arrangements are made.** 'Arrangements' is a very wide term in this context and can include any form of informal agreement for the disposal of a subsidiary company, even on normal commercial terms. Also if entitlement to profits or assets could vary in the future, for example because of options, the lowest possible percentage entitlements are taken to apply now in determining whether a group exists.

Question: Group relief

C Ltd has one wholly owned subsidiary, D Ltd. The results of both companies for the four years ended 31 March 2002 are shown below.

	12 months to 31 March			
	1999	*2000*	*2001*	*2002*
	£	£	£	£
C Ltd				
Trading profit (loss)	200	(1,700)	100	(2,000)
Schedule A	800	800	800	800
Trade charges paid	(40)	(50)	0	(60)
D Ltd				
Trading profit (loss)	(2,300)	2,000	(870)	2,400
Interest on gilts (non-trading investment) (gross)	1,800	0	1,200	1,300
Trade charges paid	(600)	(400)	(300)	(500)

Show the profits chargeable to corporation tax for both companies for all years shown, assuming that loss relief and group relief are claimed as early as possible.

Answer

C Ltd

	Accounting periods to 31 March			
	1999	*2000*	*2001*	*2002*
	£	£	£	£
Schedule D Case I	200	0	100	0
Schedule A	800	800	800	800
	1,000	800	900	800
Less s 393A(1) - current period relief		(800)	0	(800)
		0	900	0
Less charges paid	(40)	0	0	0
	960	0	900	0
Less s 393A - carryback	0	0	(900)	0
	960	0	0	0
Less group relief claim	(960)	0	0	0
PCTCT	0	0	0	0

	Accounting periods to 31 March			
	1999	2000	2001	2002
	£	£	£	£
Loss memorandum				
Loss		(1,700)		(2,000)
S 393A(1) claim: current year		800		800
		(900)		(1,200)
S 393A(1) claim: carry back				900
				(300)
Excess charges		(50)		(60)
		(950)		(360)
Group relief surrender		950		360
		0		0
D Ltd				
Schedule D Case I	0	2,000	0	2,400
Less s 393(1)(9)		(140)		
		1,860		
Schedule D Case III	1,800	0	1,200	1,300
	1,800	1,860	1,200	3,700
Less s 393A(1) - current period relief	(1,800)		(870)	
	0		330	
Less trade charges paid	0	(400)	(300)	(500)
	0	1,460	30	3,200
Less group relief claim		(950)		(360)
PCTCT	0	510	30	2,840

	Accounting periods to 31 March	
	1999	2001
Loss memorandum	£	£
Loss	(2,300)	(870)
S 393A(1) claim	1,800	870
	(500)	0
Excess charges	(600)	
	(1,100)	
Group relief surrender	960	
	(140)	
S 393(1)(9) claim	140	
	0	

Consortium relief

2.15   The definition of a consortium is given below.

> **KEY TERM**
>
> A **company is owned by a consortium** (and is known as a consortium-owned company) if:
>
> - 75% or more of its ordinary share capital is owned by companies (the members of the consortium), none of which has a holding of less than 5%, and
>
> - Each member of the consortium is entitled to at least 5% of any profits available for distribution to equity holders of the company and at least 5% of any assets so available on a winding up.

2.16 Consortium relief is a loss relief which is available:

(a) Where the surrendering company is a trading company owned by a consortium and is not a 75% subsidiary of any one company and the claimant company belongs to the consortium.

(b) Where the surrendering company is a trading company which is a 90% subsidiary of a holding company which is owned by a consortium and is not a 75% subsidiary of any one company and the claimant company is a member of the consortium.

(c) Where the surrendering company is a holding company owned by a consortium and is not a 75% subsidiary of any one company and the claimant company is a member of the consortium.

2.17 A **trading company** is one whose business consists wholly or mainly in carrying on a trade. A holding company is one whose business consists wholly or mainly in holding shares in companies which are trading companies.

2.18 **A consortium-owned company can surrender losses in proportion to the stakes of the members of the consortium.** Thus if a member holds 20% of the shares in the company, up to 20% of the company's losses can be surrendered to that member.

2.19 Consortium relief can also flow downwards. **A member of a consortium may surrender its losses to set against its share of the consortium-owned company's profits.** So, a member with a 25% stake in the consortium-owned company can surrender losses to cover up to 25% of the company's profits.

2.20 Whereas normally a surrendering company can surrender group relief without having to consider any possible s 393A(1) claim, **a loss made by a consortium-owned company must be reduced by any potential s 393A(1) claims against current period profits** (not profits of previous periods) **before it may be surrendered as consortium relief**.

2.21 Although a consortium can be established with non-UK resident companies, losses cannot, in general, be surrendered to/from a non-UK resident.

Question: Consortium relief of losses

C Ltd is owned 60% by A Ltd, 30% by B Ltd and 10% by an individual. Results for the year ended 31 March 2002 are as follows.

	A Ltd	B Ltd	C Ltd
	£	£	£
Schedule D Case I/(loss)	200,000	75,000	(50,000)
Schedule A	0	0	12,000

Compute the corporation tax liabilities of all three companies, assuming that all possible consortium relief claims are made but that C Ltd does not claim s 393A(1) relief.

Answer

A Ltd may claim £(50,000 − 12,000) × 60% = £22,800.
B Ltd may claim £(50,000 − 12,000) × 30% = £11,400.
A Ltd has one associated company (C Ltd).

A Ltd's corporation tax liability is as follows.

	£
Profits	200,000
Less consortium relief	(22,800)
Profits chargeable to corporation tax	177,200

Corporation tax	£
£177,200 × 30%	53,160
Less small companies' rate marginal relief £(750,000 − 177, 200) × 1/40	(14,320)
	38,840

B Ltd's corporation tax liability is £(75,000 − 11,400) × 20% = £63,600 × 20% = £12,720.

C Ltd's corporation tax liability is:

	£
£12,000 × 20%	2,400
Less: starting rate marginal relief £(25,000 − 12,000) × 1/40 (note)	(325)
	2,075

Note. The limits for small companies' rate marginal relief and starting rate marginal relief are divided by 2 since there are two associated companies (A Ltd and C Ltd).

C Ltd has a loss to carry forward under s 393(1) ICTA 1988 of £(50,000 - 22,800 - 11,400) = £15,800.

Tax planning for group relief

2.22 This section outlines some tax planning points to bear in mind when dealing with a group.

2.23 Group relief should first be given in this order:

1st To companies in the small companies marginal relief band paying 32.5% tax (but only sufficient loss to bring profits down to the SCR limit)

2nd To companies paying the full rate of tax at 30%

3rd To companies in the starting rate marginal relief band paying 22.5% tax (but only sufficient loss to bring profits down to the starting rate limit)

4th To companies paying SCR at 20%

5th To companies paying starting rate at 10%

2.24 Similarly, a company should make a s 393A(1) claim to use a loss itself rather than surrender the loss to other group companies if the s 393A(1) claim would lead to a tax saving at a higher rate.

2.25 Companies with profits may benefit by reducing their claims for capital allowances in a particular year. This may leave sufficient profits to take advantage of group relief which may only be available for the current year. The amount on which writing-down allowances can be claimed in later years is increased accordingly.

3 CHARGEABLE GAINS

Intra-group transfers

3.1 Companies are in a capital gains group if:

(a) At each level, there is a 75% holding, and
(b) The top company has an effective interest of over 50% in the group companies.

If A holds 75% of B, B holds 75% of C and C holds 75% of D, then A, B and C are in such a group, but D is outside the group because A's interest in D is only 75% × 75% × 75% = 42.1875%. Furthermore, D is not in a group with C, because the group must include the top company (A).

3.2 **Companies in a capital gains group make intra-group transfers of chargeable assets without a chargeable gain or an allowable loss arising**. No election is needed, as this relief is compulsory. The assets are deemed to be transferred at such a price as will give the transferor no gain and no loss (see the special rules on indexation in Chapter 8).

3.3 **Non-UK resident companies are included as members of a capital gains group. Provided the assets transferred do not result in a potential leakage of UK corporation tax, no gain/no loss transfers are possible within a worldwide (global) group of companies.** This means that it may be possible to make no gain/no loss transfers to non-UK resident companies with a branch or agency in the UK.

3.4 **If a company leaves a group while it owns assets transferred to it within the previous six years under the provisions described in para 3.2 above, then the departing company is treated as though it had, at the time of its acquisition of such assets, sold and immediately re-acquired them at their then market values**. However, the consequent gain or loss (computed using indexation allowance up to the time when the departing company acquired the assets) is brought into the departing company's tax computation for the accounting period in which it leaves the group.

3.5 The Revenue can collect the tax from the holding company if the tax is unpaid six months after its due date.

3.6 If a company leaves a group because another group company ceases to exist, the first company is not deemed to have left a group for these purposes. The tax charge also does not apply if one company acquired an asset from another, and both companies leave the group together while remaining in a group with each other.

Question: Company leaves an 'assets group'

In March 2002, Top Ltd sold to Take plc the whole of the share capital of Bottom Ltd, a 100% subsidiary. Included in the assets of Bottom Ltd is a warehouse acquired by Top Ltd in January 1984 for £96,000. This was transferred to Bottom Ltd in August 1996 for £100,000. Its market value at the date of transfer was £310,000. The indexation allowance on a sale in August 1996 would have been £73,344.

What is the effect of Bottom Ltd leaving the group? Compute Bottom Ltd's mainstream corporation tax for the year ended 31 March 2002 if it has trading income of £2,000,000.

Answer

Bottom Ltd leaves the group within six years of its acquiring the warehouse from Top Ltd. Bottom Ltd will be treated as if it had sold the warehouse at its market value in August 1996 and then immediately reacquired it.

	£	£
Proceeds (ie MV in August 1996)		310,000
Less cost: cost to Top Ltd	96,000	
indexation allowance to August 1996	73,344	
		(169,344)
Chargeable gain of Bottom Ltd, in the accounting period which includes March 2002		140,656

Top Ltd may also have a chargeable gain on the sale of its shares in Bottom Ltd.

Bottom Ltd's MCT for the year to 31.3.2002 is as follows.

	£
Schedule D Case I	2,000,000
Chargeable gain	140,656
	2,140,656
Corporation tax £2,140,565 × 30%	£642,197

Exceptions to the 'no gain/no loss' transfer price

3.7 **There are exceptions to the 'no gain no loss' transfer price for intra-group transfers of capital assets. There will be an immediate chargeable disposal:**

- Where an intra-group **transfer is in satisfaction of a debt.**

- On the **disposal of an interest in shares in a group company by way of a capital distribution.**

- **Where cash or other assets are received upon the redemption of shares in another company.**

3.8 In addition, when an asset is transferred between two group companies and is trading stock for one of those companies but not for the other, it is treated as appropriated to or from trading stock by the company for which it is trading stock. This may give rise to an immediate chargeable gain, allowable loss or trading profit or loss (see earlier in this Text).

Matching group gains and losses

3.9 Capital losses cannot be included in a group relief claim. However, **two members of a capital gains group can elect that an asset that has been disposed of outside the group is treated as if it had been transferred between them immediately before disposal.** The deemed transferee company is then treated as having made the disposal. This election may be made within two years of the end of the accounting period in which the disposal took place.

3.10 From a tax planning point of view, elections(s) should be made to ensure that net taxable gains arise in the company subject to the lowest rate of corporation tax.

Rollover relief

3.11 **If a member of a capital gains group disposes of an asset eligible for capital gains rollover or holdover relief it may treat all of the group companies as a single unit for the purpose of claiming such relief. Acquisitions by other group members within the qualifying period** of one year before the disposal to three years afterwards may therefore **be matched with the disposal.** Both the disposing company and the acquiring company must make the claim. If an asset is transferred at no gain and no loss between group members, that transfer does not count as the acquisition of an asset for these purposes.

From a group planning point of view, there should be careful timing of acquisitions/disposals to ensure that rollover/holdover relief will be available.

3.12 Claims may also be made by non-trading group members which hold assets used for other group members' trades.

Rebasing elections

3.13 Taxpayers may elect for their capital gains and losses on all assets held at 31 March 1982 to be calculated by reference to 31 March 1982 values. In the case of capital gains groups such an election must be made by the holding company on behalf of the whole group. Once made, such an election is irrevocable.

Pre-entry losses

3.14 A group might acquire a company that has capital losses brought forward, or assets which could be sold to generate capital losses. The use of such 'pre-entry' losses is restricted.

3.15 **If a company (X) joins a group (G), we must identify X's pre-entry (capital) losses. These are:**

- **Losses on disposals before X joined G.**

- **The pre-entry proportions of losses on disposals after X joined G of pre-entry assets** (assets X already owned when it joined G).

3.16 When a pre-entry asset is sold at a loss after X joins G, the pre-entry proportion of the loss is found by working out the proportion for each item of allowable expenditure (cost or enhancement expenditure) and adding up the results.

The proportion for each item of allowable expenditure is $A \times (B/C) \times (D/E)$, where:

A   is the total allowable loss

B   is the item of allowable expenditure

C   is the sum of all the items of allowable expenditure

D   is the time from when the expenditure was incurred (or 1 April 1982 if later) to when X joined G. (D is zero if X joined G before the expenditure was incurred or before 1 April 1982)

E   is the time from when the expenditure was incurred (or 1 April 1982 if later) to the disposal

The original cost of the asset is treated as incurred when the asset was acquired.

3.17 If X sells a pre-entry asset at a loss and makes an election within two years of the end of the accounting period of the disposal, the above computation is disregarded and instead the pre-entry proportion of the loss is the smaller of:

(a) The loss which would have arisen on a sale at market value when X joined G (treating a gain as a loss of £0).

(b) The loss on the actual sale.

3.18 **X's pre-entry losses** may (subject to the usual rule against carrying back capital losses) **be set against gains on assets which:**

- **X disposed of before joining G**

- **X already owned when it joined G,** or

- **X acquired after joining G from someone outside G** and which have, since acquisition, not been used except for the purposes of a trade which X was carrying on immediately before joining G and continued to carry on until the disposals giving rise to the gains.

3.19 In any one accounting period, pre-entry losses (whether of the current period or brought forward) are used (so far as possible) before other losses.

Question: Pre-entry losses

X joined the G group on 1 January 1995. X had acquired some land on 1 August 1989 for £700,000, and had incurred enhancement expenditure of £300,000 on 1 April 1992. The land was worth £600,000 on 1 January 1995. On 1 July 2001, X sold the land for £450,000. What is the pre-entry proportion of the loss?

Answer

The total allowable loss is as follows.

	£	£
Proceeds		450,000
Less: cost	700,000	
enhancement expenditure	300,000	
		(1,000,000)
Allowable loss		(550,000)

The pre-entry proportion without an election is as follows.

	£
$£550,000 \times \dfrac{700,000}{1,000,000} \times \dfrac{1.8.89-1.1.95}{1.8.89-1.7.01} \dfrac{=(65 \text{ months})}{=(143 \text{ months})}$	175,000
$£550,000 \times \dfrac{300,000}{1,000,000} \times \dfrac{1.4.92-1.1.95}{1.4.92-1.7.01} \dfrac{=(33 \text{ months})}{=(111 \text{ months})}$	49,054
	224,054

If the land had been sold when X joined the group on 1 January 1995, the loss would have been as follows.

	£	£
Proceeds		600,000
Less: cost	700,000	
enhancement expenditure	300,000	
		(1,000,000)
Allowable loss		(400,000)

The pre-entry proportion with an election would be the lower of £550,000 and £400,000, that is, £400,000.

The company wants the *lowest* possible pre-entry proportion, because that proportion's use is restricted. The company should therefore not make an election, and will then have a pre-entry proportion of £224,054. The balance of the loss, £(550,000 – 224,054) = £325,946, can be set against all gains made by X Ltd in the same or later accounting periods without restriction.

Capital gains buying

3.20 The only losses available to set against pre-entry gains **realised before a company joins a group** are:

- Losses that arise in that company before the company joins the new group, and
- Losses that arise after that time on assets that the company held when it joined the group.

> **Exam focus point**
>
> Try to remember the following summary - it will be of great help in the exam.
>
> Parent Co controls over 50% of subsidiary
> - Associated companies for upper and lower limits
>
> Parent Co owns 75% or more of subsidiary
> - Surrender trading losses, Schedule A losses, excess charges, loan deficits, excess management expenses to companies with some PCTCT for same time period
>
> Parent Co owns 75% or more of subsidiary and subsidiary owns 75% or more of its subsidiaries
> - Transfer assets between companies automatically at no gain/no loss
> - Capital gains and losses can be matched between group member companies
> - All companies treated as one for rollover relief purposes.

4 REORGANISATIONS AND LIQUIDATIONS

4.1 Companies and groups wishing to reorganise their affairs will often find that tax barriers seem to prevent straightforward commercial arrangements. This section covers the more important taxation implications of common types of transaction.

4.2 Company A may transfer a trade or business to a new company B in return for the issue of shares in B directly to the shareholders of A. A variation on this is the 'hive down' whereby a company transfers a trade or business to its own wholly-owned subsidiary in exchange for shares in the subsidiary.

4.3 Alternatively, company A might transfer its shareholding in a subsidiary to company B in return for the issue of shares in company B to company A's members.

4.4 When a trade is discontinued, unrelieved trading losses are usually lost. However, **relief is given (under s 343 ICTA 1988) where a company ceases to carry on a trade and another company begins to carry it on**, and the same persons own at least three quarters of the trade at two times, one within a year before and the other within two years after the transfer. **This relief is restricted where the transferor company is insolvent and the transferee does not take over all of the transferor's liabilities.**

4.5 **Where s 343 relief is claimed, unrelieved trading losses of the transferor are taken over by the transferee for relief against future profits of the transferred trade. In addition, capital allowances continue as if there had been no break.**

4.6 **The carry over of non-trade and capital losses is not allowed.**

4.7 There is also a relief in respect of chargeable gains. Where a business, or part of one, is transferred between companies (not in a capital gains group), chargeable assets transferred are treated as having been sold for a price giving rise to neither a gain nor a loss. This only applies if no consideration is received by the transferor (other than the transferee's assuming the liabilities of the business) and the transfer is for bona fide commercial reasons and not to avoid tax.

4.8 **The concept of a global group applies to reconstructions and amalgamations. It does not matter if either party to the scheme is not resident in the UK as long as the assets of the business transferred remain within the scope of UK corporation tax** on chargeable gains. This allows a business to be transferred on a no gain/no loss basis from one non-resident company to another non resident company as long as the business continues in the

UK or for it to be similarly transferred from a UK resident company to a non-resident company or vice versa subject to the same condition.

4.9 **Shareholders will obtain relief from capital gains tax on many reorganisations and on share for share amalgamations. Where persons holding shares or debentures in one company exchange them for shares or debentures in the same proportions in another company, the two are treated as one holding.** Thus the original and the new shares or debentures are regarded as a single asset acquired when the original shares were acquired and no disposal occurs for capital gains tax purposes.

4.10 If, on an amalgamation of two companies, their trades are kept in the original companies, there are no special tax consequences for the companies (except that the tax privileges of groups set out earlier in this chapter may become available). If one company's trade is transferred to the other company, the relief set out in Paragraph 4.7 above may be relevant.

Revenue clearance

4.11 **It is advisable to obtain advance clearance from the Revenue before undertaking a scheme of reorganisation.** Clearance should be obtained to ensure that the tax reliefs will apply, and that anti-avoidance legislation aimed at transactions in securities will not be invoked. The scheme must be carried out for bona fide commercial reasons to obtain clearances, and it must be shown that the main objectives do not include tax avoidance.

The consequences of a company's joining or leaving a group

Acquisition of a subsidiary

4.12 When a company joins a group, the following consequences ensue.

(a) It acquires several associated companies, and each existing group member has one more associated company.

(b) The tax privileges of groups set out earlier in this chapter may become available. Group relief is unavailable for losses of the new group member arising before it joined the group, nor against its pre-entry profits. The use of pre-entry capital losses may be restricted, as may be the use of group capital losses against pre-entry gains. In addition, the brought forward trading losses in the new subsidiary may be lost on a major change in the nature or conduct of its business or on a revival of a business which had become small or negligible (see Chapter 7).

Sale of a subsidiary

4.13 When a company leaves a group, the above consequences reverse. In addition, chargeable gains may arise on assets transferred to the departing company by other companies in the preceding six years, and the company selling the subsidiary may have a chargeable gain on its shares.

4.14 If a company is sold in circumstances which lead to default on the payment of its corporation tax the Inland Revenue can recover from the previous owners of that company the tax unpaid for subsequent periods if it was reasonable to infer from the terms of the transfer and the surrounding circumstances that it was unlikely the company would meet a tax liability which could have been foreseen at the time of the change in ownership.

Question: Group reorganisation

A Ltd, B Ltd and C Ltd have the following trading results for the year ended 31 March 2002.

	Profit/(loss)
	£
A Ltd	300,000
B Ltd	120,000
C Ltd	(80,000)

On 30 September 2001, A Ltd sold its 90% stake in B Ltd, realising a chargeable gain of £230,000. On 1 January 2002, A Ltd acquired an 85% stake in C Ltd. A Ltd is to claim all possible group relief.

Compute the corporation tax liabilities of all three companies for the year.

Answer

A Ltd has two associated companies during the accounting period, making the upper limit for small companies marginal relief £1,500,000/3 = £500,000.

B Ltd and C Ltd each have one associated company during their accounting periods, making the lower limit for the small companies marginal relief £300,000/2 = £150,000.

A Ltd's corporation tax liability is as follows.

	£
Schedule D Case I	300,000
Chargeable gain	230,000
	530,000
Less group relief £80,000 × 3/12	(20,000)
Profits chargeable to corporation tax	510,000
Corporation tax £510,000 × 30%	153,000

B Ltd's corporation tax liability is £120,000 × 20% = £24,000.

C Ltd has no corporation tax liability, and it has a loss of £(80,000 – 20,000) = £60,000 to carry forward.

Liquidations

4.15 As a result of a group reorganising itself if one or more companies might be put into liquidation. The general rules state that accounting periods end on each of:

(i) **the cessation of trading;**

(ii) **the passing of a resolution for winding up;**

(iii) **the expiration of 12 months from (ii) or from the end of the last accounting period;**

(iv) **the completion of the winding up;**

(v) **any other appropriate date selected by the Revenue** if the beginning or end of an accounting period is uncertain.

4.16 Thus once a company goes into liquidation a new accounting period begins and that period will run for 12 month duration until the liquidation (winding up) is complete. Ceasing to trade once in liquidation has no effect on the accounting period.

4.17 Companies in liquidation are taxed in the same way as other companies - PCTCT is calculated and taxed as normal.

4.18 Where the rate of corporation tax for the final financial year involved is not known by the time the winding up is completed, the rate for the penultimate financial year is used.

4.19 **Losses carried forward under s 393(1) ICTA 1988 cannot be carried forward beyond the date of cessation of the trade.**

4.20 The following points should also be considered.

(a) **Losses can be carried back for up to 36 months on a cessation of trade**, probably leading to repayments of corporation tax.

(b) Any trading loss to carry back from the final accounting period of trading can be augmented by unrelieved trade charges.

(c) **Capital distributions to shareholders during the liquidation will give rise to chargeable gains.**

(d) **The company's VAT registration** (see later in this text) **must be cancelled within 30 days** on cessation of trade, or penalties may arise. VAT may be due on remaining stock or on the sale of assets. Customs must also be notified when a company goes into liquidation if at that time it is still VAT registered.

5 PURCHASE OR SALE OF BUSINESS

Purchase or sale of a business.

5.1 A purchaser could acquire the business of a **'target'** company by either acquiring the 'target' company's assets or by acquiring the 'target' company's shares. The advantages/disadvantages of each method of acquiring a business are listed below.

5.2 **Advantages of buying assets**

(a) The purchaser can **choose which assets to acquire** rather than take the entire business

(b) The expenditure on plant and certain buildings will attract **capital allowances**

(c) The **capital gains base cost of the assets is the price paid** on acquisition. If shares are acquired the assets retain their original base cost, or 31.3.82 MV if higher

(d) There is some latitude to apportion the consideration over the assets acquired to best tax effect. For example plant attracts WDA at 25% but industrial buildings only 4% WDA

(e) For the purchaser who is already trading it might be possible to **argue that it is not a separate trade which is acquired but an extension of the existing trade.** This is **important where losses are being carried forward**

(f) **By acquiring assets, the liabilities** (including tax liabilities) whether known or unknown are **left behind** in the vendor company thus minimising the need for tax warranties and indemnities

5.3 **Advantages of buying shares**

(a) The **business continues uninterrupted**

(b) The 'target' company does not have to provide for tax on the profit from asset sales

(c) **Unused tax reliefs** of the 'target' company **are potentially available** for the 'target' company

(d) The **sale consideration is paid to the vendor shareholders** and not, as in the case of an asset sale, to the target company. The need to extract proceeds through a dividend or liquidation is thereby avoided

(e) **If the purchaser is a company,** a share purchase opens up the **group** tax advantages although it also increases the number of associated companies in the group by one

(f) The vendors would be able to **defer chargeable gains if the deal was paper-for-paper**

5.4 The choice of the best method of sale is partly determined by:

(a) The **vendor might be prepared to accept a sale of assets by the target company if it can shelter the resulting gains and balancing charges with capital losses and trading losses** brought forward respectively. Alternatively can the gains be sheltered by group-wide roll-over or group capital losses? If CT is payable on the gains and/or balancing charges the impact is reduced if there is brought forward ACT.

(b) **If the purchaser cannot recover (or fully recover) VAT paid on acquiring the assets this may be unattractive** (see later in this text). VAT may not actually apply provided the business is transferred as a going concern and the assets are used by the transferee in the same kind of business as before. If only some of the assets are transferred the 'going concern' point may be uncertain and will result in problems between the parties.

Reorganisation prior to sale

5.5 **The target company may pay a dividend out of distributable profits** prior to sale. Individual vendors normally bear less tax if their consideration is in the form of dividends rather than capital. A corporate shareholder pays no tax on a dividend but may pay up to 32.5% on a gain.

5.6 **Instead of paying a dividend a company could use its funds to purchase some of its own shares.** This might be convenient where one group of existing shareholders is buying out another shareholder. The vendor can then make a capital gain instead of receiving a distribution if certain conditions were satisfied.

5.7 Instead of selling the 'target' company, the 'target' company could **transfer (ie hive-down) selected assets and parts of its business to a newly formed company (Newco) and then sell the shares in Newco.** The tax legislation protects the losses in such a situation by enabling them to stick to the trade transferred (see above).

5.8 The 'target' company could transfer those assets not being sold to the holding company prior to the sale. No capital gain would crystallise provided the 75% group relationship exists.

Consideration for the disposal

5.9 The **date of disposal is normally the date of exchange of contract,** except that, where there is a condition in the contract, it is the date the contract becomes unconditional.

5.10 **Any cash element in the consideration results in an immediate chargeable gain.**

5.11 **Any shares or debentures element in the consideration will result in roll-over of the gain if:**

(a) The vendor is selling shares

(b) The purchaser is a company who issues shares or debentures to the vendor

(c) The purchaser owns or will own over 25% of ordinary share capital in the 'target' company, or there is a general offer to all shareholders in the 'target' company

(d) The exchange is for bona fide commercial reasons and not with the object of tax avoidance

In this case the vendor's base cost of the 'new' paper is cost/31.3.82 MV of the original shares with indexation running as though the new shares has been acquired when the original shares were acquired.

Losses and other reliefs

5.12 **If the 'target' company has trading losses, capital losses or surplus ACT brought forward it is important where possible not to waste them.**

5.13 The trading losses of the 'target' company can only be carried forward if the trade in which they arose continues. This carry forward is however denied if:

(a) Within a three year period there is both a change in ownership of the company and a major change in the nature of conduct of the company's trade

(b) There is a change in ownership of the company after the scale of activities has become small or negligible before it revives

5.14 Capital losses of the target can be carried forward even if there is a change in ownership of the company.

5.15 The trading losses of the 'target' company are not automatically transferred with the trade.

5.16 By hiving down the business/assets to be sold to a new subsidiary (Newco), the trading losses and capital allowances are transferred to that company, the shares in which are then sold. Losses transferred may be restricted if net liabilities of the target are not also hived down.

5.17 Chargeable assets previously transferred between group companies on a no gain/no loss basis are chargeable in the 'target' company when it leaves the group within 6 years of the transfer.

5.18 Capital allowances will be available on plant at 25% WDA on consideration. Industrial buildings allowances may be available on industrial buildings acquired.

5.19 The **'target' company may pay compensation to departing directors and/or employees**. The 'target' company will argue that this is 'wholly and exclusively' incurred. However, where the departing director/employee is also selling shares in the 'target' company the Revenue may argue that the 'compensation' is part of the consideration for sale of shares.

5.20 The director/employee may be entitled to £30,000 exemption on the compensation, but not if he has a right to the payment under his contract of employment. If he is a shareholder, the Revenue may argue that the compensation is a distribution. A defence against this argument would be that the sum is reasonable in amount having regard to the length of service and past services.

5.21 A top-up to the departing employee's pension scheme will be tax free.

5.22 Employees in the 'target' company may exchange their existing share options for options over shares in the purchaser without any tax penalty. The purchaser company must agree to the exchange, even though it need not operate its own scheme. The new options must have the same value as the old options.

Tax warranties and indemnities

5.23 Tax warranties and indemnities are only really necessary on a purchase of shares. **Warranties** are express undertakings that the company and in certain circumstances the vendor have fulfilled or will fulfil specific conditions. **Indemnities** are covenants by the vendor indemnifying the purchaser against depletion of the net assets, in consequence of specific claims against the company.

Chapter roundup

- Associated companies affect the various upper and lower limits.

- Within a 75% group, trading losses can be surrendered between UK companies.

- Within a capital gains group, assets are transferred at no gain and no loss. An election can be made for any company in a group to be treated as having made an asset disposal.

- Rollover relief is available in a capital gains group.

- Restrictions apply to the use of pre-entry losses and gains within capital gains tax groups.

- Within a consortium there is some scope for loss relief.

- There are some special reliefs for reorganisations.

- Special rules apply to accounting periods on the liquidation of a company.

- Structuring the sale/purchase of a business correctly can have major tax saving opportunities.

Quick quiz

1   List the sorts of losses which may be group relieved.

2   What is the definition of a consortium?

3   When may assets be transferred intra-group at no gain and no loss?

4   How can capital gains and losses within a group be matched with each other?

5   When may losses be carried forward on the transfer of a trade?

6   When do accounting periods end once a company is in liquidation?

7   List four advantages of buying the assets of a target business.

BPP PUBLISHING

Answers to quick quiz

1   Trading losses, excess Schedule A losses, non-trading deficits on loan relationships, excess charges on income (trade and non-trade) and excess management expenses of investment companies.

2   A company is owned by a consortium if 75% or more of its ordinary share capital is owned by companies none of which have a holding of less than 5%. Each consortium member (ie company shareholders) must have at least a 5% stake in profits and assets on a winding up in the consortium company.

3   No gain/no loss transfers are mandatory between companies in a capital gains group.

4   Two member of a capital gains group can elect that an asset which has been disposed of to a third party is treated as transferred between them prior to disposal. This election effectively allow the group to match its gains and losses in one company.

5   When a company ceases to carry on a trade and another company begins to carry on that trade and the same persons own at least 75% of the trade at two times, one within a year before and the other within two years after the transfer, then trading losses may be carried forward on the transfer of the trade.

6   A new accounting period begins once a company goes into liquidation. Subsequent accounting periods run for 12 months duration until the liquidation is complete.

7   • purchaser can choose which assets to acquire
    • capital allowances may be due
    • capital gains base cost of assets is price paid
    • liabilities need not be acquired

    (Note. more equally acceptable advantages outlined in 5.2).

Now try the questions below from the Exam Question Bank

Number	Level	Marks	Time
17	Exam	20	36 mins
18	Exam	20	36 mins

Chapter 16

OVERSEAS ASPECTS

Topic list		Syllabus reference	Ability required
1	Company residence and migration	(iv)	Comprehension
2	Double taxation relief (DTR)	(iv)	Application
3	Groups of companies	(v)	Comprehension
4	Controlled foreign companies	(iv)	Application
5	Transfer pricing	(iv)	Comprehension
6	Branch or subsidiary abroad	(iv)	Evaluation

Introduction

This chapter starts by considering which country a company lives in. We then see how relief may be given for overseas taxes suffered, how overseas companies may impact a group, how UK companies are taxed on the profits of certain overseas subsidiaries and how the transfer pricing legislation applies. Finally, we look at UK companies trading abroad.

Learning outcomes covered in this chapter

- **Identify** the significance of company residence for tax purposes

- **Calculate** the CT liability of a company which has overseas income, using the rules of double tax relief (but excluding knowledge of treaties)

- **Identify** transfer pricing problems calculating any adjustment required and state how this will be reported in its CTSA return

- **Identify** a controlled foreign company (CFC)

- **Calculate** the CT liability arising as a result of the presence of a CFC

- **Evaluate** the tax implications of the alternative methods of running an overseas operation

Syllabus content covered in this chapter

- Company residence
- Double tax relief (DTR)
- Controlled foreign companies (CFC)
- Transfer pricing
- UK companies trading abroad - subsidiary v branch

1   COMPANY RESIDENCE AND MIGRATION

Company residence

1.1   **A company is resident in the UK if it is incorporated in the UK or if its central management and control are exercised in the UK.** Central management and control are usually treated as exercised where the board of directors meets. **A UK resident company is subject to corporation tax on its worldwide profits.** It is also (unlike a non-resident company) entitled to the starting rate of corporation tax, the small companies rate and to marginal relief.

1.2   A company which would be UK resident under the rules above is nonetheless treated as not UK resident if it is to be so treated under the terms of a double taxation treaty.

1.3   **A non-UK resident company will be chargeable to corporation tax if it carries on a trade in the UK through a branch or agency.** The profits of such a company which are chargeable to corporation tax, whether or not they arise in the UK, are:

- any trading income arising directly or indirectly from the branch or agency;

- any income from property or rights used by, or held by or for, the branch or agency (other than dividends from UK companies);

- any chargeable gains arising from the disposal of assets situated in the UK.

1.4   **If a UK resident company makes investments abroad it will be liable to corporation tax on the profits made, the taxable amount being before the deduction of any foreign taxes.** The profits may be any of the following.

(a)   Interest and dividends received through paying agents.

(b)   Schedule D Case I: profits of an overseas branch or agency controlled from the UK

(c)   Schedule D Case III: income from foreign securities, for example debentures in overseas companies

(d)   Schedule D Case V: income from other overseas possessions including:

(i)   dividends from overseas subsidiaries;
(ii)   profits of an overseas branch or agency controlled abroad

(e)   Capital gains on disposals of foreign assets

Overseas dividends and interest received by a company are taxed at normal corporation tax rates.

1.5   A company may be subject to overseas taxes as well as to UK corporation tax on the same profits. Double taxation relief (see below) is available in respect of the foreign tax suffered.

Company migration

1.6   Because the overseas profits of a UK resident company are chargeable to corporation tax whereas the overseas profits of a non-UK resident company are not, UK companies might wish to transfer their residence in order to avoid paying UK corporation tax.

Only companies incorporated abroad can emigrate, because companies incorporated in the UK are automatically UK resident. To emigrate, a company must transfer its central management and control outside the UK.

1.7 **A company may freely transfer its residence out of the UK provided that:**

- **it gives notice to the Inland Revenue; and**
- **it pays the exit charge.**

1.8 **The exit charge is imposed as follows. At the time that a company ceases to be resident in the UK, it is deemed to dispose of all of its assets at their market values and immediately to reacquire them at their market values, thus giving rise to chargeable gains or allowable losses.** This deemed disposal will not apply if the company continues to carry on a trade in the UK through a branch or agency and the assets in question are:

- situated in the UK; and

- used in or for the purposes of the trade, or held for the purposes of the branch or agency.

1.9 The gain (or loss) which is deemed to arise when a company ceases to be UK resident can be postponed if:

- the company which ceases to be UK resident is a 75% subsidiary of another company immediately after the transfer;

- the holding company is resident in the UK; and

- a joint election is made in writing by the two companies within two years after the date of transfer.

1.10 If, however, the company which has left the UK disposes of any assets held at the date of emigration within the following six years, then the holding company will be deemed to make a gain equal to the whole or the appropriate part of the postponed gain. Similarly, if at any time after emigration the company ceases to be a 75% subsidiary or the holding company ceases to be UK resident then the postponed gain will crystallise.

2 DOUBLE TAXATION RELIEF (DTR)

2.1 In the UK relief for foreign tax suffered by a company may be currently available in one of three ways.

(a) **Treaty relief**

Under a treaty entered into between the UK and the overseas country, a treaty may exempt certain profits from taxation in one of the countries involved, thus completely avoiding double taxation. More usually treaties provide for credit to be given for tax suffered in one of the countries against the tax liability in the other.

(b) **Unilateral credit relief**

Where no treaty relief is available, unilateral relief may be available in the UK giving credit for the foreign tax against the UK tax.

(c) **Unilateral expense relief**

Where neither treaty relief nor unilateral credit relief is available, or unilateral credit relief is not wanted by the taxpayer (because of a lack of UK tax liability against which to obtain credit), relief for overseas tax is given by deducting the overseas tax from the overseas profits prior to including them in the profits chargeable to corporation tax.

Treaty relief

2.2 A tax treaty based on the OECD model treaty may use either the exemption method or the credit method to give relief for tax suffered on income from a business in country B by a resident of country R.

(a) Under the **exemption method,** the income is not taxed at all in country R, or if it is dividends or interest (which the treaty allows to be taxed in country R) credit is given for any country B tax against the country R tax.

(b) Under the **credit method,** the income is taxed in country R, but credit is given for any country B tax against the country R tax.

Under either method, any credit given is limited to the country B tax attributable to the income.

Unilateral credit relief

2.3 **Relief is available for overseas tax suffered on branch profits, dividends, interest and royalties, up to the amount of the UK corporation tax (at the company's average rate) attributable to that income.** The tax that is deducted overseas is usually called withholding tax. The gross income including the withholding tax is included within the profits chargeable to corporation tax.

Question: Unilateral credit relief

On 1 May 2001, AS plc receives a dividend from Bola of £80,000. This has been paid subject to 20% withholding tax. AS plc has UK trading income of £2,000,000 for the year to 31.3.02. Show that the Schedule D Case V income is £100,000 and compute the corporation tax payable.

Answer

	Total	UK	Overseas
	£	£	£
Schedule D Case I	2,000,000	2,000,000	
Schedule D Case V(W)	100,000		100,000
PCTCT	2,100,000	2,000,000	100,000
Corporation tax at 30%	630,000	600,000	30,000
Less DTR: lower of:			
(a) overseas tax: £20,000; or			
(b) UK tax on overseas income: £30,000	(20,000)		(20,000)
MCT	610,000	600,000	10,000

Working: Schedule D Case V

£80,000 × 100/(100 – 20) = £100,000.

2.4 If the overseas tax rate exceeds the UK CT rate there will be excess foreign tax. A company can:

(a) Carry the excess foreign tax back for three years
(b) Carry the excess foreign tax forward indefinitely
(c) Surrender the excess foreign tax to another group company

These apply to dividends paid on or after 31 March 2001.

2.5 Where foreign tax is carried backwards or forwards it is set against UK tax payable on foreign dividends other than dividends paid by Controlled Foreign Companies (CFCs) (see later in text) or dividends where the underlying tax has already been capped or subject to another form of limitation or relief (see below).

2.6 In respect of dividends from overseas subsidiaries the rate of foreign tax for which companies can claim relief is capped at 30% with effect from 31 March 2001.

2.7 However, from 31 March 2001 it will be possible to create UK resident **mixer companies** and relief for capped foreign tax up to a maximum of 45% will be allowed against the UK tax payable on other dividends that have not themselves been subject to the cap or any limitation on relief.

2.8 If a company has non-trading credits (income) for loan interest from abroad, and they have suffered foreign tax, then non-trading credits (income) and debits (expenses) are not netted off to give a net surplus or deficit. Instead, *all* non-trading credits and debits (UK or overseas) on loan relationships are separated out. The credits are taxable under Schedule D Case III, and the debits go against the profits which the company chooses (see below).

2.9 Companies have to take all reasonable steps to minimise their foreign tax if they are to obtain full relief against UK tax. A failure to claim all overseas tax reliefs, deductions, allowances etc will result in the UK authorities restricting the amount of DTR available.

Underlying tax relief

2.10 **In addition to the relief available for withholding tax shown above, relief is available for underlying tax relating to a dividend received from a foreign company in which the UK company owns at least 10% of the voting power, either directly or indirectly. The underlying tax is the tax attributable to the relevant profits out of which the dividend was paid.** Underlying tax is calculated as

$$\text{Gross dividend income} \times \frac{\text{foreign tax paid}}{\text{after} - \text{tax accounting profits}}$$

Relief for underlying tax is not available to individuals.

2.11 We may need to decide which accounting profits have been used to pay a dividend. If the dividend is declared for a particular year, the set of accounts for that year are used. If this information is not given, the relevant profits are those of the period of account immediately before that in which the dividend was payable.

2.12 There is an anti-avoidance provision which restricts relief for underlying tax in certain circumstances where there is a scheme the purpose, or one of the main purposes, of which is to obtain relief for underlying tax.

Question: Underlying tax relief

A Ltd, a UK company with no associated companies, holds 30,000 out of 90,000 voting ordinary shares in B Inc (resident in Lintonia).

The profit and loss account of B Inc for the year to 31 March 2002 is as follows (converted into sterling).

	£	£
Trading profit		1,000,000
Less taxation: provided on profits	300,000	
transfer to deferred tax account	100,000	
		(400,000)
		600,000
Less dividends: Net	240,000	
withholding tax (20%)	60,000	
		(300,000)
Retained profits		300,000

The actual tax paid on the profits for the year to 31 March 2002 was £270,000.

Apart from the net dividend of £80,000 received out of the above profits from B Inc on 31 May 2001 the only other taxable profit of A Ltd for its year to 31 March 2002 was £610,000 UK trading profit. A Ltd paid no dividends during the year and received no UK dividends.

Calculate A Ltd's UK corporation tax liability after double taxation relief.

Answer

A LTD: UK CORPORATION TAX LIABILITY

	£	£
Schedule D Case I		610,000
Schedule D Case V		
Net dividend	80,000	
Withholding tax at 20%		
£80,000 × 20/80	20,000	
Gross dividend	100,000	
Underlying tax		
£100,000 × $\dfrac{270,000}{600,000}$	45,000	
Gross income		145,000
PCTCT		755,000

	Total £	UK £	Overseas £
Schedule D Case I	610,000	610,000	
Schedule D Case V	145,000		145,000
PCTCT	755,000	610,000	145,000
Corporation tax £755,000 × 30%			226,500
Less small companies' marginal relief £(1,500,000 – 755,000) × 1/40			(18,625)
			207,875

The average rate of corporation tax is £207,875/£755,000 = 27.53311%.

Corporation tax at the average rate	207,875	167,952	39,923
Less DTR: lower of:			
(a) overseas tax £(20,000 + 45,000) = £65,000;			
(b) UK tax on overseas income £39,923	(39,923)		(39,923)
	167,952	167,952	0

Corporation tax of £167,952 is payable. £(65,000 – 39,923) = £25,077 of overseas tax is unrelieved (ie excess). It will be possible to carry the unrelieved tax back or forward because the dividend was received on or after 31.3.01.

2.13   Two further factors affect the computation of UK tax on overseas income against which credit for overseas tax may be claimed. These are:

- the allocation of non-trading deficits on loan relationships, charges and losses relieved against total profits under s 393A(1);

- the allocation of ACT against the corporation tax liability.

2.14 **A company may allocate its non-trading deficits on loan relationships, charges and losses relieved under s 393A(1) in whatever manner it likes for the purpose of computing double taxation relief.** (Deficits brought back can as usual only go against Schedule D Case III profits, and deficits brought forward can only go against non-trading profits, but the company can choose which Schedule D Case III or non-trading profits.) **It should set the maximum amount against any UK profits, thereby maximising the corporation tax attributable to the foreign profits and hence maximising the double taxation relief available.**

2.15 If a company has several sources of overseas profits, then deficits, charges and losses should be allocated first to UK profits, and then to overseas sources which have suffered the **lowest** rates of overseas taxation.

2.16 Losses relieved under s 393(1) must in any case be set against the first available profits of the trade which gave rise to the loss.

2.17 The limit on the set-off of ACT must be applied to each source of profits separately. For example, if the company has a foreign source of profits and a UK source of profits, the maximum ACT that may be set against the corporation tax on each source is 20% × the profits from that source.

2.18 Double taxation relief is deducted from the corporation tax liability before ACT, and ACT can only be deducted from corporation tax on a source to the extent that there is a corporation tax liability remaining on that source after double taxation relief has been deducted.

2.19 A company with a choice of loss reliefs should consider the effect of its choice on double taxation relief. For example, a s 393A(1) claim might lead to there being no UK tax liability, or a very small liability, so that foreign tax would go unrelieved. S 393(1) relief might avoid this problem and still leave very little UK tax to pay for the period of the loss.

Question: DTR and ACT

K plc is a UK resident company with ten UK subsidiaries and a subsidiary resident in Utopia. The company produced the following results for the year ended 31 March 2002.

	£
UK trading profit	1,180,000
UK chargeable gain	15,750
Dividend received from Utopian subsidiary for the year ended 31 March 2001 (amount received on 10 April 2001)	120,000
UK dividends (amounts received in June - not from group companies)	7,500
Charges paid (gross)	60,000

The Utopian subsidiary presented the following results for the year ended 31 March 2001.

	U$
Pre-tax profit (per financial accounts) (after-tax accounts profit U$400,000)	1,200,000
Less Utopian tax paid	(200,000)
	1,000,000
Less dividend paid for the year (gross)	(1,000,000)
Retained earnings	0

There are two Utopian dollars to the pound. K plc owns 80% of the share capital of its Utopian subsidiary. Dividends paid between Utopia and the UK are subject to 10% withholding tax. K plc paid a dividend of £177,000 on 1 October 2001.

There is surplus ACT to be carried forward at 1 April 2001 of £200,000.

Compute the mainstream corporation tax liability of K plc for the year to 31 March 2002.

Answer

	£
Schedule D Case I	1,180,000
Schedule D Case V (W1)	160,000
Chargeable gains	15,750
	1,355,750
Less charges	(60,000)
PCTCT	1,295,750

	£
Corporation tax £1,295,750 × 30%	388,725
Less DTR (W2)	(40,000)
	348,725
Less ACT (W2)	(192,775)
Mainstream corporation tax	155,950

Workings

1   *Schedule D Case V income*

	Tax £	Income £
Dividends received from Utopia		120,000
Add withholding tax (10/90)	13,333	13,333
		133,333
Add underlying tax £133,333 × $\dfrac{£100,000}{£500,000}$	26,667	26,667
	40,000	160,000

2   *DTR and ACT*

	Total £	UK £	Overseas £
Schedule D Case I	1,180,000	1,180,000	
Schedule D Case V	160,000		160,000
Chargeable gain	15,750	15,750	
	1,355,750	1,195,750	160,000
Less charges	(60,000)	(60,000)	
	1,295,750	1,135,750	160,000

	Total £	UK £	Overseas £
Corporation tax at 30%	388,725	340,725	48,000
Less DTR: lower of:			
(a) overseas tax £40,000;			
(b) UK tax on overseas income £48,000	(40,000)		(40,000)
	348,725	340,725	8,000
Less ACT offset (W3)	(192,775)	(184,775)	(8,000)
	155,950	155,950	0

3   *ACT offset*

	£	£
UK PCTCT × 20%		
£1,135,750 × 20%		227,150
Less: shadow ACT		
Notional FP		
£177,000 × 10/9 × 9/8	221,250	
FII for shadow purposes		
£7,500 × 10/9 × 9/8	(9,375)	
	211,875	
Shadow ACT		
£211,875 × 20%		(42,375)
Set off limit vs UK income		184,775

t	£
Overseas PCTCT × 20%	
£160,000 × 20%	32,000
Maximum ACT	
(i) £32,000	
(ii) CT left after DTR ie £8,000	
£8,000 maximum offset	
Surplus ACT b/fwd at 1.4.01	200,000
Less: amount set off = £(184,775 + 8,000)	(192,775)
Surplus ACT c/fwd at 31.3.02	7,225

Exam focus point

The layout of the above answer in working number 2 is an excellent way to present your answer in the exam. It allows you to keep the different sources (UK and overseas) of income separate for offsetting charges, losses etc.

Calculate corporation tax on the total PCTCT but allocate this to the different sources. Then claim DTR source by source and offset ACT source by source.

Unilateral expense relief

2.20   Expense relief (bringing into account only the net amount of foreign income) is not generally worthwhile if credit relief is available. However, it may not be possible to claim credit relief because of, for example, loss relief eliminating any liability to UK corporation tax. In such cases expense relief should be used.

Question: Expense relief

A Ltd has a trading profit of £110,000, foreign investment income of £15,000 (gross) and foreign tax paid of £2,500 for the year ended 31 March 2002. Show the position:

(a)   with credit relief;
(b)   with expense relief.

Answer

	Credit relief	Expense relief
	£	£
Schedule D Case I	110,000	110,000
Schedule D Case V	15,000	12,500
PCTCT	125,000	122,500

	£	£
Corporation tax on £125,000/£122,500 at 20%	25,000	24,500
Less credit relief	(2,500)	0
Corporation tax payable	22,500	24,500

2.21 Companies who have claimed DTR must notify the Revenue if the amount of foreign tax they have paid is adjusted and this has resulted in the DTR claim becoming excessive. The notification must be in writing.

Mixer companies

2.22 A mixer company is a company which holds shares in overseas subsidiaries. It is in this company that all foreign dividends are collected. A dividend is then paid to the UK company, after the different foreign tax credits have been '**mixed**' to a composite rate.

2.23 From 1 April 2001, where dividends are paid through a mixer company, the maximum DTR is related back to the dividend from the underlying company.

2.24 For each dividend the maximum DTR is given by the formula

$$\frac{D \times M}{100 - M}$$

D = amount of dividend
M = rate of corporation tax in force when dividend is paid

2.25 The above rules do not apply to dividends paid between companies in the same country, except in cases of abuse.

2.26 Special rules also deal with situations where profits are transferred between overseas companies other than through dividends effectively by restricting tax relief as if the transfer had been a dividend.

3 GROUPS OF COMPANIES

3.1 **Groups and consortia can be established through companies resident anywhere in the world. However, group relief is normally only available to, and may only be claimed from, UK resident companies.**

3.2 **EXAMPLE**

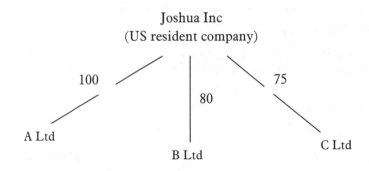

A Ltd, B Ltd and C Ltd are all UK resident companies. As the three UK companies share a common parent they will be treated as part of a group relief group despite the fact that the parent company is not UK resident. The UK companies may surrender losses to each other (but not normally to or from the overseas parent company).

3.3 **Similarly, a consortium may exist for relief purposes where one or more of the members is not resident in the UK but relief cannot be passed to or from a non UK resident company.**

Branches of companies

3.4 **Group relief is available to UK branches of overseas companies.** Branches can claim relief from UK resident group members. Alternatively, they can surrender losses, which cannot be relieved against profits in the overseas country, to such group members.

3.5 Losses incurred by overseas branches of UK companies can be surrendered as group relief only if they cannot be relieved against profits in the overseas country.

The Global Group Concept

3.6 The 'global group concept' means that instead of looking at the residence of a company one needs to look at whether the company is subject to UK corporation tax on any of its chargeable gains. Provided the assets transferred do not result in a potential leakage of UK corporation tax, no gain/no loss transfers will be possible within a worldwide (global) group of companies.

3.7 The global group concept applies to the transfer of the whole or part of a trade and extends to certain intra-group transfers of assets and to transfers of assets where one company disposes of the whole or part of its business to another company as part of a scheme of reconstruction or amalgamation.

4 CONTROLLED FOREIGN COMPANIES

4.1 A UK resident company may choose to trade abroad through an investment in a local company. Providing there are no exchange control problems and cash flow requirements do not call for the repatriation of all profits to the UK, there will generally be a benefit in accumulating income in a foreign company whose effective tax rate is lower than that of the UK company. To prevent undue tax avoidance in this way, there are special rules for 'controlled foreign companies' (CFCs).

4.2 **A controlled foreign company (CFC) is a company which:**

   (a) **is resident outside the UK; and**
   (b) **is controlled by persons resident in the UK; and**
   (c) **is subject to a 'lower level of taxation' in the country in which it is resident.**

4.3 A company is controlled by persons resident in the UK if:

   (a) two persons taken together have control of the shares, votes etc
   (b) each of the two persons has at least a 40% share of relevant joint holdings, powers etc
   (c) one of them is resident in the UK

4.4 **A lower level of tax means less than three quarters of the amount which would have been payable had the company been resident in the UK.**

Question: Controlled foreign company

Bohemia Limited is resident for tax purposes in the Cayman Islands but also trades through a branch based in Switzerland. It is owned as follows:

		%
Maurice Feischner (Swiss resident Managing Director)		25
Ace Ltd		25
Beta Ltd	UK resident companies	10
Cahill Ltd		10
Michael Brown (UK resident)		30
		100

Bohemia Ltd has chargeable profits of £875,000 in the year to 31.12.02. The tax rate in the Cayman Islands on these profits is 24%. The UK tax rate would have been 30%. The Swiss tax paid was £90,000 on the profits.

Is Bohemia Limited a controlled foreign company?

Answer

(a)   Non UK-resident? – Yes

(b)   At least 40% controlled by UK resident persons? Yes. UK residents own 75% of the company.

(c)   Subject to lower tax rate?

	Cayman Islands £	UK equivalent £
Tax payable		
£875,000 × 24%/30%	210,000	262,500
Relief for foreign tax suffered	(90,000)	(90,000)
	120,000	172,500

Tax rates: 24/30 = 80% not lower

Total tax : £210,000/£262,500 = 80% not lower

Local tax/UK tax: £120,000/£172,500 = 69.6% - lower than three quarters limit

Consequently Bohemia Limited is a CFC unless one of the exceptions apply (see below).

4.5   The CFC rules normally apply only to companies paying less than 75% of the tax they would have paid if they were resident in the UK. To avoid the CFC rules, a number of overseas countries have regimes that effectively allow companies to choose the rate of tax they pay. For accounting periods beginning after 5 October 1999 companies paying tax under such 'designer rate' tax regimes fall within the definition of a CFC regardless of the level of tax paid. The Inland Revenue has produced a list of the regimes to which these rules apply.

Apportionment of profits

4.6   **Profits of a CFC are apportioned to UK resident companies (not individuals) entitled to at least 25% of those profits.** The apportionment should be made on a 'just and reasonable' basis. Where shareholders have not changed throughout the accounting period the apportionment is based on the relevant interest.

4.7   UK companies must decide for themselves whether an apportionment is appropriate and self-assess their profits on the basis of their decision. There is an additional page to be filed together with the CT 600 tax return where a company has profits of a CFC to report. Companies failing to show the appropriate adjustments in their CT returns will be exposed to interest and penalties.

4.8 Apportioned profits are brought into the UK company's CT600 corporation tax computation as an amount of tax (after CGT). The tax rate applicable is always the full rate of corporation tax irrespective of the rate the UK company pays tax on its other profits.

Question: Apportionment of profits

In the above question how much profits would Ace Ltd be taxed on if Bohemia Ltd is held to be a CFC?

Answer

Ace Ltd would have to apportion 25% of the profit of Bohemia Ltd when calculating CT for self assessment purposes.

Ace Ltd

£875,000 × 25%   £218,750

4.9 Where CFC profits are apportioned they are reduced by 'creditable tax' which is the aggregate of:

(a) any double tax relief (see below) available in the UK in respect of foreign tax due against the chargeable profits;

(b) any income tax deducted at source on income received by the CFC;

(c) corporation tax payable in the UK on any CFC income taxable in this country.

Question: Apportionment of profits

R Inc is a controlled foreign company owned 75% by J Ltd and 25% by Mr J. Its results for the year ended 31 December 2001 were:

	£
Tax adjusted trading profits	
Under UK legislation	650,000
Under foreign legislation (foreign tax rate 8%)	500,000

Show how the profits of R Inc will be apportioned to and taxed on J Ltd. J Ltd has other profits of £2 million.

Answer

	£
UK tax adjusted profit	650,000
Apportioned to J Ltd (75%)	487,500

J Ltd's CT computation

	£	£
Tax on UK profits (£2m × 30%)		600,000
Tax on CFC		
£487,500 × 30%	146,250	
Less: foreign tax (8% × £500,000) × 75%	(30,000)	
		116,250
		716,250

Exceptions

4.10 A CFC profits do not need to be apportioned if it falls into one of the six situations outlined in paras 4.11 to 4.16.

4.11 **Its chargeable profits for the accounting period do not exceed £50,000 (this is reduced proportionately for short accounting periods).**

4.12 **It is situated in a territory which does not have a lower level of taxation.**

4.13 **It follows an acceptable distribution policy.** This applies where it distributes by way of a dividend, during or within 18 months of the period for which it is due, at least 90% of its net chargeable profits. These are net profits as computed for UK corporation tax purposes less chargeable gains and foreign tax).

4.14 **It is engaged in exempt activities** and

(a) it has a **real presence** in its territory of residence;

(b) its main activity does not consist of leasing, dealing in securities or the receipt of income such as dividends, interest or royalties and is not such that the company may be used as an invoicing route nor is the company an intra-group service company (ie which is mainly engaged in the provision of services and receives 50% or more of its income from related parties)

(c) its business is not primarily with associates in those trades which frequently involve cross-frontier transactions;

(d) it does not receive a significant amount of dividends from CFCs except where the exemption for holding companies applies.

In addition, where the company is engaged mainly in a wholesale, distributive financial or service business, less than 50% of it gross trading income is derived from connected or associated persons, from other companies potentially subject to an apportionment from the CFC or from any person connected or associated with either a UK or non-resident who satisfy the 40% test (see above).

A holding company with subsidiaries outside the territory in which it is itself resident meets the exempt activities test only if 90% or more of its income is in the form of non-tax deductible dividends from subsidiaries that are themselves exempt from the CFC rules.

4.15 **It fulfils the public quotation conditions.** This means it must be quoted on a recognised stock exchange, and dealing must have taken place within twelve months of the end of the accounting period. At least 35% of the voting power must be held by the public with no more than 85% of that power being held by all the company's principal members (defined as for close companies.

4.16 It satisfies the **motive test**. This means the transactions taking place in an accounting period must achieve a reduction in UK tax which is no more than minimal, or it was not the main purpose of these transactions was not to achieve a reduction and the reduction in UK tax by the diversion of profit from the UK was not a main reason for the company's existence during that accounting period.

4.17 There is an **advance clearance procedure** in respect of the '**exempt activities**' **test**, the '**motive**'; test and the '**acceptable distribution policy**'.

5 TRANSFER PRICING

5.1 Companies which have subsidiaries resident in countries with lower corporate tax rates than the UK may attempt to divert profits by inter-company pricing arrangements. For example, a UK company has contracted to sell goods with an invoice value of £20,000 to a foreign customer:

UK selling company ———— Goods Invoice value : £20,000 ———→ Foreign buying company

In this case all the profit on the sale arises to the UK company; alternatively the sale could be rearranged.

UK selling company ———— Goods Invoice value : £16,000 ———→ Tax haven subsidiary company ———— Goods Invoice value : £20,000 ———→ Foreign buying company

In this case £4,000 of the profit has been diverted to a subsidiary operating in a low-tax country (tax haven).

5.2 Although a company may buy and sell goods etc at any price it wishes there is **anti avoidance legislation** which **requires profit to be computed as if the transactions had been carried out at arms length.**

5.3 The transfer pricing rules apply to transactions between two persons if either:

(a) one person directly or indirectly participates in the management, control or capital of the other; or

(b) a third party directly or indirectly participates in the management, control or capital of both.

5.4 There is an exception if each of the following conditions are satisfied by both parties:

(a) the person is within the charge to UK income or corporation tax on the profits and no exemption from tax exists (if income tax then the person must be UK resident);

(b) the person is not entitled to any credit for double tax in respect of those profits;

(c) the person is not entitled to a deduction for foreign tax paid on those profits.

5.5 **The transfer pricing legislation does not apply to transactions between two UK resident traders who are both fully chargeable to corporation tax.**

5.6 A transaction between a UK company and the foreign branch of a subsidiary would however be caught if foreign tax was being paid on the branch profits and was eligible for DTR.

5.7 **Companies must self-assess their liability to tax under the transfer pricing rules and pay any corporation tax due. A statutory procedure exists for advance pricing arrangements (APAs) whereby a company can agree in advance that its transfer pricing policy is acceptable to the Revenue** – ie, not requiring a self-assessment adjustment. The APA facility is voluntary but companies may feel the need to use the facility as it provides necessary advance confirmation that their approach to transfer pricing in their self-assessment is acceptable.

6 BRANCH OR SUBSIDIARY ABROAD

6.1 Where a foreign country has a lower rate of company taxation than the UK, it can be beneficial for the UK company to conduct its foreign activities through a **non-UK resident subsidiary** if profits are anticipated (assuming that the CFC rules (see above) do not apply), and through a **branch if losses are likely to arise.**

6.2 The **profits of a foreign branch** are treated as part of the profits of the UK company and are normally included in its computation of Schedule D Case I trading profits. If, however, the operations of the overseas branch amount to a separate trade which is wholly carried on overseas, the profits are assessed under Schedule D Case V.

6.3 **Losses of a foreign branch can be surrendered as group relief** to the extent the loss cannot be relieved against profits in the overseas country. Alternatively a Schedule D Case V loss can be carried forward to set against future profits of the same trade. A Schedule D Case I loss is first set against other Schedule D Case I profits. The usual loss reliefs are then available.

6.4 The profits of a non-resident **foreign subsidiary** are only liable to UK tax when remitted to the UK, for example in the form of dividends (Schedule D Case V income). However, no relief can be obtained against the UK parent's profits for any overseas losses of a non-resident subsidiary.

Incorporation a foreign branch

6.5 Where a foreign operation is likely to show a loss in the early years followed by a profit it may be worthwhile to trade through a foreign branch whilst losses arise (these are usually then automatically netted off against the company's UK profits) and then later to convert the branch into a non-UK resident subsidiary company (so that profits can be accumulated at potentially lower rates of foreign tax).

6.6 This conversion of a foreign branch into a non-UK resident subsidiary has some important implications and the tax effects both in the UK and the overseas country need to be considered. Firstly, it may be necessary to secure the consent of the Treasury for the transaction. It is illegal for a UK resident company to cause or permit a non-UK resident company over which it has control to create or issue any shares or debentures. It is also illegal for a UK resident company to transfer to any person, or cause or permit to be transferred to any person, any shares or debentures of a non-UK resident company over which it has control.

6.7 The Treasury have published General Consents which permit certain intra-group transactions and third party transactions provided full consideration is given. Additionally certain movements of capital between EEA states are allowed automatically. Thus in practice specific Treasury consent may not be required for a transaction of the type presently under consideration.

6.8 Secondly, the conversion will constitute a disposal of the assets of the branch giving rise to a chargeable gain or loss in the hands of the UK company. A chargeable gain can be postponed where:

(a) the trade of the foreign branch is transferred to the non-UK resident company with all the assets used for that trade except cash; and

(b) the consideration for the transfer is wholly or partly securities (shares or shares and loan stock); and

(c) the transferring company owns at least 25% of the ordinary share capital of the non-resident company; and

(d) a claim for relief is made.

6.9 There is full postponement of the net gains arising on the transfer where the consideration is wholly securities. Where part of the consideration is in a form other than securities, eg cash, that proportion of the net gains is chargeable immediately.

6.10 The postponement by be indefinite. The gain becomes chargeable only when:

(a) the transfer or company at any time disposes of any of the securities received on the transfer; or

(b) the non-UK resident company within six years of the transfer disposes of any of the assets on which a gain arose at the time of the transfer.

6.11 The 'global group' concept applies to certain intra-group transfers of assets and also where one company disposes of the whole of part of its business to another company as part of a reconstruction or amalgamation scheme. Such asset transfers are on a no gain/no loss basis provided the assets transferred do not result in a potential leakage of UK corporation tax.

European Community companies

6.12 **If all or part of a trade carried on in the UK by a company resident in one EC state is transferred to a company resident in another EC state, then the transfer is deemed to be at a price giving no gain and no loss,** if all the following conditions are fulfilled.

(a) The transfer is wholly in exchange for shares or securities.

(b) The company receiving the trade would be subject to UK corporation tax on any gains arising on later disposals of the assets transferred.

(c) Both parties claim this special treatment.

(d) The transfer is for bona fide commercial reasons. Advance clearance that this condition is satisfied may be obtained.

Chapter roundup

- A company may obtain double taxation relief for overseas withholding tax, and also (if its investment is large enough) for underlying tax. The allocation of charges and losses can affect the relief available.

- The group relief rules allow groups and consortia to be established through companies resident anywhere in the world.

- Profits of a CFC are apportioned to UK resident companies entitled to at least 25% of those profits.

- The transfer pricing legislation prevents manipulation of profits between members of a group which can occur when a company chooses to buy and sell goods at a price which is not a market price.

- A UK resident company intending to do business abroad must choose between a branch and a subsidiary. If a subsidiary is chosen, it must bear in mind the rules on controlled foreign companies and on trading at artificial prices.

Quick quiz

1   When is a company UK resident?

2   How is underlying tax calculated?

3   How best should charges be allocated in computing credit relief for foreign tax?

4   What is the definition of a CFC?

5   What are the consequences of a company being treated as a controlled foreign company?

6   What steps can be taken against the use of artificial transfer prices?

7   A UK company is planning to set up a new operation in Australia that will initially be loss making. Should it set up as a branch or a subsidiary of the UK company?

Answers to quick quiz

1   A company is resident in the UK if it is incorporated in the UK or if its central management and control are exercised in the UK.

2   Underlying tax is calculated as

$$\text{Dividend plus withholding tax} \times \frac{\text{foreign tax paid}}{\text{after - tax accounting profits}}$$

3   Charges should be set-off firstly from any UK profits, then from overseas income sources suffering the lowest rates of overseas taxation before those suffering at the higher rates.

4   A CFC is a company which

(a)   is resident outside the UK
(b)   is controlled by persons resident in the UK
(c)   is subject to a lower level of taxation in the country in which it is resident.

5   Profits of a CFC are apportioned to UK resident companies (not individuals) entitled to at least 25% of the profits.

6   Although a company may buy and sell goods at any price it wishes, the transfer pricing anti-avoidance legislation requires profit to be computed as if the transactions had been carried out at arms length, in certain circumstances.

7   If losses are expected to arise then a branch operation is best.

Now try the question below from the exam question bank

Question to try	Level	Marks	Time
19	Exam	20	36 mins

Chapter 17

INVESTMENT COMPANIES AND CLOSE COMPANIES

Topic list	Syllabus reference	Ability required
1 Investment companies	(iii)	Application
2 The definition of a close company	(iii)	Application
3 The consequences of close company status	(iii)	Application

Introduction

In this chapter, we look at investment companies and close companies.

Investment companies have a special type of business: they make investments, for example in shares, and collect the income from them. An important type of investment company is the investment trust, which collects the capital of its shareholders together, buys shares and pays out the dividends on those shares to its own shareholders. Thus it gives people a way to invest across a wide spread of companies.

A close company may have any type of business, but it needs special tax treatment because it is under the control of a few people who might try to get profits out of it in non-taxable forms.

Learning outcomes covered in this chapter

- **Calculate** the total profits of a company for CT purposes
- **Calculate** the CT liability of a company (including small and intermediate companies)

Syllabus content covered in this chapter

- Close companies and close investment-holding companies; identification and consequences

1   INVESTMENT COMPANIES

1.1 **An investment company is a company whose business consists wholly or mainly in making investments and which gets the principal part of its income from investments.**

An investment company may or may not also fall within the definition of a close investment- holding company outlined below.

1.2 A housing society which acquired housing for renting with a social rather than profit purpose was held to be an investment company by the special commissioners.

1.3 **The principal overhead in an investment company's accounts will be management expenses, the costs of running the business. These are generally deductible in computing taxable profits. An unrelieved excess of such expenses in one accounting**

period may be carried forward as management expenses of the following accounting period, together with any unused capital allowances, non-trading deficits on loan relationships and excess charges incurred wholly and exclusively for business purposes. All these amounts continue to be carried forward to later periods until they are set against income and gains.

1.4 Excessive directors remuneration is not deductible for tax purposes. The Revenue may also refuse a deduction for any amounts which are not in fact expenses of management.

1.5 Capital allowances on plant and machinery are available as for a trading company, provided a written election is made to the Inspector. Balancing charges are treated as income of the business.

1.6 **The full rate of corporation tax is applied to close investment-holding companies** (see below), **irrespective of the level of profits.** Other investment companies can benefit from the starting rate, the small companies rate or marginal relief in the normal way.

Question: Investment companies

TC Ltd, a non-close investment company, has the following results for the year ended 31 March 2002.

	£
Rental income	150,000
Building society interest	8,000
Chargeable gains	100,000
Management expenses	
Property management	40,000
General	50,000
Capital allowances	
On property	800
General	1,000
Charges on income	
Business	41,000
Charitable	6,000

Unrelieved management expenses carried forward at 1 April 2001 amounted to £60,500.

Compute the mainstream corporation tax payable.

Answer

	£	£
Rents		150,000
Less: capital allowances	800	
property management expenses	40,000	
		(40,800)
Schedule A		109,200
Schedule D Case III		8,000
Chargeable gains		100,000
		217,200
Less: general management expenses	50,000	
capital allowances	1,000	
management expenses brought forward	60,500	
		(111,500)
		105,700
Less charges on income		(47,000)
PCTCT		58,700
Corporation tax payable £58,700 × 20%		£11,740

Changes in ownership

1.7 **If there is a change in ownership of an investment company, special rules apply** when any of the following occurs.

 (a) Within three years after the change, the company's (share and loan) capital is increased by at least £1,000,000 or is at least doubled.

 (b) There is a major change in the nature or conduct of the company s business within the three years before or the three years after the change in ownership.

 (c) The company s business becomes small or negligible, the ownership changes and there is then a considerable revival.

1.8 **In any of these circumstances, excess management expenses, charges and non-trading deficits on loan relationships arising before the change in ownership cannot be carried forward to after the change.** The accounting period of the change is divided into two notional accounting periods for this purpose.

1.9 When this rule does not apply, but after the change in ownership an asset is transferred to the company from another group company at no gain and no loss and that asset is then sold at a gain within the three years following the change in ownership, then excess charges, management expenses and non-trading deficits on loan relationships brought forward from before the change in ownership cannot be set against the gain.

1.10 A major change in the nature of a business occurs when there is a change in the nature of the investments held (eg a company switches from investing in shares to investing in real property). A change in a portfolio or quoted shares is not a major change in the nature of a business.

2 THE DEFINITION OF A CLOSE COMPANY

2.1 Owner-managed and family-owned companies could easily be used for tax avoidance. **Special rules apply to certain companies called close companies**, to counteract this.

> **KEY TERM**
>
> A **close company** is one that is resident in the UK and under the control of either:
>
> (a) five or fewer participators (broadly, shareholders), together with their associates (spouses, siblings, ancestors, lineal descendants and business partners); or
>
> (b) any number of its participators who are directors, together with their associates.
>
> Where there are a number of people who are associated with each other, they are grouped together so as to produce the smallest possible number of participators.

2.2 Control is given by having, or having rights to acquire, any of the following.

 (a) The ability to direct the company's affairs.

 (b) More than half of the company's share capital.

 (c) More than half of the voting power in the company.

(d) Shares which would give a right to more than half of the company's income available to participators if it were all distributed (ignoring any amount which anyone would receive as a loan creditor).

(e) The right to more than half of the company's assets available to participators on a winding up.

Participators

2.3 A 'participator' is any person having an interest in the capital or income of a company. The term includes:

(a) shareholders;

(b) persons who possess, or are entitled to acquire, share capital or voting rights in the company, such as holders of options;

(c) persons entitled to participate in distributions;

(d) persons who are entitled to ensure that income or assets (whether present or future) of the company will be applied directly or indirectly for their benefit;

(e) loan creditors other than banks acting in the ordinary course of business.

Associates

2.4 Associates of a participator are any relatives or business partners of the participator. Relatives include spouses, parents and remoter forebears, children and remoter issue, and brothers and sisters. Nephews, nieces, uncles, aunts and in-laws are not relatives for these purposes.

2.5 An associate of an associate cannot be linked to a participator: for example a man's wife's sister's shareholding cannot be added to his shareholding if he is taken as the participator. However, if his wife is taken as the participator, her husband's shares and her sister's shares are added to her shareholding.

Directors

2.6 The term 'director' includes any person who occupies the position of director, irrespective of his job description. It also includes persons in accordance with whose directions or instructions the other directors are accustomed to act, and any manager of the company who, together with associates, controls 20% or more of the ordinary share capital of the company.

Question: Associates of participators

The share capital of an unquoted company is held as follows.

	%
A	5
B, A's wife	6
C, A's daughter	3
D and E, A's brothers (jointly)	6
F, A's business partner	10
G, A's nominee	15
H, A's son	6
Seven others, unconnected to A or each other, each holding 7%	49
	100

All shares carry the same votes and the same rights to income or assets on a winding-up.

Is the company close?

Answer

A's own shareholding is increased by the shares held by his nominee and by his associates.

	%
A and his nominee G (5% + 15%)	20
B	6
C	3
D & E	6
F	10
H	6
	51

This company is therefore close as it is under the control of one participator (A) and his associates.

Exceptions to close company status

2.7 The following companies cannot be close companies.

(a) Companies not resident in the UK.

(b) Companies controlled by or on behalf of the Crown, which would not be close if the Crown's interest were ignored. The Crown includes any government department or ministry.

(c) Registered industrial or provident societies, building societies and life assurance companies.

(d) Companies controlled by one or more other companies which are not close companies, if they cannot be treated as close except by including as one of the five or fewer participators a company which is not close.

(e) A UK resident company controlled by a non-resident company unless the latter would be a close company if it were UK resident.

Quoted companies

2.8 A quoted company controlled by five or fewer participators or by its directors is not a close company if it satisfies all the following conditions.

(a) Shares (ignoring shares entitled to a fixed rate of dividend) are listed on a recognised stock exchange and there have been dealings in these shares within the preceding 12 months.

(b) At least 35% of the voting power in the company is given by such shares, which are beneficially owned by the **public**.

(c) The **principal members** do not possess more than 85% of the total voting power in the company.

2.9 For the purpose of this provision, the **public** excludes:

(a) any director, or an associate of any director, of the company;

(b) any company which is controlled by a director or directors and their associates;

(c) any associated company;

(d) any fund wholly or mainly for the benefit of present or past employees or directors;

(e) principal members (but see below).

2.10 The public specifically includes non-close companies (apart from non-UK resident companies which would be close if UK resident) and approved pension or superannuation funds (except those wholly or mainly for the benefit of present or past employees or directors), even if they are principal members.

2.11 **A principal member is one of the top five shareholders (with associates' rights included) each holding more than 5% of the voting power.** If two or more persons tie for fifth place, they all qualify as principal members. If fewer than five participators hold more than 5% of the votes each then there are fewer than five principal members.

Question: Quoted companies

The ordinary share capital of Click plc, a quoted company, is held as follows.

		%
A plc	Non-close company	25
B	Director	10
C	Manager	25
D	Director	25
E	Click plc's pension fund	4
Other unconnected shareholders, each with less than 5%		11
		100

Is Click plc a close company?

Answer

This question is answered in three stages.

(a) Is Click plc under the control of five or fewer participators or any number of participators who are directors?

C is deemed to be a director so the answer is yes, since the directors of the company hold 60% of its share capital.

(b) Do the principal members hold more than 85% of the votes?

There are only four principal members of Click plc (A, B, C and D), who together hold precisely 85% so the answer is no.

(c) Does the public hold at least 35% of the votes?

The public is made up of A plc and the unconnected shareholders, giving (25 + 11)% = 36% of the voting power. The answer is therefore yes.

The company is therefore not a close company.

3 THE CONSEQUENCES OF CLOSE COMPANY STATUS

Loans to participators

3.1 **When a close company makes a loan to one of its participators or an associate it must make a payment to the Inland Revenue equal to 25% of the loan. If the loan is repaid, the Inland Revenue will repay this tax charge.**

3.2 **For small and medium sized companies, the tax charge is due for payment nine months after the end of the accounting period.** If the loan is repaid before the tax charge is due to be paid then the requirement to account for the tax charge is cancelled. Interest runs from the due date until the earlier of payment of the tax and repayment of the loan. The loan must be notified on the company's tax return. The tax charge is subject to the quarterly payments on account regime if the company is large .

3.3 A loan for these purposes includes:

- a debt owed to the company;
- a debt incurred by a participator or his associate and assigned to the company;
- an advance of money;
- a director's overdrawn current account.

3.4 Certain loans are excluded from these provisions. These are:

- money owed for goods or services supplied in the ordinary course of the company's trade unless the credit period exceeds:

  (i) six months; or, if less
  (ii) the normal credit period given to the company's other customers;

- loans to directors and employees providing they do not exceed £15,000 in total per borrower and:

  (i) the borrower works full-time for the close company; and

  (ii) he does not have a material interest (entitlement to over 5% of the assets available for distribution on a winding up) in the close company.

3.5 If at the time a loan was made the borrower did not have a material interest but he later acquires one, the company is regarded as making a loan to him when he acquires it.

3.6 When all or part of the loan is repaid by the participator to the company, or the company writes off all or part of the loan, then the company can reclaim all or a corresponding part of the tax charge paid over to the Revenue. If the loan is repaid or written of after the due date for paying the tax charge, the tax is not repayable until nine months after the end of the accounting period of repayment or write off of the loan.

The Revenue pay interest up to the time they repay the tax. If the loan is repaid/written off before nine months from the end of the accounting period in which the loan is made, interest runs from the end of those nine months. Otherwise, it runs from the date when the tax is repayable.

3.7 Although tax is charged on the company when a loan is made to a participator, the loan is not at that stage treated as the participator's income. If the loan is later written off:

(a) The amount written off is treated as the participator's income.

(b) If the participator is a director or employee, there is no Schedule E charge because the above tax charge applies instead.

(c) The amount included within the participator's income cannot be used to cover charges paid for the purposes of avoiding a liability for tax retained on charges not paid out of taxable income.

Question: Close company loan

C Ltd, a close company which prepares accounts to 31 July each year, lends £50,000 to a shareholder in July 2000. C Ltd is required to account for a tax charge of £12,500 to the Revenue. In July 2001 the shareholder repays £20,000. In January 2002 C Ltd writes off the remaining £30,000. Compute the amount of notional tax charge recovered by C Ltd following the repayment in July 2001 and the write off in January 2002 .

Answer

(a)   The notional tax charge recovered after the repayment is $\dfrac{20,000}{50,000} \times £12,500 = £5,000$.

(b)   The notional tax charge recovered after the write off is £7,500.

Benefits in kind treated as distributions

3.8   **Benefits in kind given by a close company to participators and their associates and which are not taxable under Schedule E are treated as distributions**. The amount of the deemed distribution is what would be the Schedule E charge. The actual cost is a disallowable expense for corporation tax purposes.

Question: Benefits in kind

A close company provides a new car for a participator who is not a director or employee in April 2001. The annual benefit in kind in 2001/02 under the Schedule E rules would be valued at £3,500. No fuel is provided. What are the tax consequences?

Answer

The participator is taxed as if he had received a net dividend of £3,500 in 2001/02. The company cannot deduct capital allowances on the car or any running costs in computing its taxable profits.

Close investment-holding companies

> **KEY TERM**
>
> A **close investment-holding company** (CIC) is a close company which:
>
> - Is not a trading company, and
> - Is not a member of a trading group.

3.9   A company is a trading company for an accounting period if it exists wholly or mainly for the purpose of trading. A company will not necessarily have to trade in an accounting period in order to satisfy this test but the trade must, when it is carried on, be carried on a commercial basis.

3.10   A member of a trading group is a company which co-ordinates the administration of trading companies which it controls.

3.11   Companies which deal in land, shares or securities are treated as trading companies for this purpose. Similarly, a company which invests in property let or to be let on a commercial basis will not be treated as a CIC.

3.12   **A CIC always pays corporation tax at the full rate of 30% whatever its level of profits.** However, a CIC associated with another company still counts as an associated company for the purposes of reducing the limits for the starting rate, small companies rate and marginal relief.

Chapter roundup

- Investment companies do not trade in the ordinary way, but rather generate income from investments and in doing so incur management expenses which are deductible for corporation tax purposes.

- Close companies are companies under the control of 5 or fewer shareholders (or any number of shareholding directors).

- The rules on loans and benefits from close companies are intended to deter shareholders from using the obvious ways of extracting value from their company without paying tax.

- Close investment-holding companies are singled out for special treatment so as to deter people with substantial investments from putting their investments into a company and using the company status to defer tax liabilities.

Quick quiz

1   How may an investment company obtain relief for management expenses?

2   What is a close company?

3   What are the immediate consequences of a loan by a close company to a participator?

4   How are benefits in kind given to participators (who are not employees) of close companies treated?

5   What rate(s) of CT may apply to close investment-holding companies?

Answers to quick quiz

1   Management expenses are deductible when computing taxable profits Any unrelieved management expenses may be carried forward to be relieved in a similar fashion in the following accounting period.

2   A close company is one that is under the control of either five or fewer shareholders or any number of shareholding directors.

3   When a close company makes a loan to one of its participators it must make a payment to the Inland Revenue equal to 25% of the loan.

4   They are treated as though they were distributions by the close company.

5   CICs always pay the full rate of corporation tax (30%) irrespective of the level of their profits.

Now try the question below from the exam question bank

Question to try	Level	Marks	Time
20	Exam	20	36 mins

BPP PUBLISHING

Part E
Value added tax

Chapter 18

VALUE ADDED TAX 1

Topic list	Syllabus reference	Ability required
1 Basic principles	(vi)	Comprehension
2 The scope of VAT	(vi)	Comprehension
3 Registration	(i), (vi), (vii)	Analysis
4 Accounting for VAT	(vi)	Comprehension
5 VAT invoices and records	(vi)	Comprehension
6 The valuation of supplies	(vi)	Comprehension
7 Administration	(i), (vi)	Comprehension
8 Penalties	(vi)	Comprehension

Introduction

In this and the next chapter, we study value added tax (VAT). VAT is a tax on turnover rather than on profits.

As the name of the tax suggests, it is charged (usually at 17.5%) on the value added. If someone in a chain of manufacture or distribution buys goods for £1,000 and sells them for £1,200 he has increased their value by £200. (He may have painted them, packed them or distributed them to shops to justify his mark-up, or he may simply be good at making deals to buy cheaply and sell dearly.) Because he has added value of £200, he collects VAT of £200 × 17.5% = £35 and pays this over to the government. The VAT is collected bit by bit along the chain and finally hits the consumer who does not add value, but uses up the goods.

VAT is a tax with simple computations but many detailed rules to ensure its enforcement. You may find it easier to absorb the detail if you ask yourself, in relation to each rule, exactly how it helps to enforce the tax.

Learning outcomes covered in this chapter

- **Identify** the VAT registration/deregistration requirements and the rules and penalties in relation to VAT returns

- **Identify** the correct tax point of a supply and understand its significance

- **Discuss** the problems and opportunities inherent in a VAT group registration

- **Discuss** the most efficient method of arranging VAT registrations for groups of companies

Syllabus content covered in this chapter

- Scope
- Tax point; taxable value, payments and refunds
- Registration and deregistration: penalties
- VAT administration: registration and returns
- VAT - groups
- Applications in groups of companies. Group registrations

BPP PUBLISHING

1 BASIC PRINCIPLES

1.1 The legal basis of value added tax (VAT) is to be found in the Value Added Tax Act 1994 (VATA 1994), supplemented by regulations made by statutory instrument and amended by subsequent Finance Acts. VAT is administered by HM Customs & Excise. In legal proceedings they are called 'the Commissioners of Customs & Excise'.

1.2 VAT is a tax on turnover, not on profits. The basic principle is that the VAT should be borne by the final consumer. Registered traders may deduct the tax which they suffer on supplies to them (input VAT) from the tax which they charge to their customers (output VAT) at the time this is paid to HM Customs & Excise. Thus, at each stage of the manufacturing or service process, the net VAT paid is on the value added at that stage.

1.3 EXAMPLE: THE VAT CHARGE

A forester sells wood to a furniture maker for £100 plus VAT. The furniture maker uses this wood to make a table and sells the table to a shop for £150 plus VAT. The shop then sells the table to the final consumer for £300 plus VAT. VAT will be accounted for to HM Customs & Excise as follows.

	Cost	*Input VAT* *17.5%*	*Net sale price*	*Output VAT* *17.5%*	*Payable to HM* *Customs & Excise*
	£	£	£	£	£
Forester	0	0	100	17.50	17.50
Furniture maker	100	17.50	150	26.25	8.75
Shop	150	26.25	300	52.50	26.25
					52.50

1.4 Because the traders involved account to HM Customs & Excise for VAT charged less VAT suffered, their profits for corporation tax purposes are based on sales and purchases net of VAT.

2 THE SCOPE OF VAT

2.1 **VAT is charged on taxable supplies of goods and services made in the UK by a taxable person in the course or furtherance of any business carried on by him.** It is also chargeable on the import of goods into the UK (whether they are imported for business purposes or not, and whether the importer is a taxable person or not), and on certain services received from abroad if a taxable person receives them for business purposes.

Special rules for trade with the European Community (the EC) are covered in the next chapter.

> **KEY TERM**
>
> A **taxable supply** is a supply of goods or services made in the UK, other than an exempt supply.

2.2 A taxable supply is either standard rated or zero rated. The standard rate is 17.5% (although on certain supplies, for example the supply of domestic fuel and power, a lower rate is charged of 5%) and zero rated supplies are taxed at 0%. An exempt supply is not chargeable to VAT. The categories of zero rated and exempt supplies are listed in the next chapter.

Supplies of goods

2.3 **Goods are supplied if exclusive ownership of the goods passes to another person**.

2.4 The following are treated as supplies of goods.

(a) The supply of any form of power, heat, refrigeration or ventilation, or of water

(b) The grant, assignment or surrender of a major interest (the freehold or a lease for over 21 years) in land

(c) Taking goods permanently out of the business for the non-business use of a taxable person or for other private purposes including the supply of goods by an employer to an employee for his private use

(d) Transfers under an agreement contemplating a transfer of ownership, such as a hire purchase agreement

2.5 **Gifts of goods are normally treated as sales at cost** (so VAT is due). **However, business gifts are not supplies of goods if**:

(a) **The cost to the donor is £50 or less** and the gift is not part of a series of gifts made to the same person, or

(b) **The gift is a sample**. However, if two or more identical samples are given to the same person, all but one of them are treated as supplies.

Supplies of services

2.6 Apart from a few specific exceptions, **any supply which is not a supply of goods and which is done for a consideration is a supply of services**. A consideration is any form of payment in money or in kind, including anything which is itself a supply.

2.7 A supply of services also takes place if:

- Goods are lent to someone for use outside the business
- Goods are hired to someone
- Services bought for business purposes are used for private purposes

2.8 The European Court of Justice has ruled that restaurants supply services rather than goods.

Taxable persons

2.9 **If a company's taxable turnover exceeds certain limits then it is a taxable person and should be registered for VAT (see below)**.

3 REGISTRATION

Compulsory registration

3.1 At the end of every month a company must calculate its cumulative turnover of taxable supplies to date. However this cumulative period does not extend beyond the previous 12 months. **The company becomes liable to register for VAT if the value of its cumulative taxable supplies** (excluding VAT) **exceeds £54,000** (from 1 April 2001 onwards). The company must notify HM Customs & Excise within 30 days of the end of the month in which the £54,000 limit is exceeded. HM Customs & Excise will then register it with effect from the end of the month following the month in which the £54,000 was exceeded, or from an earlier date if they and the company agree.

Registration under this rule is not required if HM Customs & Excise are satisfied that the value of taxable supplies (excluding VAT) in the year then starting will not exceed £52,000 (from 1 April 2001 onwards).

3.2 A company is also liable to register at any time if there are reasonable grounds for believing that its taxable supplies (excluding VAT) in the following 30 days will exceed £54,000. Only taxable turnover of that 30 day period is considered **not** cumulative turnover. HM Customs & Excise must be notified by the end of the 30 day period and registration will be with effect from the beginning of that period.

3.3 **When determining the value of taxable supplies for the purposes of registration, supplies of goods and services that are** *capital assets* **of the business are to be disregarded,** except for non-zero rated supplies of interests in land.

Question: VAT registration

F Ltd's started to trade in cutlery on 1 January 2001. Sales (excluding VAT) were £4,425 a month for the first nine months and £7,100 a month thereafter. From what date should F Ltd be registered for VAT?

Answer

	£	
Sales to 31 October 2001	46,925	
Sales to 30 November 2001	54,025	(exceeds £54,000)

F Ltd must notify its liability to register by 30 December 2001 (not 31 December) and will be registered from 1 January 2002 or from an agreed earlier date.

3.4 When a company is liable to register in respect of a past period, it is the company's responsibility to pay VAT. If it is unable to collect the VAT from those to whom it made taxable supplies, the VAT burden will fall on it. A company must start keeping VAT records and charging VAT to customers as soon as it is known that it is required to register. However, VAT should not be shown separately on any invoices until the registration number is known. The invoice should show the VAT inclusive price and customers should be informed that VAT invoices will be forwarded once the registration number is known. Formal VAT invoices should then be sent to such customers within 30 days of getting the registration number.

3.5 **Notification of liability to register must be made on form VAT 1.** Simply writing to, or telephoning, a local VAT office is not enough. On registration the VAT office will send the company a certificate of registration. This shows the VAT registration number, the date of registration, the end of the first VAT period and the length of later VAT periods.

3.6 If a company makes a supply before becoming liable to register, but gets paid after registration, VAT is not due on that supply.

Voluntary registration

3.7 **A company may decide to become registered even though its taxable turnover falls below the registration limit. Unless a company is registered it cannot recover the input VAT it pays on purchases.**

3.8 Voluntary registration is advantageous where a company wishes to recover input VAT on purchases. For example, consider a company that has one input during the year which cost £1,000 plus £175 VAT; it works on the input which becomes its sole output for the year and decides to make a profit of £1,000.

(a) If it is not registered it will charge £2,175 and the customer will obtain no relief for any VAT.

(b) If it is registered it will charge £2,000 plus VAT of £350. The customer will have input VAT of £350 which he will be able to recover if he, too, is registered.

If the customer is a non-taxable person he will prefer (a) as the cost to him is £2,175. If he is taxable he will prefer (b) as the net cost is £2,000. Thus, a decision whether or not to register voluntarily may depend upon the status of customers. It may also depend on the status of the outputs and the image of the business the company wishes to project (registration may give the impression of a substantial business). The administrative burden of registration should also be considered.

Intending trader registration

3.9 **Providing that a company satisfies HM Customs & Excise that it is carrying on a business, and intends to make taxable supplies, it is entitled to be registered if it chooses.** But, once registered, it is obliged to notify HM Customs & Excise within 30 days if it no longer intends to make taxable supplies.

Exemption from registration

3.10 **If a company makes only zero rated supplies, it may request exemption from registration.** The company must notify HM Customs & Excise of any material change in the nature of supplies.

HM Customs & Excise may also allow exemption from registration if only a small proportion of supplies are standard rated, provided that the company would normally receive repayments of VAT if registered.

Group registration

3.11 **Companies under common control may apply for group registration.** The effects and advantages of group registration are as follows.

(a) Each VAT group must appoint a representative member which must **account for the group's output VAT and input VAT, thus simplifying VAT accounting** and allowing payments and repayments of VAT to be netted off. However, all members of the group are jointly and severally liable for any VAT due from the representative member.

(b) **Any supply of goods or services by a member of the group to another member of the group is, in general, disregarded for VAT purposes,** reducing the VAT accounting required.

(c) Any other supply of goods or services by or to a group member is in general treated as a supply by or to the representative member.

(d) Any VAT payable on the import of goods by a group member is payable by the representative member.

3.12 **Two or more companies are eligible to be treated as members of a group provided each of them is either established in the UK or has a fixed establishment in the UK, and:**

(a) **One of them controls each of the others,** or

(b) **One person** (which could be an individual or a holding company) **controls all of them,** or

(c) **Two or more persons carrying on a business in partnership control all of them.**

3.13 **An application to create, terminate, add to or delete a company from a VAT group may be made at any time.** Applications may be refused when it appears to HM Customs & Excise to be necessary to do so for the protection of the revenue. However, if a company is no longer eligible to belong to a VAT group because the common control test is failed, the company must leave the VAT group even if revenue might be lost.

3.14 A group registration, or any change therein, will take effect from the date the application is received by Customs although applications may have an earlier or later effect. Therefore it is possible to apply in advance for group changes and it is also possible to apply for changes having a retrospective effect. However, Customs have 90 days to refuse an application.

3.15 Customs can cancel a grouping if a company ceases to meet the eligibility requirements or a risk to the revenue arises. A risk arises where avoidance is suspected, there is a risk that tax due may not be collectable or the revenue loss goes beyond that arising as a natural consequence of grouping.

3.16 Certain 'tax planning' schemes use groups to reduce the Government's overall VAT revenue. (Normal transactions within a VAT group do not do this, because eventually supplies will be made outside the group.) Customs can deal with such schemes by directing that:

• A supply made within a group is treated as made outside the group, or

• A company within a group is treated as being outside the group for a specified period.

• A company eligible to be in a group is treated as being in the group for a specified period.

A company can appeal against a direction on the grounds that a transaction, or a change in group membership, had a genuine commercial purpose as its main purpose.

3.17 Individual companies which are within a group for company law purposes may still register separately and stay outside the VAT group. This may be done to ensure that a company making exempt supplies does not restrict the input VAT recovery of the group as a whole (see the partial exemption rules in the next chapter).

Divisional registration

3.18 **A company which is divided into several units which each prepare accounts can apply for divisional registration.** The only advantage of divisional registration is administrative convenience; the separate divisions do not become separate taxable persons and the company is itself still liable for the VAT. However, if divisions account for VAT separately it may make it more likely that VAT returns will be made on time, because data for the divisions do not have to be consolidated before returns are completed.

Broadly, the conditions for divisional registration are as follows.

(a) Each division must be registered even where that division's turnover is beneath the registration limits.

(b) The divisions must be independent, self-accounting units, carrying on different activities or operating in separate locations.

(c) Input VAT attributable or apportioned to exempt supplies (see the partial exemption rules in the next chapter) for the company as a whole must be so low that it can all be recovered (apart from VAT which can never be recovered because of the type of expenditure).

(d) Each division must make VAT returns for the same tax periods.

(e) Tax invoices must not be issued for supplies between the divisions of the same company as they are not supplies for VAT purposes.

Deregistration

Voluntary deregistration

3.19 **A company is eligible for voluntary deregistration if HM Customs & Excise are satisfied that the value of taxable supplies** (net of VAT and excluding supplies of capital assets) **in the following one year period will not exceed £52,000 (from 1 April 2001)**. However, voluntary deregistration will not be allowed if the reason for the expected fall in value of taxable supplies is the cessation of taxable supplies or the suspension of taxable supplies for a period of 30 days or more in that following year.

3.20 HM Customs & Excise will cancel a registration from the date the request is made or from an agreed later date.

Compulsory deregistration

3.21 **Companies may be compulsorily deregistered.** Failure to notify a requirement to deregister within 30 days may lead to a penalty. Compulsory deregistration may also lead to HM Customs & Excise reclaiming input VAT which has been wrongly recovered since the date on which the company should have deregistered.

3.22 Other points to note are:

(a) If HM Customs & Excise are misled into granting registration then the registration is treated as void from the start.

(b) A company may be compulsorily deregistered if HM Customs & Excise are satisfied that it is no longer making nor intending to make taxable supplies.

(c) Changes in legal status also require cancellation of registration. For example:

(i) A business being incorporated
(ii) A company being replaced by an unincorporated business

The consequences of deregistration

3.23 **On deregistration, VAT is chargeable on all stocks and capital assets in a business on which input VAT was claimed,** since the registered company is in effect making a taxable supply to itself as a newly unregistered company. If the VAT chargeable does not exceed £1,000, it need not be paid.

3.24 **This special VAT charge does not apply if the business** (or a separately viable part of it) **is sold as a going concern to another taxable person** (or a person who immediately becomes a taxable person as a result of the transfer). **Such transfers are outside the scope**

of VAT (except for assets being transferred which are 'new' or opted buildings and the transferee does not make an election to waive exemption - refer to the section on land in the next chapter).

3.25 If the original owner ceases to be taxable, the new owner of the business may also take over the existing VAT number. If he does so, he takes over the rights and liabilities of the transferor as at the date of transfer.

Pre-registration input VAT

3.26 **VAT incurred before registration can be treated as input VAT and recovered from HM Customs & Excise subject to certain conditions.**

3.27 If the claim is for input VAT suffered on goods purchased prior to registration then the following conditions must be satisfied.

(a) The goods were acquired for the purpose of the business which either was carried on or was to be carried on at the time of supply.

(b) The goods have not been supplied onwards or consumed before the date of registration (although they may have been used to make other goods which are still held).

(c) The VAT must have been incurred in the three years prior to the effective date of registration.

3.28 If the claim is for input VAT suffered on the supply of services prior to registration then the following conditions must be satisfied.

(a) The services were supplied for the purposes of a business which either was carried on or was to be carried on at the time of supply.

(b) The services were supplied within the six months prior to the date of registration.

3.29 Input tax attributable to supplies made before registration is not deductible even if the input VAT concerned is treated as having been incurred after registration.

Disaggregation

3.30 A company's registration covers all its business activities together. **The turnovers of all business activities carried on by a 'company' must be aggregated to find taxable turnover.**

3.31 **There are anti-avoidance provisions to prevent VAT benefits through the operation of one business through two or more entities. These provisions enable HM Customs & Excise to direct that any connected businesses which have avoided VAT by artificially separating should be treated as one,** whatever the reason for the separation. When deciding whether businesses are artificially separated, Customs consider the extent to which those businesses are bound by financial, economic or organisational links.

4 ACCOUNTING FOR VAT

VAT periods

4.1 **The VAT period (also known as the tax period) is the period covered by a VAT return. It is usually three calendar months.** The return shows the total input and output VAT for the tax period and must be submitted (along with any VAT due) within one month of the end of the period. (Businesses who pay VAT electronically automatically receive a seven day extension to this time limit.)

4.2 HM Customs & Excise allocate VAT periods according to the class of trade carried on (ending in June, September, December and March; July, October, January and April; or August, November, February and May), to spread the flow of VAT returns evenly over the year. When applying for registration a company can ask for VAT periods which fit in with its accounting year. It is also possible to have VAT periods to cover accounting systems not based on calendar months.

4.3 If input VAT will regularly exceed output VAT it is possible to elect for a one month VAT period. The inconvenience of making 12 returns a year will need to be weighed against the advantage of obtaining more rapid repayments of VAT.

4.4 Certain small businesses may submit an annual VAT return (see the next chapter).

The tax point

4.5 **The tax point of each supply is the deemed date of supply. The basic tax point is the date on which the goods are removed or made available to the customer, or the date on which services are completed.**

4.6 The tax point determines the VAT period in which output VAT must be accounted for and credit for input VAT will be allowed. The tax point also determines which rate applies if the rate of VAT or a VAT category changes (for example when a supply ceases to be zero rated and becomes standard rated).

4.7 **If a VAT invoice is issued or payment is received before the basic tax point, the earlier of these dates automatically becomes the tax point. If the earlier date rule does not apply and if the VAT invoice is issued within 14 days after the basic tax point, the invoice date becomes the tax point** (although the company can elect to use the basic point for all supplies if it wishes). This period may be extended to accommodate, for example, monthly invoicing; the tax point is then the VAT invoice date or the end of the month, whichever is applied consistently.

Question: Tax point

J Ltd sells a sculpture to the value of £1,000 net of VAT. The company receives a payment on account of £250 plus VAT on 25 March 2002. The sculpture is delivered on 28 April 2002. J Ltd's VAT returns are made up to calendar quarters. The company issues an invoice on 4 May 2002.

Outline the tax point(s) and amount(s) due.

Answer

A separate tax point arises in respect of the £250 deposit and the £750 balance payable.

J Ltd should account for VAT as follows.

(a) *Deposit*

25 March 2002: tax at 17.5% × £250 = £43.75. This is accounted for in the VAT return to 31 March 2002. The charge arises on 25 March 2002 because payment is received before the basic tax point (which is 28 April 2002 – date of delivery).

(b) *Balance*

4 May 2002: tax at 17.5% £750 = £131.25. This is accounted for on the VAT return to 30 June 2002. The charge arises on 4 May because the invoice was issued within 14 days of the basic tax point of 28 April 2002 (delivery date).

4.8 **Goods supplied on sale or return are treated as supplied on the earlier of adoption by the customer or 12 months after despatch. Continuous supplies of services paid for periodically have tax points on the earlier of the receipt of each payment and the issue of each VAT invoice,** unless one invoice covering several payments is issued in advance for up to a year. The tax point is then the earlier of each due date or date of actual payment.

The VAT return

4.9 The regular VAT return to HM Customs & Excise is made on form VAT 100.

4.10 Input and output VAT figures on Form VAT100 must be supported by the original or copy tax invoices, and records must be maintained for six years.

Substantial traders

4.11 **If a company does not make monthly returns, and the total VAT liability over 12 months to the end of a VAT period exceeds £2,000,000, it must make payments on account of each quarter's VAT liability during the quarter.** Payments are due a month before the end of the quarter and at the end of the quarter, with the final payment due at the usual time, a month after the end of the quarter. An electronic payment system must be used, not a cheque through the post.

4.12 For a company that who exceeds the £2,000,000 limit in the 12 months to 30 September, 31 October or 30 November, the amount of each of the two payments on account is 1/24 of the total VAT liability of those 12 months. The obligation to pay on account starts with the first VAT period starting *after* 31 March.

Question: Payments on account

Large Ltd is liable to make payments on account calculated at £250,000 each for the quarter ended 31 December 2001.

What payments/repayment are due if Large Ltd's VAT liability for the quarter is calculated as:

(a) £680,000
(b) £480,000?

Answer

(a) 30 November 2001 – payment of £250,000
    31 December 2001 – payment of £250,000
    31 January 2002 – payment of £180,000 with submission of VAT return for quarter

(b) 30 November 2001 – payment of £250,000
    31 December 2001 – payment of £250,000
    31 January 2002 – on submission of return Customs will repay £20,000.

4.13 A company who first exceeds the £2,000,000 limit in 12 months ending at some other time must pay 1/24 of the VAT liability for the first 12 months in which it exceeded the £2,000,000 limit. The obligation starts with the first VAT period which starts after those 12 months, unless the company first went over the £2,000,000 limit in the 12 months to 31 December: in that case, the obligation starts with the VAT period starting on 1 April.

4.14 If the total VAT liability for any later 12 months is less than 80% of the total liability for the 12 months used to compute the payments on account, the company can apply to use 1/24 of that smaller total. The smaller total can even be used if the 12 months have not ended, provided HM Customs & Excise are satisfied that it will be below the 80% limit. A company can leave the scheme if the latest 12 months' VAT liability was less than £1,600,000.

4.15 If a company's total annual liability increases to 120% or more of the amount used to calculate the payments on account, then the new higher annual liability is used to calculate new payments on account. The increase applies from the end of the 12 months with the new higher annual liability.

4.16 Once a company is in the scheme, the payments on account are also recomputed annually, using the liability in the 12 months to 30 September, 31 October or 30 November, even if the change is less than ± 20%. The new figure first applies to the first VAT period starting after 31 March.

4.17 For the purposes of calculating the payments on account (but not for the purposes of the £2,000,000 limit for entry into the scheme), VAT due on imports from outside the EC is ignored.

4.18 Companies can choose to switch from making quarterly to monthly returns instead of paying the interim amounts calculated by Customs. For example, the actual return and liability for January would be due at the end of February.

4.19 Companies can also choose to pay their actual monthly liability without having to make monthly returns. Customs can refuse to allow a company to continue doing this if they find it has abused the facility by not paying enough. The company will then either have to pay the interim amount or switch to making monthly returns.

4.20 A company can appeal to a VAT tribunal if Customs and Excise refuse to allow it to make monthly payments of its actual liability.

Refunds of VAT

4.21 **There is a three year time limit on the right to reclaim overpaid VAT.** This time limit does not apply to input VAT which a business could not have reclaimed earlier because the supplier only recently invoiced the VAT, even though it related to a purchase made some time ago. Nor does it apply to overpaid VAT penalties.

4.22 If a company has overpaid VAT and has overclaimed input tax by reason of the same mistake, HM Customs and Excise can set off any tax, penalty, interest or surcharge due to them against any repayment due and repay only the net amount. In such cases the normal three year time limit for recovering VAT, penalties, interest, etc by assessment does not apply.

4.23 **HM Customs and Excise can refuse to make any repayment which would unjustly enrich the claimant.** They can also refuse a repayment of VAT where all or part of the tax has, for practical purposes, been borne by a person other than the taxpayer (eg by a customer of the taxpayer) except to the extent that the taxpayer can show loss or damage to any of its businesses as a result of mistaken assumptions about VAT.

4.24 In *Marks and Spencer plc v CCE (1998)* chocolate teacakes which had been treated as standard rated were later found to be zero-rated. M&S sought a repayment of the overpaid VAT but the Tribunal thought that had M&S been aware of the true VAT position it would have remained in the same economic position by varying its prices to maintain a similar margin. It followed that M&S had, in effect, passed on most of the VAT to its customers without suffering economic loss, and it would be unjustly enriched if more than ten per cent of the overpaid VAT was repaid to it. M&S were so unhappy with this decision that the case has now been taken to the European Court of Justice.

5 VAT INVOICES AND RECORDS

5.1 **A taxable 'person' making a taxable supply to another person registered for VAT must supply a *VAT* invoice within 30 days of the time of supply, and must keep a copy.** The invoice must show:

(a) The supplier's name, address and registration number.

(b) The date of issue, the tax point and an invoice number.

(c) The name and address of the customer.

(d) The type of supply (sale, hire purchase, loan, exchange, hire, goods made from the customer's materials, sale on commission, sale or return, etc).

(e) A description of the goods or services supplied, giving for each description the quantity, the rate of VAT and the VAT exclusive amount.

(f) The rate of any cash discount.

(g) The total invoice price excluding VAT (with separate totals for zero rated and exempt supplies).

(h) Each VAT rate applicable, the amount of VAT at each rate and the total amount of VAT.

5.2 For supplies to other EC member states, item (d) may be omitted but the supplier's registration number must be prefixed by 'GB' and if the customer is VAT registered, the customer's registration number (including the state code, such as DE for Germany) must be shown.

5.3 If an invoice is issued, and a change in price then alters the VAT due, a credit note or debit note to adjust the VAT must be issued.

5.4 Credit notes must give the reason for the credit (such as 'returned goods'), and the number and date of the original VAT invoice. If a credit note makes no VAT adjustment, it should state this.

5.5 **A less detailed VAT invoice may be issued by a retailer where the invoice is for a total including VAT of up to £100** and the supply is not to another EC member state. Such an invoice must show:

(a) The supplier's name, address and registration number
(b) The date of the supply
(c) A description of the goods or services supplied
(d) The rate of VAT chargeable
(e) The total amount chargeable including VAT

Zero rated and exempt supplies must not be included in less detailed invoices.

5.6 **VAT invoices are not required for payments of up to £25 including VAT which are for telephone calls or car park fees or are made through cash operated machines. In such cases, input VAT can be claimed without a VAT invoice.**

5.7 **VAT records must be kept for six years,** although HM Customs & Excise may sometimes grant permission for their earlier destruction. They may be kept on paper, on microfilm or microfiche or on computer. However, there must be adequate facilities for HM Customs & Excise to inspect records.

5.8 All records must be kept up to date and in a way which allows:

- The calculation of VAT due
- Officers of HM Customs & Excise to check the figures on VAT returns

5.9 The following records are needed.

- Copies of VAT invoices, credit notes and debit notes issued

- A summary of supplies made

- VAT invoices, credit notes and debit notes received

- A summary of supplies received

- Records of goods received from and sent to other EC member states

- Documents relating to imports from and exports to countries outside the EC

- A VAT account

- Order and delivery notes, correspondence, appointment books, job books, purchases and sales books, cash books, account books, records of takings (such as till rolls), bank paying-in slips, bank statements and annual accounts

- Records of zero rated and exempt supplies, gifts or loans of goods, taxable self-supplies and any goods taken for non-business use

6 THE VALUATION OF SUPPLIES

6.1 **The value of a supply is the VAT-exclusive price on which VAT is charged. The consideration for a supply is the amount paid in money or money's worth.** Thus with a standard rate of 17.5%:

Value + VAT = consideration
£100 + £17.50 = £117.50

The VAT proportion of the consideration is known as the 'VAT fraction'. It is

$$\frac{\text{rate of tax}}{100 + \text{rate of tax}} = \frac{17.5}{100 + 17.5} = \frac{7}{47}$$

6.2 If the consideration for a bargain made at arm's length is paid in money, the value for VAT purposes is the VAT exclusive price. If it is paid in something other than money, as in a barter of some goods or services for others, it must be valued and VAT will be due on the value.

6.3 If the price of goods is effectively reduced with money off coupons, the value of the supply is the amount actually received.

Mixed supplies and composite supplies

6.4 **Different goods and services are sometimes invoiced together at an inclusive price (a mixed supply).** Some items may be chargeable at the standard rate and some at the zero rate. **The supplier must account for VAT separately on the standard rated and zero rated elements by splitting the total amount payable in a fair proportion between the different**

elements and charging VAT on each at the appropriate rate. There is no single way of doing this: one method is to split the amount according to the cost to the supplier of each element, and another is to use the open market value of each element.

6.5 **If a supply cannot be split into components, there is a composite supply, to which one VAT rate must be applied.** The rate depends on the nature of the supply as a whole.

6.6 A supply of air transport including an in-flight meal has been held to be a single, composite supply of transport (zero rated) rather than a supply of transport (zero rated) and a supply of a meal (standard rated). Contrast this with where catering is included in the price of leisure travel - there are two separate supplies: standard rated catering and zero rated passenger transport.

6.7 Broadly, a composite supply occurs when one element of the supply is merely incidental to the main element. A mixed supply occurs where different elements of the supply are the subject of separate negotiation and customer choice giving rise to identifiable obligations on the supplier.

Discounts

6.8 **Where a discount is offered for prompt payment, VAT is chargeable on the net amount, regardless of whether the discount is taken up** (except that for imports from outside the EC, the discount is ignored unless it is taken up). Supplies made on contingent discount terms (for example depending on the level of purchases) must be invoiced with VAT based on the full amount, an adjustment being made when the discount is earned. When goods are sold to staff at a discount, VAT is only due on the discounted price.

6.9 For goods supplied under a hire purchase agreement VAT is chargeable on the cash selling price at the start of the contract.

6.10 If a trader charges different prices to customers paying with credit cards and those paying by other means, the VAT due in respect of each standard rated sale is the full amount paid by the customer × the VAT fraction.

6.11 **When goods are permanently taken from a business for non-business purposes VAT must be accounted for on their market value.** If services bought for business purposes are used for non-business purposes (without charge), then VAT must be accounted for on their cost, but the VAT to be accounted for is not allowed to exceed the input VAT deductible on the purchase of the services.

7 ADMINISTRATION

Local VAT offices

7.1 **Local VAT offices are responsible for the local administration of VAT and for providing advice to registered 'persons' whose principal place of business is in their area.** They are controlled by regional collectors.

7.2 **Completed VAT returns should be sent to the VAT Central Unit at Southend,** not to a local VAT office.

7.3 **From time to time a registered 'person' will be visited by staff from a local VAT office (a control visit)** to ensure that the law is understood and is being applied properly. If a company disagrees with any decision as to the application of VAT given by HM Customs & Excise it can ask its local VAT office to reconsider the decision. It is not necessary to appeal formally to a tribunal while a case is being reviewed in this way. Where an appeal can be settled by agreement before being heard by a tribunal, a written settlement has the same force as a tribunal decision.

7.4 **HM Customs & Excise may issue assessments of VAT due to the best of their judgement if they believe that a company has failed to make returns or if they believe those returns to be incorrect or incomplete.** The time limit for making assessments is normally three years after the end of a VAT period, but this is extended to 20 years in the case of fraud, dishonest conduct, certain registration irregularities and the unauthorised issue of VAT invoices.

HM Customs & Excise sometimes write to companies, setting out their calculations, before issuing assessments. The company can then query the calculations.

Appeals to VAT and duties tribunals

7.5 **VAT and duties tribunals, which are independent of HM Customs & Excise, provide a method of dealing with disputes.** Provided that VAT returns and payments shown thereon have been made, appeals can be heard.

A tribunal can waive the requirement to pay all VAT shown on returns before an appeal is heard in cases of hardship. It cannot allow an appeal against a purely administrative matter such as Customs refusal to apply an extra statutory concession.

There may be a dispute over the deductibility of input VAT which hinges on the purposes for which goods or services were used, or on whether they were used to make taxable supplies. The company must show that HM Customs & Excise acted unreasonably in refusing a deduction, if the goods or services are luxuries, amusements or entertainment.

Time limits

7.6 **An appeal must be lodged with the tribunal (not the local VAT office) within 30 days of the date of any decision by HM Customs & Excise. If instead the company would like the local VAT office to reconsider their decision it should apply within 30 days of the decision to the relevant VAT office.** The local VAT office may either:

- Confirm the original decision, in which case the company has a further 21 days from the date of that confirmation in which to lodge an appeal with a tribunal, or

- Send a revised decision, in which case the company will have a further 30 days from the date of the revised decision in which to lodge an appeal with a tribunal.

7.7 Tribunal hearings are normally in public, and decisions are published. If one of the parties is dissatisfied with a decision on a point of law he may appeal to the courts. Tribunals may award costs.

8 PENALTIES

Late notification

8.1 **A company that makes taxable supplies is obliged to notify HM Customs & Excise if supplies exceed the registration limit. A penalty can be levied for failure to notify a**

liability to register by the proper date. In addition, the VAT which would have been accounted for had the company registered on time must be paid.

8.2 The penalty for late notification is based on the net VAT due from the date when the company should have been registered to the date when notification is made or, if earlier, the date on which HM Customs & Excise become aware of the liability to be registered. The rate varies as follows.

Number of months registration late by	*Percentage of VAT*
Up to 9	5%
Over 9, up to 18	10%
Over 18	15%

A minimum penalty of £50 applies.

8.3 The late registration penalty is not due if the company can show that there is reasonable excuse for the failure, and the penalty may be mitigated by HM Customs & Excise or by a tribunal.

8.4 There is no definition of 'reasonable excuse'. However the legislation states that the following are not reasonable excuses.

- An insufficiency of funds to pay any VAT due
- Reliance upon a third party (such as an accountant) to perform the task in question

8.5 Many cases have considered **what constitutes a reasonable excuse** but decisions often conflict with one another. Each case depends on its own facts. Here are some examples:

(a) Whilst **'ignorance of basic VAT law'** is not an excuse, ignorance of more complex matters can constitute a reasonable excuse.

(b) There have been a number of cases where Tribunals have accepted **misunderstandings as to the facts** as giving rise to a reasonable excuse.

(c) Although the law expressly excludes an insufficiency of funds from providing a reasonable excuse, the Tribunal will, in exceptional circumstances, look behind the shortage of funds itself and examine the case of it – this is generally restricted to cases where an unexpected event (eg bank error) has led to the shortage of funds.

Criminal fraud

8.6 **Where a person knowingly takes steps to evade VAT this amounts to criminal fraud.** The penalty for criminal fraud depends on whether the conviction is summary (by magistrates) or on indictment (by a jury). On summary conviction the maximum term of imprisonment is six months, and the maximum fine is the greater of £2,000 and three times the VAT involved. On conviction on indictment the maximum term of imprisonment is seven years and the level of fine is unlimited.

Conduct involving dishonesty (civil fraud)

8.7 This arises where a person dishonestly takes steps, or omits to take steps, in order to evade VAT. Failing to provide any information, failing to register, and therefore failing to make any VAT statement, and providing false information can count. **The penalty for civil fraud is 100% of the tax involved.** This may be mitigated by up to 100% in recognition of co-operation given during the investigation into the true VAT position. HM Customs & Excise need only show on the balance of probabilities that the conduct took place, whereas criminal fraud must be proved beyond reasonable doubt.

The unauthorised issue of invoices

8.8 **This penalty applies where a company that is not registered for VAT nevertheless issues VAT invoices.** The penalty is 15% of the VAT involved with a minimum penalty of £50, but this penalty may be mitigated.

Breaches of regulations

8.9 There are penalties for breaches of VAT regulations of any kind. The amount of penalty varies with the type and frequency of the breach concerned.

The default surcharge

8.10 **A default occurs when a company either submits its VAT return late, or submits the return on time but pays the VAT late.** It also occurs when a payment on account from a substantial trader is late. **If a company defaults, HM Customs & Excise will serve a surcharge liability notice. The notice specifies a surcharge period running from the date of the notice to the anniversary of the end of the period for which the company is in default.**

8.11 **If a further default occurs in respect of a return period ending during the specified surcharge period the original surcharge period will be extended to the anniversary of the end of the period to which the new default relates. In addition, if the default involves the late payment of VAT** (as opposed to simply a late return) **a surcharge is levied.**

8.12 The surcharge depends on the number of defaults involving late payment of VAT which have occurred in respect of periods ending in the surcharge period, as follows.

Default involving late payment of VAT in the surcharge period	*Surcharge as a percentage of the VAT outstanding at the due date*
First	2%
Second	5%
Third	10%
Fourth or more	15%

Surcharges at the 2% and 5% rates are not normally demanded unless the amount due would be at least £200 but for surcharges calculated using the 10% or 15% rates there is a minimum amount of £30 payable.

8.13 If a substantial trader is late with more than one payment (on account or final) for a return period, this only counts as one default. The total VAT paid late is the total of late payments on account plus the late final payment.

Question: Default surcharge

PP Ltd's VAT return for the quarter to 31.12.01 is late. The company then submits returns for the quarters to 30.9.02 and 31.3.03 late as well as making late payment of the tax due of £12,000 and £500 respectively.

PP Ltd's VAT return to 31.3.04 is also late and the VAT due of £1,100 is also paid late. All other VAT returns and VAT payments are made on time. Outline PP Ltd's exposure to default surcharge.

Answer

A surcharge liability notice will be issued after the late filing on the 31.12.01 return outlining a surcharge period extending to 31.12.02.

The late 30.9.02 return is in the surcharge period so the period is extended to 30.9.03. The late VAT payment triggers a 2% penalty. 2% × £12,000 = £240.

The late 31.3.03 return is in the surcharge period so the period is now extended to 31.3.04. The late payment triggers a 5% penalty. 5% × £500 = £25. Since £25 is less than the £200 de minimis limit it is not collected by Customs.

The late 31.03.04 return is in the surcharge period. The period is extended to 31.03.05. The late payment triggers a 10% penalty 10% × £1,100 = £110. This is collected by Customs since the £200 de minimis does not apply to penalties calculated at the 10% (and 15%) rate.

PP Ltd will have to submit all four quarterly VAT returns to 31.3.05 on time and pay the VAT on time to 'escape' the default surcharge regime it is currently within.

8.14 A company must submit one year's returns on time and pay the VAT shown on them on time in order to break out of the surcharge liability period and the escalation of surcharge percentages.

8.15 A default will be ignored for all default surcharge purposes if the company can show that the return or payment was sent at such a time, and in such a manner, that it was reasonable to expect that HM Customs & Excise would receive it by the due date. Posting the return and payment first class the day before the due date is generally accepted as meeting this requirement. A default will also be ignored if the company can demonstrate a reasonable excuse (see above) for the late submission or payment.

The misdeclaration penalty: very large errors

8.16 **The making of a return which understates the true liability or overstates the repayment due incurs a penalty of 15% of the VAT which would have been lost if the return had been accepted as correct.** The same penalty applies when HM Customs & Excise issue an assessment which is too low and the company fails to notify the error within 30 days from the issue of the assessment.

8.17 **These penalties apply only where the VAT which would have been lost equals or exceeds the lower of**

(a) **£1,000,000 or**

(b) **30% of the sum of the true input VAT and the true output VAT.** This sum is known as the gross amount of tax (GAT). In the case of an incorrect assessment 30% of the true amount of tax (TAT), the VAT actually due, is used instead of 30% of the GAT.

The penalty may be mitigated.

Question: Misdeclaration penalty - GAT

A company declares output tax of £100,000 and claims input tax of £30,000 on the VAT return for the quarter ended 31 March 2002. It is subsequently discovered that output tax is understated by £28,000.

Does a misdeclaration penalty arise?

Answer

The test for misdeclaration penalty is the lower of:

- 30% of GAT (Gross Amount of Tax)
  30% × £(100,000 + 28,000 + 30,000)
  = £47,400

- £1,000,000

ie £47,400

Since the error of £28,000 is less than £47,400 the error is not 'large' and hence no penalty arises.

Question: Misdeclaration penalty – TAT

A company fails to submit a VAT return for the quarter to 30 June 2001. On 31 August 2001 Customs issue an assessment showing VAT due of £200,000.

The true VAT liability for the quarter is:

	£
Output tax	370,000
Input tax	(80,000)
Net VAT due	290,000

The company pays the £200,000 of VAT assessed but does not bring the correct position to Custom's attention.

The true position is discovered during a control visit in December 2002.

Will a misdeclaration penalty apply?

Answer

The under-assessment of £90,000 will attract a penalty if it exceeds the lower of:

- 30% of TAT (True Amount of Tax)
  30% × £290,000
  = £87,000

- £1 million

ie £87,000.

The £90,000 under-assessment exceeds £87,000, thus a misdeclaration penalty will be charged at £90,000 × 15% = £13,500.

The company will have to pay the additional £90,000 due as well as the £13,500 penalty.

8.18 **Errors on a VAT return of up to £2,000 (net: underdeclaration minus overdeclaration) may be corrected on the next return without giving rise to a misdeclaration penalty or interest** (see below for details on interest).

8.19 This penalty does not apply if the company can show reasonable excuse (see above) for its conduct, or if it made a full disclosure when it had no reason to suppose that HM Customs & Excise were enquiring into its affairs.

8.20 If conduct leads to a conviction for fraud, or to a penalty for conduct involving dishonesty, it cannot also lead to a misdeclaration penalty.

The misdeclaration penalty: repeated errors

8.21 **If a company submits an inaccurate return, and the VAT which would have been lost if it had been accepted as accurate equals or exceeds the lower of**

- **£500,000**
- **10% of the GAT**

there is a material inaccuracy.

Question: Repeated errors

Bloggs Ltd submits its VAT return for the quarter to 31 December 2001 showing:

	£
Output tax	550,000
Input tax	(230,000)
Net VAT due	320,000

273

It is later established that output tax should have been £640,000.

Is the error large enough for a repeated error misdeclaration penalty?

Answer

The error is £90,000 £(640,000 – 550,000). The error falls within the repeated error misdeclaration penalty regime if it equal or exceeds:

- £500,000

- 10% of GAT (Gross amount of tax)
  10% × £(640,000 + 230,000)
  = £87,000

  ie £87,000.

Since the £90,000 error exceeds £87,000 the penalty could apply.

8.22 **Before the end of the fourth VAT period following the period of a material inaccuracy, HM Customs & Excise may issue a penalty liability notice, specifying a penalty period. The period is the eight VAT periods starting with the one in which the notice is issued.**

8.23 **If there are material inaccuracies for two or more VAT periods falling within the penalty period, then each such inaccuracy apart from the first one leads to a penalty of 15% of the VAT which would have been lost.** The penalty may be mitigated.

8.24 The penalty does not apply in the circumstances set out in Paragraphs 8.19 and 8.20 above.

If a misdeclaration penalty for a very large error is imposed for an inaccuracy it cannot also lead to a penalty for a repeated error. However, a penalty liability notice may still be issued following the inaccuracy and it may still count as the *first* material inaccuracy in a penalty period (so that the next one leads to a penalty).

Interest

8.25 **Interest** (not deductible in computing taxable profits) **is charged on VAT which is the subject of an assessment** (where returns were not made or were incorrect)**, or which could have been the subject of an assessment but was paid before the assessment was raised. It runs from the reckonable date until the date of payment.** This interest is sometimes called 'default interest'.

8.26 **The reckonable date is when the VAT should have been paid** (one month from the end of the return period), or in the case of VAT repayments, seven days from the issue of the repayment order. However, where VAT is charged by an assessment interest does not run from more than three years before the date of the assessment; and where the VAT was paid before an assessment was raised, interest does not run for more than three years before the date of payment.

8.27 In practice, interest is only charged when there would otherwise be a loss to the Exchequer. It is not, for example, charged when a company failed to charge VAT but if it had done so, another company would have been able to recover the VAT.

Repayment supplement

8.28 **Where a company is entitled to a repayment of VAT and the original return was rendered on time but HM Customs & Excise do not issue a written instruction for the**

repayment to be made within 30 days of the receipt of the return, then the company will receive a supplement of the greater of £50 and 5% of the amount due.

8.29 **If the return states a refund due which differs from the correct refund due by more than the greater of 5% of the correct refund and £250, no supplement is added.**

8.30 Days spent in raising and answering reasonable enquiries in relation to the return do not count towards the 30 days allowed to HM Customs & Excise to issue an instruction to make the repayment. The earliest date on which the 30 days can start is the day following the end of the prescribed accounting period.

Interest on overpayments due to official errors

8.31 **If VAT is overpaid or a credit for input VAT is not claimed because of an error by HM Customs & Excise, then the company may claim interest on the amount eventually refunded, running from the date on which it paid the excessive VAT** (or from the date on which HM Customs & Excise might reasonably be expected to have authorised a VAT repayment) **to the date on which HM Customs & Excise authorise a repayment.**

8.32 Interest must be claimed within three years of the date on which the company discovered the error or could with reasonable diligence have discovered it. Interest is not available where a repayment supplement is available. Interest does not run for periods relating to reasonable enquiries by HM Customs & Excise into the matter in question.

Chapter roundup

- VAT is charged on turnover at each stage in a production process, but in such a way that the burden is borne by the final consumer.

- A company may be required to register for VAT because of the level of its turnover, or it may register voluntarily.

- VAT is accounted for on regular returns. Extensive records must be kept.

- VAT is administered by HM Customs & Excise, and independent tribunals hear appeals. There is an extensive regime of penalties to ensure compliance with VAT law.

Quick quiz

1 On what transactions will VAT be charged?

2 When may a taxable person be exempt from registration?

3 How are transfers between group companies treated under a VAT registration?

4 When may a company choose to be deregistered?

5 What is the time limit in respect of pre-registration input VAT on goods?

6 Within what time limit must an appeal to a tribunal be lodged?

7 What is a default?

Answers to quick quiz

1   VAT is charged on taxable supplies of goods and services made in the UK by a taxable person in the course or furtherance of any business carried on by him.

2   If a taxable person makes only zero rates supplies it may request exemption from registration.

3   Any supplies between VAT group members are ignored for VAT purposes.

4   A company is eligible for voluntary deregistration if Customs are satisfied that the value of its taxable supplies in the following year will not exceed £52,000.

5   The VAT must have been incurred in the three years prior to the effective date of registration.

6   Within 30 days of the date of any decision by HM Customs and Excise.

7   A default occurs when a company either submits a VAT return late or submits the return on time but pays the VAT late.

Now try the question below from the Exam Question Bank

Number	Level	Marks	Time
21	Exam	20	36 mins

Chapter 19

VALUE ADDED TAX 2

Topic list		Syllabus reference	Ability required
1	Zero rated and exempt supplies	(vi)	Comprehension
2	The deduction of input VAT	(vi)	Comprehension
3	Imports, exports, acquisitions and despatches	(vi)	Comprehension
4	Special schemes	(vi)	Comprehension

Introduction

This chapter concentrates on matters which do not apply to every company. We start by looking at zero rated and exempt supplies and we see how making exempt supplies can affect the deduction of input VAT.

Imports and exports must be fitted into the VAT system. We see how this is done for transactions both within and outside the European Community. VAT needs to be applied to imports, so that people do not have a tax incentive to buy abroad, and VAT is taken off many exports in order to encourage sales abroad.

Finally, we look at special VAT schemes designed for particular types of trader, including small traders and dealers in secondhand goods.

Learning outcomes covered in this chapter

- **Identify** the significance of standard rate, zero rate and exempt supplies and those supplies outside the scope of VAT

- **Identify** the significance of EU and non EU countries when dealing with VAT

Syllabus content covered in this chapter

- Scope, including basic property transactions - 'opting to tax'
- Exemptions, zero and exempt, partial exemption
- Transactions with foreign companies including those in EU member states

1 ZERO RATED AND EXEMPT SUPPLIES

1.1 **Zero rated supplies are taxable at 0%.** A taxable supplier whose outputs are zero rated but whose inputs are standard rated will obtain repayments of the VAT paid on purchases.

1.2 Exempt supplies are not so advantageous. In exactly the same way as for a non-registered person, a **person making exempt supplies is unable to recover VAT on inputs**.

The exempt supplier thus has to shoulder the burden of VAT. Of course, it may increase prices to pass on the charge, but it cannot issue a VAT invoice which would enable a taxable customer to obtain a credit for VAT, since no VAT is chargeable on supplies.

1.3   EXAMPLE: STANDARD RATED, ZERO RATED AND EXEMPT SUPPLIES

Here are figures for three companies, the first with standard rated outputs, the second with zero rated outputs and the third with exempt outputs. All their inputs are standard rated.

	Standard rated	Zero rated	Exempt
	£	£	£
Inputs	20,000	20,000	20,000
VAT	3,500	3,500	3,500
	23,500	23,500	23,500
Outputs	30,000	30,000	30,000
VAT	5,250	0	0
	35,250	30,000	30,000
Pay/(reclaim)	1,750	(3,500)	0
Net profit	10,000	10,000	6,500

1.4   VAT legislation lists zero rated and exempt supplies. There is no list of standard rated supplies.

1.5   If a company makes a supply you need to categorise that supply for VAT as follows:
Step 1.   Look at the zero rated list to see if it is zero rated. If not:
Step 2.   Look at the exempt list to see if it is exempt. If not:
Step 3.   The supply is standard rated.

Zero rated supplies

1.6   The following are items on the **zero rated list**.

(a)   Human and animal food

(b)   Sewerage services and water

(c)   Printed matter used for reading (eg books, newspapers)

(d)   Construction work on new homes or the sale of the freehold of (or a lease over 21 years (at least 20 years in Scotland) of) new homes by builders

(e)   Sales of substantially reconstructed listed buildings, and alterations to such buildings, where such buildings are to be used for residential or charitable purposes

(f)   Services relating to ships and aircraft, and the transport of goods and passengers

(g)   The hire or sale of houseboats and caravans used as homes

(h)   Gold supplied between central banks and members of the London Gold market

(i)   Bank notes

(j)   Drugs and medicines on prescription or provided in private hospitals

(k)   Exports of goods to outside the EC

(l)   Specialised equipment used by rescue/first aid services.

(m)   Sales or hire by a charity

(n)   Clothing and footwear for young children and certain protective clothing eg motor cyclists' crash helmets

(o)   Certain supplies (eg advertising services) to charitable institutions

Exempt supplies

1.7   The following are items on the **exempt** list.

(a)   Sales of freeholds of 'old' buildings and leaseholds of land and buildings of any age including a surrender of a lease. A building is 'old' if it is three years or more since its construction in general.

(b)   Financial services

(c)   Insurance

(d)   Postal services provided by the Post Office

(e)   Betting and gaming

(f)   Certain education and vocational training

(g)   Health services

(h)   Burial and cremation services

(i)   Supplies to members by trade unions and professional bodies if in consideration only for a membership subscription

(j)   Entry fees to non-profit making sports competitions

(k)   Disposals of works of art and other items to public bodies in lieu of capital taxes

(l)   Welfare services supplied by charities

(m)   Supplies by charities, philanthropic bodies, trade unions, professional associations and non-profit making sports bodies in connection with fund raising events

(n)   Residential care services

(o)   Admission charges to certain cultural events or places

(p)   Supplies of training, retraining and work experience paid for using further education funding council funds

(q)   Investment gold

(r)   The supply of goods on which input tax was irrecoverable on purchase.

Exceptions to the general rule

1.8   The zero-rated and exempt lists outline general categories of goods or services which are either zero rated or exempt However, the VAT legislation then goes into great detail to outline exceptions to the general rule.

1.9   For example the zero-rated list states human food is zero rated. However, the legislation then states that food supplied in the course of catering (eg restaurant meals, hot takeaways) is not zero rated. Luxury items of food (eg crisps, peanuts) are also not zero rated.

1.10   In the exempt list we are told that financial services are exempt. However the legislation then states that credit management, processing services and investment advice are not exempt.

1.11   Thus great care must be taken when categorising goods or services as zero-rated, exempt or standard-rated. It is not as straightforward as it may first appear. For exam purposes you should be aware of the main items on the standard rated and exempt lists.

BPP PUBLISHING

Standard rated supplies

1.12 **As mentioned previously, there is no list of standard rated supplies. If a supply is not zero rated and is not exempt then it is treated as standard rated.** Standard rated supplies normally have a 17.5% VAT charge but some supplies are subject to a lower rate of VAT. For example fuel and power (eg gas, electricity, fuel oil, coal) for domestic or charity use (except fuel for motor vehicles) is taxed at 5%.

Land and buildings

1.13 **The construction of new dwellings or buildings to be used for residential or charitable purposes is zero rated.** The construction of new residential accommodation by the conversion of non-residential buildings is also zero rated. Zero rating extends to the construction of homes for children, the elderly, students and the armed forces, but not to hospitals, prisons or hotels, to which the standard rate applies. The sale of the freehold of a 'new' commercial building is standard rated. The definition of 'new' is less than three years old. The construction of commercial buildings is also standard rated.

1.14 Other sales and also grants, variations and surrenders of leases (including reverse surrenders, when the tenant pays the landlord) are exempt. The provision of holiday accommodation is standard rated.

1.15 Landlords may elect to treat the supply of interests in land and commercial buildings as taxable instead of exempt (the option to tax). The election covers leases, licences and sales and applies to all future supplies of the specified land and buildings. The landlord must become registered for VAT (if he is not already so registered) in order to make the election. If the land and buildings have already been let on an exempt basis, permission to exercise the option must be obtained from HM Customs & Excise. The point of making the election is that it enables the landlord to recover input VAT.

The election may be revoked after 20 years with the consent of Customs. Supplies after revocation are exempt.

2 THE DEDUCTION OF INPUT VAT

2.1 **For input VAT to be deductible, the payer must be a taxable person, with the supply being to him in the course of his business. In addition a VAT invoice must be held (except for payments of up to £25 including VAT which are for telephone calls or car park fees or which are made through cash operated machines).**

Capital items

2.2 **The distinction between capital and revenue** which is important in other areas of tax **does not apply to VAT.** Thus a manufacturer buying plant subject to VAT will be able to obtain a credit for all the VAT immediately. The plant must of course be used to make taxable supplies, and if it is only partly so used only part of the VAT can be reclaimed. Conversely if plant is sold secondhand then VAT should be charged on the sale and is output VAT in the normal way.

Non-deductible input VAT

2.3 **The following input VAT is not deductible even for a taxable person with taxable outputs.**

(a) **VAT on motor cars** not used wholly for business purposes. VAT on cars is never reclaimable unless the car is acquired new for resale or is acquired for use in or leasing to a taxi business, a self-drive car hire business or a driving school. Private use by **an employee** is non-business use (regardless of any benefit in kind charge) unless the user pays a full commercial hire charge (not just a reimbursement of costs). However, VAT on accessories such as car radios is deductible if ordered on a separate purchase order and fitted after delivery of the car. The VAT charged when a car is hired for business purposes is reclaimable, but if there is some non-business use and the hire company has reclaimed VAT on the original purchase of the car, only 50% of the VAT on hire charges can be reclaimed by the hirer. A hiring for five days or less is assumed to be for wholly business use.

VAT need not be charged on the sale of a used car except on any profit element (which, of course, is rare), unless input VAT on the original purchase of the car was recoverable.

(b) **VAT on business entertaining** where the cost of the entertaining is not a deductible Schedule D Case I expense. If the items bought are used partly for such entertaining and partly for other purposes, the proportion of the VAT relating to the entertainment is non-deductible.

In *Ernst & Young v CCE* the Tribunal held that staff entertaining was wholly for business purposes and a full input tax recovery was allowed. Customs accept this decision in respect of staff entertainment but maintain that following the case *KPMG v CCE* input tax on entertaining guests at a staff party is non-deductible.

(c) **VAT on expenses incurred on domestic accommodation for directors**

(d) **VAT on non-business items passed through the business accounts.** However, when goods are bought partly for business use, the purchaser may:

(i) Deduct all the input VAT, and account for output VAT in respect of the private use, or

(ii) Deduct only the business proportion of the input VAT.

Where services are bought partly for business use, only method (ii) may be used. If services are initially bought for business use but the use then changes, a fair proportion of the input VAT (relating to the private use) is reclaimed by HM Customs & Excise by making the purchaser account for output VAT.

A business that provides employees with mobile phones for business use can, regardless of any private use, deduct all the VAT incurred on purchase and on standing charges provided the charges do not contain any element for calls.

If a business allows its employees to make private calls without charge, then it must apportion the VAT incurred on the call charges. Any method of apportionment may be used, eg a sample of bills over a reasonable time, providing the method produces a fair and reasonable result. Apportionment must be made where the phone package allows the business to make a certain quantity of calls for a fixed monthly payment and there is no standing payment, or where the contract is for the purchase of the phone and the advance payment of a set amount of call time for a single charge.

If a business imposes clear rules prohibiting private calls, and enforces them, Customs allows a deduction of all of the VAT incurred on the call charges. Similarly, if a business tolerates only a small amount of calls, Customs allow all of the input tax incurred to be deducted.

(e) **VAT which does not relate to the** making of supplies by the buyer in the course of a **business.**

Partial exemption

2.4 A taxable person may only recover the VAT on supplies made to him if it is attributable to his taxable supplies. A person able to recover all input VAT (except the non-deductible VAT described above) is a **fully taxable person. Where a person makes a mixture of taxable and exempt supplies, he is partially exempt, and not all his input VAT is recoverable because some of it is attributable to his exempt supplies.**

The standard method of attributing input VAT

2.5 **For a company that is partially exempt, input tax must be apportioned between** that relating to **taxable supplies** (and recoverable) **and** that relating to **exempt supplies** (exempt input tax). The standard method of attributing input VAT is to:

Step 1. **Calculate how much of the input VAT relates to supplies which are wholly used or to be used in making taxable supplies:** this input VAT is deductible in full.

Step 2. **Calculate how much of the input VAT relates to supplies which are wholly used or to be used in making exempt supplies:** this is exempt input VAT.

Step 3. **Calculate how much of any remaining input VAT is deductible using the percentage (taxable turnover excluding VAT/total turnover excluding VAT) × 100%,** rounded to the nearest whole percentage above.

2.6 The following should be omitted from the calculation of the percentage mentioned in Step 3.

(a) Supplies of land
(b) Self supplies (see below)
(c) Supplies of capital goods used in the business

Question: Calculation of input tax to recover (part 1)

In the three month VAT period to 30 June 2001, A Ltd makes both exempt and taxable supplies in the order of £100,000 exempt and £300,000 taxable. Most of the goods purchased are used for both types of supply which means that much of the input VAT cannot be directly attributed to either type of supply. After directly attributing as much input VAT as possible the following position arises.

	£
Attributed to taxable supplies	1,200
Attributed to exempt supplies	600
Unattributed VAT	8,200
	10,000

How much input VAT can A Ltd recover?

Answer

The amount of unattributed VAT which is apportioned to the making of taxable supplies is

$$\frac{300,000}{400,000} = 75\% \times £8,200 = £6,150$$

A Ltd can therefore recover £1,200 + £6,150 = £7,350 of its input VAT.

The balance of input tax of £2,650 £(600 + (8,200 − 6,150)) is exempt input tax.

2.7 Alternative methods of attributing input VAT (called 'special' methods) may be agreed with HM Customs & Excise.

2.8 **Where the input VAT wholly attributable to exempt supplies plus the VAT apportioned to exempt supplies (ie the total of exempt input tax) is no more than £625 a month on average and is also no more than 50% of all input VAT, all VAT is treated as being attributable to taxable supplies and therefore fully recoverable.**

Question: De minimis limit

S Ltd makes the following supplies in the quarter ended 31 October 2001.

	£
Taxable supplies (excl. VAT)	28,000
Exempt supplies	6,000
	34,000

S Ltd analyses input tax for the period as follows.

		£
Wholly attributable to:	taxable supplies	1,500
	exempt supplies	900
Non-attributable (overheads)		1,200
		3,600

How much input tax is available for credit on S Ltd's VAT return?

Answer

	£
Wholly attributable to taxable supplies	1,500
Partly attributable to taxable supplies	

$$\frac{28,000}{28,000 + 6,000}$$

	£
ie 83% × £1,200	996
	2,496

£(900 + (1,200 − 996)) = 1,104

	£
Exempt input tax is de minimis (W1)	1,104
Input tax recoverable	*3,600*

Working 1

De minimis test

- Monthly average $\dfrac{1,104}{3}$ = £368 ie not more than £625.

- Proportion of total $\dfrac{1,104}{3,600}$ = 30.7% ie not more than 50%.

Both tests passed. Thus exempt input tax is de minimis.

Annual adjustment

2.9 An annual adjustment is made, covering the year to 31 March, 30 April or 31 May (depending on when the VAT periods end). A computation of recoverable input VAT is made for the whole year, using the same method as for individual returns. The '£625 a month on average and 50%' test is also applied to the year as a whole, and if it is passed then all input VAT for the year is recoverable.

2.10 The result for the year is compared with the total of results for the individual VAT periods:

(a) If the result for the whole year shows that less input VAT is recoverable than has been recovered period by period, the difference is accounted for as output VAT on the return for the next period after the end of the year.

(b) If the result for the whole year shows that more input VAT is recoverable than has been recovered period by period, the difference is claimed as input VAT on the return for the next period after the end of the year.

Question: Calculation of input tax to recover (part 2)

Following on from the above example A Ltd has the following results in the remaining VAT quarters of his VAT year ended 31 March 2002.

		Input VAT attributed to	
	Taxable	Exempt	
Quarter to	supplies	supplies	Unattributed
	£	£	£
30.9.01	1,500	1,000	5,000
31.12.01	2,000	500	1,800
31.3.02	1,900	850	7,000
	5,400	2,350	13,800

		Turnover	
Quarter to	Taxable		Exempt
	£		£
30.9.01	400,000		100,000
31.12.01	500,000		150,000
31.3.02	450,000		120,000
	1,350,000		370,000

Calculate the annual adjustment required and state which return it will be made on.

Answer

First we calculate the recoverable input tax in each VAT return.

			Recovered
		£	£
Return to 30.6.01			
See above Taxable		7,350	7,350
Exempt		2,650	
		10,000	

Return to 30.9.01

$\dfrac{400,000}{500,000}$ = 80% × £5,000 = Non-attributable   4,000

Wholly taxable	1,500	
Taxable total	5,500	5,500
Exempt £(1,000 + 1,000)	2,000	
	7,500	

Return to 31.12.01

$\dfrac{500,000}{650,000}$ × £1,800 = 77% (Note 2) Non-attributable   1,386

Wholly taxable	2,000	
Taxable total	3,386	
Exempt £(500 + 414)	914	
	4,300	4,300

The exempt input tax at £914 is less than £1,875 (£625 × 3 months) and 50% of total input tax (50% × £4,300 = £2,150) so is 'small' and recoverable.

Return to 31.3.02

$$\frac{450,000}{570,000} \times £7,000 = 79\% \text{ (Note 2) Non-attributable} \qquad\qquad 5,530$$

Wholly taxable	1,900	
Taxable total	7,430	7,430
Exempt £(850 + 1,470)	2,320	
	9,750	
Recovered over the VAT year		24,580

Now we do the same calculation again but using the results for the whole VAT year to 31.3.02.

Annual adjustment

$$\frac{1,350,000 + 300,000}{1,720,000 + 400,000} = 78\% \times £(13,800 + 8,200) \text{ (note 1)} \qquad 17,160$$

Wholly taxable £(5,400 + 1,200)	6,600	
Taxable total	23,760	23,760
Exempt £(31,550 – 23,760)	7,790	
	31,550	
VAT to repay to Customs on VAT return to 30 June 2002 as annual adjustment.		820

Note 1: we must include the quarter to June 2001's results.

Note 2: the percentage is always rounded up.

Irrecoverable VAT

2.11 Where all (as with many cars) or some (as with partially exempt traders) of the input VAT on a purchase is not deductible, the **non-deductible VAT is included in the cost for income tax, corporation tax, capital allowance or capital gains purposes. Deductible VAT is omitted from costs, so that only net amounts are included in accounts. Similarly, sales** (and proceeds in chargeable gains computations) **are shown net of VAT**, because the VAT is paid over to HM Customs & Excise.

Motoring expenses

Cars

2.12 **The VAT incurred on the purchase of a car not used wholly for business purposes is not recoverable** (except as in Paragraph 2.3(a) above). If accessories are fitted after the original purchase and a separate invoice is raised then the VAT on the accessories can be treated as input tax so long as the accessories are for business use.

2.13 If a car is used wholly for business purposes (including leasing, so long as the charges are at the open market rate), the input VAT is recoverable but the buyer must account for VAT on the sale of the car. **If a car is leased, the lessor recovered the input VAT when the car was purchased and the lessee makes some private use of the car** (for example private use by employees)**, the lessee can only recover 50% of the input VAT on the lease charges.**

2.14 **If a car is used for business purposes then any VAT charged on repair and maintenance costs can be treated as input VAT. No apportionment has to be made for private use.**

2.15 If an employee accepts a reduced salary in exchange for being allowed to use his employer's car privately, or pays his employer for that use, there is no supply, so VAT is not due on the salary reduction. However, VAT is due on charges for running costs. VAT is also due on charges for employee use in the rare cases where the charge is a full commercial rate so that the employer has recovered input VAT on the cost or on leasing charges in full.

Fuel for business use

2.16 **The VAT incurred on fuel used for business purposes is fully deductible as input VAT.** If the fuel is bought by employees who are reimbursed for the actual cost or by a mileage allowance, the employer may deduct the input VAT.

Fuel for private use

2.17 **When fuel is supplied for an individual's private use at less than the cost of that fuel to the business, all input VAT incurred on the fuel is allowed but the business must account for output VAT using set scale charges per VAT return period, based on the cylinder capacity of the car's engine.** The scale figures will be stated in the exam if required. However, take care to note whether the examiner has given you the VAT inclusive or the VAT exclusive scale figure. The VAT inclusive scale charges are reproduced in the tax rates and allowances tables in this text. The output VAT is the VAT inclusive scale charge $\times 7/47$ or the VAT exclusive scale charge $\times 17.5\%$.

If the employee has to pay the full cost of fuel (or more than its cost) to the employer, the employer must account for VAT on the amount paid, rather than on the scale charge.

Question: VAT and private use fuel

Iain is an employee of ABC Ltd. He has the use of a 1000 cc car for one month and an 1800 cc car for two months during the quarter ended 31 March 2002.

ABC Ltd pay all the petrol costs in respect of both cars without requiring Iain to make any reimbursement in respect of private fuel. Total petrol costs for the quarter amount to £300 (including VAT).

What is the VAT effect of the above on ABC Ltd?

Answer

Value for the quarter:

	£
Car 1	
Up to 1400 cc £242 × 1/3 =	80.67
Car 2	
1401-2000 cc £307 × 2/3 =	204.67
	285.34
Output tax:	
7/47 × £285.34	£42.50
Input tax	
7/47 × £300	£44.68

Relief for bad debts

2.18 Where a supplier of goods or services has accounted for VAT on the supply and the customer does not pay, the supplier may claim a refund of VAT on the amount unpaid. **Relief is available for VAT on bad debts if the debt is over six months old (measured from when payment is due) and has been written off in the creditor's accounts.** Where payments on account have been received, they are attributed to debts in chronological order. If the debtor later pays all or part of the amount owed, a corresponding part of the VAT repaid must be paid back to HM Customs & Excise.

2.19 **Bad debt relief claims must be made within three years**. The creditor must have a copy of the VAT invoice, and records to show that the VAT in question has been accounted for and that the debt has been written off. The VAT is reclaimed on the creditor's VAT return.

2.20 The supplier must notify any debtor who is a taxable person of his claim within seven days of the claim. The notification must state:

- The date of issue of the notice
- The date and amount of the claim
- The date and number of any VAT invoice issued in relation to each relevant supply
- The consideration due for each supply written off as a bad debt

The supplier must keep a copy of the notification along with other records relating to the bad debt relief claim.

2.21 **Debtors must repay any VAT reclaimed by them which has not actually yet been paid and on which the supplier has claimed bad debt relief.** The debtor is required to make the repayment by means of a negative entry in the VAT allowable portion of his VAT account for the period in which the bad debt relief was claimed by the supplier. The debtor's entitlement to input VAT credit is restored when payment is made to the supplier and his bad debt relief claim is reversed.

2.22 There is anti-avoidance legislation to counter abuse through assigning debts to third parties in order to reduce the amount of VAT due or to claim too much bad debt relief.

3 IMPORTS, EXPORTS, ACQUISITIONS AND DISPATCHES

3.1 The terms **import and export** refer to purchases and sales with countries **outside the EC.**

3.2 The terms **acquisition and dispatch** refer to purchases and sales with countries **in the EC.**

Imports

3.3 Imports are chargeable to VAT when the same goods supplied in the home market by a registered trader would be chargeable to VAT, and at the same rate. There is an exception for certain works of art and antiques imported from outside the EC, for which the VAT charge is calculated at an effective VAT rate of 5% on the full value.

3.4 **An importer of goods from outside the EC must calculate VAT on the value of the goods imported and account for it at the point of entry into the UK. He can then deduct the VAT payable as input VAT on his next VAT return.** HM Customs & Excise issue monthly certificates to importers showing the VAT paid on imports. VAT is chargeable on the sale of the goods in the UK in the normal way. If security can be provided, the deferred payment system can be used whereby VAT and customs duty are automatically debited to the importer's bank account each month rather than payment being made for each import when the goods arrive in the UK.

3.5 All incidental expenses incurred up to the first destination of the goods in the UK should be included in the value of imported goods. Additionally, if a further destination in the UK or another member State is known at the time the goods are imported, any costs incurred in transporting the goods to that further place must also be included in the value.

3.6 **If standard rated services are supplied in the UK by an overseas supplier** (inside or outside the EC), **VAT may be charged in the UK.**

Under the reverse charge system, certain supplies are treated as made by the UK recipient. These are:

(a) Certain advertising, banking, professional and freight transport services used by the recipient for business purposes

(b) All other services used by VAT-registered recipients for business purposes

If the recipient is VAT-registered, he must account for VAT on the supply because he is treated as making it. The point of the special category (i) is that the recipient may have to register because he is receiving the services, since the deemed supplies by him may take him over the turnover limit. Category (ii) services are only subject to the reverse charge if the recipient is VAT-registered already.

Exports

3.7 **There is a general zero-rating where a person exports goods from the EC.**

3.8 It is not sufficient merely to export goods. The zero-rating only applies if Customs 'are satisfied' that the supplier has exported the goods. Evidence of the export must therefore be retained by the trader and must take the form specified by Customs.

3.9 Evidence of export must be obtained within three months of the date of the supply. The type of evidence required by Customs varies according to the manner in which the goods are exported.

3.10 Customs expect ordinary commercial documentation, such as contracts, copy correspondence, copy invoices and consignment notes, to be available for inspection. They also expect positive proof of export clearly identifying the particular goods exported and the manner of export.

3.11 For seafreight the normal evidence is a copy of the shipped bill of lading or sea waybill certifying actual shipment, or equivalent documentation provided by the shipping company.

3.12 For air freight the evidence required is a copy of the air waybill, endorsed with the flight prefix and number and the date and place of departure.

3.13 For letter post a certificate of posting is required. If the value of the package exceeds £100, and a customs declaration is required, an export label (Form VAT 444) must be fixed to the package.

Trade in goods within the European Community

Introduction

3.14 Goods transferred between **registered persons** in different EC states are zero-rated in the seller's member state provided the seller has proof of the supply and has issued an invoice showing the purchaser's VAT reference number in the other member state. The registered person acquiring the goods has to account for VAT at the rate appropriate in the member state to which the goods are transported.

Sales (dispatches)

3.15 **Where goods are sold to another EC state, the supply is zero-rated if:**

(a) **The supply is made to a registered trader,** and

(b) **The supplier quotes his customer's VAT number on the invoice** (ie to prove that he is a registered trader), and

(c) **The supplier holds evidence that the goods were delivered to another member state.**

Where these conditions are not satisfied, the supply is subject to VAT as if the customer had been in the UK.

Purchases (acquisitions)

3.16 **Goods acquired in the UK by a VAT registered person from another EC member state are liable to VAT in this country.** Consequently, output tax has to be accounted for on the relevant VAT return. **The 'tax point' for such acquisitions is the earlier of:**

- **The fifteenth day of the month following the month of acquisition,** and
- **The date of issue of an invoice.**

3.17 The transaction is entered on the relevant VAT return as an output and an input so, subject to the partial exemption provisions, the effect is neutral. Thus the trader is in the same position as he would have been if he had acquired the goods from a UK supplier.

3.18 If the goods acquired are zero-rated or exempt under UK VAT legislation there is no requirement to account for VAT at the standard rate.

Special situations requiring registration

3.19 Exempt businesses and non-taxable organisations must register for VAT in the UK if their acquisitions of goods from other EC member states exceeds £54,000 in any calendar year or if they have reason to believe that the value of such acquisitions in the next 30 days will exceed £54,000.

3.20 A person in another EC member state who makes mail order supplies to non-taxable persons in the UK exceeding £70,000 in any calendar year must register for VAT in the UK. **These rules are often referred to as the 'distance selling' provisions.**

3.21 A UK company making mail order supplies to non registered customers in other EC states, where it is responsible for the delivery of the goods to other EC states, must register in that other member state if the annual value of such supplies to persons in that EC state exceeds 35,000 ECU or 100,000 ECU (approx. £24,500 or £70,000) depending which EC state is involved.

Reporting requirements

3.22 **All persons registered for VAT who make supplies of goods to other EC member states are required to complete a statement (usually referred to as an 'ESL' - EC Sales List) at the end of each calendar quarter showing their total of such sales to each customer in the return period and showing:**

- **The VAT registration number of the supplier**
- **A two digit prefix indicating the member state of the acquirer of the goods**
- **The VAT registration number of each acquirer,** and
- **The total value of all supplies within the calendar quarter made to each acquirer.**

3.23 A penalty of £100 can be imposed for a material inaccuracy on the ESL, but this will only be imposed after there have been two previous material inaccuracies and Customs have both given a written warning and issued a notice. A penalty can also be levied for failure to submit an ESL.

3.24 The information in the statement will be exchanged with the VAT authorities in other EC member states for audit and control purposes.

3.25 Traders must provide the necessary data for the compilation of trade statistics on the movement of goods between EC countries. **The form used for the collection of this data is known as the supplementary statistical declaration (SSD) or more commonly the Intrastat and this form records the movement of goods, not supplies of services**.

3.26 Traders whose dispatches of goods to, or arrivals of goods from, other EC countries in a calendar year exceed a threshold must supply details of consignments processed each month on SSDs. The threshold for both arrivals and dispatches is £233,000. Nil returns do not have to be submitted.

3.27 The SSD must be submitted within ten working days of the end of a calendar month. If submitted electronically the submission deadline is extended to the end of the month following the period in question.

Warehousing

3.28 Customs may approve the use of premises as a 'customs warehouse'. Once within the warehousing regime, import VAT only becomes payable on the removal of the goods from the warehouse.

3.29 The benefits of warehousing include:

(i) The deferment of payment of VAT up to the time that the goods are removed rather than when the goods are physically imported into the UK.

(ii) Goods re-exported to customers outside the EC will not constitute a chargeable event giving rise to a charge to VAT.

(iii) Goods which are found to be faulty on arrival can be returned to the supplier before VAT is paid. This will result in a reduction in administrative costs.

Fiscal warehousing

3.30 Fiscal warehousing allows VAT-free trading in qualifying EC commodities, eg specified metals, foodstuffs and chemicals. VAT is payable when the commodities are removed from the warehouse. Payment of VAT on supplies of some services in these and other warehousing regimes may also be deferred.

3.31 The regime applies to eligible goods on which the VAT chargeable on importation (in the case of goods imported from outside the member states) has been paid. Where eligible goods subject to the regime are changed into other eligible goods by some operation, they continue to be entitled to remain under the fiscal warehousing arrangements. However, where eligible goods are changed into ineligible goods, they become chargeable to VAT as if they had been removed from the fiscal warehouse at that time.

3.32 Supplies of services are zero-rated if they are wholly performed on, or in relation to, goods subject to the regime for example, storage or repackaging.

3.33 VAT is payable by the person who removes the goods, or pays the duty.

Certain services

3.34 **When certain advertising, banking, professional and freight transport services are supplied *by* a UK registered trader, either to a person outside the EC or to a VAT registered trader in another EC state, they are treated as supplied in the recipient's state. They are therefore outside the scope of UK VAT, and no VAT is charged.**

3.35 The same rule applies to a supply of work done on goods by a UK trader, where the work is supplied to a VAT-registered trader in another EC state and the goods leave the UK: the supply is outside the scope of UK VAT. If a UK-registered trader gets someone in another EC state to do work on goods and the goods then leave the other state, the UK trader will account for UK VAT on the work under the reverse charge system.

4 SPECIAL SCHEMES

The cash accounting scheme

4.1 **The cash accounting scheme enables companies to account for VAT on the basis of cash paid and received.** That is, the date of payment or receipt determines the return in which the transaction is dealt with. **The scheme can only be used by a company whose annual taxable turnover (exclusive of VAT) does not exceed £600,000.** A company can join the scheme only if all returns and VAT payments are up to date (or arrangements have been made to pay outstanding VAT by instalments).

4.2 If the value of taxable supplies exceeds £750,000 in the 12 months to the end of a VAT period a company must leave the cash accounting scheme immediately.

The annual accounting scheme

4.3 **The annual accounting scheme is only available to companies** who regularly pay VAT to Customs and Excise, not to companies who normally get repayments. It is available for companies **whose taxable turnover (exclusive of VAT) for the 12 months starting on their application to join the scheme is not expected to exceed £600,000.** Companies cannot apply to join until they have been registered for at least 12 months. The year for which each return is made may end at the end of any calendar month.

4.4 **Under the annual accounting scheme companies file annual VAT returns but throughout the year they must make payments on account of their VAT liability by direct debit.** If annual turnover is £100,000 or more, the company must pay 90% of the previous year's net VAT liability during the year by means of nine monthly payments commencing at the end of the fourth month of the year. If taxable turnover in the previous year was up to £100,000, quarterly payments are required, each of 20% of the previous year's net VAT liability. In this case the payments are made at the end of the fourth, seventh and tenth months of the year. However, if the sum due does not exceed £400, the quarterly interim payment need not be made.

Late payment of instalments is not a default for the purposes of the default surcharge.

4.5 **An annual VAT return must be submitted to HM Customs & Excise along with any payment due within two months of the end of the year.**

4.6 It is not possible to use the annual accounting scheme if input VAT exceeded output VAT in the year prior to application. In addition, all returns must have been made up to date. Annual accounting is not available where VAT registration is in the name of a VAT group or a division.

4.7 If the expected value of taxable supplies exceeds £750,000 notice must be given to HM Customs & Excise within 30 days and the company may then be required to leave the scheme. If the £750,000 limit is in fact exceeded, it must leave the scheme.

4.8 If a company fails to make the regular payments required by the scheme or the final payment for a year, or has not paid all VAT shown on returns made before joining the scheme, it may be expelled from the scheme. Customs can also prevent a company using the scheme 'if they consider it necessary to do so for the protection of the revenue'.

4.9 Advantages of annual accounting:

- Only one VAT return each year so fewer occasions to trigger a default surcharge

- Ability to manage cash flow more accurately

- Avoids need for quarterly calculations for partial exemption purposes and input tax recovery

4.10 Disadvantages of annual accounting:

- Need to monitor future taxable supplies to ensure turnover limit not exceeded

- Timing of payments have less correlation to turnover (and hence cash received) by business

- Payments based on previous year's turnover may not reflect current year turnover which may be a problem if the scale of activities have reduced

The secondhand goods scheme

4.11 **The basic idea of the secondhand goods scheme is to restrict the amount of VAT due on goods sold under the scheme to VAT on the profit margin, rather than on the entire amount charged on reselling the goods. The trader has to account for VAT at 7/47 of the difference between the buying price (including any VAT he paid) and the selling price. The scheme applies to works of art, collectors' items and antiques and to all secondhand goods, apart from precious metals and gemstones. A company does not have to use the scheme: it can account for VAT in the normal way if it chooses.** The scheme cannot be used for goods that were acquired as the result of the transfer of a business as a going concern unless the goods were already eligible for the scheme before the transfer.

4.12 No VAT invoice is issued, so a customer cannot reclaim the input VAT suffered.

Question: Secondhand goods scheme

A Ltd carries on a trade in secondhand pianos. On 5 November 2001 it sells a piano to Anne for £3,500. A Ltd had purchased the piano through an advertisement in a local paper from Scott for £2,100 on 10 October 2001. A Ltd spent £500 on repairs and tuning in respect of the piano.

What is A Ltd's output tax liability on the sale?

Answer

Under the margin scheme A Ltd's output tax is:

	£
Selling price	3,500
Less: purchase price	(2,100)
Margin	1,400

VAT @ 7/47 × £1,400 = £209

Costs of repair and tuning are ignored although any input tax incurred by A Ltd on these is recoverable in the normal way.

4.13 **A dealer in large volumes of low value goods (purchase price £500 or less per item) can account for VAT of 7/47 of his total margin for a period (netting off profits and losses), instead of working out each profitable margin individually and ignoring losses.** This global accounting cannot be used for motor vehicles, motorcycles, caravans, motor caravans, aircraft, boats, outboard motors, horses or ponies.

4.14 **The scheme can only be applied where the goods were bought from a person who did not charge VAT on the supply or from one who was operating the secondhand goods scheme.** It can also be used by an agent who acts in his own name and is therefore treated as actually buying and selling goods himself.

4.15 Goods sold under the scheme are not subject to the usual rules on trade with other EC member states. There is no VAT on their acquisition and sales to traders in other states are taxed just like sales in the UK. Exports to outside the EC are zero rated. Imports from outside the EC (apart from cars) cannot be included in the scheme.

Chapter roundup

- Some supplies are taxable (either standard rated or zero rated). Others are exempt. A company making both taxable and exempt supplies may be unable to recover all of its input VAT.

- Imports from outside the EC are subject to VAT and exports to outside the EC are zero rated. Taxable acquisitions from other EC states are also subject to VAT and sales to registered traders in other EC states are zero rated.

- Special schemes include the cash accounting scheme and the annual accounting scheme. These schemes make VAT accounting easier for certain types of company.

Quick quiz

1 What input VAT is never deductible?

2 What is partial exemption?

3 What relief is available for bad debts?

4 Are goods exported from the EC standard-rated or zero-rated?

5 What are the turnover limits for the annual accounting and cash accounting schemes?

Answers to quick quiz

1 VAT on:

- motor cars
- business entertaining
- expenses incurred on domestic accommodation for directors
- non-business items passed through the accounts
- items which do not relate to making business supplies

2 Where a 'company' makes a mixture of taxable and exempt supplies it is partially exempt and cannot recover input tax incurred by the business in full.

3 Where a supplier has accounted for VAT on a supply and the customer fails to pay, then the supplier may claim a refund of the VAT accounted for to Customs but never actually collected from the customer.

4 In general, exports from the EC are zero-rated.

5 Turnover not exceeding £600,000 to join the schemes. Once turnover exceeds £750,000 must leave the schemes.

Now try the question below from the exam question bank

Question to try	Level	Marks	Time
22	Exam	20	36 mins

Exam question and answer bank

1 **TREE LTD** *36 mins*

(a) Tree Ltd, a company with no associated companies, had the following results for the eighteen months to 31 December 2001:

	£
Trading profits	180,000
Chargeable gain - realised 1.6.01	172,000
Gift aid donation - paid 30.9.01	5,000
Gift aid donation - paid 30.9.00	22,000
Schedule A	36,000
Dividend received 30.3.01	27,000

The Schedule A income was rental income which accrued evenly over the period.

Requirement

Compute the corporation tax liability in respect of the profits arising in the eighteen months to 31 December 2001. (14 marks)

(b) Dealers plc a company with no associated companies, had profits chargeable to corporation tax of £420,000 for its year ended 31 December 2001.

Requirement

Compute Dealers plc's mainstream corporation tax liability for the year. (3 marks)

(c) Springer Ltd, a company with no associated companies, had profits chargeable to corporation tax of £6,200 in the year to 31 December 2001.

Requirement

Calculate Springer Ltd's mainstream corporation tax liability for the year. (3 marks)

Total Marks = 20

2 **HOGG LTD** *23 mins*

(a) Hogg Ltd prepares accounts for the year to 31 December 2001. In June 2001 it estimates that its corporation tax liability for the year will be £500,000. In January 2002 it revises its estimate to £520,000. In September 2002 it submits its return and self-assessment, showing a total liability of £525,000. The company has always paid corporation tax at the full rate.

Requirement

State the amounts and due dates for the payment of corporation tax by Hogg Ltd in respect of the year to 31 December 2001. (7 marks)

(b) In 2005 Hogg Ltd changes its accounting date to 31 October 2005. Assume that the liability for the ten months to 31 October 2005 is expected to be £600,000.

Requirement

State the due dates for and the amount of instalments of corporation tax that Hogg Ltd will be required to pay in respect of this period. · (6 marks)

Total Marks = 13

3 TRADERS LTD

22 mins

Traders Ltd's profit and loss account for the year to 31 March 2002 was as follows.

	£		£
General expenses	73,611	Gross trading profit	246,250
Repairs and renewals	15,000	Bad debts recovered	
Legal and accountancy charges	1,200	(previously written off)	373
Subscriptions and donations	2,000	Commissions	1,900
Bad debts written off	500	Profit on sale of investment	5,265
Directors' remuneration	20,000		
Salaries and wages	18,000		
Patent royalties	5,000		
Depreciation	15,000		
Rent and rates	1,500		
Net profit	101,977		
	253,788		253,788

Notes

(i)   *General expenses include the following.*

	£
Travelling expenses of staff, including directors	1,000
Entertaining suppliers	600

(ii)   *Repairs and renewals include the following.*

	£
Redecorating existing premises	300
Renovations to new premises to remedy wear and tear of previous owner (the premises were usable before these renovations)	500

(iii)   *Legal and accountancy charges are made up as follows.*

	£
Debt collection service	200
Staff service agreements	50
Tax consultant's fees for special advice	30
45 year lease on new premises	100
Audit and accountancy	820
	1,200

(iv)   *Subscriptions and donations include the following.*

	£
Donations under the gift aid scheme	200
Donation to a political party	500
Sports facilities for staff	500
Contribution to a local enterprise agency	200

(v)   The commissions received were not incidental to the trade.

(vi)   The chargeable gain arising on the sale of investments was £770.

(vii)   The patent royalties were paid gross to another UK company.

Requirement

Compute Traders Ltd's profits chargeable to corporation tax for the accounting period to 31 March 2002, and the corporation tax liability thereon. **12 marks**

4 HARDY LTD

18 mins

Hardy Ltd, makes accounts to 30 June. Despite substantial investment in new equipment, business has been indifferent and the company will cease trading on 31 December 2001. Its last accounts will be prepared for the six months to 31 December 2001.

The tax written down value of fixed assets at 1 July 1997 was as follows.

Pool	£
General	25,700 ✓
Cars	6,300 ✓

Fixed asset additions and disposals have been as follows.

		£
20.9.97	Plant cost	2,300 ✓
25.9.97	Computer cost	4,400 ✓
15.7.98	Car for managing director's use cost	13,400 ✓
14.7.00	Plant sold for	340 ✓
10.5.01	Computer sold for	2,200 ✓

An election to depool the computer was made when it was acquired in 1997. Private use of the managing director's car was agreed at 20% for all years. ✓

At the end of 2001, the plant would be worth £20,000, the managing director's car £10,600 and the other cars £4,000.

The company is one that qualifies for first year allowances.

Requirement

Calculate the capital allowances for the periods from 1 July 1997 to 31 December 2001. **10 marks**

Assume that the maximum possible capital allowances are claimed as early as possible.

5 **W LTD (PILOT PAPER)** *36 mins*

W Ltd, a company engaged in the manufacture of machine tools, prepares its accounts annually at 31 March.

The following information relates to transactions during the year ended March 2002.

During the years 1999 and 2000 the company invested heavily in plant and machinery, mainly to take advantage of the first year allowances (FYA) available to it under the capital allowances system. This has resulted in a low pool value brought forward and the company has decided to sell plant which is now surplus to its requirements.

The various values brought forward at 1 April 2001 are:

General pool	Expensive car (1)	Expensive car (2)	Computer SLA
£36,000	£22,000	£30,000	£18,000

The following transactions took place during the year ended 31 March 2002:

Disposals
- Two items in the general pool were sold for £60,000
  In each case the selling price was less than the original cost

- Expensive car (2) was sold for £22,000

- The computer, which had been de-pooled under the Short Life Asset (SLA) rules, was sold for £20,000

Purchases:
- A new lorry was bought for £18,000

- A piece of machinery was bought for £20,000
  This could, if wished, be treated as a SLA

The factory in which the trade is carried on was bought new on 1 April 1993 for £120,000 and an extension costing £40,000 was added on 1 April 1995. An initial allowance was not claimed on either of these payments. On 1 April 2001 the factory was sold for £100,000 and, on the same day, the company took occupation of a second-hand factory for which they paid £210,000. This factory had been bought by the original owners for £180,000 on 1 April 1991 and first used by them on that date.

The company is one which qualifies for FYA where appropriate and if claimed.

Requirements

(a) Calculate the maximum possible capital allowances (including industrial buildings allowances) which could be claimed by W Ltd in respect of the year ended 31 March 2002.　**14 Marks**

(b) State clearly how you have treated the purchases of the lorry and the new piece of machinery.　**2 Marks**

(c) State clearly why you have chosen this approach given that there are two possible approaches, one of which produces significantly higher capital allowances than the other.　**4 Marks**

　　Total Marks = 20

6　**CUCKOLD LTD**　*45 mins*

(a) Cuckold Ltd makes up accounts to 31 March each year. It is considering the purchase of an additional, secondhand factory on 1 April 2002. It has decided to spend £150,000 and the following details refer to four possible factories which could each be acquired for that sum. All are equally suitable for Cuckold Ltd's purposes and all have been used for qualifying industrial purposes throughout their lives.

	Original cost to first owner	*Date of first use*
	£	
(i)	100,000	1 April 1978
(ii)	80,000	1 April 1977
(iii)	160,000	1 April 2000
(iv)	120,000	1 April 1994

Requirement

Advise Cuckold Ltd of the amount of industrial buildings allowances which would be available as a result of purchasing each of the above factories, indicating the periods for which the allowances would be available. Which building would you advise it to purchase?　**10 marks**

(b) Having acquired a factory Cuckold Ltd intends to incur further capital expenditure on the following items.

(i)　Installation of display lighting in a showroom where customers will view his products
(ii)　Thermal insulation of the factory
(iii)　Construction of a canteen, within the factory premises, for the use of the workforce

Requirement

Advise Cuckold Ltd of the extent to which capital allowances would be available in respect of the above items of expenditure. Cuckold Ltd is a small or medium sized enterprise for FYA purposes.　**6 marks**

(c) Acorn Ltd had purchased a new industrial building on 1 July 1991 for immediate use for £200,000. During a period of recession from 1 April 1993 to 30 September 1995 the building was rented out for the storage of furniture. On 1 October 1995 manufacturing re-commenced. On 31 May 2001 the building was sold for £150,000.

The building was not situated in an enterprise zone. Acorn Ltd prepared accounts to 31 December each year.

Requirement

Calculate the balancing adjustment arising on the sale of the building.　**9 Marks**

　　Total Marks = 25

7　**SCHEDULE A**　*20 mins*

P Ltd starts to let out property on 1 July 2001. The company has the following transactions.

(a) On 1 July 2001, it lets an office block which it has owned for several years. The tenant is required to pay an initial premium of £20,000 for a 30 year lease, and then to pay annual rent of £4,000, quarterly in advance. The office is let unfurnished.

(b) On 1 October 2001 it buys a badly dilapidated office block for £37,000. During October, it spends £8,000 on making the office habitable. It lets it furnished for £600 a month from 1 November 2001, but the tenant leaves on 31 January 2002. A new tenant moves in on 1 March 2002, paying

£2,100 a quarter in arrears. Water rates are £390 a year, payable by P Ltd. P Ltd also pays buildings insurance of £440 for the period from 1 October 2001 to 31 August 2002. P Ltd financed the purchase (but not the repairs) with a bank loan at 15% interest. P Ltd decides to claim the renewals basis. It replaces some furniture on 1 May 2002, at a cost of £350. The tenant is responsible for all repair costs and council tax.

Requirement

Compute P Ltd's Schedule A income for the year to 31.3.02.   **11 marks**

---

8   **FERRARO LTD**   *18 mins*

Ferraro Ltd has the following results.

	y/e 31.12.97 £	y/e 31.12.98 £	9m to 30.9.99 £	y/e 30.9.00 £	y/e 30.9.01 £
Trading profit (loss)	10,000	34,480	6,200	4,320	(100,000)
Bank deposit interest accrued	100	200	80	240	260
Rents receivable	3,000	1,200	1,420	1,440	1,600
Capital gain				12,680	
Allowable capital loss		5,000			9,423
Patent royalties (gross)	1,000	1,000	0	1,000	1,500

Requirement

Compute all profits chargeable to corporation tax, claiming loss reliefs as early as possible. State any amounts carried forward as at 30 September 2001.   **10 marks**

---

9   **GAINS**   *9 mins*

E Ltd disposed of assets as follows.

(a)   On 1 January 2001 it sold a car which had been used by a company director at a loss of £10,700. ✗

(b)   On 28 February 2001 it sold some shares at a loss of £16,400. ✓

(c)   On 1 May 2001 it sold some shares and realised a gain of £7,200. ✓

(d)   On 1 October 2001 it sold some shares at a loss of £2,000. ✓

(e)   On 1 December 2001 it sold a picture to a collector for £50,000, making a gain of £3,000. ✓

(f)   On 1 March 2002 it sold a racehorse called Edwina's Boy which was used for publicity purposes, making a gain of £10,000. ✗

Requirement

What loss, if any, is available to be carried forward at the end of its year ended 31 March 2002.   **5 Marks**

---

10   **HARDUP LTD**   *27 mins*

Hardup Ltd made the following disposals in the year ended 31 March 2002.

(a)   On 12 May 2001 it sold an office block for £120,000. The company had bought the offices for £65,000 on 1 July 1988.

(b)   On 18 June 2001 it sold a plot of land for £69,000. It had bought it for £20,000 on 1 April 1982 and had spent £4,000 on defending its title to the land in July 1985.

(c)   On 25 June 2001 the company exchanged contracts for the sale of a workshop for £173,000. Completion took place on 24 July 2001. It had bought the workshop for £65,000 on 16 October 1983.

Requirement

Compute Hardup Ltd's capital gains for the year end 31.3.02.   **15 marks**

Indexation factors

July 1988 – May 2001	0.635
April 1982 – June 2001	1.160
July 1985 – June 2001	0.838
October 1983 – June 2001	1.025
October 1983 – July 2001	1.031

11   GREEN LTD   *18 mins*

Green Ltd made the following purchases of ordinary shares in Read plc, a quoted company.

Year	Number	Cost
		£
1971	1,000	900
1973	400	580
1978	800	1,000
1980	600	680

On 30 June 2001 the company sold 1,600 shares for £7,000. The market value of the shares on 31 March 1982 was £1.40 a share.

On 26 May 2001 Green Ltd sold 6,000 quoted ordinary shares in Greengage Supermarkets plc for £42,000. Its previous dealings in these shares had been as follows.

3 July 1969 -82	Purchased 750 shares for £200.
17 November 1973 -82	Purchased 1,000 shares for £1,350.
18 June 1975 -82	One for one bonus issue.
7 May 1980 -82	Purchased 1,400 shares for £3,900.
30 January 1983 -82	One for two rights issue at 160p taken up.
15 January 1986 -85	Purchased 450 shares for £1,560.

The value of the shares on 31 March 1982 was £1.50 a share.

Requirement

Compute the capital gain on the disposal of shares.   **10 Marks**

Indexation factors

	1.198		1.113
March 1982 - May 2001	1.150	January 1983 - May 2001	1.067
March 1982 - June 2001	1.155	January 1986 - May 2001	0.774
	1.204		0.814

12   WOLF LTD   *14 mins*

Wolf Ltd carried out the following capital transactions:

(a)   On 30 June 2001 it assigned the lease of a commercial building for £20,750; the lease expires on 30 June 2018.

   The company had acquired the lease for £8,000 on 1 January 1994.

(b)   On 28 July 2001 it sold a racehorse for £25,000. The horse had been bought for £3,000 on 1 July 1995.

(c)   On 5 August 2001 it sold 500 unquoted shares in Nicoletta Ltd for £4,250. The company had bought the shares for £600 on 3 July 1977. The value on 31 March 1982 was £3.50 a share.

Wolf Ltd had allowable losses of £2,219 brought forward at 1 April 2001.

Requirement

Prepare a statement showing Wolf Ltd's capital gains for its year ended 31 March 2002.   **8 Marks**

Indexation factors

March 1982 - August 2001	1.217
January 1994- June 2001	0.238
July 1995 - July 2001	0.177

13   **K LTD**   *45 mins*

During its accounting period of 12 months to 31 March 2002, K Ltd, a UK resident company with no associated companies, made the disposals which are detailed below. The company also had trading profits of £1,450,000 and dividends received of £29,700.

Requirement

Compute the amount to be included in the corporation tax computation of K Ltd in respect of capital gains, and the increase in the company's corporation tax liability consequent on its having made these disposals.

(a)   *30 November 2001*

Sold a property that had been used in the trade for £170,335. This had been acquired on 31 May 1982 at a cost of £85,000. This cost had been funded using the full proceeds of the sale of an asset on the same day with rollover relief being claimed. The original asset had been acquired in 1978 at a cost of £50,000.

(*Note.* It was not possible to use market value at 31 March 1982 for a sale made in May 1982.)

(b)   *31 January 2002*

Sold a painting, which had been hanging in the boardroom, for £5,800. This had cost £10 in January 1984.

(c)   *14 February 2002*

Sold a storage warehouse, which had not qualified for industrial buildings allowances, for £90,000. This had cost £28,000 in January 1980 and had a market value at 31 March 1982 of £35,000.

(d)   *3 March 2002*

Sold a holding of shares in Z plc for £20,000. This holding had been acquired in January 1980 at a cost of £32,000 and the market value at 31 March 1982 was £28,000.

(e)   On 15 February 2002 £85,000 was invested in new fixed plant and machinery. It is the company's policy to defer gains where possible.

Use the following RPI factors.

March 1982 - May 1982	0.028	March 1982 - February 2002	1.254
May 1982 - November 2001	1.175	March 1982 - March 2002	1.260
January 1984 - January 2002	1.056		

25 Marks

14   **EMPLOYMENT AND SELF-EMPLOYMENT**   *20 mins*

Requirement

Discuss the factors to be taken into consideration when deciding whether a person is employed or self-employed for the purposes of income tax.   **11 Marks**

15   **TAKER**   *18 mins*

Taker is employed at an annual salary of £35,000. He is not in a pension scheme, but receives the following benefits in 2001/02.

(a)   He has the use of an 1,800 cc petrol engined motor car, which cost £20,000 in 1999. Fuel is provided for both business and private motoring, and Taker contributes £500 a year (half the cost of fuel for private motoring) for fuel. Annual business mileage is 2,400 miles.

(b)   He makes occasional private calls on the mobile phone provided by his employer.

(c)   He usually borrows his employer's video camera (which cost £600) at weekends, when he uses it to record weddings and parties for friends. He receives no payment for this, and he supplies blank tapes himself.

(d)   He has an interest free loan of £3,000 from his employer. Take the official rate of interest to be 6.25%.

(e)   His employer pays £4,000 a year to a registered childminder with whom the employer has a contract. The childminder looks after Taker's three year old son.

In 2001/02, Taker pays expenses out of his emoluments as follows.

(a)   He pays subscriptions to professional bodies (relevant to his employment) of £180.

(b)   He makes business telephone calls from home. The cost of business calls is £45. The cost of renting the line for the year is £100, and 40% of all Taker's calls are business calls.

(c)   He pays a golf club subscription of £150. He does not play golf at all, but goes to the club to discuss business with potential clients. These discussions frequently lead to valuable contracts.

Requirement

Compute Taker's Schedule E income for 2001/02.   **10 Marks**

---

16   PAYE (PILOT PAPER)   *36 mins*

The advertising company of which you are chief accountant is about to reorganise the method of remunerating certain members of staff. Until recently a number of individuals had been acting as freelance agents. They were not on the company's payroll, and had been paid gross.

As a result of a major investigation by the Inland Revenue the company has been advised that these individuals should now become employees subject to the rules of Schedule E.

It is the intention that each of these individuals will be given the use of a company-owned motor car and provided with fuel to cover both business and private mileage. A number of them will need to move house and the company has undertaken to give each person affected an amount of £5,000 towards their relocation costs. In addition, some of them will be given interest-free loans in order to enable them to refurnish their new homes.

This will be the first time your company has provided this range of benefits (apart from motor cars which are provided to the directors). The Board is anxious to ensure that it will be complying with the rules for both quantifying and reporting the benefits in kind. It also wishes to be in a position to explain to these new staff members the effect of the benefits on their monthly PAYE deduction.

Requirements

(a)   Prepare a report to the head of payroll, briefly setting out the rules for quantifying each of the above benefits. Your report must also deal with:

   •   the compliance rules for returning details of the benefits to the Inland Revenue, and

   •   the company's responsibilities under income tax self assessment rules, making references to the documentation, deadlines and penalties.   **15 Marks**

(b)   Prepare a brief information sheet for staff members, explaining the method by which they will be taxed on their benefits in kind and the effect of this on their PAYE Code Numbers.   **5 Marks**

                                                                                              Total Marks = 20

---

17   H, S AND N   *36 mins*

H Ltd has owned 60% of the issued ordinary share capital of S Ltd since its incorporation, the remaining 40% being held by Mr S. Both companies have always prepared accounts to 30 June, their most recent accounts showing the following.

	H Ltd		S Ltd	
	Year ended 30.6.00	Year ended 30.6.01	Year ended 30.6.00	Year ended 30.6.01
	£	£	£	£
Adjusted trading profit	2,000		30,000	100,000
Adjusted trading loss		(48,000)		
Charges paid (gross)			12,000	12,000

On 1 January 2000, H Ltd acquired 80% of the issued ordinary share capital of N Ltd, a company which had always prepared accounts to 31 December.

N Ltd's accounts for the period of 1 January 2000 to 30 June 2001 show the following.

	£
Adjusted trading profit, before capital allowances	65,250
Chargeable gain, after indexation allowance on land bought in 1982 and sold in February 2001	20,000

N Ltd had a written down value on plant at 1 January 2000 of £5,000 and had incurred expenditure as follows.

		£
3 February 2000:	new car to be used by the managing director of N Ltd 80% for business, 20% for private use	16,000
4 January 2001:	new plant	31,000
20 March 2001:	secondhand machine bought on hire purchase, the cash price being £8,000, a deposit of £2,000 being paid on the above date followed by 24 monthly instalments of £300, commencing 20 May 2001.	

No dividends were paid or received. None of the new plant was computer or technology equipment.

Requirement

Compute the mainstream corporation tax payable by H Ltd, S Ltd and N Ltd for the above periods of account, assuming all available claims and surrenders are made to minimise the mainstream corporation tax payable by the group. **20 marks**

---

18   D LTD (PILOT PAPER) *36 mins*

The following information relates to events and transactions involving D Ltd, a UK resident company, 90% of whose share capital is owned by T Ltd, another UK resident company. D Ltd made up accounts for the year ended 31 December 2001.

(a)   In May 1994 D Ltd had sold a building for £280,000 which had cost £120,000 in May 1980 and which had a market value (MV) of £130,000 at 31 March 1982. On the occasion of this disposal D Ltd had made a global election to use MV at 31 March 1982 for all sales of assets held at that date.

Of the proceeds, £270,000 was used to purchase new plant and machinery and the maximum possible holdover relief was claimed. This plant and machinery was scrapped in May 2001 and £10,000 was recovered for its scrap value.

(b)   In June 1997 the ownership of a factory was transferred to D Ltd from its parent company, T Ltd, at the agreed market value of £260,000. The factory had cost T Ltd £180,000 in June 1989. In May 2001, T Ltd sold 20% of its holding in D Ltd, reducing the holding to 70%.

(c)   In June 2001, D Ltd sold, for £320,000, an office block which had been held as an investment property and let. It had cost £180,000 in June 1978 and its MV at 31 March 1982 was £150,000.

(d)   In September 2001, D Ltd sold for £180,000 two plots of land which had been used for the purpose of the trade. These are part of a block of nine plots which had been bought by D Ltd in June 1992 for a total amount of £500,000. The market value of the seven unsold plots at 30 September 2001 was £1,200,000.

Requirements

(a)   Compute any chargeable gain or allowable loss arising from each of the above events. **16 Marks**
(b)   Explain briefly whether any of the above gains could be deferred. **4 Marks**

Total Marks = 20

Indexation factors which may be used.

March 1982 – May 1994	0.822
June 1989 – June 1997	0.365
June 1997 – May 2001	0.108
March 1982 – June 2001	1.204
June 1992 – September 2001	0.267

19   **M LTD (PILOT PAPER)**   *36 mins*

M Ltd is a UK resident company which owns controlling interests in two other UK resident companies and in two non-resident companies.

It also has the following interests in three non-resident companies:

Company	Shareholding	Rate of Withholding tax	Profits post tax y/e 31.03.02	Foreign tax paid
	%	%	£	£
A Inc	6	15	400,000	80,000
B P G	8	25	900,000	300,000
C S A	32	20	800,000	200,000

M Ltd had experienced a prolonged period of poor trading and, as a result of losses brought forward from earlier years, its chargeable Schedule DI income for the year ended 31 March 2002 is only £20,000.

During the year, patent royalties of £75,000 had been paid and these had been added back in arriving at the adjusted Schedule DI income. These patent royalties were paid to another UK company.

The only other income received by M Ltd during the year consisted of dividends from the above three companies, each of which had substantial undistributed profits. The figures (net of withholding tax) were:

	£	Date received
A Inc	170,000	1.6.01
B P G	150,000	10.9.01
C S A	120,000	31.12.01

Requirements

(a) Compute the MCT payable by M Ltd in respect of the year ended 31 March 2002. Your answer should show clearly your treatment of the patent royalties payment and of the foreign taxes suffered. You should explain why you are dealing with items in a particular way and you should use a columnar layout.   **16 Marks**

(b) Explain briefly what the taxation implications would be if C S A were deemed to be a controlled foreign company   **4 Marks**

                                                                          Total Marks = 20

20   **HUIS PLC**   *36 mins*

(a) Huis plc is a close company. On 31 May 2001, six months before the company's year end, it lent £45,000 to Sartre, a shareholder. Sartre is not an employee of the company. The loan carried a market rate of interest.

The company advised Sartre on 31 March 2003 that he would not be required to repay the loan.

Requirement

Set out the tax consequences of the transactions with Sartre, giving the dates on which any amounts are payable to the Inland Revenue.   **12 marks**

(b) Beauvoir Ltd is a close investment-holding company. It has had the following results for the last two years.

	Year ended 31.3.01	Year ended 31.3.02
	£	£
Schedule A	14,000	25,000
Schedule D Case III	20,000	100,000
Management expenses	36,000	45,000
Dividends received in August from non-group companies	16,000	27,000

Requirement

Compute the company's mainstream corporation tax for both years.   **8 marks**

                                                                          Total Marks = 20

21   **SIGNING UP**   *36 mins*

Requirements

(a)   When is a company that does no business with anyone outside the UK required to register for VAT?

(b)   What are the effects of group registration?

(c)   What are the conditions for divisional registration?

(d)   In what ways may the tax point for a supply of goods be established?

Total Marks = 20

22   **CAVE LTD**   *36 mins*

(a)   For the quarter ended 31 March 2002 Cave Ltd had the following transactions.

	£
Sales at the standard rate	1,700,000
Sales at the zero rate	400,000
Plant sold in the UK	100,000
Plant sold outside the EC	50,000
Exempt sales	800,000
Purchases at the standard rate	600,000
Purchases at the zero rate	100,000
Wages	900,000

The above amounts do not include any VAT.

Requirement

Compute the amount of VAT which Cave Ltd would be required to pay to HM Customs & Excise for the quarter.   **15 marks**

(b)   What relief is available for output VAT already paid in respect of a transaction which subsequently becomes a bad debt?   **5 marks**

Total Marks = 20

1   TREE LTD

(a)   Tree Ltd

	Year to 30.6.01 £	Six months to 31.12.01 £
Trading profits (12/18: 6/18)	120,000	60,000
Chargeable gain	172,000	
Schedule A (12/18: 6/18)	24,000	12,000
Less: charge on income	(22,000)	(5,000)
Profits chargeable to corporation tax	294,000	67,000

Year to 30.6.01
Corporation tax (W1)
FY 00
£220,500 × 30%   66,150

Less 1/40 (1,125,000 – 243,000) × $\dfrac{220,500}{243,000}$ (20,008)

FY 01
£73,500 × 30%   22,050

Less 1/40 (375,000 – 81,000) × $\dfrac{73,500}{81,000}$ (6,669)

                                                                        61,523

Six months to 31.12.01 (W2)
£67,000 × 20%   £13,400

(b)   Dealers plc's profits for small companies rate purposes are £420,000 so tax is payable at the marginal rate in both FY00 and FY01.

	FY 2000 and FY 2001 £
Profits chargeable to corporation tax	420,000
'Profits'	420,000
Upper limit	1,500,000
Lower limit	300,000
Corporation tax	
FY 2000 and 2001	£
£420,000 × 30%	126,000
Less small companies marginal relief	
£(1,500,000 – 420,000) × 1/40	(27,000)
Mainstream corporation tax	99,000

(c)   Springer Ltd's 'profits' are £6,200. This means they qualify for the starting rate in both FY 2001 and FY 2000:

	£
FY 2000 and FY 2001	
£6,200 × 10%	620

Workings

1   Tax rate: year to 30.6.01

The year to 30.6.01 falls into FY00 and FY01

	FY00 (9/12) £	FY01 (3/12) £
PCTCT	220,500	73,500
'Profits' (£294,000 + £27,000 × 100/90)	243,000	81,000
Small companies lower limit	225,000	75,000
Small companies upper limit	1,125,000	375,000

As 'profits' are between the small companies' upper and lower limits in both financial years, small companies marginal relief applies in both financial years.

Note. As tax rates are the same in FY2000 and FY 2001, it is not strictly necessary to split the computation of tax between the financial years. However, you should spilt the years as shown here if you find it easier to compute the corporation tax in this way.

2 The six month period to 31.12.01 falls in the financial year 2001. As profits of £67,000 are above the starting rate upper limit of £25,000 and below the small companies rate lower limit of £150,000 for this period, the small companies rate applies.

2 HOGG LTD

(a) The due dates for the payment of corporation tax by Hogg Ltd in respect of the year to 31.12.01 are:

	£	£
14 July 2001 1/4 × (88% × £500,000)		110,000
14 October 2001 1/4 × (88% × £500,000)		110,000
14 January 2002 1/4 × (88% × £520,000)	114,400	
plus underpaid 2 × £(114,400 − 110,000)	8,800	
		123,200
14 April 2002 1/4 × (88% × £520,000)		114,400
1 October 2002 balance of instalments 88% × £525,000		
− £110,000 − £110,000 − £123,200 − £114,400		4,400
Balance of tax 12% × £525,000		63,000
Total		525,000

(b) The due dates for the payment of corporation tax instalments by Hogg Ltd in respect of the ten months to 31 October 2005 are:

14 July 2005	£180,000
14 October 2005	£180,000
14 January 2006	£180,000
14 February 2006 (4th month of next accounting period)	£60,000 (balance)

Tutorial note: The amount of the instalments is $^3/n \times CT = {}^3/10 \times £600,000 = £180,000$.

3 TRADERS LTD

CORPORATION TAX COMPUTATION

	£	£
Net profit per accounts		101,977
Add: entertaining	600	
tax consultancy	30	
lease on new premises	100	
gift aid donation	200	
political donation	500	
patent royalties payable	5,000	
depreciation	15,000	
		21,430
		123,407
Less: commissions (chargeable under Schedule D Case VI)	1,900	
profit on sale of investment	5,265	
		(7,165)
Schedule D Case I		116,242
Schedule D Case VI		1,900
Chargeable gain		770
		118,912
Less charges paid (patent royalties and gift aid)		(5,200)
Profits chargeable to corporation tax		113,712

The profits for small companies rate purposes are below the lower limit, so the small companies rate applies.

The corporation tax liability is £113,712 × 20%	£22,742

4   HARDY LTD

	FYA £	Pool £	Car pool £	Expensive car £	Short life asset £	Allowances £
1.7.97 – 30.6.98						
Brought forward		25,700	6,300			
WDA @ 25%		(6,425)	(1,575)			8,000
		19,275	4,725			
Additions	2,300				4,400	
FYA @ 50%	(1,150)				(2,200)	3,350
		1,150				11,350
		20,425	4,725		2,200	
1.7.98 – 30.6.99						
Additions				13,400		
WDA		(5,106)	(1,181)	(3,000)	(550)	9,837
		15,319	3,544	10,400	1,650	
1.7.99 – 30.6.00						
Transfer		3,544	(3,544)			
		18,863				
WDA		(4,716)		(2,600)	(413)	7,729
		14,147		7,800	1,237	
1.7.00 – 30.6.01						
Disposals		(340)			(2,200)	
		13,807			(963)	
Balancing charge					963	(963)
WDA		(3,452)		(1,950)		5,402
		10,355		5,850		4,439
1.7.01 – 31.12.01						
Disposals		(24,000)		(10,600)		
		(13,645)		(4,750)		
Balancing charges		13,645		4,750		(18,395)

Note. The private use of the car by the managing director does not affect the company's capital allowances.

5   W LTD

Note. The planning element in this question is to recognise that by NOT claiming a FYA on the lorry and by NOT depooling the new piece of machinery as a short-life asset, the capital allowances are significantly greater.

(a)   (i)   **Plant and machinery**

	General pool £	Expensive car (1) £	Expensive car (2) £	SLA £	Allowances £
TWDV b/f	36,000	22,000	30,000	18,000	
Additions	38,000				
Disposals	(60,000)		(22,000)	(20,000)	
	14,000	22,000	8,000	(2,000)	
Less: WDA @ 25%/ (restricted)	(3,500)	(3,000)			6,500
Balancing allowance			(8,000)		8,000
Balancing charge				2,000	(2,000)
TWDV c/f	10,500	19,000	-	-	12,500

(ii) **Industrial buildings allowances**

Factory one

	£
Cost	120,000
Y/e 31.3.94/31.3.95	(9,600)
	110,400
Y/e 31.3.96	
Addition	40,000
	150,400
WDA @ 4% cost	(6,400)
	144,000
Y/e 31.3.97 – 31.3.01	
5 × £6,400	(32,000)
Residue before sale	112,000

The factory was sold for £100,000, so a balancing allowance of £12,000 is available.

Factory two

Industrial buildings allowances are available on the lower of the original cost (£180,000) and the purchase price (£210,000), ie on £180,000.

Allowances are available over the remaining tax life of the building = 15 (25 – 10) years.

∴ the industrial buildings allowance available in the year ended 31.3.02 is:

$$\frac{£180,000}{15} = £12,000$$

Capital allowances

The maximum capital allowances for the year ended 31 March 2002 are therefore £36,500 (£12,500 + £12,000 + £12,000).

(b) First year allowances have not been claimed in respect of the lorry or the new piece of equipment. In addition, an election has not been made to de-pool the new piece of equipment. This avoids the balancing charge that would otherwise arise on the general pool.

(c) The position if FYAs were claimed and a SLA election made would be:

	Gen Pool £	FYA £	SLA £	Total £
1 April 2001 b/f	36,000	-	-	
Purchases		18,000	20,000	
FYA 40%		(7,200)	(8,000)	15,200
Disposals	(60,000)			
Bal Charge	(24,000)			(24,000)
Allowances as before:				
Expensive car (1)				3,000
(2)				8,000
SLA charge				(2,000)
Total capital allowances				200
First method capital allowances				12,500
Difference				12,300

The IBAs would be unchanged.

Clearly this is less beneficial than the position shown where no FYA's are claimed and a SLA election is not made.

6 **CUCKOLD LTD**

(a) Cuckold Ltd should acquire factory (i), as shown in the working below.

Factory (ii) is clearly unattractive since, with its tax life expired, industrial buildings allowances cannot be claimed. Factories (iii) and (iv) have greater total allowances available than factory (i) but the annual allowance is much smaller.

Working: industrial buildings allowances on alternative factories

	Factory (i)	Factory (ii)	Factory (iii)	Factory (iv)
Residue after sale*	£100,000	£80,000	£150,000	£120,000
Remaining tax life**	1 yr	0	23 yrs	17 yrs
Allowances available	£100,000	0	£150,000	£120,000
in y/e 31.3.2003	1 yr		23 yrs	17 yrs
	= £100,000		= £6,522	= £7,059

*   The residue after sale is the lower of the price paid by the new purchaser and the original cost.

**   The tax life of an industrial building begins when it is first brought into use and ends 25 years later (except for expenditure incurred before 6 November 1962, when the relevant period is 50 years rather than 25 years).

(b)   (i)   *Showroom display lighting*

Expenditure on display lighting will be eligible for plant and machinery capital allowances. The most important general test in determining whether expenditure is eligible is the 'functional test'. This asks whether the item concerned fulfils a *function* in the carrying on of the trade or merely forms part of the setting *in* which the trade is carried on.

This test was used with regard to lighting in *Cole Bros Ltd v Phillips 1982*, where lighting equipment which produced higher levels of lighting than normal and which was specialised in order to display goods to customers was held to be plant.

Expenditure on plant and machinery is eligible for a first year allowance of 40%. The balance of the expenditure is then eligible for a 25% writing down allowance in subsequent years on a reducing balance basis.

(ii)   *Thermal insulation*

Expenditure on thermal insulation for a qualifying industrial building is specifically allowed as expenditure on plant and machinery: thus a first year allowance followed by writing down allowances will be available as described above. When the building is eventually sold, the disposal value of the thermal insulation is taken to be zero, so no balancing charge can arise in respect of it.

(iii)   *A factory canteen*

Expenditure on a factory canteen will qualify for industrial buildings allowances. The definition of an industrial building includes any building or structure provided by the person carrying on a qualifying trade (that is, one using a building that qualifies for industrial buildings allowances) for the welfare of workers employed in the trade.

(c)   Industrial building allowance given prior to sale.

	£	£
Cost (1.7.91)		200,000
Allowances:		
CAP to 31.12.91 - 4%	8,000	
CAP to 31.12.92 - 4%	8,000	
CAP to 31.12.93 - 4% (notional) (note)	8,000	
CAP to 31.12.94 - 4% (notional) (note)	8,000	
CAP to 31.12.95 - 4%	8,000	
CAP to 31.12.96 - 4%	8,000	
CAP to 31.12.97 - 4%	8,000	
CAP to 31.12.98 - 4%	8,000	
CAP to 31.12.99 - 4%	8,000	
CAP to 31.12.00 - 4%	8,000	
		(80,000)
Residue before sale		120,000

$$\text{Adjusted net cost } (£200{,}000 - £150{,}000) \times \frac{89}{119} = £37{,}395$$

Balancing charge:

Allowances given (£80,000 − £8,000 − £8,000)	64,000
Less: adjusted net cost	(37,395)
	26,605

Note. Although notional allowances reduce the allowable expenditure they are not actually given as a deduction from profits.

7 SCHEDULE A

P LTD: SCHEDULE A INCOME

	£	£	£
First house			
Premium £20,000 × [1 − 0.02 (30 − 1)]			8,400
Rent £4,000 × 9/12			3,000
			11,400
Second house			
Rent £600 × 3		1,800	
Rent £2,100 × 1/3		700	
		2,500	
Less: water rates £390 × 6/12	195		
insurance £440 × 6/11	240		
repairs: capital	0		
furniture: in year to 31.3.03	0		
		(435)	
			2,065
Schedule A income			13,465

The interest on the loan is dealt with under the loan relationship rules. It is not a Schedule A expense.

8 FERRARO LTD

	Accounting periods				
	12m to 31.12.97	12m to 31.12.98	9m to 30.9.99	12m to 30.9.00	12m to 30.9.01
	£	£	£	£	£
Schedule D Case I	10,000	34,480	6,200	4,320	0
Schedule D Case III	100	200	80	240	260
Schedule A	3,000	1,200	1,420	1,440	1,600
Chargeable gain (12,680 − 5,000)	0	0	0	7,680	0
	13,100	35,880	7,700	13,680	1,860
Less s 393A - current	0	0	0	0	(1,860)
	13,100	35,880	7,700	13,680	0
Less charges	(1,000)	(1,000)	0	(1,000)	0
	12,100	34,880	7,700	12,680	0
Less s 393A - c/b				(12,680)	(0)
PCTCT	12,100	34,880	7,700	0	0

The loss carried forward against future profits of the same trade is £100,000 − £ (12,680 + 1,860) + £1,500 trade charges = £86,960.

The allowable capital loss of £9,423 during the year ended 30 September 2001 is carried forward against future chargeable gains.

9 GAINS

Motor cars are exempt assets, so the loss brought forward from the year ended 31 March 2001 is £16,400.

The position for the year ended 31 March 2002 is as follows.

	£
Gains	
Shares	7,200
Picture	3,000
	10,200
Less loss on shares	(2,000)
	8,200
Less loss brought forward	(8,200)
Chargeable gains	Nil

The racehorse is a chattel and is an exempt asset.

The loss carried forward at 31 March 2002 is £(16,400 − 8,200) = £8,200.

10   HARDUP LTD

CAPITAL GAINS COMPUTATION

	£
Office block (W1)	13,725
Plot of land (W2)	18,448
Workshop (W3)	41,375
Taxable gains	73,548

Workings

1   *The office block*

	£
Proceeds	120,000
Less cost	(65,000)
	55,000
Less indexation allowance 0.635 × £65,000	(41,275)
Chargeable gain	13,725

2   *The plot of land*

	£
Proceeds	69,000
Less: cost	(20,000)
expenditure in July 1985	(4,000)
	45,000
Less indexation allowance	
1.160 × £20,000	(23,200)
0.838 × £4,000	(3,352)
	18,448

3   *The workshop*

	£
Proceeds	173,000
Less cost	(65,000)
	108,000
Less indexation allowance 1.025 × £65,000	(66,625)
	41,375

The date of disposal for chargeable gains purposes is the date that the disposal becomes unconditional. In this case the date of exchange, not the date of completion.

11   **GREEN LTD**

The disposal of Read plc shares

	Cost £	31.3.82 value £
Proceeds	7,000	7,000
Less: cost (see below)	(1,806)	
31.3.82 value 1,600 × £1.40		(2,240)
Unindexed gain	5,194	4,760
Less indexation allowance 1.204 × £2,240	(2,697)	(2,697)
	2,497	2,063

The chargeable gain is £2,063.

The 1982 holding

	No of shares	£
1971 purchase	1,000	900
1973 purchase	400	580
1978 purchase	800	1,000
1980 purchase	600	680
	2,800	3,160
Less sale	(1,600)	(1,806)
1982 holding carried forward	1,200	1,354

The disposal of Greengage Supermarkets plc shares

(a)   *The FA 1985 pool*

	£
Proceeds $\dfrac{450}{6,000}$ × £42,000	3,150
Less cost (W1)	(1,560)
	1,590
Less indexation allowance £(2,830 − 1,560) (W1)	(1,270)
Chargeable gain	320

(b)   *The 1982 holding*

	Cost £	31.3.82 value £
Proceeds $\dfrac{5,550}{6,000}$ × £42,000	38,850	38,850
Less: cost (W2)	(7,075)	
31.3.82 value (W3)		(8,510)
Unindexed gain	31,775	30,340
Less indexation allowance (W3)	(9,943)	(9,943)
Gain	21,832	20,397

The total chargeable gain is £(320 + 20,397) = £20,717.

Workings

1   *The FA 1985 pool*

	No of shares £	Cost £	Indexed cost £
Pool starts:			
15.1.86 purchase	450	1,560	1,560
Indexed rise to May 2001 0.814 × £1,560			1,270
	450	1,560	2,830
Disposal	(450)	(1,560)	(2,830)
FA 1985 pool carried forward	0	0	0

2   *The 1982 holding*

	No of shares	£
July 1969 purchase	750	200
November 1973 purchase	1,000	1,350
	1,750	1,550
June 1975 bonus issue	1,750	0
	3,500	1,550
May 1980 purchase	1,400	3,900
	4,900	5,450
January 1983 rights issue	2,450	3,920
	7,350	9,370
Disposal	(5,550)	(7,075)
1982 holding carried forward	1,800	2,295

3   *The indexation allowance for the 1982 holding*

	£
The cost of the rights shares sold is	
$2,450 \times \dfrac{5,550}{7,350} = 1,850 \times £1.60$	2,960
The 31 March 1982 value of shares owned at 31 March 1982 and sold is	
$4,900 \times \dfrac{5,550}{7,350} = 3,700 \times £1.50$	5,550
	8,510

	£
$1.113 \times £2,960$	3,294
$1.198 \times £5,550$	6,649
	9,943

Summary

	£
Gain on Reed plc shares	2,063
Gain on Greengage shares	20,397
Taxable gains	20,460

12   WOLF LTD

(a)   *The lease*

	£
Proceeds	20,750
Less $\dfrac{66.470 \ (17 \text{ years})}{80.361 \ (24\frac{1}{2} \text{ years})} \times £8,000$	(6,617)
Unindexed gain	14,133
Less indexation allowance $0.238 \times £6,617$	(1,575)
	12,558

The percentage for 24½ years is $79.622 + (81.100 - 79.622) \times 6/12 = 80.361$.

(b)   *The racehorse*
This is a wasting chattel and is therefore exempt.

(c)   *The Nicoletta Ltd shares*

	Cost £	31.3.82 value £
Proceeds	4,250	4,250
Less cost/31.3.82 value	(600)	(1,750)
Unindexed gain	3,650	2,500
Less indexation allowance $1.217 \times £1,750$	(2,130)	(2,130)
	1,520	370

The chargeable gain is £370.

(d) *Summary*

	£
Net gains £(12,558 + 370)	12,928
Less losses brought forward	(2,219)
Chargeable gains	10,709

13   K LTD

(a) *The property*

The rolled over gain was as follows.

	£
Proceeds	85,000
Less cost	(50,000)
	35,000
Less indexation allowance – 0.028 × £50,000	(1,400)
Rolled over gain	33,600

Because the first asset was acquired before 31 March 1982 and disposed of before 6 April 1988, and the second asset was acquired after 31 March 1982 and disposed of after 5 April 1988, only half of this gain is deducted from the cost of the second asset.

	£	£
Proceeds		170,335
Less cost	85,000	
Less half of rolled over gain	(16,800)	
		(68,200)
		102,135
Less indexation allowance to November 2001 – 1.175 × £68,200		(80,135)
Chargeable gain		22,000

(b) *The painting*

There will be no chargeable gain, because the painting is a chattel sold for not more than £6,000.

(c) *The warehouse*

	£
Proceeds	90,000
Less 31.3.82 value (clearly gives a lower gain than cost)	(35,000)
	55,000
Less indexation allowance to February 2002 – 1.254 × £35,000	(43,890)
	11,110
Less gain held over	(6,110)
Chargeable gain (proceeds not re-invested)	5,000

(d) *The shares in Z plc*

	Cost	31.3.82 value
	£	£
Proceeds	20,000	20,000
Less cost/31.3.82 value	(32,000)	(28,000)
Loss	(12,000)	(8,000)

The allowable loss is the lower loss, £8,000.

(e) Rollover relief can be claimed to defer the gain on the storage warehouse. As £5,000 of the proceeds from the sale of the warehouse were not reinvested in fixed plant, £5,000 of the gain is immediately chargeable, leaving £6,110 (£11,110 – £5,000) to be rolled over. It would not have been possible to rollover any of the gain on the sale of the other property used in the trade because the proceeds not reinvested, £85,355 (£170,355 – £85,000) was bigger than the gain arising.

(f) *Summary*

	£
The investment property	22,000
The painting	0
The warehouse	5,000
The shares in Z plc	(8,000)
The gilt edged securities	0
Net chargeable gains	19,000

(g) *Increase in corporation tax liability*

	Without disposals £	With disposals £
Schedule D Case I	1,450,000	1,450,000
Chargeable gains	0	19,000
Profits chargeable to corporation tax	1,450,000	1,469,000
Dividends plus tax credits		
£29,700 × 100/90	33,000	33,000
Profits for small companies rate purposes	1,483,000	1,502,000
Corporation tax		
£1,450,000/£1,469,000 × 30%	435,000	440,700
Less small companies' marginal relief		
£(1,500,000 – 1,483,000) × 1,450,000/1,483,000 × 1/40	(416)	0
	434,584	440,700

The increase in the corporation tax liability due to the disposals is £(440,700 – 434,584) = £6,116.

14 EMPLOYMENT AND SELF-EMPLOYMENT

The factors to consider in deciding whether someone is employed or self-employed for income tax purposes are as follows.

(a) How much control is exercised over the way work is done? The greater the control, the more likely it is that the worker is an employee.

(b) Does the worker provide his own equipment? That would indicate self-employment.

(c) If the worker hires his own helpers, that indicates self-employment.

(d)· If the worker can profit by his own sound management, or lose money through errors, that indicates self-employment.

(e) If there is a continuing obligation to provide work for the worker, and an obligation on the worker to do whatever job is offered next, that indicates employment.

(f) If the worker accepts work from many independent sources, that indicates self-employment.

(g) If the worker can work whenever he chooses, that indicates self-employment.

These tests are summed up in the general rule that there is employment when there is a contract of service, and self-employment when there is a contract for services.

15 TAKER

Schedule E income

	£	£
Salary		35,000
Car £20,000 × 35%		7,000
Fuel (partial contribution gives no reduction)		2,460
Mobile telephone		0
Use of video camera £600 × 20%		120
Loan: does not exceed £5,000		0
Childminder		4,000
		48,580
Less: professional subscriptions	180	
cost of business telephone calls	45	
		(225)
Schedule E income		48,355

16 PAYE

(a) To: The Head of Payroll
From: Chief Accountant
Date: 1 April 2001
Subject: Benefits in kind

Introduction

The purpose of this report is to set out the rules for quantifying for tax purposes the various benefits that we will be providing to certain members of staff. It also deals with the compliance rules for returning details of benefits to the Revenue and the company's responsibilities under the income tax self-assessment rules to employees. The requirement to pay NIC on certain benefits is also discussed.

Quantifying various benefits

Cars and car fuel

For employees earning £8,500 or more a year and directors, a car provided by reason of the employment gives rise to a taxable benefit. The taxable benefit each year is found as follows:

£ (Price of car – capital contributions) × % × age factor

The price of the car is the sum of:

(i)   The list price of the car (up to a maximum of £80,000) at the time of first registration, including charges for delivery and standard accessories, and

(ii) The price (including fitting) of all optional accessories provided when the car was first provided to the employee or, if fitted later, costing at least £100 each.

The cost of mobile telephones and equipment needed by a disabled employee are not included.

Capital contributions are payments by the employee in respect of the price of the car or accessories. The maximum deductible capital contributions is £5,000: contributions beyond that total are ignored.

The 'percentage' for 2001/02 depends on the **business** mileage in the tax year:

Business mileage	First car
Less than 2,500	35%
At least 2,500, less than 18,000	25%
At least 18,000	15%

If the car is at least four years old at the end of the tax year, then the age factor is ¾ . Otherwise it is 1.

The benefit is pro rated on a time basis if the car is not available for a continuous period of at least 30 days in the tax year. The mileage factor limits of 2,500 and 18,000 are also pro rated in such cases.

The benefit is reduced by any payment the user must make for the private use of the car (as distinct from a capital contribution to the cost of the car).

If we provide fuel for the company cars there will be a further benefit on a set scale in addition to the car benefit. No taxable fuel benefit will, however, arise if the employee or director reimburses the company with the cost of ALL fuel used for private purposes. Unlike most benefits, a reimbursement of only part of the cost of such fuel does not reduce the scale charge.

The fuel benefit is reduced in the same way as the car benefit if the car is not available for 30 days or more, but it is not adjusted for business mileage.

Relocation costs

There will be no taxable benefit for any employee or director in respect of the first £8,000 of relocation costs. Thus the proposed £5,000 payment will be tax-free for the recipients.

Interest free loans

No taxable benefit will arise in respect of interest free loans which do not exceed £5,000 at any time in a tax year. For employees earning in excess of £8,500 per annum and directors, the taxable benefit of loans in excess of £5,000 is the amount of the loan multiplied by the Inland Revenue's official rate of interest. If any part of the loan is written off a taxable benefit will also arise equal to the amount written off in a tax year.

Compliance rules for reporting benefits to the Revenue

A form P11D quantifying benefits in kind must be completed for each director and employee earning £8,500 or more a year. These forms must be submitted to the Inland Revenue by 6 July following the end of the tax year.

Company responsibilities under the income tax self assessment rules

Employees must be given details of the information included in their P11D by 6 July following the end of the tax year. This will enable employees to complete their self-assessment returns and as such are cross referenced into those returns. Penalties may be imposed on the company if the P11D returns are incorrect or late.

National Insurance Contributions (NICs)

Class 1A NICs are due to be paid by the company no later than 19 July following the end of the tax year in which any benefits-in-kind were provided to employees. These NICs are calculated at a rate of 11.9 % on the value of the benefit as outlined above. Class 1A NICs must be returned on Form P11D(b).

(b) INFORMATION SHEET FOR STAFF MEMBERS

The purpose of this information sheet is to set out how you will be taxed on any benefits in kind you receive from the company and to explain how these benefits will effect your PAYE code.

There will be no taxable benefit in respect of the first £8,000 of relocation costs you receive and there will be no taxable benefit in respect of any interest free loans if the total loans made to you do not exceed £5,000. However, if you earn at least £8,500, your company car will give rise to a taxable benefit and there will be a further benefit in respect of fuel provided for private use. There will also be a taxable benefit in respect of loans in excess of £5,000 and in respect of any loan written off.

The tax on taxable benefits will be collected throughout the year under the PAYE system. The way the Revenue collect the tax is to deduct the taxable value of your benefits from the allowances given to you in your PAYE code. This means that at each pay date you will be taxed on a proportion of the value of your benefits and that at the end of the year you should have paid the correct amount of income tax.

You could, however, find that you still owe some tax at the year end. This will occur if the Revenue underestimate the taxable value of the benefits included in your PAYE code. It may also occur if the taxable value of your benefits exceed allowances as the company is then restricted in the amount of tax that it can deduct from your cash pay on each pay day.

Example

If you are provided with a 1995 cc car with a list price of £15,000 and you drive 20,000 miles on business the benefit in kind will be calculated as:

	£
£15,000 × 15% =	2,250
If any private petrol is paid for by the company	2,460
Taxable benefit-in-kind	4,710

Tax at 22% on this equals £1,036 which would be collected over the tax year at £86 per month.

17   H, S AND N

H Ltd: corporation tax computations for the accounting periods of 12 months to

	30.6.00	30.6.01
	£	£
Schedule D Case I	2,000	
Less loss of y/e 30.6.01, s 393A(1) ICTA 1988	(2,000)	
Chargeable profits	0	0
MCT payable	£0	£0

S Ltd: corporation tax computations for the accounting periods of 12 months to

	30.6.00	30.6.01
	£	£
Schedule D Case I	30,000	100,000
Less charges	(12,000)	(12,000)
Chargeable profits	18,000	88,000

S Ltd: corporation tax computations for the accounting periods of 12 months to

	30.6.00	30.6.01
	£	£
Corporation tax		
FY 1999		
£18,000 × 20% × 9/12	2,700	
FY 2000		
£18,000 × 20% × 3/12	900	
FY 2000		
£88,000 × 20% × 9/12		13,200
FY 2001		
£88,000 × 20% × 3/12		4,400
MCT payable	3,600	17,600

Note. There are three associated companies so the lower limit for small companies rate purposes is £100,000 in FY 1999, FY 2000 and FY 2001. The upper limit for starting rate purposes in FY 2000 and FY 2001 is £16,667. The small companies rate therefore applies in each of the financial years.

N Ltd: corporation tax computations for the accounting periods of 12 months and 6 months to

	31.12.00	30.6.01
	£	£
Adjusted profit split 12:6	43,500	21,750
Less capital allowances (W2)	(4,250)	(17,569)
Schedule D Case I	39,250	4,181
Chargeable gain	0	20,000
	39,250	24,181
Less group relief surrendered by H Ltd (W1)	(19,625)	(24,000)
Chargeable profits	19,625	181

	£	£
Corporation tax		
FY 1999 and FY 2000		
(£19,625 × 20% x 3/12) + (£19,625 x 20% x 9/12)	3,925	
FY 2000 and FY 2001		
£181 × (3/6 × 10% + 3/6 x 10%)		18
MCT	3,925	18

Workings

1   *Group relief*

	£
Loss of H Ltd y/e 30.6.01 available for group relief	48,000
Surrendered to N Ltd	
6 months to 31.12.00 restricted to 6/12 × £39,250	(19,625)
6 months to 30.6.01 restricted to 6/12 × £48,000	(24,000)
	4,375
Less s 393A(1) claim by H Ltd	(2,000)
Loss of H Ltd carried forward	2,375

Group relief is not available for S Ltd because it is only a 60% subsidiary.

2   *Capital allowances*

	FYA £	Pool £	Expensive car £	Allowances £
12 months to 31.12.00				
WDV brought forward		5,000		
Addition: car			16,000	
WDA 25%/£3,000		(1,250)	(3,000)	4,250
		3,750	13,000	
6 months to 30.6.01				
WDA 25% × 6/12		(469)	(1,500)	1,969
Additions: plant	31,000			
machine on HP	8,000			
	39,000			
FYA 40%	(15,600)			15,600
		23,400		17,569
WDV carried forward		26,681	11,500	

Note. Writing down allowances are pro-rated in a short period of account but first year allowances are not.

18   **D LTD**

(a)   (i)   Sale of building in May 1994

	£
Disposal proceeds	280,000
Less: M82 value	(130,000)
	150,000
Less: indexation (£130,000 × 0.822)	(106,860)
Gain	43,140

An amount equal to the proceeds not reinvested, £10,000, was immediately chargeable. The remainder, (£33,140) was held over and is chargeable on the disposal (ie the scrapping) of the plant and machinery in May 2001.

(ii)   *Transfer of building*

The transfer of the building from T Ltd in June 1997 would have been made on a no gain/no loss basis for chargeable gains purposes.

On the sale of 20% of T Ltd's holding in D Ltd in May 2001 T Ltd and D Ltd cease to be members of the same capital gains group. The gain that would have arisen in June 1997 on the transfer of the factory for its market value then crystallises.

	£
Market value in June 1997	260,000
Less: cost	(180,000)
	80,000
Less: Indexation (£180,000 × 0.365)	(65,700)
Chargeable gain	14,300

The gain of £14,300 is chargeable in the year that D Ltd and T Ltd ceased to be members of the same group, the year ended 31 December 2001.

(iii)

	£
Sale proceeds	320,000
Less: M82 value	(150,000)
Unindexed gain	170,000
Less: indexation	
(£150,000 × 1.204) (restricted)	(170,000)
	Nil

Tutorial note 1. As a rebasing election had previously been made, the March 1982 value must be used in this computation.

Tutorial note 2. Indexation cannot turn a gain into a loss, it can only reduce the gain to £nil.

(iv) *Disposal of two plots of land*

	£
Sale proceeds	180,000
Less: Cost ($£500,000 \times \dfrac{180,000}{180,000 + 1,200,000}$)	(65,217)
Unindexed gain	114,783
Less: indexation (£65,217 × 0.267)	(17,413)
Chargeable gain	97,370

(b) It is not possible to rollover the gain of £33,140 which was previously held over on the acquisition of the plant and machinery.

It is not possible to rollover the gain that crystallises when D Ltd and T Ltd cease to be members of the same group.

No deferral is possible on the investment property because it is not a gain arising on a business asset.

Rollover relief will be available to defer the gain arising on the disposal of the two plots of land providing a qualifying asset is purchased in the period commencing one year before and ending three years after the disposal and also dependant on how much of the £180,000 proceeds are reinvested in the new asset.

19 M LTD

(a) Year ended 31 March 2002

	Total £	UK £	A Inc £	B PG £	C SA £
Schedule D Case I	20,000	20,000			
Schedule D Case V (W1)	587,500	-	200,000	200,000	187,500
	607,500	20,000	200,000	200,000	187,500
Less: Charge on income	(75,000)	(20,000)	(55,000)	-	-
Profits chargeable to corporation tax	532,500	-	145,000	200,000	187,500
CT @ 30%	159,750	-	43,500	60,000	56,250
Less: DTR (W2)	(136,250)	-	(30,000)	(50,000)	(56,250)
Mainstream corporation tax	23,500	-	13,500	10,000	-

In order to maximise the set off of double tax relief, charges are allocated firstly to UK profits and then to overseas sources of income that have suffered the lowest rate of overseas tax. There are five associated companies so the full rate of corporation tax applies.

(b) If C SA were deemed to be a controlled foreign company (CFC), then an amount equal to M Ltd's interest in C SA's profits would be included in M Ltd's profits chargeable to corporation tax. This would be equal to £256,000 (ie £800,000 × 32%) in the year to 31.3.02.

The tax on C SA's profits would be calculated using the supplementary page for CFCs contained in Form CT600. This tax would be due for payment on the same date(s) as the rest of M Ltd's CT.

If C SA were to distribute at least 90% of its profits to M Ltd, M Ltd would be taxable on the dividends received in any accounting period. The CFC rules would not then apply.

Workings

1   *Dividend from C SA*

Since M Ltd's shareholding in C SA is at least 10%, relief for underlying tax is available:

	£
Dividend from C SA	120,000
Withholding tax (× 20/80)	30,000
	150,000

Underlying tax

$$£150,000 \times \frac{200,000}{800,000}$$ 37,500

Gross dividend	187,500

2   *Overseas dividends*

			Net £	Tax credit £	Gross £
A	Inc	(15%)	170,000	30,000	200,000
B	PG	(25%)	150,000	50,000	200,000
C	SA	(20%)	120,000	67,500	187,500

3   *Double tax relief*

		A Inc £	B pg £	C Sa £
Lower of				
(i)	UK tax	43,500	60,000	56,250
(ii)	Overseas tax	30,000	50,000	*67,500
		£30,000	£50,000	£56,250

* Underlying tax + withholding tax.

Note: The main point in this question is to ensure that any deductible charges are first deducted from UK income with the balance of charges being deducted from that part of foreign income bearing the LOWEST rate of foreign tax. This allows a maximisation of the foreign tax credits.

20   HUIS PLC

(a)   The loan to Sartre will lead to Huis plc being required to pay £45,000 × 25% = £11,250 to the Inland Revenue. This is payable at the same time as the mainstream corporation tax for the accounting period, so it is payable by 1 September 2002 although if Huis plc is a 'large' company the tax on the loan is subject to the quarterly instalment regime.

When the loan is written off on 31 March 2003 the company will be entitled to a refund of the £11,250. This refund will be due nine months after the end of the accounting period of the write off, ie it will be due on 1 September 2004.

In the year in which the loan is written off, 2002/03, the amount of the loan written off will be treated as Satre's income.

(b)   Because Beauvoir Ltd is a close investment-holding company, the full rate of corporation tax applies. Excess management expenses are carried forward.

		Year ended 31.3.01 £	Year ended 31.3.02 £
Schedule A		14,000	25,000
Schedule D Case III		20,000	100,000
		34,000	125,000
Less management expenses	- current	(34,000)	(45,000)
	- brought forward (note)		(2,000)
PCTCT		0	78,000

Note: £2,000 carried forward from y.e. 31.3.01

Mainstream corporation tax at 30%	£23,400

21 **SIGNING UP**

(a) *Compulsory registration*

A company making taxable supplies becomes liable to register for VAT if, at the end of any period not exceeding 12 months, the value of its taxable supplies exceeds £54,000 from 1 April 2001 onwards. The company must notify HM Customs & Excise within 30 days of the end of the 12 month period. They will then register the company with effect from the end of the month following the 12 month period, or from an agreed earlier date.

A company is also liable to register at any time if there are reasonable grounds for believing that its taxable supplies in the following 30 days will exceed £54,000. HM Customs & Excise must be notified by the end of the 30 day period and registration will be with effect from the beginning of that period.

When determining the value of a company's taxable supplies for the purposes of registration, supplies of goods and services that are capital assets of the business are disregarded, except for non-zero rated supplies of interests in land. Supplies which are taken into account are valued excluding VAT.

(b) *Group registration*

Companies each of which is established or has a fixed establishment in the UK and which are all under common control, may apply for group registration. The effects of group registration are as follows.

(i) Each VAT group must appoint a representative member which must account for the group's output VAT and input VAT. However, all members of the group are jointly and severally liable for any VAT due from the representative member.

(ii) Any supply of goods or services by a member of the group to another member of the group is, generally, disregarded for VAT purposes. This may result in a considerable cash flow advantage to group registration.

(iii) Any other supply of goods or services by or to a group member is treated as a supply by or to the representative member, although any special status of the representative member is ignored if the company supplying the goods or services does not also have that special status.

(iv) Any VAT payable on the import of goods by a group member is payable by the representative member.

(c) *Divisional registration*

A company which is divided into several self-accounting units can apply for divisional registration. Divisional registration is for administrative convenience; the separate divisions do not become separate taxable persons and the company is itself still liable for the VAT. The conditions for divisional registration are as follows.

(i) Each division must be registered even if that division's turnover is beneath the registration limits.

(ii) The divisions must be independent, self-accounting units, carrying on different activities or operating in separate locations.

(iii) Input VAT attributable to exempt supplies by the company as a whole must be so low that it can all be recovered (apart from VAT which can never be recovered because of the type of expenditure).

(iv) Each division must make VAT returns for the same VAT periods, though non-standard VAT periods may be allowed.

(v) VAT invoices must not be issued for supplies between divisions of the same company as they are not supplies for VAT purposes.

(d) The basic tax point is the date on which goods are removed or made available to the customer.

If a VAT invoice is issued or payment is received before the basic tax point, the earlier of these dates automatically becomes the tax point. If an earlier tax point does not apply and the VAT invoice is issued within 14 days of the basic tax point, the invoice date becomes the tax point (although the company can elect to use the basic tax point for all its supplies if it wishes). This 14 day period may be extended to accommodate, for example, monthly invoicing: the tax point is then the VAT invoice date or the end of the month, whichever is applied consistently.

Goods supplied on sale or return are treated as supplied on the earlier of adoption by the customer or 12 months after despatch.

22   **CAVE LTD**

(a)

	£	VAT £
Outputs at standard rate £(1,700 + 100)	1,800,000	315,000
Outputs at zero rate £(400 + 50)	450,000	
Total taxable outputs	2,250,000	
Exempt outputs	800,000	
Total outputs	3,050,000	

Proportion of taxable outputs (exclude capital goods) =
  2,100/2,900 = 73% (round to nearest whole percent above)

	£	
Inputs chargeable at 17.5%	600,000	
VAT = £105,000 × 73%		(76,650)
VAT to be accounted for		238,350

(b)   Where a supplier of goods or services has accounted for VAT on a supply, the customer does not pay within six months (from when payment is due), and the debt is written off in the creditor's accounts, the supplier may claim a refund of VAT on the amount unpaid. Where payments on account have been received, later debts are regarded as bad before earlier ones. The consideration must not be in excess of market value.

Scenario question and answer bank

1   X LTD (PILOT PAPER)   *80 mins*

(a)   X Ltd is a UK resident company which manufactures household appliances. Until 1995 its shares were wholly owned by the members of the Smith family. During 1995 80% of the shares were acquired by Z Ltd, a UK company which owns a chain of retail outlets selling household appliances. The remaining 20% of the shares continue to be held by Mr J Smith, aged 43, who is employed as general manager of X Ltd.

The directors of X Ltd are also directors of Z Ltd.

For the purpose of this scenario you are the chief accountant of X Ltd.

At a meeting arranged by you with the directors of X Ltd held in April 2001, you are provided with their estimates of the results for the year to 31 March 2002, together with additional information which may have a bearing on the taxation liability of the company. They express surprise that you have requested this information at such an early stage.

The estimates are as follows.

		£
Income	Trading profits	820,000
	Loan interest receivable (see below)	5,000
	Patent royalties received	10,000 (gross)
	Rental income	15,000
Payments	Loan interest payable (see below)	12,000
	Gift Aid	4,000

Notes

1   The loan interest receivable was in respect of a loan of £50,000 made by X Ltd to a major supplier S Ltd, two years ago.

2   The loan interest payable was on a loan from a finance company (which was not a bank) to finance the purchase of equipment.

3   Patent royalties were received net of tax from an individual trader.

In addition to the above, you establish that the company had a corporation tax (CT) liability of £270,000 for the year ended 31 March 2001 based on chargeable income of £900,000.

It had surplus advance corporation tax (ACT), generated in the year to 31 March 1999, brought forward at 31 March 2001 of £30,000. The directors had decided to pay a dividend of £624,000 during May 2001 in respect of the year ended 31 March 2001. There was no FII received in any year.

Requirements

Prepare a report to the directors of X Ltd.

(i)   Producing your calculation of the estimated corporation tax liability of the company for the year ended 31 March 2002;   **8 Marks**

(ii)   Illustrating, by means of a schedule, how and when this liability will be settled;   **6 Marks**

(iii) Advising them of the effect of paying the dividend in May 2001;   **3 Marks**

(iv)   Explaining why it is necessary to have reliable estimates of the chargeable income;   **2 Marks**

(v)   Advising them of their statutory obligations under the Corporation Tax Self Assessment (CTSA) system.   **3 Marks**

Presentation and style   **5 Marks**
                                                                                   Total Marks = 27

Note that your calculations, in arriving at the corporation tax liability and the schedule of payments should be shown in appendices attached to your report.

The schedule of payments should cover the period for April 2001 to January 2003.

(b)   During the year to 31 March 2002 X Ltd's parent company, Z Ltd, experienced cash flow problems. On 31 December 2001 Z Ltd sold its holding in X Ltd to B Ltd, a UK company which already owned two UK subsidiaries. You are aware that X Ltd owned an asset which had been transferred to by Z Ltd under group arrangements in August 1997. The gain on this transaction at the time of the transfer was £30,000.

BPP
PUBLISHING

Scenario questions

In May 2002 you have a meeting with the directors of B Ltd who have been provided with a copy of your report made to X Ltd in April 2001 and they provide you with the following information:

- Apart from the trading profit, which was £810,000, all of the other estimates shown in Part (a) were accurate.

- The supplier, S Ltd, to whom the loan of £50,000 was made, became insolvent on 31 January 2002 and nothing was recoverable.

- During January 2002, the directors of B Ltd considered that Mr Smith, the general manager of X Ltd, was unsatisfactory and dismissed him, making him a gratuitous payment of £24,000. This has not been treated as a deduction in the reported profits of X Ltd. Mr Smith later sold his 20% holding in X Ltd to B Ltd.

Requirements

Prepare a report for the directors of B Ltd;

(i) Producing your calculation of the corrected corporation tax liability for the year ended 31 March 2002 and indicating whether there has been an over or under payment of corporation tax to date;

6 Marks

(ii) Explaining the reasons for the difference between the projected and actual liability for the year ended 31 March 2002;   **4 Marks**

(iii) Explaining how the over/under payment will affect the quarterly payment position by producing a revised schedule of payments.   **5 Marks**

Presentation and style   **4 Marks**

Total Marks = 19

Total Marks = 46

Any detailed calculations should be shown in appendices attached to your report.

2   HAPPY MAIDS LTD   *80 mins*

Happy Maids Ltd, a newly formed company, commenced trading on 1 June 2001. Happy Maids Ltd provides a custom cleaning service for domestic and commercial premises. Happy Maids Ltd charges between £6 and £10 per hour for the services of its staff who in turn clean the premises to the customer's specifications using equipment and cleaning products supplied by Happy Maids Ltd. Happy Maids Ltd pays its staff between £4 and £6 per hour.

Happy Maids Ltd has already invested in the services of a leaflet mailing business to deliver brochures to premises in its target area. This service cost £1,000 in June 2001 but resulted in sufficient advance orders to justify the taking on of 10 staff members initially. In the four months since the business started, on 1 June 2001, Happy Maids Ltd has invoiced £25,250 for cleaning services and has paid staff wages of £18,000.

Happy Maids Ltd invoices at the end of each month for the services provided in the month then ending. It requires payment within 7 days. However, it is noticeable that only 50% of customers pay on time. One customer has not yet paid anything. As a result Happy Maids Ltd is considering offering a 5% discount on the invoice value for payment within the 7 day period.

Happy Maids Ltd's main expense is the wages bill for cleaners. The company has also incurred the costs of ten cleaning packages made up of industrial vacuum cleaners, brushes, attachments etc plus uniforms at a cost of £495 each. These will be written off through the profit and loss account on a replacement basis. It also purchases cloths, polishes, cleaning solutions etc and the costs of these are running at approximately £200 per month. Happy Maids Ltd's major outlay was for £5,000 in June 2001 on a new small van which is driven by one of its employees to transport cleaners who do not have their own cars. Cleaners who use their own cars are paid a mileage allowance by the company. The company also purchased a computer in July 2001 for £1,000 which is used to produce invoices, payslips and letters for the business.

There are minimal overhead costs at present as Beth, one of Happy Maids Ltd's directors, runs the business from her home.

Beth has no knowledge of financial matters but as an ex-home economics teacher feels she will be able to 'keep the books' herself. However she is completely ignorant of tax law and has contacted you to seek your advice with regard to the impact of tax on the business.

All the above amounts exclude VAT.

Requirements

(a)   Write a letter to Beth to explain

- the impact of VAT on the business
- the tax implications of taking on 10 members of staff
- the treatment of the mileage allowances paid to staff using their own cars   **17 Marks**

(b)   Assuming that Happy Maids Ltd registered for VAT on the 1 June 2001 prepare a draft of the first quarters VAT return if turnover in that period was £20,000.   **6 Marks**

(c)   Prepare a computation of the taxable profit if Happy Maids Ltd makes up the first set of accounts for the four months to 30 September 2001.   **8 Marks**

(d)   Outline the treatment of bad debts for Schedule D Case I purposes.   **2 Marks**

(e)   Discuss the effect on VAT if Happy Maids Ltd goes ahead with its plan to offer a 5% discount for prompt payment of its invoices   **4 Marks**

Presentation and style   **9 marks**

Total Marks = 46

Scenario question answers

1   X LTD (PILOT PAPER)

(a)   To: The Directors of X Ltd
      From: Chief Accountant
      Subject: Estimated corporation tax liability of X Ltd and due dates of payment of corporation tax
      Date: 30 April 2001

Introduction

The purpose of this report is to estimate the corporation tax liability of X Ltd for the year to 31 March 2002 and to set out the dates by which X Ltd will have to pay corporation tax.

It is necessary to make the most precise estimates of the corporation tax (CT) liability for the year to 31 March 2002 to allow us to make accurate quarterly payments during the current period.

Failure to make adequate payments on their due dates could result in interest and penalties for the company imposed by the Inland Revenue.

Thus at our recent meeting you used your management accounting expertise to provide accurate estimates of our profits for the year ahead from which I have estimated out likely CT liability.

Estimated corporation tax liability

As you will see from Appendix 1, I have used the estimates of the company's results for the year to 31 March 2002. I have used these estimates to calculate that corporation tax of £237,200 will be due in respect of the year.

On 1 April 2001 the company had brought forward ACT of £30,000. Subject to the maximum set off limit, this ACT can be set against the CT liability arising in the period to 31 March 2002. The maximum ACT set off will be equal to 20% of the company's profits chargeable to corporation tax. I have estimated this as £166,800 in Appendix 1.

However, the maximum set off of ACT must reduced by any 'shadow' ACT that arises on a dividend paid during the accounting period. If X Ltd pays a dividend of £624,000 during May 2001, shadow ACT of £156,000 will arise and the set off of brought forward ACT in the year to 31 March 2002 will be restricted to £10,800. Although the remaining unrelieved ACT will be carried forward for relief in future periods, this clearly has cash flow disadvantages and we should consider carefully whether it might be worth reducing the amount of dividend to be paid next month.

Due dates of payment of corporation tax

As X Ltd pays corporation tax at the full rate it is required to pay its corporation tax liability in quarterly instalments commencing during the accounting period concerned. The system of paying corporation tax by quarterly instalments is being phased in. 72% of the corporation tax liability due for the year to 31 March 2001 was due in instalments. However, this percentage increases to 88% for the year to 31 March 2002, and then 100% for the subsequent periods.

I have set out the amounts of tax payable on various dates in Appendix 2. The amounts for the year to 31 March 2002 are based on the estimates that you gave me earlier this month. It is important to note that interest runs from the due date on under or overpaid instalments. The Revenue may impose penalties if it believes that the company has deliberately or flagrantly failed to pay instalments of sufficient size. This means that it is very important that we make reliable estimates of chargeable income.

It will be important that we carefully monitor the CT which we need to pay by instalments because, as you can see, these will have a significant cash flow effect throughout the year.

May I draw your attention to the significant outflow of nearly £128,000 during January 2002 when the balance of tax for the year ended 31 March 2001 falls due in addition to a quarterly instalment for the year ended 31 March 2002.

Statutory obligations under the corporation tax self assessment (CTSA) system

Under the CTSA system we are normally obliged to file a CT return for each period by the later of:

(i)   3 months after a notice requiring the return was issued
(ii) 12 months after the end of the accounting period

Thus the return for the year ended 31 March 2002 will be due on 31 March 2003 assuming the Revenue issue a timely notice. The Revenue has a further 12 months to decide whether or not to enquire into the return.

We are required to keep the records on which a return is based, normally until six years after the end of an accounting period. The standard of records maintained is high and goes beyond the Company Act requirements. If the Revenue enquire into a return we may also be required to produce documents.

If you wish any further clarification on any of the items discussed above please do not hesitate to contact me.

Signed: Chief Accountant

Appendix 1

Estimated CT liability for the year ended 31 March 2002

	£
Schedule D Case I (£820,000 – £12,000)	808,000
Schedule D Case III	5,000
Taxed income	10,000
Schedule A	15,000
Less: Gift Aid	(4,000)
Profits chargeable to corporation tax	834,000

FY 2001

	£
£834,000 × 30% (W1)	250,200
Less: ACT (W2)	(10,800)
Less: Income tax suffered (W3)	(2,200)
Estimated CT payable	237,200

Workings

1   *Upper limit*

As there are two associated companies, the upper limit is £750,000 and the full rate of corporation tax applies.

2   *ACT*

	£
Notional franked payment (× 100/80)	780,000

Shadow ACT @ 20% = £156,000

	£
Maximum set off (£834,000 × 20%)	166,800
Less: Shadow ACT	(156,000)
Maximum offset surplus ACT b/f	10,800

3   *Income tax suffered*

Patent royalties £10,000 × 22%	£2,200

Note that payments under the gift aid scheme are made gross and interest paid to/received from UK companies is paid/received gross.

Appendix 2: Schedule of payments of CT

Year to 31 March 2001

CT liability   £270,000

72% × £270,000 = £194,400 is due in four quarterly instalments of £48,600 commencing on 14 October 2000.

28% × £270,000 = £75,600 is due nine months after the end of the accounting period, 1 January 2002.

Year to 31 March 2002

CT liability   £237,200

88% × £237,200 = £208,736 is due in four quarterly instalments of £52,184 each commencing on 14 October 2001. The balance of 12% × £237,200 = £28,464 is due nine months after the end of the accounting period, 1 January 2003.

The schedule of payments of CT from April 2001 is therefore:

	Date	Amount due £
3rd instalment for y/e 31.3.01	14.4.01	48,600
4th instalment for y/e 31.3.01	14.7.01	48,600
1st instalment for y/e 31.3.02	14.10.01	52,184
Balancing payment for y/e 31.3.01	1.1.02	75,600
2nd instalment for y/e 31.3.02	14.1.02	52,184
3rd instalment for y/e 31.3.02	14.4.02	52,184
4th instalment for y/e 31.3.02	14.7.02	52,184
1st instalment for y/e 31.3.03	14.10.02	(amount not calculated)
Balancing payment for y/e 31.3.02	1.1.03	28,464

(b) To: The Directors of B Ltd

From: Chief Accountant

Subject: Actual corporation tax liability of X Ltd for the year to 31 March 2002 and due dates of payment of corporation tax

Date: 1 May 2002

Introduction

The purpose of this report is to advise the directors of B Ltd of X Ltd's actual liability to corporation tax for the year ended 31 March 2002 and to set out the dates by which payment of corporation tax is due. In my report dated 30 April 2001 the CT liability was estimated at £237,200. A number of events have taken place since that estimate was made which have resulted in the liability being less than the forecast figure.

Actual corporation tax liability for the year ended 31 March 2002

As outlined in Appendix 1 the calculation of X Ltd's actual corporation tax liability for the above year is £231,800 as opposed to the estimated corporation tax liability for the year of £237,200. The reasons for the difference between the actual and estimated liability are as follows:

(i) As Z Ltd sold its shares in X Ltd during the period, the gain that would have arisen at the time of the transfer of the chargeable asset from Z Ltd to X Ltd crystallises. This means that chargeable profits increase by £30,000.

(ii) Actual trading profits are £10,000 below the estimate and an additional deduction of £24,000 can be made in respect of the compensation payment made to Mr Smith

(iii) A loan of £50,000 became irrecoverable. This amount is deducted firstly from Schedule D Case III income and then from total profits.

However the reduction of the actual chargeable profits to £780,000 means that it is not possible to set off any of the surplus ACT brought forward.

Payment of corporation tax

88% of the actual corporation tax liability for the year is due in quarterly instalments as shown in Appendix 2. To date quarterly instalments have been overpaid by a total of £3,564. The company will receive interest on this overpaid amount and will only need to pay tax of £47,432 on 14 July 2002. The balancing payment which is due on 1 January 2003 will be £27,816 rather than the £28,464 originally estimated.

Appendix one

Actual corporation tax liability for the year ended 31 March 2002

	£
Schedule D Case I	
(£810,000 – £12,000 – £24,000)	774,000
Taxed income	10,000
Schedule A	15,000
Chargeable gain	30,000
Less: Gift Aid	(4,000)
	825,000
Less: Non-trade deficit (£5,000 – £50,000)	(45,000)
Profits chargeable to corporation tax	780,000

FY 2001

	£
£780,000 × 30% (WI)	234,000
Less: ACT (W2)	-
Less: income tax suffered	(2,200)
CT liability	231,800

Workings

1   There are 5 associated companies. Thus the upper limit becomes £300,000. Full rate of CT is thus still due.

2   ACT

	£
Maximum set-off (£780,000 × 20%)	156,000
Less: Shadow ACT (part one)	(156,000)
Set-off of ACT b/f	Nil

Appendix two: due dates for the payment of tax

Year ended 31 March 2002

88% × £231,800 = £203,984 is due in four quarterly instalments of £50,996. The due dates are as follows.

Dates	Amount due £	Amount paid £	Overpaid £
14.10.01	50,996	52,184	(1,188)
14. 1.02	50,996	52,184	(1,188)
			(2,376)
14.4.02	50,996	52,184	(1,188)
			3,564
14.7.02	50,996		
	(3,564)		
	47,432		
1.01.03	27,816		

2   HAPPY MAIDS LTD

(a)

Mrs Beth Jones	Huntley Accountants
Happy Maids Ltd	2 The High Street
24 Haldane Road	Jesmond
Jesmond	Newcastle NE1
Newcastle. NE2	

Dear Beth,

TAXATION QUERIES

I outline below the impact of taxation on the various aspects of Happy Maid Ltd's business which we discussed at our recent meeting.

Impact of VAT on the Business

> VAT is charged on
> - supplies
> - of taxable goods and services
> - made in the UK
> - by a taxable person
> - in the course or furtherance of business.

The provision of cleaning services by Happy Maids Ltd is a taxable supply of services for VAT and will be subject to VAT at the standard rate of 17.5% once the company becomes a 'taxable person'.

A 'Taxable person' is someone who is or should be registered for VAT. Essentially the company needs to be registered for VAT once its turnover exceeds a certain threshold (currently £54,000), although it can register voluntarily before the compulsory date if it wishes. If the level of turnover remains fairly similar to that incurred in the first 4 months the company will have to register early in the new year when the turnover of £54,000 is due to be exceeded. The company could register voluntarily at any time before this date. The compulsory registration date must not be missed as penalties can be imposed by Customs and Excise.

Let us say that by the 28 February 2002 the company's cumulative turnover to date totalled £54,100 and thus exceeded the compulsory registration threshold. The company would have to notify Customs of this fact and apply to register for VAT by 30 March 2002. Customs would register the company for VAT from 31 March 2002. Once registered for VAT the company must charge 17.5% VAT on all invoices to customers. This will result in a 17.5% price increase for all domestic customers. However, commercial customers will not be affected by the price increase if they are registered for VAT and can recover the VAT that has been charged to them.

Once registered, Happy Maids Ltd can recover VAT paid by it on acquisitions for the business. It will also have to complete quarterly VAT returns showing the VAT charged to customers (output tax) in the quarter, the VAT suffered on purchases (input tax) and the net amount payable or repayable. VAT returns must be completed accurately and submitted with any payment due within one month of the quarter end to avoid interest or penalties being imposed on the company.

Tax implications of employees engaged by the company.

There are two taxes to consider for any company taking on an employee – Income Tax and National Insurance Contributions (NIC).

The costs of employing staff are fully deductible expenses when calculating the Schedule D Case I profit of the business. Such costs will include wages, mileage allowances and NIC costs. Every pay day the company must also deduct the income tax and NIC payable by its employees under the PAYE system.

Special code numbers for each of the employees will be used together with tax calculation tables (both of which are issued by the Inland Revenue) to work out how much tax to deduct from each pay packet and these amounts are then paid over to the Inland Revenue 14 days after the end of each tax month.

When an employee leaves a form P45 must be prepared. This shows the employee's code and the tax paid to date.   The P45 is given to the new employer who sends a section of it to his tax office. If a new employee is taken on without a P45 then form P46 must be completed and sent to the tax office.

At the end of the tax year the employer must by 31 May give each employee a P60 showing the pay and tax deducted in the tax year. These amounts are summarised on form P35 and sent to the

Revenue by 19 May. In addition forms P11D or P9D (dependant on amount paid to employee) must be completed giving details of benefits in kind made available to employees in the year and copies must be given to the employee.

Penalties and interest may be incurred if taxes are not paid on time or forms submitted on time.

Employee business mileage allowances

If an employee uses his own car on employer's business and is paid a mileage allowance for doing so strictly this mileage allowance is taxable income for the employee (and tax deductible as a business expense for the employer). The employee may make a claim to deduct any motoring expenses incurred wholly, exclusively and necessarily in the performance of his duties from his taxable income.

However, as an alternative to the above, employees can take advantage of the Authorised Mileage Rates which the Revenue have laid out dependant on the engine size of the car and the business miles travelled. The employee can receive tax free mileage allowances up to the authorised rates. Any excess allowance received is a taxable benefit. Allowances received in excess of the authorised mileage rates are also subject to Class I national insurance contributions.

I hope my letter have explained clearly the problem areas you raised in our meeting. However if you wish me to clarify any of the points made or if you have any other queries please do not hesitate to contact me.

Yours sincerely,

N. Advisor

(b)   **Draft VAT return for the quarter to 31 August 2001**

	£	£
Output tax		
£20,000 × 17.5%		3,500
Input tax		
Leaflet mailing	1,000	
Cleaning packages 10 × £495	4,950	
Cleaning products £200 × 3	600	
Van	5,000	
Computer	1,000	
	12,550	
× 17.5%		(2,196)
VAT payable		1,304

(c)   **Schedule D Case I profit for the four months to 30 September 2001**

	£	£
Turnover		25,250
Expenses:		
Wages	18,000	
Brochure delivery service	1,000	
Cleaning products £200 × 4	800	
Capital allowances (W1)	3,000	
		(22,800)
Schedule D Case I		2,450

Note: Turnover is the net of VAT figure

Scenario question answers

Working

1   Capital allowances 4 months to 30.9.2001

	£	General pool £	Total allowances £
B/fwd		Nil	
Additions			
Van	5,000		
FYA 40%	(2,000)		2,000
		3,000	
Computer	1,000		
FYA 100%	(1,000)		1,000
		Nil	
C/fwd		3,000	
Total allowances			3,000

Notes

- FYAs are not restricted for a 4 month period

- No WDAs are available on assets on which an FYA was available in the period.

- The computer qualifies for a 100% FYA since the business meets the definition of small.

- The 'cost' of additions is net of VAT since all VAT has been recovered in (b). If there was any irrevocable VAT then the 'cost' for capital allowance purposes would include this amount.

(d)   Only bad debts incurred in the course of a business are deductible for Schedule D Case I purposes. General bad debt provisions are not deductible but specific provisions and write-offs against individual debts are deductible.

(e)   Where a discount is offered for prompt payment VAT is chargeable on the net amount, regardless of whether or not the discount is taken up.

Thus for a supply by Happy Maids Ltd for £500 plus VAT where a 5% prompt payment discount is available VAT will be calculated as follows.

£500 × 95% × 17.5%

Thus if the invoice is paid promptly the following will be due from the customer.

	£
£500 less 5% discount	475
VAT	83
	558

If the invoice is not paid promptly

	£
Amount in full	500
VAT	83
	583

BPP PUBLISHING

Objective test questions and answers

OBJECTIVE TEST QUESTION 1

Dex Ltd prepares accounts for the year to 31 March 2002. On 22 December 2002 a notice to file a corporation tax for the year was issued. By what date must Dex Ltd file its CT return?

A   31 March 2003

B   22 March 2003

C   1 January 2004

D   22 December 2003

OBJECTIVE TEST QUESTION 2

An employee leaving an employment is given a four part:

A   P60

B   P35

C   P45

D   P11D

OBJECTIVE TEST QUESTION 3

For how long must records and accounts be kept for VAT purposes?

A   Two years

B   Three years

C   Four years

D   Six years

OBJECTIVE TEST QUESTION 4

A company's turnover from the start of trade on 1 April 2001 was as follows

	Turnover £
April 2001 – June 2001	3,800 per month
July 2001	5,000
August 2001 – July 2002	6,700 per month

By what date must the company notify C and E that it is liable to register for VAT.

A   31 March 2002

B   31 January 2002

C   28 February 2002

D   2 March 2002

OBJECTIVE TEST QUESTION 5

In 2000 A Ltd bought one of its directors a computer for £4,000 both for private and business use at home.

What taxable benefit, if any, arises in 2001/02 on the director in respect of the computer?

A   £800

B   £300

C   £500

D   £NIL

OBJECTIVE TEST QUESTION 6

Which of the following assets sold by B Ltd at a gain in the year to 31 March 2002 is exempt from tax on chargeable gains.

A   Quoted shares

B   An office used wholly for business purposes

C   Treasury stock

D   Machinery bought for £20,000 and sold for £40,000

OBJECTIVE TEST QUESTION 7

Olly Ltd exports furniture to customers in other EC member states, which , if any, of Olly Ltd's exports to customers in other EC states may be zero rated?

A   Exports to registered customers only

B   Exports to non-registered customers only

C   Exports to both registered and non-registered customers

D   None of Olly Ltd's exports to EC member states may be zero-rated

OBJECTIVE TEST QUESTION 8

Zeta Ltd has always made up accounts to 31 December each year. It is a 'large' company. For the year ended 31 December 2001 how much of its corporation tax liability must be paid by instalments?

A   60%

B   72%

C   88%

D   100%

OBJECTIVE TEST QUESTION 9

Under Schedule E an expense is, in general, allowed as a deduction from earned income if it meets the definition 'wholly,   and   incurred in the performance of duties'.

The missing words are:

A   exceptionally and only

B   exclusively and only

C   exclusively and necessarily

D   exceptionally and normally

OBJECTIVE TEST QUESTION 10

Which of the following payments made on a termination of employment are entirely or partly exempt from tax?

A   Payment for doing extra work during the period of notice

B   Payment in lieu of notice as stated in contract of employment

C   Payment for work done to date

D   Payment on account of injury at work which has resulted in the termination of employment

OBJECTIVE TEST QUESTION 11

JoJo Ltd provides it's sales director with a brand new company car available for private use on his promotion on 1 June 2001. The car cost £35,000 plus VAT and is driven 2,100 business miles by the director during 2001/02.

The benefit in kind under Schedule E for the director is

A   £7,292

B   £8,568

C   £11,995

D   £14,394

OBJECTIVE TEST QUESTION 12

Which of the following non cash vouchers are exempt from NIC?

(i)   Childcare vouchers.
(ii)   Luncheon vouchers up to 15p per day.
(iii) Transport vouchers where the employee is 'lower paid'.

A   (ii) only

B   (ii) and (iii) only

C   (iii) only

D   All of them

OBJECTIVE TEST QUESTION 13

XYZ Ltd takes an order from Mr Smith to manufacture and deliver to him a cabinet made to his requirements on 1 March 2001. The cabinet is finished on 4 June 2001 and delivered to Mr Smith on 6 June 2001. An invoice is raised on 12 June 2001 which Mr Smith pays on 4 August 2001.

What is the tax point of the supply?

A   4 June 2001

B   6 June 2001

C   12 June 2001

D   4 August 2001

OBJECTIVE TEST QUESTION 14

Y Ltd declares output tax of £100,000 and claims input tax of £32,000 for the quarter ended 30 June 2001. It is subsequently discovered that output tax was understated by £30,000.

How much misdeclaration penalty will be charged?

A   Nil

B   £50 minimum penalty

C   £4,500

D   £9,000

OBJECTIVE TEST QUESTION 15

J Jones and Son Ltd completed the construction of a 5 storey office block in March 2001. On 2 May 2001 they granted a 99 year lease of the building to ABC Ltd for £1.2 million.

Which statement best describes the VAT position regarding this transaction?

A   Standard-rated supply. VAT due at 17.5%

B   Exempt supply. No VAT to charge. Option to tax not available for leases

C   Exempt supply with option to tax available to charge VAT at 17.5%

D   Zero-rated supply of newly constructed building by the constructor

OBJECTIVE TEST QUESTION 16

Due to a computer error Alpha Ltd's VAT return for the quarter ended 30 June 2001 showed VAT due of £120,000 when really £150,000 was due. The VAT return was submitted on 21 July 2001.

Customs discovered the error made on 5 December 2001 during a control visit.

Alpha Ltd paid the extra £30,000 due on 20 December 2001.

Interest will run on the £30,000 due from

A   30 June 2001

B   21 July 2001

C   1 August 2001

D   5 December 2001

OBJECTIVE TEST QUESTION 17

Which of the following are exempt supplies for VAT?

(i)   Funeral services
(ii)   Insurance
(iii) Drugs and medicines on prescription
(iv)   Health services

A   All of them

B   (i) and (ii) only

C   (i), (ii) and (iii) only

D   (i), (ii) and (iv) only

OBJECTIVE TEST QUESTION 18

Complete the following sentence.

'A company has .... days from the end of an enquiry to amend its self assessment in accordance with the Revenue's conclusions.'

A   7

B   21

C   30

D   60

OBJECTIVE TEST QUESTION 19

Xera Ltd files the return for the year ended 31 December 2001 on 15 January 2003.

All previous returns had been filed on time.

What penalty will be charged (if any)?

A   Nil

B   £50

C   £100

D   £200

OBJECTIVE TEST QUESTION 20

A company has a corporation tax liability for the eight month period to 30 November 2001 of £2,000,000. Previously 31 March was the accounting date.

How much corporation tax must be paid on 14 October 2001?

A   Nil (tax not due on this date)

B   £440,000

C   £540,000

D   £660,000

OBJECTIVE TEST QUESTION 21

What is the maximum amount a 40 year old employee earning £100,000 per annum can contribute to an approved occupational pension scheme in 2001/02 on which tax relief can be claimed?

A   £14,310

B   £15,000

C   £19,080

D   No maximum

OBJECTIVE TEST QUESTION 22

Pete earns a salary of £18,000 pa. During 2001/02 he had two loans from his employer:

(i)   £3,000 interest free to buy a season ticket to allow travel to work by train.
(ii) £40,000 loan at 3% to purchase a holiday home in France.

The official rate of interest is 10%. What is the Schedule E benefit in kind in respect of the loans?

A   Nil

B   £2,800

C   £3,100

D   £4,300

BPP PUBLISHING

OBJECTIVE TEST QUESTION 23

Family Co Ltd is a close company. It makes a loan of £100,000 to Fred who is the shareholding Managing Director on 2 January 2002. The company makes up accounts to 31 December. The company pays small companies rate tax.

How much tax must the company pay in respect of the loan and when?

A   £20,000 on 14.4.2002

B   £20,000 on 1.10.2003

C   £25,000 on 14.4.2002

D   £25,000 on 1.10.2003

OBJECTIVE TEST QUESTION 24

A Ltd is a UK holding company which owns shares in the following subsidiaries:
80% of B Ltd (UK retailer)
60% of C Ltd (UK wholesaler)
55% of D Ltd (UK insurance company)
55% of X Inc (overseas manufacturer with no UK business establishment)
40% of E Ltd (UK retailer)

Which companies could be included in a VAT group registration if the group wishes to include as many companies as possible?

A   A, B, C, D, X and E

B   A, B, C, D, X

C   A, B, C, D

D   A, B, C

OBJECTIVE TEST QUESTION 25

Prospector Ltd started to trade on 1 January 2002 and registered for VAT on 1 March 2002. Prior to trading the company incurred the following expenses:

		Gross cost £
1 March 2001	Accounting advice on the impact of trading	9,000
1 May 2001	Purchase of office equipment	25,000
21 September 2001	Marketing advice on forthcoming adverts	10,000
1 December 2001	Christmas Party for potential customers	10,000

How much VAT can Prospector Ltd recover as pre-registration input tax?

A   £8,043

B   £6,553

C   £5,213

D   £3,723

OBJECTIVE TEST QUESTION ANSWER 1

A   Twelve months after the end of the accounting period (as this was later than 3 months after the notice to file a return was issued).

OBJECTIVE TEST QUESTION ANSWER 2

C

OBJECTIVE TEST QUESTION ANSWER 3

D

OBJECTIVE TEST QUESTION ANSWER 4

D   Turnover to 31 January 2002 exceeds the registration limit of £54,000. The company must notify C & E of its liability to register within 30 days.

OBJECTIVE TEST QUESTION ANSWER 5

B   £4,000 × 20% – £500 = £300

OBJECTIVE TEST QUESTION ANSWER 6

C   A gain on Treasury stock is dealt with under the loan relationship rules.

OBJECTIVE TEST QUESTION ANSWER 7

A   Exports to registered customers may be zero rated.

OBJECTIVE TEST QUESTION ANSWER 8

C

OBJECTIVE TEST QUESTION ANSWER 9

C

OBJECTIVE TEST QUESTION ANSWER 10

D   Payment on injury is fully exempt. All the other payments are fully taxable since the employee is contractually entitled to receive them.

OBJECTIVE TEST QUESTION ANSWER 11

B

	£
Cost	35,000
Irrecoverable VAT	6,125
	41,125

£41,125 × 25% × 10/12 = £8,568

2,100 miles over 10 months is equivalent to > 2,500 miles over 12 months hence 25%.

BPP
PUBLISHING

OBJECTIVE TEST QUESTION ANSWER 12

D

OBJECTIVE TEST QUESTION ANSWER 13

C   The tax invoice was issued within 14 days of the basic tax point. Hence the invoice date is the tax point.

OBJECTIVE TEST QUESTION ANSWER 14

A   The test for MP is the lower of:

(a)   30% £(100,000 + 32,000 + 30,000) = £48,600
(b)   £1 million

ie £48,600

The error of £30,000 is below this threshold - thus no penalty charged.

OBJECTIVE TEST QUESTION ANSWER 15

C

OBJECTIVE TEST QUESTION ANSWER 16

C   Interest runs from the due date for the VAT return in which the under-declaration was made.

OBJECTIVE TEST QUESTION ANSWER 17

D   Drugs and medicines on prescription are zero-rated.

OBJECTIVE TEST QUESTION ANSWER 18

C

OBJECTIVE TEST QUESTION ANSWER 19

C   Return less than 3 months late.

OBJECTIVE TEST QUESTION ANSWER 20

D   88% × £2,000,000 = £1,760,000

$$\frac{3}{8} \times £1,760,000 = £660,000$$

OBJECTIVE TEST QUESTION ANSWER 21

A   15% × earning cap of £95,400 = £14,310.

OBJECTIVE TEST QUESTION ANSWER 22

C

	£
Loans @ official rate	
£43,000 @ 10%	4,300
Less: interest paid	
£40,000 @ 3%	(1,200)
	3,100

The total of non-qualifying loans exceeds £5,000 so a taxable benefit arises in respect of both of the loans.

OBJECTIVE TEST QUESTION ANSWER 23

D   25% × loan is payable.

Due on normal due date for small company

ie. 1 October 2003 for y/e 31.12.2002.

OBJECTIVE TEST QUESTION ANSWER 24

C   X inc is overseas and as it has no business establishment in the UK cannot be in a VAT group. E Ltd is only held as to 40% thus insufficient holding to be in the group.

All other companies can be included in a VAT group registration (although may wish to exclude D Ltd since making exempt supplies - question asked for max number so include D Ltd to get answer needed).

OBJECTIVE TEST QUESTION ANSWER 25

C   The accountancy service is over 6 months before registration. The Christmas Party is entertaining. Thus both not allowed. £(25,000 + 10,000) × 7/47 = £5,213.

BPP PUBLISHING

List of key terms
and index

Note: **Key Terms** and their references are given in **bold**.

BPP
PUBLISHING

REVIEW FORM & FREE PRIZE DRAW

All original review forms from the entire BPP range, completed with genuine comments, will be entered into one of two draws on 31 January 2002 and 31 July 2002. The names on the first four forms picked out on each occasion will be sent a cheque for £50.

Name: _____ **Address**: _____

_____

How have you used this Text?
(Tick one box only)

☐ Self study (book only)

☐ On a course: college (please state)_____
_____

☐ With 'correspondence' package

☐ Other _____

Why did you decide to purchase this Text?
(Tick one box only)

☐ Have used BPP Texts in the past

☐ Recommendation by friend/colleague

☐ Recommendation by a lecturer at college

☐ Saw advertising

☐ Other _____

During the past six months do you recall seeing/receiving any of the following?
(Tick as many boxes as are relevant)

☐ Our advertisement in CIMA *Insider*

☐ Our advertisement in *Financial Management*

☐ Our advertisement in *Pass*

☐ Our brochure with a letter through the post

☐ Our website www.bpp.com

Which (if any) aspects of our advertising do you find useful?
(Tick as many boxes as are relevant)

☐ Prices and publication dates of new editions

☐ Information on product content

☐ Facility to order books off-the-page

☐ None of the above

Which BPP products have you used?

Text ☐ **Kit** ☐ **Passcard** ☐ **MCQ cards** ☐ **Tape** ☐ **Video** ☐

Your ratings, comments and suggestions would be appreciated on the following areas

	Very useful	*Useful*	*Not useful*
Introductory section (Key study steps, personal study)	☐	☐	☐
Chapter introductions	☐	☐	☐
Key terms	☐	☐	☐
Quality of explanations	☐	☐	☐
Questions and answers in each chapter	☐	☐	☐
Chapter roundups	☐	☐	☐
Quick quizzes	☐	☐	☐
Exam focus points	☐	☐	☐
Question bank	☐	☐	☐
Objective test bank	☐	☐	☐
Answer bank	☐	☐	☐
Index	☐	☐	☐
Icons	☐	☐	☐
Mind maps	☐	☐	☐

	Excellent	*Good*	*Adequate*	*Poor*
Overall opinion of this Study Text	☐	☐	☐	☐

Do you intend to continue using BPP products?   ☐ Yes   ☐ No

Please note any further comments and suggestions/errors on the reverse of this page. The BPP author of this edition can be e-mailed at: suecann@bpp.com

Please return this form to: Alison McHugh, CIMA Range Manager, BPP Publishing Ltd, FREEPOST, London, W12 8BR

REVIEW FORM & FREE PRIZE DRAW (continued)

Please note any further comments and suggestions/errors below.

FREE PRIZE DRAW RULES

1   Closing date for 31 July 2002 draw is 30 June 2002. Closing date for 31 January 2002 draw is 31 December 2001.

2   Restricted to entries with UK and Eire addresses only. BPP employees, their families and business associates are excluded.

3   No purchase necessary. Entry forms are available upon request from BPP Publishing. No more than one entry per title, per person. Draw restricted to persons aged 16 and over.

4   Winners will be notified by post and receive their cheques not later than 6 weeks after the relevant draw date.

5   The decision of the promoter in all matters is final and binding. No correspondence will be entered into.

See overleaf for information on other
BPP products and how to order

CIMA Order

To BPP Publishing Ltd, Aldine Place, London W12 8AW

Tel: 020 8740 2211. Fax: 020 8740 1184

www.bpp.com Email publishing@bpp.com

Order online www.bpp.com

Mr/Mrs/Ms (Full name)

Daytime delivery address

Postcode

Email

Daytime Tel

Date of exam (month/year)

	7/01 Texts	1/01 Kits	1/01 Passcards	9/00 Tapes	7/00 Videos	8/01 i-Pass / 1/02 i-Pass	1/02 i-Learn	7/01 MCQ cards
FOUNDATION								
1 Financial Accounting Fundamentals	£20.95	£10.95	£5.95	£12.95	£25.95	£24.95		£5.95
2 Management Accounting Fundamentals	£20.95	£10.95	£5.95	£12.95	£25.95	£24.95		£5.95
3A Economics for Business	£20.95	£10.95	£5.95	£12.95	£25.95	£24.95		£5.95
3B Business Law	£20.95	£10.95	£5.95	£12.95	£25.95	£24.95		£5.95
3C Business Mathematics	£20.95	£10.95	£5.95	£12.95	£25.95	£24.95		£5.95
INTERMEDIATE								
4 Finance	£20.95	£10.95	£5.95	£12.95	£25.95	£29.95	£19.95	£5.95
5 Business Tax (FA 2001)	£20.95 (9/01)	£10.95 (1/02)	£5.95 (1/02)	£12.95 (01)	£25.95 (01)	£29.95	£19.95	£5.95
6 Financial Accounting	£20.95	£10.95	£5.95	£12.95	£25.95	£29.95	£19.95	
6I Financial Accounting International	£20.95	£10.95						
7 Financial Reporting	£20.95	£10.95	£5.95	£12.95	£25.95	£29.95		
7I Financial Reporting International	£20.95	£10.95						
8 Management Accounting - Performance Management	£20.95	£10.95	£5.95	£12.95	£25.95	£29.95	£19.95	£5.95
9 Management Accounting - Decision Making	£20.95	£10.95	£5.95	£12.95	£25.95	£29.95	£19.95	£5.95
10 Systems and Project Management	£20.95	£10.95	£5.95	£12.95	£25.95	£29.95	£19.95	
11 Organisational Management	£20.95	£10.95	£5.95	£12.95	£25.95	£29.95	£19.95	
FINAL								
12 Management Accounting - Business Strategy	£20.95	£10.95	£5.95	£12.95	£25.95			
13 Management Accounting - Financial Strategy	£20.95	£10.95	£5.95	£12.95	£25.95			
14 Management Accounting - Information Strategy	£20.95	£10.95	£5.95	£12.95	£25.95			
15 Case Study	£20.95			£12.95	£25.95			
(1) Workbook		£19.95						
(2) Toolkit for 11/01 exam: available 9/01		£19.95						
(3) Toolkit for 5/02 exam: available 3/02								

Total

POSTAGE & PACKING

Study Texts

	First	Each extra
UK	£3.00	£2.00
Europe***	£5.00	£4.00
Rest of world	£20.00	£10.00

£

Kits/Passcards/Success Tapes

	First	Each extra
UK	£2.00	£1.00
Europe***	£2.50	£1.00
Rest of world	£15.00	£8.00

£

Breakthrough Videos

	First	Each extra
UK	£2.00	£2.00
Europe***	£2.00	£2.00
Rest of world	£20.00	£10.00
MCQ cards	£1.00	£1.00

£

Grand Total (Cheques to *BPP Publishing*) I enclose a cheque for (incl. Postage)

£

Or charge to Access/Visa/Switch

Card Number

Expiry date

Start Date

Issue Number (Switch Only)

Signature

We aim to deliver to all UK addresses inside 5 working days. A signature will be required. Orders to all EU addresses should be delivered within 6 working days. All other orders to overseas addresses should be delivered within 8 working days.